ISBN 978-1-334-33155-8
PIBN 10764427

This book is a reproduction of an important historical work. Forgotten Books uses
state-of-the-art technology to digitally reconstruct the work, preserving the original format
whilst repairing imperfections present in the aged copy. In rare cases, an imperfection in
the original, such as a blemish or missing page, may be replicated in our edition. We do,
however, repair the vast majority of imperfections successfully; any imperfections that
remain are intentionally left to preserve the state of such historical works.

1 MONTH OF
FREE
READING

at
www.ForgottenBooks.com

By purchasing this book you are eligible for one month membership to ForgottenBooks.com, giving you unlimited access to our entire collection of over 1,000,000 titles via our web site and mobile apps.

To claim your free month visit:
www.forgottenbooks.com/free764427

English
Français
Deutsche
Italiano
Español
Português

www.forgottenbooks.com

Mythology Photography **Fiction**
Fishing Christianity **Art** Cooking
Essays Buddhism Freemasonry
Medicine **Biology** Music **Ancient**
Egypt Evolution Carpentry Physics
Dance Geology **Mathematics** Fitness
Shakespeare **Folklore** Yoga Marketing
Confidence Immortality Biographies
Poetry **Psychology** Witchcraft
Electronics Chemistry History **Law**
Accounting **Philosophy** Anthropology
Alchemy Drama Quantum Mechanics
Atheism Sexual Health **Ancient History**
Entrepreneurship Languages Sport
Paleontology Needlework Islam
Metaphysics Investment Archaeology
Parenting Statistics Criminology
Motivational

SAMUEL B. GARRETT

BOND GENEALOGY

A History

Of the Descendants of

JOSEPH BOND

Born 1704, in Wiltshire, England;
Died 175–, in North Carolina.

Also a brief account of many of the descendants of
JOHN BOND, his brother, who also emigrated
to America; the two being sons of Benjamin and Ann (Paradise) Bond, of
Wiltshire, England.

Compiled and Copyright 1913 by
Samuel Bond Garrett,
Muncie, Ind.

PRICE FIVE DOLLARS.

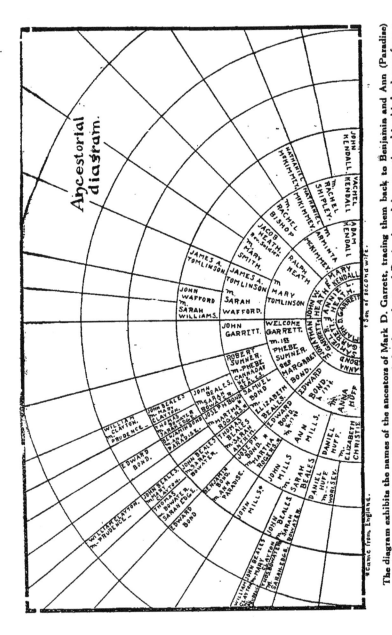

Ancestorial diagram.

The diagram exhibits the names of the ancestors of Mark D. Garrett, tracing them back to Benjamin and Ann (Paradise) Bond, of Wiltshire, England. In like manner any of the descendants of Benjamin and Ann mentioned in this book may form a similar chart naming their progenitors back to the same source.

BOND HISTORY.

CHAPTER I.
Ancestors of JOSEPH BOND, Page 7.

CHAPTER II.
JOSEPH BOND, Page 9.

CHAPTER III.
Third Generation, Page 11.

CHAPTER IV.
Fourth Generation, Page 24.

CHAPTER V.
Fifth Generation, Page 47.

CHAPTER VI.
Sixth Generation, Page 95.

CHAPTER VII.
Seventh Generation, Page 172.

CHAPTER VIII.
Eighth Generation, Page 226.

CHAPTER IX.
JOHN BOND, a Brother to JOSEPH, Page 230.

Edward Bond.

Benjamin Bond, married Ann Paradise.

- **John**
  Born 1701,
  in England.
  - Benjamin .... Abraham, Amos, Elizabeth.
  - Abraham .... John, Levi, Mary.
  - John .... Allen, Hannah, Rebecca, Mary, John.
  - Edward .... Susan, Sarah, Mary, Benjamin, Alice, Martha, Elizabeth, Ruth, Hannah, Levi.
  - Isaac .... Rebecca, Mary, Joshua, Israel, Abraham, Susley, Reuben.

- **Joseph**
  Born 1704,
  in England.
  - Edward .... Benjamin, Keziah, John, William, Edward, Anna, Jesse, Joshua, Joseph.
  - Benjamin .... Martha, Silas, Elizabeth, Ruth, Eli.
  - Ruth (Walton) ...... Joseph, Mary, Abraham, David, Martha, Gabriel, Bathsheba, Amos, John.
  - Stephen .... Ruth, Martha, Mary, Patience, Charity, Stephen, Keziah, Nathan, Benjamin, Rebecca, Isaac, Ann, Rachel, Joseph.
  - Ann (Cohorn).
  - Samuel .... Martha, Margaret, Joseph, Thomas, Sarah, Samuel, Dorcas, Rachel, Mordecai, Elizabeth, Ornon, Ruth.
  - John .... Martha, Joseph, Benjamin, Joel, Isaac, Elizabeth, William, Jane.

FOREWORD.

The work of compiling data for a genealogy of a branch of the BOND family was begun in the year 1884 and has been pursued at intervals during twenty-five years. It has required no small amount of patience and perseverance to secure the historical facts herein narrated. No attempt has been made to present anything like "write-up" of any individual; on the contrary the biographies are very brief, this being necessary, otherwise the volume might become too large to suit our purpose. A number of abbreviations are used in the work, the list of which should be learned by the reader. The place of birth is not always given, but frequently can be ascertained by reference to the parents and their place of residence.

After the name heading each family, appears, in parenthesis, the name of his or her ancestors of each generation running back to the immigrant JOSEPH BOND, or JOHN BOND, as the case may be. Both being sons of BENJAMIN and ANN (PARADISE) BOND.

A name in parenthesis thus "Anna (HUFF) Bond" denotes that her maiden name was Huff. Each name is given a number, in light type where the birth is noted; when this number is carried forward to where the marriage of the person named is recorded the number is here placed in black type, so they can be readily found. The light and black numbers will be found throughout the work, including the index.

The aim has been to record the facts as a matter of history of our kindred. That errors will be found is to be expected and cannot be avoided; for these we ask the indulgence of the reader.

Now, dear reader, if you are a member of this numerous Bond family or in any way interested therein, buy a copy of this history and familiarize yourself with its contents, and receive much benefit and pleasure therefrom.

THE AUTHOR.

ABBREVIATIONS USED IN THIS BOOK.

abt.   about.

b.   born.

ch.   child or children.

d.   died or deceased.

d. s. p.   died without issue.

dau.   daughter.

m.   married.

mo. or m.   month.

mtg.   meeting. (An abbreviation used by the Friends or Quakers in the records kept by them, in their meetings of business.

n. f. k.   nothing further known.

res.   residence or resided.

s. p.   sine prole, without issue.

w.   wife, widow, or widowed.

yr.   year.

CHAPTER I.

THE ANCESTORS OF JOSEPH BOND.

The branch of the Bond family in America whose history the writer has undertaken to briefly narrate is of English origin. The English stock coming originally from Saxony to England about the time of William the Conqueror.

A generation ago almost any one of the older members of the family could readily trace their ancestors to Joseph Bond, who, they said, came from England and married Martha Rogers, who also came on the same ship.

At the present time there are very few of the Bonds who can trace their lineage even this far, and many cannot even name their great-grandparents with any certainty.

The research that I have made to learn the earlier history of these people has not been as fruitful as I could wish, yet the labor has been crowned with a measure of success, and I submit the results with the hope that there may be, in this and future generations, a few readers who will derive some satisfaction from its perusal.

———

I quote from "Wiltshire Notes and Queries," a quarterly magazine devoted to historical and genealogical matters, in which abstracts of Friends' records in Wiltshire, England, have been published:

"Benjamin Bond, son of Edward Bond, of Bewley, Laycock parish, and Ann Paradise, of Slaughterford, were married 2 mo. 20, 1686, at Slaughterford."

"Edward Bond, of Calne, drugget maker, son of Benjamin Bond, of Bidston, was married 4 mo. 29, 1720, to Mary Smith, at Chippenham."

From another copy of the magazine:

"John Bond, son of Benjamin and Ann Bond, of Bidiston, was born 2 mo. 21, 1701."

"Joseph Bond, son of Benjamin and Ann Bond, of Devizes, Wilts, born 8 mo. 6, 1704."

From the Chester Monthly Meeting Records, of Chester, Pennsylvania, 10 mo. 25, 1721:

"John Bond produced a certificate from Lavington Monthly Meeting in the county of Wilts in Great Britain:

" 'From our Monthly Meeting of the South West Division (commonly called Lavington Monthly Meeting), in the County of Wilts, South Britain, to ffriends in Pensilvania:

" 'Dear ffriends & Brethren. These are to certifie you that our friend John Bond who has an intention to settle a mong you has faithfully served his apprentiship within the verge of this meeting and has behaved himself soberly and religiously and therefore we tenderly recommend him to you and we also find nothing but Clearness respecting marriage. With Salutation of Dear Love we rest your friends and Brethren.

" 'Signed in behalf of said Monthly Meeting this 10th of 1st mo., 1720.

" 'HENRY SANGER,	EDWARD GYE,
' 'THOMAS KING,	JOHN GYE,
' 'JOHN MOORE,	SAMUEL RUTTY,
' 'JOHN CALLAWAY.' "	

A LETTER WRITTEN BY BENJAMIN BOND.

"Unto ffriends in Pensilvania or Elsewhere in America, unto whose hand this may come. Greeting:

"Whereas my son John Bond has an Intention to settle amongst you, These may Certifie that I do give my consent to it and hope he will adhear to the advice of honest ffriends where ever his Lott may be Cast, and Being well sattisfied that he is Clear from any Engagement with woman on the account of marriage I do Allow him to take a wife Amongst you when he shall see meet without my ffurther approbation; So with the Salutation of Endeared Love I Remain your well wishing ffriend and Brother in the unchangeable Truth.

"BENJA. BOND.

"Bidestone near Chippenham, County Wilts, the 13th of the first mo., 1720–21."

John Bond received a certificate from Chester Monthly Meeting 9 mo. 26, 1722, to Abington Monthly Meeting, Philadelphia County.

From minutes of Abington Monthly Meeting:

11 mo. 28, 1722: "John Bond produced a certificate from Chester Monthly Meeting."

12 mo. 22,·1724: "John Bond and Sarah Cadwalader declared the second time their intention of marriage."

1st mo. 29, 1725: "The marriage was reported orderly."

8th mo. 21, 1731: "A certificate was granted to John Bond in order to Visit his friends in Old England."

6 mo. 28, 1732: "John Bond produced a certificate from Chippenham Mo. Mg. in Wiltshire in Old England, which was Read & Rec'd."

CHAPTER II.

JOSEPH BOND.

1. JOSEPH BOND, son of Benjamin and Ann Bond, of Devizes, Wilts (England), was born 8 mo. 6, 1704. Our knowledge of his early history is very meager indeed. In the preceding chapter it is shown that his father was a Quaker or Friend and so was his brothers, John and Edward, yet I find no evidence among the Friends' records of Pennsylvania or North Carolina that Joseph had a membership in that religious society. The date of his coming to America has not been learned, although there is a tradition that he came in 1735. There is no doubt about his coming that early. He arrived at Philadelphia and was bound or put under contract to someone to labor for his passage to this country. After gaining his liberty he and Martha Rogers were married, though I have not found any proof of this marriage in any of the records in Philadelphia or among Friends. The lack of his name being mentioned in any of the Friends' records makes it very evident that he had lost his membership, if he ever had one, before coming to America. After his marriage he lived in Bucks County, Pa., for some years. Joshua Bond, late of Jay County, Ind., who was a grandson of Joseph, wrote under date of 12th day of the 1st mo. 1862, a biographical sketch of himself. This manuscript gives a ray of light on the present subject. I here quote from him:

"My granfather Bond name was Joseph and granmothers name Martha Rogers before she was married. The both came

from ingland in one ship when yong and after working to pay
their passage the married. Granmother was thought to be a
kinswoman of John Rogers the Marter."

Joshua was 81 years old when he wrote the above, which I have
tried to quote verbatim et literatim. .

In a manuscript left by Edward Bond Sr., son of Joseph, in
which he is writing about the last sickness and decease of his
sister, Ruth Walton, he mentions his father thus:

"She was the Daughter of Joseph Bond and Martha his wife
who lived in the early part of their time in Bucks County in or
near richland township pennsylvania who afterward moved to
new garden North Carolina & there deceast, and was Buried at
new garden, Guilford county."

There is evidence that he moved from Bucks County, Penn.,
to North Carolina when his son Edward was between ten and
eleven years old. This would fix the date at 1750 or 1751. This
was at a time when a great many of the Friends or Quakers were
moving from Pennsylvania, Maryland, Massachusetts and Virginia and settling in North Carolina. New Garden Meeting
was established in 1751, as was also that of Cane Creek in Ala-
mance County. New Garden Meeting was probably held in
some of their dwellings for a year or two. It was about 1752
that Richard Williams with his wife, Prudence Beals, and two
children settled at New Garden, and it was Williams that gave
the site for the meeting house.

The date of his decease or that of his wife has not been ascertained. Their son John, who was probably the youngest child,
was born in May, 1755, and from the evidence at hand I believe
neither he nor his wife lived long after this date. I visited the
cemetery at New Garden, now Guilford College, in the year 1908,
and endeavored to locate their graves. I was shown the plot of
ground where the earliest graves were located, but found no
marks whereby I could establish which grave contained their
remains. So we here state briefly, or rather restate, that Joseph
Bond was grandson of Edward Bond, of England, and son of
Benjamin Bond and wife, Ann Paradise, of Wiltshire, England.
He was born in England, emigrated to America—Pennsylvania
—about 1735, married Martha Rogers, lived in Bucks County,
Penn., moved to Roan, now Guilford Co., N. C., about 1751,

died before 1760.   Buried at New Garden, now Guilford College.
Children:
2.   I.   Edward Bond, b. Sept. 26, 1740.
3.   II.· Benjamin Bond, b. 1742.
4. III.   Ruth Bond (Walton), b. 1744-45.
5.   IV.   Stephen Bond, b.
6.   V.   Ann Bond (afterwards Cohorn or Cochran); n..f. k.
7.   VI.   Samuel Bond, b. Dec. 2, 1753.
8. VII.   John Bond, b. May 30, 1755.
The history of each of'the above children, except that of Ann,
will be found in the succeeding pages.

CHAPTER III.

THIRD GENERATION.

2.   EDWARD BOND (son and probably oldest child .of
Joseph and Martha Bond) was born in Bucks Co., Penn., Sept.
26, 1740; moved with his parents to North Carolina 1750 or 1751,
where they settled near New Garden, now Guilford College.
My knowledge of his history has been almost altogether obtained
from the following sources and records, viz:.   The records of the
Friends kept by their monthly meeting; deed records; from the .
writings of his friends, and his own manuscripts.   I will quote
from some of these various records so the reader can be in possession of many facts connected with his history.
Feb. 28, 1758.   Minutes of New Garden Monthly Meeting:.
"Edward Bond requests to come under the care of Friends; we
therefore appoint Thomas Thornburg and Nathan· Dicks to inquire into his conversation and else may (be) needful and make
report at our next meeting."   From the records of March: "The
Friends appointed at our last .meeting to inquire concerning
Edward Bond make report; they find nothing to obstruct, his
request is therefore granted."
January 27th, 1759, he makes request to be joined as a member
of said meeting and April 28, 1759, this request is granted.
In 1763 he desired the concurrence of the meeting to travel in
company with William Hunt and Zachariah Dicks, upon a religious visit to friends in South Carolina, which the meeting

approved, and the clerk was requested to give him a copy of the minutes on behalf of the meeting.

MARRIAGE CERTIFICATE.

"Whereas Edward Bond of New Garden in Roan County, North Carolina, son of Joseph Bond, dec'd, and Ann Mills, daughter of John Mills of the same place, having declared their intention of marriage with each other before several monthly meetings of the people called Quakers, held at New Garden in the county aforesaid, and nothing appearing to obstruct, were left to their liberty to accomplish their marriage according to good order, the which they did on the 16th day of the 8th mo. 1764, in the 'presents' of many witnesses 12 of whose names are herein 'writed' to-wit:"

"SARAH MILLS.	JOHN MILLS.
"SARAH HUNT.	WILLIAM HUNT.
"ANN BALDWIN.	JAMES MENDENHALL.
"RUTH HUNT.	RICHARD BEESON.
"MARY BEALES.	WILLIAM BALDWIN.
"SARAH KNIGHT.	JONATHAN HARROLD."

Deep River meeting was established in 1760 and it is probable that he became a member of that particular meeting. He bought of Anthony Hoggatt in 1774, 100 acres of land for the sum of thirty and five pounds current and lawful money. This land was on the long branch, the east side of the east fork of Deep River, Guilford County, N. C.

In 1767 he was appointed overseer of Deep River Meeting. Deep River Monthly Meeting was set off from New Garden Aug. 8, 1778. From this date on his name is often used on committees of Deep River Monthly Meeting of which he was a member from this date until his removal to Indiana Territory in the year 1810.

In the year 1793 he went on an extended visit among Friends and kindred and also visiting Friends' meetings in Virginia and Pennsylvania, traveling on horseback, being gone from home more than four months. Among his manuscripts is a detailed account of this trip; a diary of each day's travel or visit. Starting August 15, 1793, he reached home December 24th of the same year. On the third day of his travel he reached the home of his cousin Edward Bond in Bedford County, Va. The following day being the first day of the week (Sunday), he attended Goose Creek Meeting and remained here until second day (Monday). He was accompanied on this trip as far as Yorktown, Pa., by John Wickersham, who was also on a like visit to friends in Pennsylvania. He says: "Second day morning we set out again on our journey. Cousin Edward Bond went with us to his daughter's, Mary McFarson (McPherson) and Cousin Alin Bond, John Bond's son Alin, also went and set us in the road." This Allen Bond was eldest son of John and Margaret (Allen) Bond. John was the first cousin, being the son of his uncle John.

He mentions passing through Lynchburg; crossing the James River; crossing the mountains at Rockfish Gap; taking a wrong road and passing through Stantown (Staunton), and on the 23d they arrived at "Margaret Bond's at 'Shanadore' (Shenandoah) River." He writes: "She being my cousin John Bond's widow we staid there with her and her children, who were nearly grown up, til the next day, then we went to her brother Joseph Alin's —and from there to his son Joseph Alin's, who was married to cousin Edward's (Bond) oldest daughter Susannah."

"From there we went to cousin Isaac Bond's and staid all night. Isaac Bond was married to his second wife. He hath two daughters by his first wife. One of them lives with him and the other lives near Middle Town in Bucks County in Pennsylvainia, with Jesse Willson, who's wife is a relation of her's." Sunday, the 25th of August, he mentions about it being the first day of the week, he went with his relations and other Friends to meeting called Smith Creek Meeting. He says he "was very much stript and very poor in this meeting and had a sick afternoon at Jackson Alin's, who was married to cousin Edward Bond's daughter Sarah."

From here they went to Opecon (Opequon) and on through Winchester, Va., crossed the Potomac and the mountains and on the 30th arrived at Jonathan Jessop's in Yorktown, Pa. Quoting again from his record:

"Here we met with our friend Ann Jesop, who had been living with her son Jonathan some months, but was now making ready to go back to New Garden to her own home."

"I had between 40 & 50 l (pounds) in money that E. Macy sent by me to Jonathan, which I carried safe and give to him and took a receipt."

, and I parted at this town. He went up towards
.d I went down to my brother Benjamin Bond's
ip (Fawn township) joining to Maryland 25 miles,
where ι .... l him and his family in midling good health, and
very glad to see me. This is a poor barron and hilly part of the
country. I thought it some like Thomas Creek."

"The next day (1st of 9 mo.) being first day of the week I went
with them to meeting which was small and I thought poor. I
staid at my brother's about ten days and plowed some. I
seemed to have a good deal of satisfaction for the most part since
I left home and felt great contentment such I thought I had
never known before. Yet I was not without exercise particu-
larly about going to meeting for fear something should appear
for me to speak in the meeting which I had almost set a resolu-
tion against complying with while I was from home."

While here at his brother's he first heard of the "plague"
which was then epidemic in Philadelphia. It continued for
many weeks and hindered him and a great many of the Friends
from attending the yearly meeting which was held in that city
the latter part of September. The disease was very fatal and
but few people ventured into the city at that time.

He left his brother's September 10th and during the next thirty
days he visited friends and relatives in the counties of Chester,
Delaware, Montgomery and Bucks. He attended meeting every
First day and often went to mid-week meeting. He frequently
makes mention of the Philadelphia sickness; was near Philadelphia but did not enter the city. He tells of a number of people who went to the city, some of whom took sick and died there,
others returning to the country died at home. It was reported
that a hundred had died in one day of the disease.

He visited his cousin Benjamin Bond and Benjamin's two
sons, Abraham and Amos, and his daughter, the wife of Adam
Barton. He says Abraham lived in Delaware County near
Chester. He also visited Elizabeth, the widow of his cousin
Abraham Bond, deceased. She had three children, John and
Levi and daughter Mary. Says he did not get to see her or John,
as John was gone to Nova Scotia. Levi and Hannah, his wife,
live in Newtown, Bucks County. Their children, Abraham,
Robert, Thomas, Elizabeth and Jane. He arrived back to his
brother Benjamin's Oct. 10th and from there went with some

friends to the yearly meeting at Baltimore and returned again to his brother's.

Oct. 23, he left his brother Benjamin Bond's in York County to visit his sister, who then lived in the western part of the State in Washington County. There being several settlements of Friends in Fayette and Washington Counties. He attended numerous meetings and visited families all over that part of the State and as far west as Wheeling, Va. It was the 9th of December when he parted with his sister and brother-in-law, Benjamin and Ruth Walton, and started on his journey homeward. Benjamin Townsend and several other Friends accompanied him on his homeward journey as far as Frederick County, Va., where they all attended Hopewell Quarterly Meeting. Here he met some of his cousins from Smith Creek who kept him company to his cousin Margaret Bond's. From here he reached home in a little more than five days, arriving on Christmas eve, Dec. 24, 1793, and found his wife and children well and glad to see him.

In the year 1809 he went on a journey, traveling on horseback to Indiana Territory, to visit his sons Jesse and William, who had moved there two years previous. He was accompanied on this trip by Adam Davis. He left an extensive written account of this trip in which he describes the daily occurrences. Tells with whom they stopped each night, the cost if any and other details. They traveled into Greyson County, Va., crossed New River and through Abington, Va., which town he "supposes has two hundred houses;" into Tennessee over Clynch mountain and by way of Richmond, Ky., to Cincinnati. There is enough matter in his account of this trip to fill ten large pages. He left home July 17, 1809, and was twenty days in reaching the home of his son Jesse, who lived near Richmond where Earlham College now is.

During his stay he attended quarterly meeting at Waynesville, Ohio. He says the house was so full he did not get in the first day he was there. He visited many meetings and families and also viewed the unsettled parts of the country west and north of his son Jesse's. He returned home by the same route, being gone from home nine or ten weeks.

The following year he and his son Joseph and their families moved to Indiana Territory and settled on a farm on the middle fork of White Water some six miles N. N. E. of Richmond. Here he cleared the land and made a farm. The ground for Goshen Meeting house and the graveyard was donated by him for the purpose for which it is still used. We find among his papers the following account of his coming to the territory and also of the coming of some of his children:

"We set out on our journey from No. Carolina to go to White Water in the Indiana Territory the 18th of the 9th mo. 1810, and came there on the 27th of the 10th mo. 1810. Our son Joseph and his wife came with us. Joshua Bond with his family came to us on the 5th day of the 11th mo. 1811, from 'Greyson' County Virginia. Edward Bond 'Juner' came the same time to his brother Jesse and hath since settled on the 'purchase' with his family. Abram Bunker came to us the 1st of 3rd mo. 1815 with his wife and five children."

"Daniel North & wife from Surry County N. Carolina set on his journey the 6th of 11th mo. 1819 and got here to White Water, Wayne County, Indiana, the 29th of 12th mo. 1819."

As previously noted he was married on August 16, 1764, to Ann Mills, of Guilford County, N. C. She was the daughter of John and Sarah (Beales) Mills, John Mills being the son of a John Mills, who emigrated from England to Philadelphia and afterwards settled on Opequon Creek, near Winchester, Va. Sarah Beales was born May 29, 1713, and was the daughter of John and Sarah (Bowater) Beales. This later John Beales being the son of John and Mary (Clayton) Beales (sometimes spelled Beals–Bales). Sarah Bowater was the daughter of Thomas and Sarah Bowater nee Edge, who came from England. Mary Clayton was the daughter of William and Prudence Clayton. These ancestors of Ann Bond nee Mills were all of them so far as known Quakers. Ann was born in 5th mo. (May) 1745 O. S. in Frederick County, Va., moving with her parents to North Carolina about 1751 or 1752. She died in Wayne County, Indiana, April 3, 1826, her husband Edward Bond having passed away nearly five years prior to her decease. He having died May 6, 1821. Interment was made in the graveyard which he had donated and laid out on his farm for the purpose of burial and for a meeting house, called Goshen, near Middleborough, Wayne County, Indiana.

The children of Edward, and Ann (Mills) Bond:

9.   I.   Benjamin, b. July 4, 1765.

10.   II.   Keziah, b. June 29, 1767; d. s. p.

11.   III.   John, b. June 15, 1769.

12.   IV.   William, b. Nov. 16, 1771.

13.   V.   Edward, b. Jan. 24, 1774.

14.   VI.   Anna, b. Sept. 19, 1776.

15.   VII.   Jesse, b. March 24, 1779.

16.   VIII.   Joshua, b. Nov. 28, 1781.

17.   IX.   Joseph, b. Feb. 20, 1785.

With one exception all of these reared families. Keziah married Daniel North and moved in 1819 to Indiana. She died about 1847, leaving no issue.

3. BENJAMIN BOND, son of Joseph and Martha (Rogers) Bond, was born in Bucks County, Pennsylvania, in the year 1742. It is probable that he moved with his parents to North Carolina and that after their decease he and his sister Ruth went back to Pennsylvania where they found homes among friends. From the Abington (Penn.) Monthly Meeting records of Friends we extract the following: "4th mo. 24th, 1769. Benjamin Bond requests to be received into membership and Horsham meeting gives a good account of him." 6 mo. 26, 1769, he is admitted into membership. 11 mo. 26, 1770 "Horsham Meeting requests a certificate for Benjamin Bond who inclines to take a 'voige' to North Carolina." 12 mo. 31, 1770 a certificate signed for him to New Garden, North Carolina. 9th mo. 30, 1771 he returns the certificate endorsed by New Garden, N. Carolina, Meeting.

This visit to his brothers and friends was taken before his marriage. The certificate in due time was received by New Garden, N. C., Monthly Meeting, and when he desired its return to him the meeting appointed William Stanley to indorse and sign it on behalf of the meeting.

From the records of Abington Mo. Mtg. of Friends we obtain the following data:

"4th mo. 17th, 1778. Benjamin Bond, of the township of Horsham in the County of Philadelphia, son of Joseph Bond of North Carolina, deceased, and Mary Walton, daughter of Thomas Walton, of the Mannor of Moorland, in the county and province aforesaid, were married at Horsham Meeting. Thomas and Mary Walton sign as her parents. One Edward and Susannah Bond also witnesses."

Some time after this they settled in Fawn Township, York

County, of the same State, where they lived till his decease in August, 1826. At this time several of the children were married. The widow and children moved to Indiana. She died in Wayne County, Indiana, Aug. 7, 1845. Children:

18.   I.   Martha Bond, b. abt. 1779; d. Feb. 25, 1854; did not marry.

19.   II.   Silas, b. July 15, 1783.

20.   III.   Elizabeth (afterwards Strawbridge).

21.   IV.   Ruth (afterwards Vore), b. Dec. 15, 1787.

22.   V.   Eli, b. Jan. 26, 1790.

4. RUTH BOND, daughter of Joseph and Martha (Rogers) Bond, was born in Bucks County, Pennsylvania, about 1744-5. She married (date not known) Benjamin Walton, a Friend or Quaker. They lived some years in Eastern Pennsylvania, Bucks County, but later, prior to 1793, moved to a new settlement of Friends in Washington County of the same State. She died June 2, 1805, in the 61st year of her age. The date of his decease and birth is wanting. The Waltons were a numerous and prominent people in Pennsylvania. Residence, Pennsylvania. The children of Benjamin and Ruth (Bond) Walton moved from Pennsylvania to Ohio and Indiana. Children:

23.   I.   Joseph Walton, b. ————; n. f. k.

24.   II.   Mary Walton (Townsend).

25.   III.   Abraham Walton, b. 1761.

26.   IV.   David Walton, did not marry.

27.   V.   Martha Walton; married Joseph John; n. f. k.

28.   VI.   Gabriel Walton, b. Nov. 17, 1777.

29.   VII.   Bathsheba Walton, married John Dinza; n. f. k.

30.   VIII.   Amos Walton.

31.   IX.   John Walton.

The further history of Gabriel and Abraham Walton will be found in this book; of the others nothing further is known. There is a tradition that Benjamin Walton was the son of one of the three brothers that came from England on the same ship with Joseph Bond.

5. STEPHEN BOND. Date of birth not known. That there was a Stephen Bond, son of Joseph and Martha, there is sufficient evidence. The record here produced is a copy of the one contained in the birth and marriage record of the Westfield (N. C.) Monthly Meeting of Friends. From the fact that Joseph

Bond had a son Stephen and the further fact that Samuel Bond, brother of Stephen, lived also at Westfield, I am led to believe that this Stephen is the same, and son of Joseph. It will be noticed that he has a son named for Joseph and a daughter named for Martha, besides other names for near relatives. So I am quite sure I make no mistake in placing his family in this page, although after exchanging hundreds of letters with different families of Bonds all over the country I find no positive trace of any of his descendants. His son Stephen died in childhood and whatever became of the other sons and daughters I am at a loss to know. Who he married is not known to the writer. The record gives her Christian name, "Maiden." The children:

32.   I.   "Ruth Bond daughter of Stephen and Maiden his wife was born ye 19th of ye 2 mo. 1773."

33.   II.   "Martha their daughter was born ye 5th of ye 12 mo. 1774."

34.   III.   "Mary their daughter was born ye 5th of ye 12 mo. 1776."

35.   IV.   "Patience their daughter was born ye 7th of ye 10 mo. 1778."

36.   V.   "Charity their daughter was born ye 19th of ye 8 mo. 1780."

37.   VI.   "Stephen their son was born ye 26th of ye 8 mo. 1782."

38.   VII.   "Keziah their daughter was born ye 6th of ye 6 mo. 1784."

39.   VIII.   "Nathan their son was born ye 6th of ye 6 mo. 1786."

40.   IX.   "Benjamin and

41.   X.   "Rebecca, twins, son and daughter, were born ye 30th of ye 6 mo. 1788."

42.   XI.   "Isaac their son was born ye 27th of ye 11 mo. 1790."

43.   XII.   "Ann their daughter was born ye 27th of ye 7 mo. 1793."

44.   XIII.   "Rachel their daughter was born ye 18th of ye 1 mo. 1796."

45.   XIV.   "Joseph their son was born ye 1st of ye 4 mo. 1798."

"Stephen Bond (Jr.) deceased 12 of ye 7 mo. 1796."

"Mary Bond, daughter of Stephen Bond and Maiden his wife, and William Thomas, of Grayson County, Virginia, son of Joseph and Sarah Thomas, were married ye 23rd of ye 2 mo. 1798." N. f. k.

The further history of Stephen Bond's descendants is wanted.

7. SAMUEL BOND, son of Joseph Bond and Martha his wife, was born 12 mo. 2nd, 1753; married January 11, 1775: Elizabeth Beales, born May 25, 1755, daughter of Thomas and Sarah Antrim Beales. She became an eminent minister among Friends, preaching the gospel for more than sixty years. Her father, Thomas Beales, was a noted preacher of his day; he was the son of John and Sarah (Bowater) Beales. Therefore, Elizabeth, wife of Samuel Bond, was first cousin to Ann (Mills), wife of Edward Bond. They resided in Surry County, North Carolina, where their family of 12 children were born. He died there January 29, 1812. The widow and all the children moved to Indiana. She lived to be 92 years old, passing away in Wayne County, Indiana, April 13, 1848. The following marriage certificate was copied from the records kept by New Garden Monthly Meeting of the Religious Society of Friends, called Quakers:

"Whereas Samuel Bond of Surry County, North Carolina, son of Joseph Bond, deceased, & Elizabeth Beales, daughter of Thomas Beales of the same place, having declared their intention of marriage with each other before several monthly meetings of the people called Quakers held at New Garden in Guilford County, North Carolina, aforesaid, according to the good order used among them, and nothing appearing to obstruct, was left to their liberty to accomplish their marriage according to good order. Which they did ye 11th of ye 1 mo. 1775, at a meeting of said people at Toms Creek in the 'presents' of many witnesses, 12 of whose names are herein inscribed, to-wit:

"MARGARET CARR.	MIRIAM CARR.
"ANN HIATT.	JOHN HIATT.
"LYDIA BRYANT.	JOSEPH HIATT.
"SUSANNA HIATT.	ISAAC JONES.
"MARY JESSOP.	THOMAS JESSOP, JR.
"THOMAS MILLS.	THOMAS CARR."

The children of Samuel and Elizabeth Bond:

46.   I.   Martha (Ballard), b. Oct. 14, 1775.
47.   II. Margaret (Garrett), b. Sept. 11, 1777.

48.   III.   Joseph S., b. Aug. 9, 1779.
49.   IV.   Thomas, b. Dec. 5, 1781.
50.   V.   Sarah, b. Feb. 7, 1784; d. s. p. July 25, 1786.
51.   VI.   Samuel, b. April 12, 1786.
52.   VII.   Dorcas (Baldwin), b. Feb. 16, 1788.
53.   VIII.   Rachel (Teagle), b. Sept. 11, 1790.
54.   IX.   Mordecai, b. Sept. 28, 1792; d. inft. Jan. 14, 1794.
55.   X.   Elizabeth (Baldwin), b. Jan. 21, 1795.
56.   XI.   Ornon, b. July 9, 1798.
57.   XII.   Ruth (Teagle), b. Feb. 7, 1802.

8. JOHN BOND, son of Joseph and Martha, was born May 30, 1755; married January 28, 1778: Jane Beeson, daughter of Benjamin and Elizabeth Beeson, of Guilford County, North Carolina. She died January 9, 1792. They were members of Centre Monthly Meeting of Friends or Quakers, but in January 1, 1781, they moved their membership to Deep River Mo. Mtg. In June 1784 he was disowned from membership and little has been learned of his history since that date. There is, however, a tradition among his descendants that after his wife died he married Elizabeth Beeson, by whom he had one child; name and sex not known to them. There were eight children born to them before Jane's death. They (the children) retained membership in the meeting and must have moved their membership back to Centre Meeting, for in 1795 they moved their membership from Centre to New Hope Monthly Meeting, Green County, Tenn. In the minutes of New Hope Monthly Meeting of Tennessee we find recorded in 1795 where the five sons of John Bond moved their rights of membership from Centre Monthly Meeting of North Carolina to New Hope Monthly Meeting, Green County, Tenn. The sons' names: Joseph, Benjamin, Joel, Isaac and William. Their sisters' membership may also have been moved at the same time, but their record being kept in a separate book by the women and the book not being found I am unable to say what became of them. The children all being minors at that time it is reasonable to believe that John had married again and moved his family to the new settlement of Quakers in East Tennessee. A few years later two of these sons were disowned from membership and all moved away from the neighborhood, and no further mention is made of them in the minutes or records. About a hundred years after these occurrences the writer, after several

years' search and inquiry, located in Kentucky, Missouri and
other states the descendants of four of these sons of John Bond.

Through the courtesy of Miss Susan E. Davis, of Wayne
County, Ky., I became the possessor of the original marriage
certificate of John Bond and Jane Beeson, and as a matter of
curiosity as well as history I herewith reproduce it as nearly as
can be done:

"Whereas John Bond son of Joseph and Martha Bond Both
Deceased; of the County of Giulford in the Province of North C
and Jean Beeson Daughter of Benj. and Elizabeth Beeson of the
County and provine affordsaid Having Declaired their intentions
of Marriage Before Several Monthly Meetings of the people
called Quakers at Center Meeting House in county affordsaid
Having consent of parents and Relations therein concerned:
their said proposials of marriage was allowed of by the said meeting . . . Now therefore to certifie all whom it may concern
that for the full accomplishing of their said Intentions this 28
Day of the first month in the year of our Lord one thousand seven
hundred and seventy eight they the said John Bond and Jane
Beeson appeared in a publick assembly of the affordsaid people
met together for Divine Worship and they further service at one
of their meeting houses on pole cat in the affordsaid county . .
. . . then and there the same John Bond takeing the said
Jane Beeson by the hand Did in a Solomn mannar openly Declare
that he took the said Jane Beeson to be his wife, promise through
Divine assistance to be unto her a Loving and true Husband
untill it should please the Lord by Death to separate them and
in Like manner the said Jane Beeson Did openly in the same
assembly Declair that she took the said John Bond to be her
husband promising through Divine assistance to be unto him a
true and Loving Wife until it should please the Lord to separate
them or words to that effect . . . . . Moreover the said
John Bond and Jane Beeson. She according to the custom of
marriage assume the name of her Husband as a further proof
there of did then and there to these presents set their hands . .

JOHN BOND.
JEAN BOND.

And we whose names are hereunder written Being present at
the Solomnization of the said marriage and Superscription, have

as witnesses hereunto set our names the day and year above written."

SARAH REYNOLDS.   MARY REYNOLDS.
HANNAH REYNOLDS.   NANCY (?)
ELI POWELL.   CLOVIE (?) BAILY.
MARIAM LAMB.   RUTH LAMB.
HENRY POWELL.   WILLIAM BEALS.
DAVID REYNOLDS.   HENRY LAMB.
ELIZABETH NORTON.   CHARITY JACKSON.
EVE CRAFORD.   MARGARET CHAMNESS.
ELIZABETH POWELL.   SARAH LAMB.
MARY JESSOP.   ELIZABETH BEESON.
JEMIMA HASKET, SR.   JEMIMA HASKET, JR.
JOSHUA LAMB.   SARAH CRAFFORD.
BENJAMIN BEESON.   ELIZABETH BEESON.
EDWARD BOND.   CHARITY JACKSON.
ISAAC BEESON.   ISABEL BEESON.
WILLIAM BEESON.   ELISABETH BEESON.
MARY BEESON.   JAMES BROWN.
JOHN BEALS.   PETER DICKS.
ABRAHAM HASKET.   JACOB ELLOT.
    JEREMIAH REYNOLDS.

Recorded in Friends book of GEORG THASHER (?).
Records belonging to Center WILLIAM JESSOP.
Monthly Meeting by Benja- ——————— CHAMNESS.
min Coffin in page 21.

The children of John Bond and Jane his wife:
58.   I.   Martha, b. Aug. 19, 1778.   N. f. k.
59.   II.   Joseph, b. Feb. 29, 1780.
60.   III.   Benjamin, b. Oct. 19, 1781.
61.   IV.   Joel, b. Jan. 18, 1784.
62.   V.   Isaac, b. Dec. 27, 1785.
63.   VI.   Elizabeth, b. Dec. 18, 1787.
64.   VII.   William, b. Dec. 5, 1789.
65. VIII.   Jane, b. Jan. 7, 1792.

Here ends the third generation, or the grandchildren of Joseph and Martha Bond.

BOND HISTORY

CHAPTER IV.

FOURTH GENERATION.

Great-grandchildren of

JOSEPH BOND

Beginning with children of Benjamin,
son of Edward and Ann.

Ending with children of William,
son of John and Jane.

Numbering from 66 to 297.

9. BENJAMIN BOND (Edward-Joseph), born July 4, 1765;
married June 12, 1799: Mary Williams, born Jan. 4, 1770, daughter of Owen and Catherine Williams of Stokes County, N. C.
She died July 22, 1826; he died in Henry County, Ind., Oct. 10,
1839. He was born near Deep River, Guilford County, N. C.
From the Deep River Mo. meeting records we learn that Benjamin Bond, son of Edward and Ann, married Mary Williams,
daughter of Owen and Catherine Williams, at Muddy Creek
Meeting in Stokes County, N. C., 18th of 6 mo., 1799. Witnesses were: Job Coggshall, Rachel Jones, Richard Jones, Mary
Haisley, Jonathan Sell, Sarah Pike, William Manlove, Elizabeth Patterson, Henry Willett, Abigail Comer, Samuel Schooley,
Mary Pike. He moved to Wayne County, Ind., in the year 1827,
and later settled in Henry County of the same State, where he
spent the remaining portion of his life.

The following sketch was written by William P. Hastings,
who married a granddaughter of the subject:

"Grandfather Benjamin Bond I knew from my earliest recollection until his death. They lived less than a mile from where I
was born and brought up. He lived with his son Jonathan and
his daughter Tabitha; neither son nor daughter were married.
Elam Bond, a son of Huldah, was bound to Jonathan, and was
the remaining member of the family at the time of Benjamin's

death. Benjamin had composed rhymes, generally historical of the events recorded in the Old Testament. His favorite was the account of Samson and Delilah. Being afflicted with rheumatism so that he could not sleep a great deal of the time, he spent much of his time in singing his songs. Of course the tunes were also original with him. They were very much like the chanting tone used by Quaker preachers three-quarters of a century ago. He has been dead something over 63 years. I still remember the similarity though but a child at the time. I remember that I went to the house to see him for the last time. The impression of seeing his dead face was deep and lasting. I remember that while living Benjamin Bond wore drab clothes cut in Quaker fashion of a hundred years ago; perhaps they were not quite the Quaker garb that was most common at the time of my recollection of him. The coat and vest were longer and the hat, which was also drab in color, was softer, broader brimmed and turned up at the sides as we see the hat in the picture of Nathan Hunt. He was smooth shaved, as were all the Friends at that time, both old and young. As I remember him he was bald with some gray hair remaining about his temples and the base of his head. His face was rounder and fuller than your grandfather's (Edward Bond) as I remember him. He was good-natured and we little children liked him and called him 'Grandfather Bond' whenever we spoke of him, and it so turned out that I married his granddaughter. "Wm. P. Hastings."

"March, 1903."

The children of Benjamin and Mary Bond were:

66.   I.   Edward, b. March 8, 1800.
67.   II.   Jonathan W., b. Oct. 15, 1801.
68. III.   Jedediah, b. Aug. 19, 1804.
69. IV.   Tabitha (Newby), b. May 3, 1808.
70.   V.   Nathan Hunt Bond, b. Dec. 30, 1813.

11. JOHN BOND (Edward-Joseph), son of Edward and Ann Bond, of Guilford County, N. C., was born June 15, 1769; married Dec. 8, 1791: Mary Huff, born Sept. 3, 1767, daughter of Daniel and Elizabeth (Christie) Huff. To this union was born ten children. She died March 1, 1809, in Stokes, now Yadkin County, N. C. He died Dec. 5, 1860, in Henry County, Ind., to which place he had arrived only a few weeks before his decease. He resided in Surry County and when Yadkin County

was organized and cut off from Surry it left him in Yadkin County. He was a member of Deep Creek Monthly Meeting and was a minister of some note. He twice traveled on horseback to Indiana on religious visits among the Friends.

His second wife, to whom he was married about 1813, was Rachel Hobson, widow of Stephen Hobson, and daughter of Thomas and Elizabeth Vestal.

Under date of November 19th, 1902, Hannah W. Osborn (at that time aged nearly 86 years), of Centre, N. C., wrote as follows:

"When I first became familiar with the transactions of North Carolina Yearly Meeting (of Friends or Quakers) about seventy-five years ago, John Bond was an active member in the meeting. He was a minister and belonged to Deep Creek Mo. Mtg. in Surrey County. I never knew the name of his wife, who was mother of his children, nor the name of any of his children, except one daughter, Anna. When her father was 82 years old she married John Hutchens, leaving her father alone, but it seems even at that ripe age he did not find it good to be alone, so married Anna Macy, daughter of John and Anna Macy, a worthy maiden of about 60, who was in need of a home and employment, and withal, fitted to be the household companion of such a man, installed her mistress of his sufficiently supplied house while he continued to cultivate his farm with his own hands. After living on some 10, 12 or more years, I regret I can't call to mind just how many, they disposed of their farm and moved to Indiana . . . to the sore regret of his friends. For he had continued so vigorous that they had hoped to see him live out his 100 years."

The children of John and Mary:

71.   I. William Bond, b. Sept. 18, 1792.

72.   II. Anna (Hutchens), b. Aug. 26, 1794; d. March 10, 1858; s. p.

73.   III. John, b. Aug. 7, 1796.

74.   IV. Nathan, b. June 6, 1798; d. July 5, 1800, in childhood.

75.   V. Mary (Hobson), b. July 5, 1800.

76.   VI. Elizabeth (Keys), b. Dec. 2, 1801.

77.   VII. Jesse, b. Nov. 9, 1803.

78.   VIII. Joshua, b. Nov. 4, 1805.

79. IX. Caleb, b. June 3, 1807; d. May 8, 1867, s. p., in Wayne Co., Ind.

80. X. Joseph, b. March 1, 1809.

12. WILLIAM BOND (Edward-Joseph), born Nov. 16, 1771, in Guilford County, N. C.; married Dec. 13, 1792: Charlotte Hough, born Nov. 11, 1773, daughter of William and Mary Hough. They resided in North Carolina until 1807, when they moved to Wayne County, Indiana Territory, and about 1810 moved to Henry County and a few years later settled in Laporte County, Ind., where the city of Laporte now is. He died Sept. 19, 1838; she died Dec. 25, 1852. Deep River, N. C., Mo. Mtg. marriage records contains on page 141 their marriage certificate; among the witnesses appear the following: Edward Bond, Anna Bond, William Hough, Sarah Hough, John Bond, Ruth Bond, Edward Bond, Jr., Martha Bond, Israel Hough, Jacob Dobbins, Mary Bond, Lydia Keys. Their children:

81. I. Anna Bond, b. Sept. 23, 1793; d. July 11, 1794, inft.

82. II. Mary (Wasson), b. May 9, 1795.

83. III. Sarah, b. Jan. 28, 1798; d. Aug. 11, 1816; s. p.

84. IV. Lydia (Wasson), b. Feb. 3, 1800.

85. V. Jesse, b. Feb. 14, 1803.

86. VI. Charlotte (Stanton), b. Aug. 9, 1806.

87. VII. William, b. Nov. 20, 1810.

88. VIII. John, b. March 3, 1813.

89. IX. Ira, b. July 25, 1815; d. Sept. 3, 1843, s. p.

13. EDWARD BOND, JR. (Edward-Joseph), son of Edward and Ann (Mills) Bond, was born on Deep River, Guilford County, N. C., Jan. 24, 1774; married May 17, 1795: Anna Huff, born Feb. 18, 1777, daughter of Daniel and Elizabeth (Christie) Huff. To this union was born eleven children. She died Sept. 22, 1839; he died March 14, 1856; both in Wayne County, Ind. After their marriage they settled in what is now Yadkin County, N. C., then Surry County. They moved to Indiana Territory in 1811, arriving at his father's in Wayne County on Nov. 5 of that year. They entered land where the town of Webster now is, where they lived the rest of their days. They built a cabin into which they moved the day before Christmas. The cabin was soon abandoned and a comfortable house entered. Then some years later they built a substantial frame house, which to this day, after something like eighty years' service, is a well preserved residence and looks very much like it did a half century ago except for some minor changes and the replacing of the plaster and pebble outside with weather-boarding. The land for the Friends' meeting house and graveyard was taken from his farm as well as the greater part of the town of Webster. After the division of Friends in 1828 into two societies, viz.: Orthodox and Hicksites, he and several of his children were affiliated with the Hicksite branch of Friends. Children:

90.   I.   Daniel Bond, b. Oct. 5, 1796.

91.   II.   Benjamin, b. Nov. 15, 1797.

92. III.   Keziah (Underwood), b. July 17, 1799.

93.   IV.   Elizabeth (Roberts), b. May 6, 1801.

94.   V.   Rachel, did not m.; b. Dec. 1, 1804; d. Feb. 1, 1851; s. p.

95.   VI.   Edward, b. Jan. 11, 1809; d. Dec. 22, 1840; not m.; s. p.

96. VII.   John, b. July 3, 1810; d. June 28, 1829; not m.; s. p.

97. VIII.   Huldah (Payne), b. May 22, 1812.

98.   IX.   Anna (Garrett), b. May 1, 1815.

99.   X.   Elias, b. June 25, 1817.

100.   XI.   Gideon, b. Aug. 18, 1820; d. June 11, 1839; s. p.

14. ANNA BOND (Edward-Joseph), b. at Deep River, Guilford County, N. C., Sept. 19, 1776; married June, 1803: Abram Bunker, born Aug. 1, 1768, son of Reuben and Judith (Macy) Bunker; a native of Nantucket Island, Mass. This Reuben Bunker was son of Reuben and Judith (Chase) Bunker. Judith Macy, above mentioned was the daughter of John and Eunice (Coleman) Macy, and the later John Macy was the son of John and Judith (Worth) Macy, also natives of Nantucket Island, Mass. I am not informed as to the particular place in North Carolina where Abram and Anna (Bond) Bunker resided from the time of their marriage until they moved to Indiana Territory, where they arrived March 1, 1815, with their then five children. They settled a few miles north of Richmond, near where her father then resided. Children:

101.   I.   Keziah Bunker (m. Fry), b. March 29, 1804; d. July 22, 1875, leaving no issue.

102.   II.   Thomas Bunker, b. Nov. 20, 1805.

103. III.   Phebe Bunker (Fisher), b. Dec. 24, 1807.

104. IV. David Bunker, b. Oct. 23, 1810.

105. V. Anna Bunker, b. May 13, 1812; d. March 8, 1832; s. p.

106. VI. Daniel Bunker, b. July 15, 1816.

15. JESSE BOND (Edward-Joseph), born Feb. 24, 1779, in Guilford County, N. C.; married 1802: Phebe Commons, born 1779, daughter of Robert and Ruth (Hayes) Commons. She died June 30, 1845; he passed away in his 84th year Nov. 4, 1862. He began preaching when quite young and became an eminent minister among Friends. In July, 1802, he removed his membership from Deep River Monthly Meeting in Guilford County, to Mount Pleasant Monthly Meeting in Grayson County, Va. In 1807 he emigrated to Indiana and became one of the early pioneers in Indiana Territory. He and his brother William were the first of the Bond family to settle in Wayne County, Indiana; others soon followed. He first settled on the farm where Earlham College now is, but in a few years moved on a farm a mile south of Greensfork. When White Water Monthly Meeting was established at Richmond in 1815 he was the first recorded minister. His son, William C. Bond, under date of July 20, 1885, wrote as follows about his parents, Jesse and Phebe Bond:

"They came to Wayne County, Indiana, in 1807; settled on where now is Earlham College. They raised eleven children, all married and had families before the parents died, and all living on good farms in Indiana. I, William, went a few days ago to the old farm at Earlham, the place of my birth, drank at the spring; saw the relics of the old chimley, and was shown one of the old apple trees that Jesse, my father 'hilled' on a drag from Ludlow's nursery, Cincinnati, about 1807, has some apples on it, another was cut down last spring, the stump about two feet across.

"Richmond had but three houses. Saulsbury was the county seat. I have heard Jesse Bond tell of he and John Charles taking warm blankets and hot bricks to the jail at Saulsbury to keep good young men from freezing, put in for muster fines in them days."

Quakers, being conscientious against war, would not muster and would suffer themselves to be put in jail rather than pay the fine that was imposed upon those who did not muster, as required by law.

107.   I.   Nathan, b. Aug. 16, 1803.
108.   II.   Robert, b. Dec. 23, 1804.
109.   III.   John, b. July 24, 1806.
110.   IV.   William C., b. Aug. 23, 1808.
111.   V.   Enos, b. July 22, 1810.
112.   VI.   Isom, b. Aug. 29, 1813.
113.   VII.   Ruth, b. May 12, 1815.
114. VIII.   Hannah, b. Jan. 27, 1818.
115.   IX.   Isaac, b. Feb. 27, 1820.
116.   X.   Jesse, Jr., b. April 4, 1822.
117.   XI.   Lydia, b. Dec. 3, 1824.

16. JOSHUA BOND (Edward-Joseph), son and eighth child of Edward and Ann (Mills) Bond, was born in Guilford County, N. C., Nov. 23, 1781; married Oct. 10, 1805, in Grayson County, Va.: Ruth Coffin, born 1781, daughter of Libini and Hephzibah (Starbuck) Coffin, and Libini Coffin was the son of William and Priscilla (Paddock) Coffin, and William Coffin was the son of William, Sr. Priscilla Paddock was daughter of Nathaniel and Ann Paddock. This is as far as the lineage has been obtained. After his marriage Joshua Bond lived a few years in Grayson County, Va., where he built a saw mill, which he operated in addition to his farming. In 1811 he moved to Indiana, first settling near Middleboro, in Wayne County. As I have in my possession a copy of a biography written by himself I will here let him tell the story of his life. He left quite a number of manuscripts on various subjects; some about the division and dissensions among the Society of Friends, one about the hardships and afflictions that he and his family had passed through. I will only here publish the one paper, his history, which I try to reproduce in his own language. His first wife, who was the mother of his children, died Nov. 23, 1847. His second wife was Mary Walton, widow of his cousin, Abraham Walton. Her maiden name was Allison; she died April 17, 1877. Joshua Bond died Sept. 11, 1876, aged nearly 95 years.

JOSHUA BOND'S HISTORY WRITTEN BY HIMSELF.

"This 12th day of the 1st month 1862 I have a mind to leave a small account of the life and labours of Joshua Bond ritten by himself. I was born and raised on north carrolina gilford county near the east fork of deepriver. I was born on the 28th day of the 11 month 1781 in a large settlement of friends my fathers name was Edward Bond my mothers name was Ann the daughter of John Mills and Sarah her name was Bales when young—my grandfather Bond name was Joseph and grandmother name Martha Rogers when young. the both came from Ingland in one ship when yong and after working to pay their passage the married—grandmother was thought to be a kinswoman of John Rogers the marter—my parents was studdy attenders of friends meeting and was greatly concernd to bring up their children two industry onistery and thruth. now I am in my eighty first year of life. I desire to expres something of what I have passed through I was brought up to farming but my father had a saw mill bilt when I was about sixteen. and I helped him tend the mill for sevrel years and we fixt up a cotton picking mechene at the mill the first that was nigh so there I was right in to publick business I got well larnt to tend the saw, and picking mechene and to measure boards so when I left my parents I came over the blue ridge mountains into new Virginia and perchased a mill seat on a stream called little reediland right in the wild woods a mild or more from a bous and about ninety miles from my fathers and I went onto my land to work in the spring of 1805, and I hiard a yong man by the month to work with me. though some times I worked a lone one time I worked a week without speaking with any body and I worked on and bilt me a cabin and a saw mill—and I found a yong women not fur off that needed a home her parents were broken up her name was Ruth Coffin so I married her the 6th day of the 10th month 1805 at friends meeting cald mountpleasent—which was about six miles from where I lived but friends soon a greed that there might be meeting held at my hous so there was a few friends met at my hous till we bilt a hous to meet at—so we lived there till we had three children—and I had bilt a grist mill nigh my saw mill and cleared a small plantation— and my parents came to my hous a moving to indiana territory

in the year 1810 so I concluded to leave new. virginia and cum
to Indiana territory so I fixt and came the fall of 1811 and was
five weeks on the road and it rained o good-dale of the time—"

"we got to fathers on the middle fork of white watter the fifth
day of the 11 month 1811 and I soon bilt me a cabin clost by
fathers and went to hewing houslogs for some of the neighbors
but it want long till a neighbor hired me to bild him a saw mill
on the middle fork of white watter a bout a half mild from my
hous, and it want long till he hired me to help him bild a fulling
mill the first I suppose in the territory of Indiana and I was the
head workman in bilding sevrel saw mills. a bout the settlement
of white watter and I bilt a fulling mill over in the Ohio state
near new paris and I was head workman in starting the first
carding mechene in indiana that I know of and I was head workman in bilding a fulling mill on greens fork near Washington and
a nother away out west of mill ford—and I pershed a mill seat
clost too my bous and bilt the first oil mill that I know of in the
state of Indiana I made the oil that was used on that big brick
meeting house at whitewatter—

"and I bilt me a grist mill and fulling mill and fixt in a carding
mechene and had the making of oil grinding carding and fulling
carried on for sevrel years. and I helped bild the brick meeting
house at goshen—and we had a great dale of company for sevrel
years and some of my family had become weakly we thought it
best to sell and move out near winchester we lived at white
watter twentyone year—I bought a sawmill near Winchester
randolf county that was out ov repair and I repaird it and dun
a good dale of sawing but I soon parted with it—I bought a plantation also there joining the town on the north side of winchester
that was out of repair and I repaird it and I had the first thrashing meshene bilt that I knew of while I lived their. I staid on
that plantation by winchester a bout three years—and friends
had there meetings at my hous a good dale of the time—then i
perched land in the wilderness of Jay county indiana where I
now live and took sum hired hands and a wagon load of per-
vision and bedding and tools to work with and cum into Jay
county in the fall ov 1835 to prepare bildings to move. too we
crost the massasinaway at the boat yards by words then went
on through the wilderness and crost butternut then crost the
sallimony up a buve the mouth of butternut so came down on

the north side till we came to William swallers who had cum a
little before from his hous we had to cut our road a bout one
mild to my land from near the massasinaway we had a narrow
crukid road turning round big logs and running over little ones
and through the bushes and over them also when we got onto
my land we stopped the wagon and went to looking for a place
to bild a house and a place to git watter while we bilt.

"So we dug for water at the edge of a masha looking place
and got watter in a bout four feet and it raised and run out and
has run watter for us everesence so we went to work and put
up a small cabin to camp in while we would hew logs and bild
a hous we got the logs hued and hold together and the founda-
tion laid all reddy for raising and the weather coald and we went
home nigh to winchester and brought out my hogs to git fat on
hickery nuts, and I was a sleding out property on the snow in
the winter and moved my famoly from near winchester the first
of the third month 1836 and we ware two days a coming the
way was narrow and cruked and the second day it snoad very
much and loaded the bushes down so it was difficult gitting a
long we crost the sallimony at william Bunches I went back
the next day for a nother load, and sum hands came out from
winchester to help us raise our hous so we got our hous up and
got into it right quick then went to clearing ground for corn
and to plant a orchard when we got the ground reddy we marked
it of for planting our corn I planted my apple seed and pear
seed then I cracked my peach stones and planted them in a
bout every fifth row and a bout every fifth hill in the row and
planted the rest of the ground in corn my peach trees came
up most as soon as the corn so the ware tended with the corn
so the peach trees groad famous and had peaches on them the
third summer but the first crop of corn got bload down in a
time that a most spilt the corn so I had to go in near winchester the next winter for corn. and in the spring had to go into
whitewater a bout six miles north of Richmond for corn I left
wheat groing on that plantation near winchester so when har-
vest came we had wheat and by the next spring we had land
cleared so that I soad a little spring wheat and it was good I
had to let my horses and cattle and sheep all run to the woods
the horses and cattle I often found from one to two miles from
home and sum times near twice that far I lost three hors beasts

the three I suppose was worth one hundred and fifty dollars for
I paid sixty dollars for one of them a little before and the other
two I raised and the cattle I lost I suppose was worth over one
hundred dollars. and we had to bring the sheep up every even-
ing and pen them clost to the house to keep the wolves from get
ting them, but there was fifteen of the sheep died the first summer so I had but five left the did well, we killed a number of red-
belleyed snakes and the first summer after that the want so plenty
their backs ware plack their shape was a bout like the black
viper them snakes was said to be very pisen and the first summer that I lived in these woods in Jay county the first meeting
of friends was held at my hous onst a week for a considerable
time but when there got to be a number of famolies moved in
then we bilt a hous to meet at and the first election that I remember being inpen (in Penn) township was hel in my mill
house I had bilt a hors mill to grind grain for my neighbors and
myself I had a pare of hand mill stones brought out to Jay before I moved my famoly into Jay that my neighbors and I
ground with till I bilt a hors mill I have ground a number of
grists for the poor and afflicted without any pay and I have
tended to the mill all night sum times to benefit the publick
now the reader may notice that I have been endeavoring to
benifit the publick ever cence I was a man   it is a great and
good thing to be truthful a doing our dutyes to benifit the Soul
and boddy of our selves and our fellow beings the first man that
died in this settlement was Aaron Rigby and I had the making
of his coffin and I helped to bild the first bridge over the sali-
mony that I knew of   so I was a trying to do sum good in the
world and not do any harm   I moved my thrashing mechene
to where I now live (and there was some loads of wheat brought
in the sheef and taken away in flour) and have it in uce yit and
the grinding mill is yit in uce—this 3 day of the 4 mo 1862"

"JOSHUA BOND."

I have not been able to obtain the complete record of births
and deaths. Children:

118.   I.   Anna (Coffin).
119.   II.   Abijah, b. Feb. 12, 1808, in Grayson Co., Va.
119½.   III.   Deborah, d. 1833-35, at Winchester, and buried
at Goshen, Wayne Co., Ind.; did not m.
120.   IV.   Phebe (Crow).

121.	V.	William, b. Nov. 25, 1819, in Wayne Co., Ind..
122.	VI.	John, d. s. p when young man.
123.	VII.	Hephzibah and
124.	VIII.	Elizabeth, twins, d. s. p.
125.	IX.	Joshua, d. s. p.
126.	X.	Daniel, d. s. p. **1194990**
127.	XI.	Mary, did not m.; d. s. p.

17. JOSEPH BOND (Edward-Joseph), the youngest of the children of Edward and Ann Bond, was born in Guilford County, North Carolina, Feb. 20, 1785; married Dec. 14, 1809; in same county: Sarah Mendenhall, born Dec. 19, 1790, daughter of Aaron and Mariam (Rich) Mendenhall. To this union was born ten children. She died Feb. 18, 1848; he died Aug. 18, 1864. He moved to Indiana Territory in 1810, accompanying his father; settled in the same neighborhood near Middleboro, where he spent the remainder of his life. Children:

128.	I.	Aaron, b. Aug. 8, 1811.
129.	II.	Isaac, b. Nov. 4, 1812.
130.	III.	Achsah (Jones), b. Dec. 10, 1814.
131.	IV.	Dinah (Hiatt), b. Dec. 2, 1816.
132.	V.	Mahlon H., b. Nov. 2, 1818.
133.	VI.	Marian (Brown), b. Nov. 17, 1820; m. Charles Brown; no issue.
134.	VII.	Ann (Jones), b. Dec. 8, 1822.
135.	VIII.	Peter, b. Oct. 17, 1824.
136.	IX.	Susannah, b. Feb. 25, 1828.
137.	X.	Esther, b. July 21, 1834.

19. SILAS BOND (Benjamin-Joseph), born in York County, Pa., July 15, 1783. He was married three times, his last wife surviving him. He died Feb. 23, 1858, in Wayne County, Ind.; buried on his home farm graveyard near Middleboro. He married first: Hannah Kennard, in Pennsylvania. To them was born three children. She died February, 1811, in Pennsylvania. Their children:

138.	I.	Benjamin, b. 1807.
139.	II.	Eli, b. 1809.
140.	III.	Silas Walton, b. Jan. 26, 1811.

His second wife was Lydia Alloway, born Jan. 27, 1786; died July 22, 1853; their children:

141.	IV.	Mary, b. Aug. 2, 1816.

142.   V.   John, b. Nov. 31, 1817.

143.   VI.   Milton, b. Nov. 7, 1819.

144.   VII.   Lydia, b. Nov. 6, 1821.

145.   VIII.   Stephen, b. July 21, 1824.

146.   IX.   Solomon, b. Aug. 5, 1826.

147.   X.   Jesse, b. Nov. 21, 1828.

Silas lived in Pennsylvania several years, then moved to Barnesville, Belmont County, O. The son Solomon was born there. They soon after moved to Wayne County, Ind., where they settled on a farm near Chester, where he resided for many years.

20. ELIZABETH BOND (Benjamin-Joseph), born in York County, Pennsylvania, about 1785; married Joseph Strawbridge; he was born Jan. 24, 1773, and died July 29, 1851, in Wayne County, Ind. She died 1826. After her decease he married second wife. I am not in possession of much of the data of this family. Her children so far as known were:

148.   I.   Mary Strawbridge; she m. Stephen Grave; n. f. k.

149.   II.   Sarah Strawbridge, m. Henry Jay son of John and Mary Jay; n. f. k.

150.   III.   Joseph B. Strawbridge; n. f. k.

151.   IV.   Benjamin Strawbridge; n. f. k.

152.   V.   Martha Strawbridge; m. Brown; n. f. k.

153.   VI.   Elizabeth Strawbridge; m.; n. f. k.

154.   VII.   Jesse Strawbridge.

155.   VIII.   Thomas Clarkson Strawbridge, b. Aug. 1, 1820; d. Feb. 3, 1879; buried in Goshen graveyard, northeast of Richmond.

21. RUTH BOND (Benjamin-Joseph), born in York County, Pa., Dec. 15, 1787; married about the year 1807: Isaac Vore, born April 3, 1783, son of Jacob and Mary. He died Feb. 24, 1862; she died Aug. 1, 1878. The date of their moving to Indiana is not known, but from a copy of a letter written and signed by them both we learn that he had entered land in Wayne County prior to the date of this letter, which was dated at Deercreek, Harford County, Maryland, Oct. 6, 1817. The letter was written to her uncle, Edward Bond, and desired him to lease the land if possible; if that could not be done to have some of their timber deadened. So there is little doubt of their arrival in Indiana soon after this date. Children:

156.   I.   Jacob Vore.
157.   II.   Mary Vore; married, but left no issue.
158.   III.   Eliza Vore (Gauze).
159.   IV.   Ruth Vore (Horney).
160.   V.   Anna Vore, d. in childhood.
161.   VI.   Rebecca Vore, d. s. p.
162.   VII.   Isaac Vore, d. s. p.
163.   VIII.   Martha Vore, d. s. p.

22.   ELI BOND (Benjamin-Joseph), born Jan. 26, 1790, in York County, Pennsylvania; married in same county Feb. 4, 1822: Mary Adkins, daughter of Jonathan and Sarah Adkins, She was born Feb. 6, 1800; died Feb. 13, 1884; he died Aug. 7, 1859. Residence Pennsylvania, Indiana and Iowa; moved to Iowa about the year 1847. Children:

164.   I.   William Arment, b. June 13, 1823; d. July 6, 1833; s. p.
165.   II.   Ruth W., b. Feb. 6, 1825.
166.   III.   Titus, b. April 8, 1827.
167.   IV.   Sarah A., b. May 10, 1829.
168.   V.   Calvin, b. Nov. 2, 1831; d. March 3, 1851; s.-p.
169.   VI.   William Arment (2nd), b. Aug. 2, 1834.
170.   VII.   Benjamin, b. July 31, 1837.
171.   VIII.   Eliza Ann, b. June 18, 1841; m. March, 1888, Joseph H. Stephens; she has no children.
172.   IX.   Mary Etta, b. March 17, 1845.

24.   MARY WALTON (Ruth-Joseph), daughter of Benjamin and Ruth (Bond) Walton; married Dec. 9, 1790: David Townsend, son of Francis and Rachel, both of Luzerne Township, Fayette County, Pennsylvania. They were married at Westland Meeting (Friends). Among the witnesses to this marriage were Benjamin, Ruth, Abraham and Martha Walton. N. f. k.

25.   ABRAHAM WALTON (Ruth-Joseph), son of Benjamin and Ruth (Bond) Walton, born 1761; had three wives; residence Pennsylvania and Indiana; died in Huntington County, Ind., 1849. He was at one time a resident of Wayne County, Ind., near Chester. First married May 29, 1794, Mary Heald, daughter of Nathan and Rebecca Heald, of Washington County, Pennsylvania. To this union was born seven children:

173.　　I.　Ruth Walton.
174.　　II.　Anna Walton (Armstrong).
175.　III.　Eber Walton; n. f. k.
176.　IV.　Abraham Walton, Jr.
177.　　V.　Rachel Walton (Votaw).
178.　VI.　Achsah Walton.
179.　VII.　Amos Walton.
His second wife was Phebe Shaw.　Children:
180.　VIII.　Leslie Walton.　Four others died infants.

In the year 1836 he married the third wife in Beaver County, Pennsylvania: Mary Allison.　Children:

181.　IX.　Ellis Walton.
182.　　X.　Elvira Walton, b. June 18, 1840.
183.　XI.　Eliza Walton.
184.　XII.　Joseph Walton.

28.　GABRIEL WALTON (Ruth-Joseph), son of Benjamin and Ruth (Bond) Walton, born Nov. 17, 1777; married March 12, 1802: Mary Townsend, daughter of Benjamin Townsend, a Quaker preacher of Chester County, Pennsylvania. She became a preacher of some note herself. She was born Sept. 8, 1781, and died Nov. 15, 1862; he, Gabriel Walton, died April 18, 1845.　Children:

184.　　I.　Edith Walton, b. in Columbiana County, O., December 10, 1802; m. John Wathey; had two children.

185.　　II.　Bathsheba Walton, b. May 16, 1804; m. Henry Criss; she died Oct. 20, 1852; four children.

186.　III.　Levi Walton, b. April 10, 1807; d. Nov. 7, 1811; s. p.

187.　IV.　Joseph Townsend Walton, b. Feb. 25, 1809; d. July 31, 1848; m. Annie Wiseman; had seven children.

188.　　V.　Jesse Walton, b. March 28, 1812; d. Nov. 9, 1842; m. Esther Wiseman; no children.

189.　VI.　Morris Walton, b. March 12, 1814; d. Sept. 27, 1872; had two wives and seven children.

190.　VII.　Eli Walton, b. April 19, 1816; m.; had one son.

191.　VIII.　Moses Walton, b. March 12, 1818; m. Eliza Chandler; had three children.

192.　IX.　Amos Walton, b. Jan. 21, 1820; married; two children.

193. X. William Walton, b. March 12, 1822; married; six children.

194. XI. Maria Walton, b. Aug. 6, 1823; m. Isaiah C. Shaw; residence Stark County, Ohio.

I have some further data of the Walton family, but it seems unnecessary to carry it farther in this history of the Bonds.

46. MARTHA BOND (Samuel-Joseph), daughter and eldest child of Samuel and Elizabeth (Beals) Bond, born in Surry County, North Carolina, Oct. 14, 1775; married Nathan Ballard, born in Virginia, April 22, 1778; she died in 1813 in Grayson County, Va.; he died July 29, 1838, at Richmond, Ind. Children:

195. I. Ahira Ballard; m. Mary Thomas; he d. and left one daughter, who d. s. p.

196. II. Sarah Ballard, b. 1803.

197. III. Rhoda Ballard, b. Aug. 23, 1805.

198. IV. Samuel Ballard, twin brother of

199. V. David Ballard, did not. m.

200. VI. Elizabeth Ballard.

All born in Grayson County, Va. Moved to Wayne County, Ind., a short time after their mother's decease.

47. MARGARET BOND (Samuel-Joseph), daughter of Samuel and Elizabeth (Beals) Bond, born in Surry County, North Carolina, Sept. 11, 1777; married Feb. 19, 1812: Welcome Garrett, of Surry Co., N. C., born Aug. 24, 1758. He died near Wesfield, Ind., Sept. 29, 1842, age 84 years; she died same place, Aug. 14, 1862, in her 85th year. He was the son of John Garrett. He had been previously married to Phebe Sumner and reared a large family. In the year 1834 he moved to Indiana. They lived a short time in Wayne County, then moved to Hamilton County, near Westfield. To Welcome and Martha (Bond) Garrett was born four children:

201. I. Rachel Garrett, b. April 23, 1813.

202. II. Jonathan Garrett, b. Dec. 12, 1814.

203. III. Hiram Garrett, b. Nov. 10, 1816.

204. IV. Jesse Antrim Garrett, b. Oct. 23, 1818; d. June 19, 1819, in infancy.

The author, in August, 1909, published a history and genealogy of Welcome Garrett and his descendants from both of his wives; which includes seven generations, and containing the names of more than a thousand descendants. The work also contains much valuable data relating to other branches of the Garrett family.

48. JOSEPH S. BOND (Samuel-Joseph), born in Surry County, N. C., Aug. 9, 1789; married Dec. 2, 1802: Rachel Harrold, born Dec. 23, 1780, daughter of John and Phebe Harrold; she died Oct. 28, 1842; he died Nov. 18, 1840, both in Indiana, to which State they moved in the year 1812, bringing certificates from Westfield Monthly Meeting of Friends to White Water Monthly Meeting at Richmond, Indiana Territory, as it was then. To them was born twelve children:

205.	I.	Darius, b. Dec. 26, 1803.
206.	II.	Eunice, b. Oct. 8, 1805; d. Jan. 24, 1870; s. p.
207.	III.	John H., b. Dec. 6, 1807.
208.	IV.	Mordecai, b. Sept. 24, 1809.
209.	V.	Joseph, b. July 29, 1811, in North Carolina.
210.	VI.	Amos, b. April 9, 1814, in Indiana.
211.	VII.	Levi, b. Nov. 4, 1815.
212.	VIII.	Elihu, b. April 28, 1817.
213.	IX.	Rachel, b. March 13, 1819; d. March 20, 1840; s. p.
214.	X.	Zimri, b. Dec. 25, 1820.
215.	XI.	Infant.
216.	XII.	Levina, b. Jan. 5, 1826.

49. THOMAS BOND (Samuel-Joseph), born Dec. 5, 1781, in Surry County, N. C.; married Mary Nation, born Sept. 30, 1782. He died Sept. 27, 1845, in Indiana. He moved to Indiana in 1813 with a certificate dated February of that year from Westfield (N. C.) Monthly Meeting. May 17, 1832, a certificate was received at New Garden Monthly Meeting, Ind., from Duck Creek Monthly Meeting for Thomas Bond and sons, Hiram and Pleasant. His children:

217.	I.	Amer, b. Sept. 2, 1805.
218.	II.	Betsey, b. Jan. 4, 1807.
219.	III.	Jesse, b. Oct. 7, 1808.
220.	IV.	Thomas, Jr., b. March 4, 1811.
221.	V.	Hiram, b. Jan. 7, 1814.
222.	VI.	Pleasant, b. March 4, 1817.
223.	VII.	Asenath, b. March 26, 1819; d. s. p.
224.	VIII.	Phebe, b. July 30, 1821.

225. IX. Mary, b. July 14, 1826; m. Benjamin Lamb; has no living issue.

51. SAMUEL BOND, JR. (Samuel-Joseph), son of Samuel and Elizabeth (Beals) Bond, was born in Surry County, N. C., April 12, 1786; married June 22, 1808: Charity Beeson, born Aug. 3, 1789, daughter of Amasa and Mary (Harrold) Beeson. This marriage is of record in the record book of Westfield Monthly Meeting of Surry County, N. C. This meeting granted him a certificate to Fairfield Monthly Meeting, Highland County, Ohio, on Nov. 10, 1810. They moved to Wayne County, Ind., not long after and settled near Webster. He died Oct. 6, 1858; she died Feb. 3, 1870. Tracing her ancestors, I find that her father, Amasa Beeson, was son of William and Mary, and this William was the son of Reuben and Charity Beeson. The children of Samuel and Charity Bond:

226. I. Amasa, b. Dec. 26, 1809.
227. II. Samuel, b. Dec. 27, 1811.
228. III. Ellis, b. Feb. 17, 1814.
229. IV. Ann, b. Oct. 24, 1816.
230. V. Ruth, b.
231. VI. Jonathan, b. Nov. 17, 1821; not. m.; d. s. p.
232. VII. Rhoda, b. April 8, 1824.
233. VIII. Lydia, b. Oct. 19, 1827.
234. IX. Jesse, b. Jan. 29, 1832.

52. DORCAS BOND (Samuel-Joseph), born Feb. 16, 1788, in Surry County, N. C.; died in Indiana about 1830; she married John Baldwin, born March 30, 1788, son of Daniel and Mary (Benbow) Baldwin, and this Daniel Baldwin was the son of William Baldwin and wife Elizabeth. This William Baldwin died Aug. 19, 1809. His father was John Baldwin, who died Jan. 19, 1767, and wife Ann, who died Nov. 9, 1741, O. S. Whether Dorcas Bond, the subject of this sketch, came to Indiana before her marriage or afterwards I am not informed. She died, leaving six children:

235. I. Joel Baldwin.
236. II. Eli Baldwin.
237. III. Rhoda Baldwin, did not marry.
238. IV. Ann Baldwin.
239. V. Eliza W. Baldwin.
240. VI. George W. Baldwin, b. 1829.

53. RACHEL BOND (Samuel-Joseph), born Sept. 11, 1790, in Surry County, N. C.; died in Wayne County, Ind., March 17, 1863; she married Thomas Teagle. To this union was born eight children:

241.   I.   Ornon Teagle.

242.   II.   Diadama Teagle; m. Sept. 12, 1839, Thomas Baldwin, res. Randolph Co., Ind.

243.   III.   Margaret Teagle, b. Oct. 1, 1820; d. 1904-5; m. Curtis Keener.

244.   IV.   Lorenzo Teagle.

245.   · V.   Delila Teagle.

246.   VI.   Orthaniel Teagle.

247.   VII.   Elmina Teagle.

248. VIII.   Isaac A. Teagle; n. f. k.

55. ELIZABETH BOND (Samuel-Joseph), born Jan. 21, 1795, in Surry County, N. C.; moved to Wayne County, Ind., with mother; married Isaiah Baldwin, date of his birth or decease not at hand. She died Jan. 25, 1841; her children:

248a.   I.   Nathan I., b. Jan. 15, 1817.

248b.   II.   Elizabeth, b. Feb. 3, 1826.

248c.   III.   Ann, b. Nov. 19, 1827.

248d.   IV.   Eunice, b. Aug. 30, 1831.

248e.   V.   Rachel, b. Jan. 25, 1834.

56. ORNON BOND (Samuel-Joseph), born in Surry County, N. C., July 9, 1798; married July 18, 1818, in Wayne County, Ind.: Anna Hunt, born June 23, 1800; she died Aug. 7, 1843; he died Jan. 16, 1873. He resided in Wayne County several years, then settled on a farm in Hamilton County, Ind., near East Branch Meeting of Friends, where he lived many years. Children:

249.   I.   Riley, b. July 11, 1819.

250.   II.   Eliza, b. Jan. 22, 1821.

251.   III.   Asher, b. June 14, 1824; d. March 19, 1843; s. p.

252.   IV.   Jane, b. Nov. 18, 1827.

253.   V.   Nathan, b. Oct. 27, 1829.

254.   VI.   John, b. Nov. 30, 1832.

255.   VII.   Jesse, b. Jan. 5, 1835.

256. VIII.   Joel, b. Jan. 17, 1838.

257.   IX.   Martha, b. Dec. 9, 1842.

57. RUTH BOND (Samuel-Joseph), the youngest child of

Samuel and Elizabeth Bond, born in North Carolina, Feb. 7, 1802. Moved with her mother's family to Wayne County, Ind., in 1812. Married Dec. 9, 1819: Joseph Teagle, born Sept. 21, 1782; he died 1836. To this union there were six children. She married a second husband Jan. 26, 1842, Ezekiel Haisley, by whom she had one child. He died 1857. She died July 20, 1869. Her children:

258.   I.   Matilda Teagle, b. Sept. 29, 1820; d. April 30, 1834; s. p.

259.   II.   Elizabeth Teagle, b. Oct. 12, 1822.

260.   III.   Martha Ann Teagle, b. Nov. 3, 1824.

261.   IV.   Allen Teagle, b. Jan. 19, 1827.

262.   V.   Agatha Teagle, b. Dec. 29, 1830.

263.   VI.   Eli Teagle, b. May 17, 1833.

The one by her second husband:

264.   VII.   Mary Haisley, b. May 11, 1843.

59. JOSEPH BOND (John-Joseph), second child and eldest son of John and Jane (Beeson) Bond, was born Feb. 29, 1780, in Guilford County, N. C. His parents being Friends or Quakers he had a birthright membership in that society. In the year 1795, when he was 15 years of age, a certificate of membership from Center Monthly Meeting of Friends of Guilford County, N. C., to New Hope Monthly Meeting of Green County, Tenn., was granted to Joseph Bond and his four brothers, Benjamin, Joel, Isaac and William. It is supposed that his father moved at that time from North Carolina to Tennessee, taking his children and moving their membership in the meeting, the father not being a member at the time. When in 1797 Lost Creek Monthly Meeting was established he and his brothers became members of that meeting, located in Jefferson County, Tenn. At the age of 17 years he married out of the meeting, contrary to the rules of the society, and thereby lost his membership. The records of Lost Creek Monthly Meeting, page 16, dated Nov. 18, 1797, read as follows:

"The preparative meeting complains of Joseph Bond for accomplishing his marriage contrary to the good order used among Friends. Also hath moved quite from among Friends, directly after he was married. This meeting therefore disowns him from being a member of our society until he comes

to a sight and sence of his misconduct and condemns the same
to the satisfaction of Friends, which that he may is desired on
his behalf."

It does not appear of record that he ever came back to apologize. From this time on no traces of him could be found in the
records of the monthly meeting. During the interval of twenty
years from 1884 to 1905 I wrote perhaps several hundred letters
in which inquiry was made for the descendants of this Joseph
Bond or those of his brothers. Finally locating many of them
in Missouri, some in Illinois and others in Kentucky. From'
these I learned that soon after his marriage Joseph Bond and
his father-in-law settled in Wayne County, Kentucky, near the
Cumberland River. Here is where he reared his family and
here his remains were buried. He died Feb., 1853. We learn
from his grandchildren that he, Joseph Bond, married (1797)
Abigail Hinds. She died about 1841. She was the daughter of
Joseph (?) Hinds, whose wife was a Ludlow. The children of
Joseph and Abigail Bond were:

265.   I.   Joel, b. Aug. 13, 1798.
266.   II.   Sarah, b. Dec. 12, 1799.
267.   III.   John.
268.   IV.   Jane, b. Sept. 7, 1803.
269.   V.   Samuel.
270.   VI.   Malinda.
271.   VII.   Matilda.
272.   VIII.   Joseph, Jr.
273.   IX.   Elizabeth, b. March 29, 1815.
274.   X.   Martha, b. Sept. 24, 1817; d. April 18, 1863.
275.   XI.   Hannah, b. Sept. 22, 1819; d. 1878.

60. BENJAMIN BOND (John-Joseph), born Oct. 19, 1781,
in Guilford County, N. C.; born a Quaker; his membership in
Center Monthly Meeting in North Carolina was changed in
1795 to New Hope Monthly Meeting in Green County, Tenn.,
and two years later to Lost Creek Monthly Meeting in Jefferson County, Tenn. The minutes of this last meeting says of
Benjamin Bond, under date of Feb. 2, 1801:

"Grassy Valley preparative meeting (located a few miles N. E.
of Knoxville) complains of Benjamin Bond for attending a marriage consummated contrary to discipline and dancing, and
using bad language."

This was continued through the meetings held in March, April and May, when he was disowned from being a member. I have not been successful in learning the further history of this Benjamin Bond, except that he married and was the father of a family and lived in Tennessee at least a few years. He had sons:

276.   I.   James (?).
277.   II. Benjamin, Jr. (?).
278.   III. William, and others whose names I have not learned.

William, it is said, was called "Whig Billy Bond" and that he married his first cousin, Clara, daughter of Isaac Bond. I have been unable to obtain further definite knowledge of his family or their present place of abode.

61. JOEL BOND (John-Joseph), son of John and Jane (Beeson) Bond, born Jan. 18, 1784, in Guilford County, N. C.; moved to Jefferson County, Tenn., in 1795, and a few years later settled in Wayne County, Ky., where he married Jane Hinds, born in Maryland, Nov. 20, 1787, daughter of Joseph Hinds (called "Miller" Joe Hinds) and wife Betsey. This Joseph Hinds being a brother to Abigail Hinds, who previous to this had married Joseph Bond, a brother to Joel. About the year 1835 he moved from Kentucky to Miller County, Mo. However, he lived a year or two in Breckenridge County, Ky., before going to Missouri. He died in Miller County, Mo., Feb. 1, 1856. His residence was west of Spring Garden. It has been said of him that he did not own slaves, as did some of his brothers. So far as learned the children's names were as follows:

279.   I.   William M., b. Oct. 2, 1815.
280.   II.   Stephen W.
281.   III. Benjamin, said to have not married.
282.   IV.   Joel, Jr.
283.   V.   Lewis G.
284.   VI.   Margaret.
285.   VII. Elizabeth.

62. ISAAC BOND (John-Joseph), son of John and Jane (Beeson) Bond, was born in Guilford County, N. C., Dec. 27, 1785; moved with his father's family to Jefferson County, Tenn., in 1795. He was born a Quaker and reared among them. He later moved to Wayne County, Ky., where he married Anna Holmes. About 1845 he moved from Kentucky to near Hickory Hill, Cole County, Mo. He served as a soldier, so it is said, during the war of 1812, and when a minor he. was bound out to Joseph Hinds. He died in Cole County, Mo., Aug. 27, 1856. He had a plantation and was the possessor of slaves. His children were:

286.   I.   Jane, b. 1807.
287.   II. Mahala.
, 288. III. Daughter, name not learned, but she married Charles McKinney.
289.   IV. Clara, who married her cousin, "Whig Billy" Bond, or William Bond, son of Benjamin; see history William Bond.
290.   V.   John J., m.; history wanted.
291.   VI. Perry; has issue; n. f. k.
292.   VII. Barton S., b. about 1827; d. Aug. 20, 1880.
293.   VIII. Amner Beeson, b. 1823.

64. WILLIAM BOND (John-Joseph), son of John. and Jane (Beeson) Bond, was born in Guilford County, N. C., Dec. 5, 1789; died in Cole County, Mo., Oct. 11, 1875. Moved from North Carolina to Jefferson County, Tenn., in 1795, and a few years later settled in Wayne County, Ky., where he married Charity Hinds, born Aug. 9, 1789, daughter of Joseph and Betsy Hinds. She died Jan. 30, 1866, in Cole County, Mo., to which place they moved about the year 1836, and settled near Hickory Hill. He was a soldier in the war of 1812. When in his minority was bound to his brother Joseph. Children:

294.   I.   Margaret Ann, b. Sept. 16, 1816.
295.   II. John Washington, b. March 24, 1821.
296.   III. Isaac Beeson, b. June 5, 1826.
297.   IV. William Shelby, b. March 22, 1829.

This completes the list of great-grandchildren of Joseph and Martha. End of fourth generation.

CHAPTER V.

FIFTH GENERATION.

66. EDWARD BOND (Benjamin–Edward–Joseph), born March 8, 1800, in Guilford County, N. C.; married May 25, 1825, Nancy Ann Hayworth, born Oct. 21, 1803, daughter of Henry and Elizabeth; occupation, farmer; he died Sept., 1847; she died 1843. He moved from North Carolina in 1827 to Henry County, Ind.; a few years later they settled in Lee County, Iowa. Children:

298. I.   Henry H., b. Nov. 17, 1826; did not m.
299. II. Lucinda, b. March 8, 1828; did not m.
300. III. Athalinda, b. June 6, 1830.
301. IV. Jedediah, b. April 16, 1832.
302. V.   Benjamin Franklin, b. Jan. 30, 1836; did not m.; d. August 23, 1880.
303. VI. Elizabeth Ann, b. March 3, 1843; did not m.

67. JONATHAN W. BOND (Benjamin–Edward–Joseph), born Oct. 15, 1801; married, settled on a farm at Cadiz, Henry County, Ind., where he lived many years; he died Oct. 1, 1877. They left no living issue.

68. JEDEDIAH BOND (Benjamin–Edward–Joseph), born Aug. 19, 1804, in Guilford County, N. C.; married Dec. 5, 1832, Elmina Stanley, born Feb. 10, 1812, daughter of Richard and Abigail (Foster) Stanley; she died March 3, 1847; he died Aug. 25, 1893, aged 89 years. At the time of his marriage he lived in Wayne County, Ind., where the eldest child was born. He moved to Lee County, Iowa, where he resided several years; returning to Indiana he settled on a farm near Lewisville, Henry County, where he lived until his decease. By this marriage he had six children. He married second Feb. 21, 1850: Dinah Bond, nee Kenworthy, widow of Isom Bond. To this union there was one child. Children:

304. I.   . Luzena S., b. Oct. 6, 1833, in Wayne Co., Ind.
305. II. Semirah, b. Feb. 6, 1836, at Newport, now Fountain City, Ind.; d. July 27, 1837, in infancy.
306. III. Martha Jane, b. July 14, 1839, in Lee County, Ia.
307. IV. Rebecca C., b. April 27, 1841; m. 1868, John Lowry; she d. Sept. 25, 1869, s. p.
308. V.   Angelina G., b. June 15, 1843, in Lee Co., Iowa.
309. VI. Elmina, b. Aug. 13, 1846, in Henry Co., Ind.

The child of the second marriage was:

310. VII. E. Mary, b. Jan. 30, 1854.

Further tracing the ancestors of the first wife, Elmina Stanley, I find that Richard Stanley, her father, was the son of Samuel and Sarah (Williams) Stanley, and Samuel was the son of William and Elizabeth and William was the son of James and Catherine Stanley.

69. TABITHA BOND (Benjamin–Edward–Joseph), born May 3, 1808, in Guilford County, N. C.; moved with her parents to Indiana in 1832; married May, 1840: Elias Newby, born Oct. 16, 1798, son of Joseph and Penelope Newby, of North Carolina; he died March 27, 1881; she died Nov. 6, 1896, in Henry County, Ind.; residence near Cadiz; his occupation, farmer. Children:

311.   I.   Eliza Newby and

312.   II.   Elizabeth Newby, twins, b. Feb. 14, 1841, in Henry Co., Ind,

70. NATHAN HUNT BOND (Benjamin–Edward–Joseph), born in Guilford County, N. C., Dec. 30, 1813; moved to Wayne County, Ind., 1832; married Dec. 30, 1835, Abigail Beard, of Union County, Ind., born March, 1817, daughter of William and Rachel Beard; she died Sept. 9, 1885; he died Nov. 16, 1883, at Pilot Grove, Lee County, Iowa. Residence, North Carolina, Indiana, Iowa; moved to Iowa before September, 1840. Ch:

313.   I.   Mary Etta, b. Dec. 16, 1837, in Wayne Co., Ind.

314.   II.   Rachel Ann, b. Sept. 24, 1840, in Lee Co., Iowa.

315. III.   William Penn, b. March 12, 1843, in Lee Co., Iowa.

316.   IV.   Tabitha J., b. Oct. 15, 1845; d. Aug. 13, 1847, in Lee Co., Iowa.

317.   V.   Hannah J., b. May 15, 1848, in Union Co., Ind.

318.   VI.   Elihu B., b. April 1, 1852, in Lee Co., Iowa.

71. WILLIAM BOND (John–Edward–Joseph); born in North Carolina, probably Surry County, Sept. 18, 1792; married Elizabeth Wiles, born Dec. 26, 1789, daughter of Luke and Frances Wiles. He moved to Indiana, whether before or after marriage I am not informed. He entered land in N. W. quarter Section 5, Township 17, Range 11, in Henry County, Ind., in July, 1827, where he resided until his decease, June 23, 1874; she died June 9, 1868. Children:

319.   I.   John, b. Nov. 3, 1820.

320.   II.   Amelia, b. Nov. 19, 1822.

321. III. Gulielma, b. July 15, 1824.

322. IV. Frances, b. Jan. 12, 1826.

323. V. Mary Ann, b. Dec. 13, 1827.

324. VI. Asenath, b. Jan. 6, 1830. *m Joel Adams - 1853*

325. VII. Elizabeth, b. Jan. 13, 1834; m. Samuel Brown, son of Isaac and Mary Brown; she died leaving no issue.

72. ANNA BOND (John–Edward–Joseph), b. Aug. 26, 1794; married 1851, John Hutchins, a preacher; she died March 10, 1858, s. p.

73. JOHN BOND, JR. (John–Edward–Joseph), son of John and Mary (Huff) Bond, born in Surry County, N. C., Aug. 7, 1796; married Millie Reynolds; both died in North Carolina; he died Aug. 8, 1818. Children:

326. I. Daughter, name not learned; d. s. p.

327. II. Nathan J., m. Rhoda Hutchins; they both d. s. p. in Southern Missouri.

75. MARY BOND (John–Edward–Joseph), born July 5, 1800; married Stephen Hobson in North Carolina. Children as reported follow:

328. I. David Hobson.

329. II. William Hobson.

330. III. Jesse Hobson.

331. IV. Mary Hobson.

332. V. Anna Hobson; she m. Elam Jessop. N. f. k.

She died Aug. 31, 1831. Stephen Hobson, it is said, married four times and raised several sets of children. Moved to Indiana and later to California. N. f. k.

76. ELIZABETH BOND (John–Edward–Joseph), daughter of John and Mary (Huff) Bond, was born in Surry County, N. C., Dec. 2, 1801; married Oct. 19, 1826: Benjamin P. Keys, son of Joseph and Mary (Pickett) Keys, of Surry County, N. C. Their children were all born near Rockford, Surry County. She died there July 30, 1833. He moved to Indiana in 1835, bringing the four children, and settled on a farm on White river four miles east of Winchester. He died Aug. 4, 1872. Children:

333. I. John Keys, b. Dec. 27, 1827.

334. II. Joseph Keys, b. April 30, 1830.

335. III. Mary Keys, b. Sept. 17, 1831.

336. IV. Daniel H. Keys, b. May 23, 1833.

77. JESSE BOND (John–Edward–Joseph), born in Surry

County, N. C., Nov. 9, 1803; married in Henry County, Ind.: Rachel Hobson, born 1819 (?), daughter of George and Deborah (Marshall) Hobson. He entered eighty acres of land in Henry County, Ind., in 1826. He died 1853; she died 1855; both died near Savannah, Mo. Further history wanting. Children:

337.   I.   George, b. Jan. 25, 1837.
338.   II.   Mary Ann, b. about 1838; d. 1855.
339.   III.   John, b. Aug. 6, 1840.
340.   IV.   Stephen, b. Sept. 8, 1843.

78. JOSHUA BOND (John–Edward–Joseph), son of John and Mary (Huff) Bond, born in Surry County, N. C., Nov. 14, 1805; married Rachel Davis, of same county, born Nov. 6, 1803, daughter of William Davis. He settled on a farm in Surry County. We find in Deed Record 'T', page 153, a conveyance of real estate by John Bond to Joshua Bond, March 31, 1827, for the "consideration of the mutual love a parent hath for a child and for the better support and maintainance of the same, 43 acres on the waters of Deep Creek on the east side of a branch of Deep Creek." Signed by John Bond. Witnesses, Caleb Bond, Daniel Vestal. Another deed from the same to the same and same date conveyed 60 acres. He died in North Carolina Sept. 3, 1859. She moved to Iowa in 1860, where she died March, 1876. Children:

341.   I.   Abel, b. Dec. 22, 1825.
342.   II.   Enos, b. Sept. 18, 1827.
343.   III.   William, b. Oct. 17, 1829.
344.   IV.   John, b. July 23, 1832.
345.   V.   Simpson, b. July 17, 1834.
346.   VI.   Mary, b. May 4, 1839.
347.   VII.   Anna, b. Jan. 8, 1842; d. Nov. 23, 1858, in N. C., s. p.

80. JOSEPH BOND (John–Edward–Joseph), son of John and Mary (Huff) Bond, born in Surry County, N. C., March 1, 1809; married Aug. 7, 1833, in Randolph County, N. C.: Naomi Cox, born Nov. 14, 1816, daughter of Mahlon and Catherine Cox. Six weeks after their marriage he moved to Henry County, Ind., and two years later moved to a farm in Parke County, Ind., where he died April 7, 1879; she died Oct. 10, 1905, in North Platte, Neb. Children:

348.   I.   Matilda, b. June 1, 1834.

349.   II.   John, b. Sept. 8, 1836; a soldier in Ninth Ind. Battery; he died July 6, 1864, s. p.

350.   III.   A son, b. March 2, 1839; d. 1839.

351.   IV.   Anna, b. April 26, 1840.

352.   V.   Nathan, b. March 1, 1843.

353.   VI.   Mary, b. July 23, 1845.

354.   VII.   Mahlon, b. Nov. 24, 1847.

355.   VIII.   Daniel H., b. Jan. 10, 1850.

356.   IX.   William, b. Dec. 9, 1853; d. infant.

357.   X.   A son, b. Feb. 9, 1855; d. infant.

358.   XI.   Adam, b. Feb. 16, 1856.

82.   MARY BOND (William–Edward–Joseph), daughter of William and Charlotte (Hough) Bond, born in North Carolina May 9, 1795; with her parents moved to Wayne County, Ind., in 1807, and a few years later they settled in Laporte County, Ind.   She married Calvin Wasson, a minister of the gospel among Friends; he was son of Archibald, of Irish descent; born Feb. 14, 1795; died Dec. 14, 1870; she died March 3, 1870.   Children:

359.   I.   William Wasson; m. Elizabeth Ellis; 4 ch.; n. f. k.

360.   II.   Nathan Wasson; m. Maria Cox; 3 ch.; n. f. k.

361.   III.   Elizabeth Wasson; m. Asa Hockett; 3 ch.

362.   IV.   Sarah Wasson; m. Abijah Ridgeway; 4 ch.; res., Amboy, Ind.

363.   V.   Mary J. Wasson; m. Thomas Branson.

364.   VI.   Eliza Wasson; m. Eleazer Carter.

365.   VII.   Rev. Calvin H. Wasson, b. Feb. 24, 1832; d. March 27, 1904; m. Abbie Morris; res., New Castle, Ind.

366.   VIII.   Asa Wasson; m. Jennie Vestal; 4 ch.; res., Tippecanoe Co., Ind.   N. f. k.

84.   LYDIA BOND (William–Edward–Joseph), born Feb. 3, 1800, in North Carolina; died Jan. 29, 1853, in Laporte, Ind. She moved to Indiana with her parents in 1807 and some years later to Laporte County, Ind.; married Jehiel Wasson, born Jan. 16, 1800, son of Archibald Wasson.   Children:

367.   I.   Jesse Wasson, b. Oct. 22, 1821.

368.   II.   Charlotte Wasson, b. Nov. 28, 1823.

369.   III.   Nancy Wasson, b. Sept. 30, 1825.

370.   IV.   Asenath Wasson, b. March 8, 1828.

371.   V.   Mary Wasson, b. March 10, 1831; m. James Posd k; she d. Aug. 26, 1854, s. p.

372. VI. Sarah Wasson, b. Jan. 17, 1834.
373. VII. Noah Wasson, b. March 14, 1836; d. April 16, 1855.
374. VIII. Elizabeth Wasson, b. Sept. 13, 1838; d. Jan. 12, 1839.
375. IX. Martha A., and
376. X. Lydia E. Wasson, twins, b. Aug. 23, 1840.
377. XI. Eliza Wasson, b. July 21, 1843.

85. JESSE BOND (William–Edward–Joseph), son of William and Charlotte (Hough) Bond; born in North Carolina Feb. 14, 1803; his father moved to Indiana Territory in 1807, first stopping in Wayne County a few years, then moved to Laporte County. Jesse married April 4, 1822: Mary Vore, daughter of Jacob and Mary Vore. Residence, Laporte, Ind. He died March 16, 1882. Children:

378. I. Lydia, b. Jan. 21, 1823.
379. II. Sarah, b. March 11, 1824; d. March 21, 1902; not m.
380. III. Isaac Vore, b. Dec. 2, 1825.
381. IV. Elisha, b. Sept. 16, 1827; d. Oct. 9, 1827, inft.
382. V. Silas, b. Sept. 17, 1828.
383. VI. William, b. May 13, 1830.
384. VII. Eliza A., b. Sept. 22, 1832; did not m.

86. CHARLOTTE BOND (William–Edward–Joseph), born in North Carolina Aug. 9, 1806; reared in Indiana; married April 10, 1834: Elijah Stanton, born Nov. 26, 1802; he died Jan. 11, 1885, in Santa Barbara, Cal., to which place they had moved from Laporte, Ind., in 1868; she died. Children:

385. I. Louise Elvira Stanton, b. Nov. 30, 1841.

87. WILLIAM BOND (William–Edward–Joseph), son of William and Charlotte (Hough) Bond; born in Wayne (one report says Henry) County, Ind., Nov. 26, 1810; moved with parents a few years later to Laporte County, same State. He married Mary Hitchcock, nee Mitchell; she died April, 1873; he died July 1, 1884; residence Indiana, Kansas. Children:

386. I. Fannie, d. in St. Louis, 1853.
387. II. William Henry, b. July 19, 1840.
388. III. Ira Mandaville, b. April, 1843; not m.
389. IV. Philip Quincy, b. Sept. 15, 1846.
390. V. Thomas Leonidas, b. Dec. 22, 1849.

88. JOHN BOND (William–Edward–Joseph), born May 2,

1814; reared in Laporte County, Ind. Married first Nancy Kennedy; to them was born two children. He died Jan. 28, 1881, at Lake City, Minn. Children:

391. I. Irene, b. 1837.
392. II. Melissa, b. 1839.

He married second: Nancy Barnett; children:

393. III. Jesse R., b. Sept. 5, 1847.
394. IV. Lorenzo D., b. April 22, 1849.
395. V. Charlotte, b. Aug. 18, 1851.
396. VI. Alfred P., b. Dec. 22, 1852.
397. VII. Emily, b. Feb. 11, 1855.
398. VIII. William T., b. Jan. 11, 1857; d. April 2, 1885; s. p.
399. IX. Calvin S., b. June 26, 1861; d. Feb. 5, 1885; s. p.
400. X. Benjamin, d. in childhood.

90. DANIEL BOND (Edward-Edward-Joseph), son of Edward and Anna (Huff) Bond, born in Surry County, N. C., May 10, 1796; moved to Wayne County, Ind., with his parents in 1811; married 1819: Mary Hussey, born March 13, 1797, daughter of Christopher and Sarah (Brown) Hussey, of Ohio. She died Sept. 30, 1837; he died Aug. 17, 1839, in Randolph County, Ind. Children:

401. I. Christopher, b. June 28, 1821.
402. II. Levina, b. March 11, 1824.
403. III. Sarah, b. May 31, 1826.
404. IV. Cyrus, b. Aug. 8, 1828.
405. V. Eunice, b. June 28, 1830.
406. VI. Simon, b. Oct. 21, 1832.
407. VII. Pleasant, b. June 27, 1835.
408. VIII. Peninah, b. June 11, 1837; d. April 11, 1858; not m.

91. BENJAMIN BOND (Edward-Edward-Joseph), born Nov. 15, 1797, in Surry County, N. C.; moved to Wayne County, Indiana Territory, in 1811; married March 18, 1828: Ellen Goldsmith, born Jan. 26, 1802. They resided at New Garden, near what is now Fountain City, Wayne County, Ind., for five years; moved to Williamstown, Grant County, Ky., where they only remained three months; returned to Indiana and entered land in Randolph County, Ind., in 1837, where they lived till 1854, when they moved to Hennepin County, Minn., where they lived many years. He died in

Labette County, Kas., Jan. 12, 1875; she died in Pulaski County, Ky., March 4, 1897. Children:

409. I. Erastus, b. Jan. 8, 1829; d. Jan. 30, 1829, inf.

410. II. Samson, b. Jan. 7, 1830.

411. III. Jacob Sylvanus, b. Feb. 11, 1832; d. Feb. 14, 1833, inf.

412. IV. Pelatiah, b. Feb. 8, 1834.

413. V. Hezekiah, b. Aug. 29, 1836.

414. VI. David, b. June 26, 1838; d. June 17, 1839.

415. VII. Benjamin, b. April 6, 1840, near Lynn, Randolph County, Ind.; d. while a soldier in Co. F, Third Cavalry Reg. Ind. Vol., Nov. 25, 1861, at Budd's Ferry, Md. Buried in Crown Hill Cemetery, Indianapolis, Ind.; not m. He first enlisted April 15, 1861, and served in Co. I, Eighth Reg. Ind. Vol. Inft., in the three-months term of service.

416. VIII. Daniel, b. April 2, 1842.

417. IX. Edward, b. May 5, 1845.

92. KEZIAH BOND (Edward-Edward-Joseph), born in Surry County, N. C.; July 17, 1799; moved with her parents to Wayne County, Ind., 1811; married 1816: Lewis Underwood, born in South Carolina, Dec. 9, 1789; he was a soldier in the war of 1812. They settled in Randolph County, Ind., in 1823, and in 1856 moved to Adair County, Iowa. He died July 26, 1865; she died May 17, 1866. Children:

418. I. Andrew Underwood, b. Dec. 28, 1818.

419. II. Jane Underwood, b. March 28, 1821; d. Feb. 5, 1843, s. p.

420. III. Susannah Underwood, b. Jan. 28, 1823.

421. IV. Exum Underwood, b. May 12, 1825.

422. V. Lucinda Underwood, b. Aug. 4, 1827.

423. VI. Elvina Underwood, b. March 24, 1829; m. Barnabas Payne; she d. 1870, s. p.

424. VII. Enoch Underwood, b. March 2, 1830; d. April 2, 1830.

425. VIII. Annet Underwood, b. May 17, 1831.

426. IX. Huldah Matilda Underwood, b. Oct. 4, 1833.

427. X. Anna Delano Underwood, b. Dec. 3, 1835; d. s. p.

428. XI. Elizabeth Lurana Underwood, b. July 29, 1837.

429. XII. Anderson Underwood, b. April 10, 1835; d. inf.

430. XIII. Keziah L. Underwood, b. Aug. 21, 1845; d. inf.

93. ELIZABETH BOND (Edward-Edward-Joseph), born in Surry County, N. C., June 5, 1801; moved with her parents to Wayne County, Ind., in 1811; married Dec. 5, 1816: Solomon Whitson Roberts, born April 14, 1795, in South Carollina, son of Thomas (born 1759) and Ann (Whitson) Roberts. This Thomas Roberts was son of Walter and Rebecca (Williams) Roberts. Walter, it is said, came from Wales, first to Bucks County, Pa., then to Frederick County, Va.; later the family moved to South Carolina. Immediately after their marriage Solomon W. and Elizabeth settled on a farm a mile west of Richmond, where they lived until 1853, when they moved to a farm five miles southeast of Pendleton, Ind. They were Friends and members of the Hicksite branch of that society. He died April 6, 1857; she died Nov. 8, 1884. Children:

431. I. Esther Roberts, b. July 11, 1818; d. Dec. 29, 1840, s. p.

432. II. Mary Roberts, b. Sept. 25, 1820; m. Charles Haines; she d. Dec., 1895, s. p.

433. III. Thomas W. Roberts, b. Dec. 16, 1822.

434. IV. Daniel H. Roberts, b. Nov. 10, 1824.

435. V. Milton Roberts, b. Sept. 13, 1826; d. March 28, 1850, s. p.

436. VI. Anna Roberts, b. Aug. 3, 1828; d. April 29, 1853, s. p.

437. VII. Edward Roberts, b. Feb. 4, 1830; m. 1856, Mary Ann Allen; she d. Nov., 1906; he d. Feb. 2, 1905, s. p.

438. VIII. Elihu Roberts, b. Jan. 13, 1832; d. June 8, 1858, s. p.

439. IX. Eunice Roberts, b. Nov. 10, 1833; d. April 29, 1869, s. p.

440. X. Solomon Roberts, b. April 18, 1836; d. Nov. 21, 1837, inf.

441. XI. Caleb Roberts, b. Jan. 27, 1838; d. Feb. 13, 1841, s. p.

442. XII. Hannah Roberts, b. Feb. 10, 1840; d. April 13, 1853, s. p.

443. XIII. Artemus Roberts, b. Oct. 28, 1841.

97. HULDAH BOND (Edward-Edward-Joseph), daughter of Edward and Anna (Huff) Bond, born in Wayne County,

Ind., May 22, 1812; married Barnabas Payne, born Aug. 18, 1812, son of Benjamin and Rhoda (Mason) Payne.. Benjamin Payne died in Stokes County, N. C. To this union was born eight children. She died Oct. 24, 1854. He married second time to Elvina Underwood, a cousin to his children. They had no issue. Residence North Manchester, Wabash County, Ind. Occupation farmer. He died July 6, 1866. Children:

444.   I.   Emily Jane Payne, b. Dec. 18, 1839; d. June 10, 1840, s. p.

445.   II.   Elias Payne, b. June 20, 1841.

446.   III.   Orlando Payne, b. Jan. 1, 1844; d. Dec. 20, 1852, s. p.

447.   IV.   Luzena Payne, b. May 12, 1845.

448.   V.   Albert Payne, b. Nov. 13, 1846; d. s. p.; not m.

449.   VI.   Anna Payne, b. April 12, 1848.

450.   VII.   Jesse Payne, b. Dec. 13, 1850; m.; no ch.; res. 1909, Los Angeles, Cal.

451. VIII.   Mahlon Payne, b. Sept. 25, 1852.

98. ANNA BOND (Edward–Edward–Joseph), born in Wayne County, Ind., May 1, 1815; married Dec. 4, 1834; (262) Jonathan Garrett, born Dec. 12, 1814, son of Welcome and Margaret (Bond) Garrett, then of Westfield, Surry County, N. C. He was born in North Carolina and emigrated to Indiana in 1832. To this union was born six children. She died in Sept., 1849, at Webster, Wayne County, Ind. He married second in 1856: Mary Shutes, nee Gray, and settled in Hamilton County, Ind., near Westfield. To this later union was born three sons, who died sine prole when young, unmarried. He died Aug. 24, 1899, aged 84 years. The children of Jonathan and Anna (Bond) Garrett:

452.   I.   Leander P. Garrett, b. Nov. 27, 1835.

453.   II.   Melissa Garrett, b. March 21, 1837; not m.

454.   III.   Vilena Garrett, b. Jan. 15, 1839.

455.   IV.   Caleb S. Garrett, b. March 12, 1840; d. Dec. 4, 1891, in Tacoma, Wash.; did not m.; was soldier almost continuously from April 18, 1861, to Oct. 12, 1891, when he was retired.

456.   V.   Salathiel Garrett, b. Feb. 5, 1843; d. April 16, 1864, while a prisoner of war at Tyler, Tex.; member of Co. F, Sixteenth Reg. Ind. Vol. Inft.; wounded at Sabine Cross Roads, La.

457.   VI.   Samuel Bond Garrett, b. Nov. 21, 1844.

99. ELIAS BOND (Edward–Edward–Joseph), son of Edward and Anna (Huff) Bond, was born in Webster, Wayne County, Ind., June 25, 1817; married April 24, 1842: Lydia Hutchins, born Sept. 26, 1823, daughter of Dr. Johnson and Susannah (Adams) Hutchins. They lived in Blackford County, then Wayne County, and about 1856-7 moved to a farm near Pendleton, Madison County, Ind. She died there July 9, 1871. He moved to Hamilton County, where he deceased March 31, 1904, aged 86 years. Children:

458.   I.   Solomon R., b. May 31, 1843.

459.   II.   Artemas J., b. Dec. 6, 1844; d. s. p. Oct. 21, 1861, in army. Eighth Ind. Vol. Inft.

460.   III.   Sarah Elizabeth, b. May 23, 1847.

461.   IV.   William H., b. Aug. 20, 1849; d. Dec. 15, 1863; s. p.

462.   V.   Anna Jane, b. Sept. 6, 1851.

463.   VI.   Jeremiah, b. Aug. 22, 1854.

464.   VII.   Mary Etta, b. May 11, 1857.

465.   VIII.   Martha Ellen, b. Jan. 26, 1859.

466.   IX.   Melissa Alice, b. Nov. 11, 1861; d. infancy.

467.   X.   Elias Edward, b. April 16, 1864.

468.   XI.   Dora May, b. Feb. 18, 1869; d. Aug. 31, 1872; childhood.

102. THOMAS BUNKER (Anna–Edward–Joseph), son of Abram and Anna (Bond) Bunker, born in North Carolina, Nov. 20, 1805; moved with parents to Wayne County, Ind., 1815; married Hepsey Swain (?). Children:

469.   I.   Ira Bunker, b. Nov. 16, 1836; m. Sept. 26, 1857: Minerva Benson. Children:

    (a) William C. Bunker, b. June 22, 1858.

    (b) Floretta E. Bunker, b. June 13, 1860.

    (c) Florence P. Bunker, b. Aug. 9 1865; des.
       Perhaps others. He d. Feb. 14, 1865.

470.   II.   Frank Bunker, m.; d. 1857; n. f. k.

471.   III.   Anna Bunker, m. Robert Neff; n. f. k.

103. PHEBE BUNKER (Anna–Edward–Joseph), daughter of Abram and Anna (Bond) Bunker, born in North Carolina, Dec. 24, 1807; married June 6, 1837, in Wayne County, Ind.: Edward Fisher; he died March 11, 1882; she died Aug. 22, 1875. Residence, Wayne County, Ind. Children:

472. I.   Ellis N. Fisher, b. Jan. 7, 1839; d. Dec. 28, 1891.

473. II. Daniel B. Fisher, b. Oct. 21, 1840.

474. III. Esther J. Fisher, b. Oct. 29, 1842; d. 1863.

475. IV. Alexander N. Fisher, b. Nov. 23, 1844.

476. V.   Ann Fisher, b. Jan. 7, 1847; d. 1891, in Texas.

477. VI. Theodore F. Fisher, b. Jan. 26, 1849.

104. DAVID BUNKER (Anna–Edward–Joseph), son of Abram and Anna (Bond) Bunker, born Oct. 23, 1810, in North Carolina; moved with his parents to Wayne County, Ind., in 1815, and in 1835 moved to Washington County, Iowa; married first, Miriam Hunt. Children:

478. I.   Anna Bunker, b. July 30, 1834.

479. II. Jesse Bunker, b. March 16, 1836.

480. III. Martha Jane Bunker, b. Sept. 23, 1838.

481. IV. Abram Bunker, b. April 7, 1841.

482. V.   William Henry Harrison Bunker, b. 1843; d. inft.

He married second, May 16, 1844: Julia Ann Holsinger Smith; he died June, 1886. Children:

483. VI. Mariam Bunker, b. Jan. 9, 1847.

484. VII. David Bunker, b. Feb. 23, 1850.

485. VIII. Phebe Ann Bunker, b. Oct. 25, 1852.

486. IX. Mary Elizabeth Bunker, b. July 23, 1856.

106. DANIEL BUNKER (Anna–Edward–Joseph), son of Abram and Anna (Bond) Bunker, born July 15, 1816, in Wayne County, Ind.; married Rebecca Hunt, born Dec. 4, 1820, daughter of Jesse and Marion (Wilson) Hunt. She died Oct. 15, 1854; he died Oct. 19, 1847. Children:

487. I.   Keziah Bunker, d. infancy.

488. II. Phebe Ann Bunker, d. infancy.

489. III. John C. Bunker.

490. IV. Nancy Melissa Bunker.

491. V.   Ann Eliza Bunker, b. Oct. 19, 1846.

107. NATHAN BOND (Jesse–Edward–Joseph), eldest son of Jesse and Phebe (Commons) Bond; born in Grayson County, Va., Aug. 16, 1803; moved with his parents to Wayne County, Ind., 1807; married July 21, 1825: Tamer Kenworthy, born 1806, in Warren County, Ohio, daughter of Robert Kenworthy, of Williamsburg, Wayne County, Ind. He moved onto a farm near Greensfork, where he also owned and operated a woolen mill and a sawmill. Carding and spinning wool and sawing lumber was carried on by him for many years. He died Nov. 22, 1888; she died June 12, 1889. Children:

492.   I.   Jonathan K., b. May 3, 1827.
493. II. Ruth Ann, b. Feb. 7, 1829.
494. III. Mary J., b.

108. ROBERT BOND (Jesse–Edward–Joseph), son of Jesse and Phebe (Commons) Bond, born in Grayson County, Va., Dec. 23, 1804; moved with parents to Wayne County, Ind., 1807; married April 20, 1826: Rachel Thornburg, born 1808 in Tennessee, daughter of Henry Thornburg. He resided on a farm one mile south of Greensfork; very successful and possessed many acres rich land. He died March 28, 1864; she died 1867. Children:

495.   I.   Henry T., b. Feb. 10, 1827.
496.   II. John, b.
497. III. Lewis T.
498. IV. Emily, b. 1831; d. 1855.
499.   V. Milton.
500. VI. Abner D., b. April 19, 1836.
501. VII. Lydia E., b. July 10, 1842.
502. VIII. Larkin T., b. March 16, 1847; d. 1882.

109. JOHN BOND (Jesse–Edward–Joseph), born in Grayson County, Va., July 24, 1806; moved with his parents to Wayne County, Ind., the following year, where he was brought up and lived the remainder of his life; married Jan. 17, 1828: Mary Barnard, born Nov. 26, 1811, daughter of Obed and Margaret Barnard. Occupation, farming. Residence, south of Greensfork, Wayne County, Ind. He died 1867; she died 1890. Children:

503.   I.   Margaret, b. Nov. 22, 1828.
504.   II. William Harlan, b.
505. III. Orlinda Elizabeth, did not m.
506. IV. Phebe J. N. f. k.

110. WILLIAM C. BOND (Jesse–Edward–Joseph), son of Jesse and Phebe (Commons) Bond, born Aug. 23, 1808, in Wayne County, Ind., on a farm where Earlham College now is; married Sept. 23, 1830: Hannah Locke, born Dec. 27, 1812, daughter of William and Damaris (Mills) Locke. He settled on a farm at the town of Greensfork. She died Aug. 17, 1888; he died Nov. 6, 1901, aged 93 years. Children:

507. I.   Oliver S., b. June 29, 1831.

508. II.   Damaris, b. Sept. 29, 1833.

509. III. Larkin T., b. Dec. 6, 1835.

510. IV.   Francenia, b. Dec. 10, 1837.

511. V.   Eliza J., b. Aug. 24, 1848.

512. VI.   Martha E., b. Aug. 4, 1853.

111. ENOS BOND (Jesse–Edward–Joseph), son of Jesse and Phebe (Commons) Bond, born in Wayne County, Ind., Nov. 22, 1810; married Feb. 21, 1830: Susan Hoover, born May 1, 1813, daughter of Jacob and Catherine Hoover; to this union was born nine children. Occupation, farmer; residence, Wayne and Henry Counties, Ind. She died May 15, 1869; he died Feb. 27, 1893. Children:

513.   I.   Calvin, b. Dec. 23, 1831.

514.   II.   Mary Ann, b. Nov. 25, 1833.

515.   III. William Commons, b. Oct. 29, 1835; d. Dec. 3, 1856, s. p.

516.   IV.   Hannah, b. Jan. 4, 1838.

517.   V.   Isom, b. April 21, 1840.

518.   VI.   Catherine, b. Sept. 1, 1842.

519.   VII. Eli, b. Aug. 11, 1844; d. May 16, 1905; did not m.

520. VIII.   Jesse, b. July 30, 1846.

521.   IX.   Phebe, b. Aug. 20, 1849.

112. ISOM BOND (Jesse–Edward–Joseph), born in Wayne County, Ind., Aug. 29, 1813; married Dinah Kenworthy; he died Miami County, Ind., 1847. Children:

522.   I.   Rebecca Ann, b. June 6, 1837.

113. RUTH BOND (Jesse–Edward–Joseph), born May 12, 1815, in Wayne County, Ind.; married May 8, 1834: Williams Nicholson, born Nov. 7, 1809, son of John and Mary (Williams) Nicholson. They settled on a farm a few miles southeast of New Castle, in Henry County, Ind., where he became a prosperous farmer and useful and influential citizen. She died March 9, 1888; he died April 22, 1890. Children:

523.   I.   Jesse Nicholson, b. March 22, 1835.

524.   II.   Merrit Nicholson, b. Oct. 19, 1836.

525.   III. Rachel Nicholson, b. Aug. 12, 1838.

526.   IV.   Reason Nicholson, b. May 27, 1841.

527.   V.   Nathan Nicholson, b. March 24, 1843.

528.   VI.   Martha Nicholson, b. Jan. 17, 1846.

529. VII.   Charles Nicholson, b. June 26, 1857; d. Oct. 5, 1861, s. p.

114   HANNAH BOND (Jesse–Edward–Joseph), born Jan. 27, 1818, in Wayne County, Ind.; married April 28, 1836: John Wilson, born May 12, 1816, died Oct. 7, 1852; she died Nov. 25, 1900.   Residence, north of Greensfork, Wayne County, Ind. Children:

530.   I.   Lydia Wilson, b. March 14, 1837.
531.   II.   Oliver Wilson, b. Feb. 3, 1839.
532.   III.   Martha E. Wilson, b. Sept. 21, 1840.
533.   IV.   Phebe B. Wilson, b. Sept. 21, 1842; d. July 1, 1857; s. p.
534.   V.   Adaline Wilson, b. Jan. 18, 1845.
535.   VI.   Jesse B. Wilson, b. Jan. 29, 1847; d. Dec. 28, 1870; did not m.
536.   VII.   Eliza A. Wilson, b. July 12, 1849; d. April 1, 1875; s. p. -
537. VIII.   James Addison Wilson, b. March 10, 1851.

115.   ISAAC BOND (Jesse–Edward–Joseph), son of Jesse and Phebe (Commons) Bond, born Feb. 27, 1820, in Wayne County, Ind.; married Feb. 1, 1844: Catherine Eargood; she died April 27, 1849, leaving three children.   He married second, 1851, Millicent Mendenhall, of Wayne County, Ind.; two children. Residence, Miami County, Ind.   He died July 19, 1890; farmer; Children:

538.   I.   Lewis, b. Oct. 15, 1844.
539.   II.   Arthur, b. Dec. 10, 1846.
540.   William, b. Nov. 27, 1848; d. March 23, 1876.
Children of second marriage:
541.   IV.   Clara, b. 1858.
542.   V.   Lydia, b. 1865.   N. f. k.

116.   JESSE BOND (Jesse–Edward–Joseph), son of Jesse and Phebe (Commons) Bond, born in Wayne County, Ind., April 4, 1822; married Sept. 30, 1841: Jane Cox.   She died Feb. 24, 1856. Children:

543.   I.   Robert, b. Sept. 27, 1842.
544.   II.   Emaline, no issue, b. Dec. 17, 1846.
545.   III.   David, b. July 25, 1849.
546.   IV.   Riley, b. 1844; d. 1844.
547.   V.   Charles, b. Nov. 29, 1851.

Jesse married second June 11, 1857, Harriet Hough. Children:

548.   VI.   Ira, b. April 8, 1858; m.; dec; no living issue.

549.   VII.   Nellie, b. Jan. 20, 1863; d. s. p.

550.   VIII.   Albert, b. Oct. 11, 1865; m.

551.   IX.   Ruth, b. Jan. 6, 1868; d. Nov. 19, 1898.

a551.   X.   Benjamin, b. Dec. 27, 1871.

Jesse Bond married third March 7, 1894, Mrs. Belle Titus, nee King. P. O. 1908, Mexico, Ind.

117. LYDIA BOND (Jesse–Edward–Joseph), daughter of Jesse and Phebe (Commons) Bond, born Dec. 3, 1824, in Wayne County, Ind.; married Dec. 21, 1843: Oliver Mendenhall, born Jan. 26, 1820, son of William and Rebecca (Coffin) Mendenhall. They settled on a farm on Blue river, near New Castle, Ind. She died Oct. 6, 1903. Children:

552.   I.   Orilla Mendenhall, b. Dec. 28, 1844.

553.   II.   Jesse Mendenhall, b. Nov. 11, 1846.

554.   III.   William Mendenhall, b. June 23, 1850.

555.   IV.   Mattie Mendenhall, b. Dec. 4, 1857.

556.   V.   Emily Mendenhall, b. 1848; d. s. p. 1864.

557.   VI.   Luther Mendenhall.

558.   VII.   Charles Mendenhall.

118. ANNA BOND (Joshua–Edward–Joseph), eldest child of Joshua and Ruth (Coffin) Bond, born 1806 in Grayson County, Va.; moved to Indiana with her parents in 1811; married Greenby Coffin; she died Sept. 7, 1835; was buried at Goshen graveyard, Wayne County, Ind. One child:

559.   I.   Deborah Coffin, b. Aug. 11, 1835, in Randolph Co., Ind., near Winchester.

119. ABIJAH BOND (Joshua–Edward–Joseph), son of Joshua and Ruth (Coffin) Bond, born in Grayson County, Va., Feb. 12, 1808; moved to Indiana with parents in 1811, lived in Wayne and Randolph Counties and moved into Jay County, near Pennville, in 1835, where he lived until he was 91 years old. He died Aug. 26, 1899. Married 1850: Mary Ann Perry, born 1830, daughter of Nathan and Lydia (Thomas) Perry; she died Aug. 13, 1867. Children:

560.   I.   Lydia E., b. Feb. 21, 1851.

561.   II.   John Joshua, b. Sept. 12, 1853.

562.   III.   Ruth Jane, b. Oct. 10, 1855; d. May 15, 1884.

563.   IV.   Susan Palena, b. April 23, 1858.

564. V. Sarah Elizabeth, b. Jan. 7, 1861.

565. VI. Phebe Ann, b. May 7, 1863; d. Feb. 1, 1884.

566. VII. Minerva Arena, b. Nov. 23, 1866; d. Sept. 18, 1871.

120. PHEBE BOND (Joshua–Edward–Joseph), daughter of Joshua and Ruth (Coffin) Bond, born Feb. 16, 1812, in Wayne County, Ind.; married Jan. 12, 1839, at Pennville, Jay County, Ind.: Joshua Crow, born Jan. 29, 1795; he died Jan. 29, 1853; she died April 7, 1884. Residence, Jay County, Ind. Children:

567. I. Ruth Anna Crow, b. Oct. 9, 1840; d. Dec. 7, 1852, s. p.

568. II. Daniel Bond Crow, b. June 6, 1842.

569. III. Abel Lee Crow, b. March 9, 1844; d. Aug. 7, 1892.

570. IV. Abijah Thomas Crow, b. Nov. 15, 1846.

571. V. Reuben C. Crow, b. March 24, 1848.

572. VI. Mary Deborah Crow, b. Oct. 10, 1850.

573. VII. Jesse Bond Crow, b. May 2, 1853.

121. WILLIAM BOND (Joshua–Edward–Joseph), born in Wayne County, Ind., Nov. 25, 1819; married March 10, 1845: Lavina McCoy; a few years later moved to Cedar County, Mo.; occupation, farmer; he died Nov. 4, 1877; she died Oct. 7, 1881. Children:

574. I. John Thomas, b. Dec. 13, 1845; d. March 16, 1850, in childhood.

575. II. Mary Elizabeth, b. March 16, 1851.

128. AARON BOND (Joseph–Edward–Joseph), eldest son of Joseph and Sarah (Mendenhall) Bond, born near Middleboro, Wayne County, Ind., Jan. 8, 1811; married Feb. 2, 1834: Amy Wright, daughter of Raford and Ursula Wright. He by occupatiou was a millwright, and moved to Huntington, Ind., where he helped to build the first sawmill on Richland Creek. He died at Dora, Wabash County, July 18, 1877. He had ten children by this wife and one by a second marriage. He married second July 25, 1855: Elizabeth B. Leedy, born April 4, 1817, died Nov. 23, 1865. Children by first wife:

576. I. James W., b. Dec. 29, 1834; d. Sept. 28, 1835, infancy.

577. II. Louisa, b. July 2, 1836.

III. Mary Jane, b. March 22, 1838; d. June 6, 1855, s. p.

578. IV. Ellis Marshall, b. May 28, 1840; d. Oct. 26, 1840.

579.   V.   Zilpha Ann, b. Dec. 24, 1841.

580.   VI.   Melissa Ellen, b. Aug. 8, 1844; d. Oct. 10, 1854,
s. p.

581.   VII.   ⁻Joseph R., b. Jan. 27, 1846; d. Nov. 27, 1867., s. p.

582.   VIII.   Ursula Harriet, b. March 7, 1848.

583.   IX.   Sarah Elizabeth, b. March 16, 1850; d. March 15,
1852.

584.   X.   Wright, b. July 14, 1854; d. Aug. 19, 1854, inft.

One child by second marriage:

585.   XI.   Henry D., b. March 23, 1856; d. July 23, 1877.
N. f. k.

129. ISAAC BOND (Joseph–Edward–Joseph), son of Joseph
and Sarah (Mendenhall) Bond, born in Wayne County, Ind.,
Nov. 4, 1812; married Jan. 11, 1836: Sarah Hiatt. To this union
were born six children. He died Aug. 17, 1876. The widow
married Feb. 9, 1878: Jason Holloway. She died Nov. 16, 1883,
Jason Holloway died April 11, 1884. The children of Isaac and
Sarah Bond:

586.   I.   Cyrus, b. Dec. 25, 1836; d. 1839, childhood.

587.   II.   Lydia, b. June 29, 1839.

588.   III.   Emily, b. Nov. 16, 1841; d. Jan. 21, 1870.

589.   IV.   Susannah, b. May 18, 1843; d. s. p.

590.   V.   Rosanna, b. Sept. 14, 1845.

591.   VI.   Mary, b. Dec. 24, 1847.

130. ACHSAH BOND (Joseph–Edward–Joseph), daughter
of Joseph and Sarah (Mendenhall) Bond, born in Wayne County,
Ind., Dec. 10, 1814; married Nov. 3, 1832: Sylvanus Jones, son
of Micajah; he was born Oct. 6, 1809, in North Carolina; he died
Feb. 28, 1896; she died March 6, 1903, aged 88 years. Their
long lives were mostly spent in or near Richmond, Ind. Children:

592.   I.   Joseph Jones, b. Sept. 6, 1833.

593.   II.   Sarah Jones, b. March 12, 1835.

594.   III.   Elizabeth Jones, b. Feb. 11, 1837.

595.   IV.   Abigail Jones, b. Nov. 1, 1838.

596.   V.   Mahlon Jones, b. Dec. 27, 1841.

597.   VI.   Caleb Jones, d. inft.

598.   VII.   Susannah Jones, b. Aug. 24, 1845; d. Dec., 1858,
s. p.

599.   VIII.   Abijah Jones, b. Jan. 20, 1848.

600.   IX.   William Jones, b. June 20, 1850; d. Dec., 1858, s. p.

601.   X.   Ann Jones, d. infant.

602.   XI.   Jemima Jones, b. Sept. 24, 1854.

603.   XII.   Mary Jones, b. Feb. 16, 1857.

131. DINAH BOND (Joseph–Edward–Joseph), born Dec. 2, 1816, in Wayne County, Ind.; married Feb. 6, 1836: Joseph Hiatt, born Dec. 8, 1811; she died Sept. 28, 1851. She had ten children. He married second wife: Mary Cook, nee Bond, widow of John Cook and daughter of Silas Bond. He died April 1882. Children:

604.   I.   Mary Ann Hiatt, b. Nov. 25, 1836; d. Nov. 28, 1836; inft.

605.   II.   Emaline Hiatt, b. Nov. 1, 1837; d. March 14, 1845, in childhood.

606.   III.   Sylvester Hiatt, b. Aug. 24, 1839; d. April 14, 1840.

607.   IV.   Amanda Elvira Hiatt, b. Feb. 8, 1841.

608.   V.   Eleanor Hiatt, b. April 14, 1842; d. June 17, 1842.

609.   VI.   Joseph Hiatt, b. March 20, 1843; d. Aug. 21, 1845.

610.   VII.   James Hiatt, b. April 26, 1846; d. same date.

611. VIII.   Sarah A. Hiatt, b. Oct. 14, 1847.

612.   IX.   Abigail Hiatt, b. Aug 2, 1849.

613.   X.   Solomon Hiatt, b. Sept. 28, 1851; d. Jan. 13, 1875, s. p.

132. MAHLON H. BOND (Joseph–Edward–Joseph), son of Joseph and Sarah (Mendenhall) Bond, born Nov. 2, 1818, in Wayne County, Ind., near Middleboro, near which place he made his home throughout life. He and his eldest son, Ezra, were soldiers during the war in Co. H, 84th Reg. Ind. Vol. Inft. He married March 28, 1839: Susan Mullin, born March 29, 1822. She was the mother of six children. She died Dec. 1, 1850. He married second Oct. 30, 1851: Martha P. Bennett, by whom he had four children. He died March 21, 1891. Children by first wife:

614.   I.   Ezra, b. May 15, 1840.

615.   II.   Mary A., b. Aug. 12, 1842.

616.   III.   Esther D., b. Sept., 1844.

617.   IV.   Rachel, b. June 25, 1846; d. Sept. 9, 1847, inft.

618.   V.   Willard P., b. June 23, 1848; now d.; was a soldier in the regular army; had no issue.

619.   VI.   Lydia E., b. Feb. 2, 1853; d. March 15, 1853.

621. VIII. Ann E., b. Feb. 2, 1853; d. March 17, 1853.

622.   IX.   Mahlon C. Perry, b. March 4, 1854.

623.   X.   Anna P., b. Nov. 25, 1855.

134. ANN BOND (Joseph–Edward–Joseph), born Dec. 8, 1822, in Wayne County, Ind.; married Oct. 24, 1839: Elihu Jones, born March 8, 1818, son of Micajah Jones; he died Nov. 19, 1850; she died Dec. 5, 1907. They had five children:

624.   I.   A son, b. Sept. 30, 1840; d. Oct., 1840, inft.

625.   II.   Jesse Jones, b. Jan. 31, 1843.

626.   III.   Martha Jones, b. Nov. 10, 1844.

627.   IV.   Amos Jones, b. Feb. 7, 1847.

628.   V.   Joseph B. Jones, b. Aug. 26, 1849.

The widow, Ann (Bond) Jones, married second, Oct. 4, 1856: Peter Wright, also a resident of Wayne County, born March 3, 1810, died April 13, 1899. Their children:

629.   VI.   Thomas Wright, b. Aug. 4, 1857.

630.   VII.   Edward Wright, b. Oct. 11, 1859.

631. VIII. Charles J. Wright, b. Nov. 1, 1861.

632.   IX.   Ellen Wright, b. Aug. 17, 1865.

135. PETER BOND (Joseph–Edward–Joseph), son of Joseph and Sarah (Mendenhall) Bond, born Oct. 17, 1824, in Wayne County, Ind., where he resided until his decease; he was a blacksmith by trade; married Sept. 5, 1850: Martha Fulgham, born Dec. 11, 1831, daughter of Frederick and Piety (Parker) Fulgham; he died Aug. 31, 1881. She married David Little and for third husband Alpheus Test. She died April 28, 1901. The children of Peter and Martha Bond:

633.   I.   Erastus, b. Oct. 21, 1851.

634.   II.   Fredricka Jane, b. June 11, 1855; d. Nov. 21, 1875, s. p.

635.   III.   Miriam, b. Nov. 1, 185–; d. Oct. 24, 1864, in childhood.

636.   IV.   Charles Francis, b. April 18, 1860.

637.   V.   Josiah Rockwell, b. Sept. 16, 1862; d. Aug. 6, 1864.

638.   VI.   Marcanna, b. Jan. 4, 1866.

639.   VII.   Sarah, b. Oct. 27, 1870.

640. VIII. Henry Herbert, b. June 12, 1874; d. June 16, 1874, inft.

136. SUSANNAH BOND (Joseph-Edward-Joseph), born Feb. 25, 1828, near Middleboro, Ind.; married Sept. 17, 1846: John Brown, residence Arba, Wayne County, Ind. She died May 4, 1908. To this union was born ten children, five d. s. p.:

641. I. Nancy Brown, b. July 21, 1848; m. Aug. 12, 1888: Mahlon Jones; res. Arba, Ind.

642. II. Martha Ann Brown, b. June 3, 1853; m. Oct. 12, 1875: Samuel A. Rupe. Address Ridgeville, Ind. Three sons.

0642. III. Mary Jane Brown, b. Oct. 12, 1863; m. Aug. 12, 1877: Jonathan A. Rush. Eight ch.

643. IV. Joshua Brown, b. Sept. 24, 1866; m. Cora Somers. Address Crete, Ind. Three ch.

644. V. Sarah Adaline Brown, b. Nov. 29, 1870; m. Oct. 8, 1907: Joseph P. Skinner, of Fountain City, Ind. R. F. D.

137. ESTHER BOND (Joseph-Edward-Joseph), youngest child of Joseph and Sarah (Mendenhall) Bond, born July 21, 1834, in Wayne County, near Middleboro; married Dec. 25, 1851, Jonathan Jay. Children:

645. I. Sarah Jay.

646. II. Perry (?) Jay. N. f. k.

138. BENJAMIN BOND (Silas-Benjamin-Joseph), son of Silas and Hannah (Kennard) Bond, born 1807, in York County, Pa.; moved to Union County, Ind.; married March 28, 1832: Lydia Test, born March 17, 1813, daughter of Samuel and Sarah (Maxwell) Test. He was a manufacturer of woolen goods. He moved into Richmond, Ind., in 1848; died by acdent Nov. 22, 1850. Children:

647. I. Martha, b. Feb. 22, 1833.

648. II. Hannah, b. Nov. 7, 1834.

649. III. Sarah, b. Dec. 16, 1837.

650. IV. Elizabeth, b. Feb. 7, 1839.

651. V. Mary, b. Oct. 7, 1841.

652. VI. William, b. Oct. 9, 1844.

653. VII. Susan, b. Feb. 17, 1847.

654. VIII. Esther, b. Feb. 2, 1850.

139. ELI BOND (Silas-Benjamin-Joseph), born in York County, Pa., about 1809; married 1847 at Galena, Ill.: Sarah

Denio. He died 1852 at Galena, Ill. The widow and son, Silas W., moved to Iowa Falls, Ia., in 1872. Children:

    655.   I. Mary Stevens, b. Oct. 1848; d. July, 1885.

    656. II. Silas Walter, b. April 2, 1850, at Galena, Ill.

    140. SILAS WALTON BOND (Silas-Benjamin-Joseph), son of Silas and Hannah (Kennard) Bond, born Jan. 26, 1811, in York County, Pa.; moved to Wayne County, Ind.; married: Jan. 14, 1835: Rebecca Williams, born June 9, 1816, daughter of Daniel and Margaret (Jeans) Williams. They lived several years in Indiana, near Richmond. In 1848 they moved to Galena, Ill. In 1865 they located in Iowa Falls, Ia., where they lived many years. He died Feb. 23, 1907, age 96 years, they having lived together seventy-two years; she died March 16, 1910, in her 94th year. Children:

    657.   I. Daniel, b. Nov. 28, 1835.

    658. II. Josiah, b. June 10, 1838.

    658½. III. Charles, b. 1840; d. s. p.

    659. IV. Mary, b. 1842; d. s. p.

    660.   V. Martha E., b. Nov. 20, 1844.

    661. VI. Adaline, b. Dec. 24, 1848.

    662. VII. Emma J., b. April 4, 1859.

    141. MARY BOND (Silas-Benjamin-Joseph), daughter of Silas and Lydia (Alloway) Bond, born Aug. 2, 1816; married John Cook; resided in Indiana. Further history wanting.

    142. JOHN BOND (Silas-Benjamin-Joseph), son of Silas and his second wife, Lydia (Alloway) Bond, born Nov. 30, 1817, in York County, Pa.; married; data wanted. Moved to Iowa, where he deceased. N. f. k.

    143. MILTON BOND (Silas-Benjamin-Joseph), son of Silas and Lydia (Alloway) Bond, born Nov. 7, 1819; married Nov. 1, 1838: Sarah Cook, born Oct. 4, 1816; he died Aug. 6, 1862; she died July 12, 1902. Residence Indiana. Children:

    663.   I. John W., b. Sept. 28, 1839.

    664. II. Lucinda B., b. Oct. 21, 1841.

    665. III. William P., b. May 9, 1844; dec. while a prisoner in the army at Vicksburg, Miss., Jan. 14, 1863.

    144. LYDIA BOND (Silas-Benjamin-Joseph), born Nov. 6, 1821; married Jefferson Zeek; residence Wayne County, Ind. Children:

    666.   I. Silas Zeek, b. Sept. 23, 1844.

667.   II.   William A. Zeek, b. Nov. 18, 1846.
668.   III.   Clayton B. Zeek, b. April 30, 1849.
669.   IV.   Milton J. Zeek, b. July 19, 1852.
669½.   V.   Stephen Zeek, b. Sept. 29, 1854; dec.
670.   VI.   Lydia Mary Zeek, b. April 29, 1857.

145. STEPHEN BOND (Silas-Benjamin-Joseph), b. July 21, 1824; married Sarah Graham, born Aug. 24, 1827; she died March 23, 1884; he died Sept., 1857, in Jo Daviess County, Ill. Residence Indiana, Illinois. Children:

671.   I.   John, b. Feb. 22, 1848.
672.   II.   Jesse, b. June 2, 1850.
673.   III.   Benjamin Franklin, b. Dec. 19, 1852.

146. SOLOMON BOND (Silas - Benjamin - Joseph), born Aug. 5, 1826, at Barnesville, Belmont County, Ohio; moved to Wayne County, Ind., with his parents when a small boy; in 1870 he moved to Darlington, Ind., and in 1892 lived at Boxley, Hamilton County, Ind.; he married Nov. 28, 1848: Eliza Williams, daughter of William and Mary Williams. She died Feb. 23, 1902; he died Sept. 21, 1902. Children:

674.   I.   Albert S., b. Aug. 19, 1849; d. Nov., 1875; did not marry.
675.   II.   John, b. Sept. 9, 1851; d. Dec., 1851, infant.
676.   III.   Elwood Darlington, b. Aug. 27, 1852; d. Oct. 10, 1870; did not marry.
677.   IV.   Willis H., b. Aug. 11, 1854.
678.   V.   Rosco P., b. Oct. 10, 1856.
679.   VI.   Mary E., b. Oct. 11, 1859.
680.   VII.   Lydia E., b. March 7, 1868.
681.   VIII.   Sarah A., b. July, 1870; d. Oct., 1870, in infancy.

147. JESSE BOND (Silas - Benjamin - Joseph), youngest child of Silas and Lydia Bond, born Nov. 21, 1828; married Hannah L. Wright, born April 21, 1830. He died 1894; she died Oct. 28, 1892. Children:

682.   I.   Alice, b. Nov. 2, 1851.
683.   II.   Lydia, b. July 23, 1853.
684.   III.   William, b. May 31, 1855.
685.   IV.   Annie, b. Jan. 19, 1866.

156. JACOB VORE (Ruth-Benjamin-Joseph), eldest son of Isaac and Ruth (Bond) Vore, born in Pennsylvania; moved to

Indiana and later to Kansas City, Mo.; married Sarah Kirk. Children:

686. I. Mary Vore.
687. II. William Vore.
688. III. Elizabeth Vore.
689. IV. James Vore. Probably others. N. f. k.

158. ELIZA VORE (Ruth-Benjamin-Joseph), daughter of Isaac and Ruth (Bond) Vore; married Solomon Gause; residence Richmond, Ind. Children:

690. I. Isaac V. Gause.
691. II. Ruth Ann Gause.
692. III. James Gause. N. f. k.

159. RUTH VORE (Ruth-Benjamin-Joseph), daughter of Isaac and Ruth (Bond) Vore; married Solomon Horney. Residence Richmond, Ind. Children:

693. I. Eliza Horney; m. John C. Cornell, an eminent minister in Society of Friends (Hicksite).
694. II. Isaac Horney; m. Harriett Rhoads. N. f. k.

165. RUTH WALTON BOND (Eli - Benjamin - Joseph), daughter of Eli and Mary (Adkins) Bond, born Nov. 26, 1825, in York County, Pa.; moved to Indiana and later to Iowa; married 1843, Arthur Sullivan; she died Nov., 1902. Children:

695. I. Harvey Sullivan.
696. II. Anna Sullivan.
697. III. Sarah Sullivan.
698. IV. Mary Sullivan.

166. TITUS BOND (Eli-Benjamin-Joseph), born Feb. 6, 1825; married 1851, Amelia Collins. He d. s. p. Nov. 10, 1852. N. f. k.

167. SARAH ADKINS BOND (Eli-Benjamin-Joseph), born May 10, 1829; married in Wayne County, Ind., Sept. 21, 1840: David R. Taylor, born Dec. 16, 18—. His residence 1903, Richmond, Ind. She died Nov., 1854. Children:

699. I. Virginia Ann Taylor, b. Jan. 28, 1848.
700. II. William Henry Taylor, b. Feb. 28, 1850.
701. III. Infant.

169. WILLIAM ARMENT BOND (Eli-Benjamin-Joseph), born Aug. 2, 1834; married 1853, Abigail A. Reeder. He was lieutenant in 1st Iowa Inft. (colored); d. at Helena, Ark., July 24, 1864. Four children. Two living in 1907. Children:

702.   I.   Calvin T., b. April 9, 1855.

703.   II.   Sarah Lizzie, b. June 18, 1856.

*704·   III.   Charles B., b. July 1, 1857; d. drowned accidentally July 20, 1884.

704.   IV.   Florence, b. June 13, 1860.

170.   BENJAMIN BOND (Eli-Benjamin-Joseph), son of Eli and Mary (Adkins) Bond, born July 31, 1837; married Jan., 1858: Martha Burt. Residence Dillon, Mont. Children:

705.   I.   Dr. H. A.

706.   II.   C. C.

707.   III.   Clifford.

708.   IV.   Ada.

709.   V.   Mary Adel.

710.   VI.   Belle.

711.   VII.

171.   ELIZA A. BOND (Eli-Benjamin-Joseph), born June 18, 1841; married March, 1888: Joseph H. Stephens; she living 1907; no issue.

172.   MARY ETTA BOND (Eli-Benjamin-Joseph), youngest of the family of Eli and Mary (Adkins) Bond, born March 17, 1845; married June, 1861: Edward A. Baldwin. Children:

715.   I.   Son.

182.   ELVIRA WALTON, daughter of Abraham and Mary (Allison) Walton, born June 18, 1840; married March 22, 1857: Sylvester McCoy; they had two children; he died Dec. 24, 1860. Children:

I.   Mariana McCoy, b. 1858.

II.   Florence McCoy, b. 1860.

She married second husband Jan. 15, 1870: Daniel Regester; he died Dec. 29, 1874. Children:

III.   Elmer E. Regester, b. Aug. 31, 1871. Address 1903, Hood River, Ore.

IV.   Wilbur S. Regester, b. Feb. 23, 1875; P. O. 1903, Kent, Oregon.

She married third husband Jan. 8, 1876: Levi Johnson; he died Feb. 17, 1900. Her address 1903, Hood River, Ore. Residence Indiana and Oregon.

196.   SARAH BALLARD (Martha-Samuel-Joseph), daughter of Nathan and Martha (Bond) Ballard, born 1803, in Grayson County, Va.; married John Vore; she died Grayson County,

(Martha–Samuel–Joseph)

Va., Sept. 22, 1832. The family then moved to Wayne County, Ind. Children:

716.   I.   Azel Vore, b. Nov. 19, 1823.
717.   II.   Nathan Vore, b. June 18, 1825; d. 1828.
718. III.   Eli Vore, b. Jan. 18, 1827.
719.   IV.   Rhoda Vore. b. Dec. 26, 1829; d. July 11, 1845, s. p.

Azel Vore above mentioned married May 8, 1851: Elizabeth Lamb. Residence Wayne County, Ind. They had seven children:

720. Sarah Ann.   722. Isaac.   724. Phineas Albert.
721. Thomas.   723. Mary Jane.   725. Gilbert.
726. Cora.

The above named Eli Vore married Dec. 21, 1852: Lucy J. Birdwell. Their children:

727. Charles Milton Lacy Vore.

He married second wife, Lydia Ann Smith, by whom he had one child:

728. Rewell Vore.

197. RHODA BALLARD (Martha–Samuel–Joseph), daughter of Nathan and Martha (Bond) Ballard, born in Grayson County, Va., Aug. 23, 1805. She was raised in the family of her aunt and uncle, John and Dorcas (Bond) Baldwin, near Richmond, Ind. Married March 8, 1828: Benjamin Fulghum, of Wayne County, Ind., a native of Goldsboro, N. C. He died May 10, 1877, at Cambridge City, Ind.; she died Jan. 18, 1866, at Richmond. Children:

729.   I.   Martha Fulghum, b. Feb. 26, 1829; d. Sept. 4, 1832, in childhood.

730.   II.   Frank Fulghum, b. Oct. 29, 1830; d. Sept. 13, 1832.

731. III.   Charles Fulghum, b. Aug. 22, 1832; d. Sept. 22, 1832.

732.   IV.   Hannah Fulghum, b. Aug. 29, 1833; m. Hiram Hadley.

733.   V.   Caroline Fulghum, b. Dec. 29, 1835; m. 1856, Charles Hollingsworth.

734.   VI.   Eliza B. Fulghum, b. Oct. 20, 1837; m. Sept. 21, 1868, at Richmond, Ind.: Harrison Clarkson.

735. VII. William A. Fulghum, b. Aug. 3, 1840; m. Harriet White.

736. VIII. Albert Fulghum, b. Jan. 1842; m. Harriet Pitts.

737. IX. Mary Fulghum, b. March 5, 1844; m. Robert Stewart.

738. X. John Allen Fulghum, b. July 17, 1846; d. infancy.

739. XI. Naomi C. Fulghum, b. Oct. 19, 1849; m. David Morris.

199. SAMUEL BALLARD (Martha–Samuel–Joseph), son of Nathan and Martha (Bond) Ballard, b. in Grayson County, Va.; when a child was brought to Wayne County, Ind.; married Millicent White; residence, Indianapolis, Ind. Children:

740. I. Mary Ballard.

741. II. David Ballard.

742. III. Cornelius Ballard. Several others. N. f. k.

200. ELIZABETH BALLARD (Martha–Samuel–Joseph), daughter of Nathan and Martha (Bond) Ballard, born in Grayson County, Va.; m. ———— Furnace. Residence Waynesville, Ohio. N. f. k.

201. RACHEL GARRETT (Margaret – Samuel – Joseph), daughter of Welcome and Margaret (Bond) Garrett, b. in Surry County, N. C., April 22, 1813; married Jan. 6, 1831: David McKinney; she died July 8, 1840, at Westfield, Hamilton County, Ind.; he died Nov. 22, 1873, in Jasper County, Iowa. Children:

743. I. Margaret McKinney, b. Nov. 2, 1831, in North Carolina.

744. II. Amelia McKinney, b. May 16, 1833; d. inft.

745. III. Alfred McKinney, b. Aug. 2, 1834.

746. IV. Mary McKinney, b. Oct. 10, 1836.

747. V. William Barron McKinney, b. Jan. 17, 1839. Res., Newton, Iowa.

202. JONATHAN GARRETT (Margaret–Samuel–Joseph), son of Welcome and Margaret (Bond) Garrett, born in Surry County, N. C., Dec. 12, 1814. In 1832, emigrated to Wayne County, Ind., where he married Dec. 8, 1834: Anna Bond, born May 1, 1815, daughter of Edward and Anna (Huff) Bond, of Webster, Ind. He was a farmer by occupation. Residence, Wayne, Randolph and Hamilton Counties, Ind. He died at Westfield, Ind., Aug. 24, 1899, aged 84 years; she died Sept. 1849. In 1856 he married second: Mrs. Mary Shutes, nee Gray; she died

Sept. 21, 1904. Six children by first marriage. Three by last'
Children:

748. I. Leander P. Garrett, b. Nov. 27, 1835.

749. II. Melissa Garrett, b. March 31, 1837; did not m.

750. III. Vilena Garrett, b. Jan. 15, 1839.

751. IV. Caleb Garrett, b. March 12, 1840; served during the war in Co. C, Eighth Reg. Ind. Vol. Inft.; d. by accident Dec. 4, 1895, at Tacoma, Wash. Did not m.

752. V. Salathiel Garrett, b. Feb. 5, 1843, in Randolph Co., Ind.; served in Co. F, Sixteenth Reg. Ind. Vol. Mounted Inft.; d. April 15, 1864, of wounds received at battle of Sabine Cross Roads, La.; did not m.

753. VI. Samuel Bond Garrett, b. Nov. 21, 1844. The writer of this genealogy.

The children of the second wife are:

754. VII. Rufus Garrett, b. June 2, 1856; d. Oct. 4, 1875, s. p.

755. VIII. Isaac Garrett, b. Aug. 20, 1859; d. Nov. 19, 1874, s. p.

756. IX. Thomas Garrett, b. March 2, 1861; d. Jan. 9, 1875, s. p.

203. HIRAM GARRETT (Margaret–Samuel–Joseph), son of Welcome and Margaret (Bond) Garrett, born in Surry County, N. C., Nov. 10, 1816; died in Hamilton County, Ind., Nov. 8, 1855. Moved to Indiana in 1834. Married March 11, 1839: Mary Reynolds, born Jan. 12, 1816, daughter of Thomas and Charity (Wells) Reynolds. They settled on a farm three miles southeast of Westfield, where they remained during life. She died Dec. 19, 1877. Children:

757. I. Rachel Elma Garrett, b. Oct. 28, 1840; m. Dec. 18, 1861, Milton Davis; d. s. p., Oct. 13, 1870.

758. II. Thomas Welcome Garrett, b. June 30, 1842; d. s. p. June 18, 1863; was a soldier.

759. III. Charity Margaret Garrett, b. Oct. 25, 1844; m. Randolph Gibson.

760. IV. Jesse Antrim Garrett, b. July 1, 1846; d. s. p. Dec. 12, 1852.

761. V. Sarah Anna Garrett, b. Feb. 17, 1848.

762. VI. Jonathan Wilson Garrett, b. Aug. 28, 1849; d. s. p. Sept. 5, 1860.

763. VII. Hiram Ellis Garrett, b. Jan. 5, 1851; d. s. p. Jan. 30, 1878.

764. VIII. Mary Elizabeth Garrett, b. Feb. 11, 1852.

765. IX. Phebe Ann Garrett, b. March 12, 1855; m. Charles W. Cassey; res., 1909, Los Angeles, Cal.

205. DARIUS BOND (Joseph S.–Samuel–Joseph), born Dec. 26, 1803, in North Carolina; married in Indiana: Betsey Hockett; born Aug. 19, 1809, daughter of Stephen and Margaret Hockett, he died in Indiana Sept. 3, 1837. The family soon after moved to Iowa. She died in Iowa, 1886. Children:

766. I. John S., b. May 23, 1828.

767. II. Elwood, b. 1829; d. 1867.

768. III. Reuben, b. July 16, 1831.

769. IV. Eunice, b. 1833.

770. V. Matilda, b. abt. 1837.

207. JOHN H. BOND (Joseph S.–Samuel–Joseph), born near Westfield, N. C., Dec. 6, 1807; moved to Indiana 1812; married Emily Hockett, born Nov. 13, 1811; she died Feb. 7, 1892; he died Sept. 28, ——, in Randolph County, Ind. Children:

771. I. Asa, b. Nov. 13, 1829.

772. II. Eli, b. Oct. 27, 1831.

773. III. Levi, b. Oct. 24, 1833.

774. IV. Lydia, b. Jan. 8, 1836.

775. V. Hiram, b. Jan. 3, 1839.

776. VI. Darius, b. Aug. 29, 1841.

777. VII. Jesse, d. inft.

778. VIII. Rhoda, b. Jan. 19, 1849.

779. IX. Irene, b. Jan. 3, 1854.

208. MORDECAI BOND (Joseph S.–Samuel–Joseph), born near Westfield, Surry County, N. C., Sept. 24, 1809; married in Indiana, 1831: Rachel Marshall, born Sept. 22, 1814. He died in Iowa Aug. 8, 1849. Children:

780. I. Infant.

781. II. Stephen, b. April 19, 1833; d. infant.

782. III. Lavina, b. Oct. 21, 1834.

783. IV. Elmina, b. Oct. 29, 1836; d. July 7, 1852, s. p.

784. V. Joseph S., b. Nov. 6, 1838; d. Jan. 25, 1860.

785. VI. Elizabeth, b. Aug. 22, 1841; did not m.

786. VII. Eunice, b. Dec. 26, 1843.

787. VIII. Joshua M., b. Jan. 16, 1846.

788.   IX.   William M., b. Sept. 1, 1848.

209.   JOSEPH BOND (Joseph S.–Samuel–Joseph), son of Joseph S. and Rachel Bond, b. near Westfield, N. C., July 29, 1811; moved to Indiana 1812; married June 20, 1832: Elizabeth Harrold, residence, Randolph County, Ind.; four children to this union, none living. He married second, Sarah Mendenhall. He died July 5, 1884. Children:

789.   I.   Ruth W., b. July 20, 1845.

790.   II.   Margaret, b. July 9, 1848.

791.   III.   Mary J., b. Jan. 6, 1852.

792.   IV.   Samuel, b. March 24, 1859. All deceased.

210.   AMOS BOND (Joseph S.–Samuel–Joseph), son of Joseph S. and Rachel (Harrold) Bond, born in Indiana April 9, 1814; married Nov., 1839: Lucy Coggeshall. He died in Grant County, Ind., Feb. 28, 1896. Children:

793.   I.   Enos, b. Dec. 14, 1840; m.; no ch.; d. 1884.

794.   II.   Joseph Addison, b. April 2, 1843; d. in army; did not m.

795.   III.   Hannah C., b. April 24, 1846; not m.; res., Marion, Ind.

796.   IV.   Rachel, d. aged 7 years. N. f. k.

211.   LEVI BOND (Joseph S.–Samuel–Joseph), son of Joseph S. and Rachel (Harrold) Bond, born Nov. 4, 1815, in Indiana; m. Dec. 1, 1840: Lydia Williams, born Sept. 9, 1817, daughter of John and Mary (Cook) Williams. He died Dec. 24, 1893; she died July, 1909; both at Webster, Wayne County, Ind., which place had been their home for many years. He was interested in the history of his ancestors and delighted in talking about Bonds and Beals long since deceased. Only son survives:

797.   I.   Jehiel, b. Jan. 30, 1842.

212.   ELIHU BOND (Joseph S.–Samuel–Joseph), born April 28, 1817, in Wayne County, Ind.; married Feb. 15, 1843: Amy Ellis, daughter of Amos and Sarah Ellis. He died June 7,1870. Children:

798.   I.   Mary, b. Nov. 2, 1844.

He married second Charlotte ————, born March 11, 1822. Children:

799.   II.   Willis.

214.   ZIMRI BOND (Joseph S.–Samuel–Joseph), born Dec. 25, 1820, in Indiana; died April 14, 1887, in Fort Scott, Kas.;

first married Emily Branson, by whom he had four children; all died young. Second wife was Julia Ann Mendenhall, born Jan. 25, 1835, daughter of Aaron and Hannah (Clark) Mendenhall. Children:

800.   I.   Elizabeth E., b. Nov. 3, 1859.

801.   II.   Webster, b. March 20, 1861; d. Aug. 21, 1862, inft.

802.   III.   Albert, b. Jan. 17, 1863.

803.   IV.   William R., b. Feb. 13, 1865; d. March 9, 1865, inft.

Children by second wife:

804.   V.   Linetta H., b. March 20, 1866.

805.   VI.   Fred E., b. Dec. 13, 1867.

806.   VII.   Orpha O., b. Jan. 31, 1870; d. Aug. 12, 1873, s. p.

807.   VIII.   Daisy E., b. Dec. 22, 1874; d. Feb. 17, 1877; child.

808.   IX.   Forice M., b. May 4, 1877.

216.   LAVINA BOND (Joseph S.-Samuel-Joseph), born Jan. 5, 1826; married Elisha Harrold, born Aug. 5, 1826; he died Aug. 24, 1909; she died April 24, 1904, in Ringold County, Iowa, to which place they had moved in 1871. Children:

809.   I.   John Wesley Harrold, b. June 10, 1848; d. s. p. Feb. 12, 1849.

810.   II.   Joseph Macy Harrold, b. Feb. 27, 1850; d. Sept. 23, 1850, infant.

811.   III.   Mary Melissa Harrold, b. May 30, 1852.

812.   IV.   Emilia Ann Harrold, b. May 3, 1854.

813.   V.   Levi Milton Harrold, b. Feb. 5, 1857; d. June 18, 1894.

814.   VI.   Eunice Leah Harrold, b. April 30, 1860.

815.   VII.   Catherine R. Ella Harrold, b. May 1, 1864.

816.   VIII.   Oliver Oscar Harrold, b. April 21, 1869.

217.   AMER BOND (Thomas-Samuel-Joseph), eldest son of Thomas and Mary (Nation) Bond, born Sept. 2, 1805, near Westfield, N. C.; moved to Indiana when a child; married June 7, 1827: Mary Pickett, born Sept. 30, 1808; she died Nov. 9, 1858; he died 1855. She was the daughter of Joseph and Priscilla Pickett. Children:

817.   I.   Priscilla, b. Nov. 1, 1828.

818.   II.   Jonathan, b. Nov. 21, 1831; d. Dec. 21, 1833, inft.

819.   III.   Thomas, b. May 12, 1834.

820.   IV.   Caleb, b. Oct. 3, 1836.

821.   V.   Sarah A., b. Aug. 30, 1839; d. Oct. 27, 1858, s. p.

822.   VI.   Mary Jane, b. Sept. 27, 1841; d. Dec. 21, 1902; m.; no children.

823.   VII.   Martha Ellen, b. June 27, 1844; m. Edward Trickey; no ch.

824.   VIII.   Mahlon, b. Nov. 30, 1850.

825.   IX.   Rhoda S., b. Jan. 19, 1853; d. s. p. May 24, 1854.

218.   BETSEY BOND (Thomas-Samuel-Joseph), daughter of Thomas and Mary (Nation) Bond, born in Surry County, N. C., Jan. 4, 1807; moved to Indiana a few years later; married July 5, 1827: Exum Palin; he died Aug. 16, 1878; she died May 9, 1894. They settled on a farm near Newtown, Fountain County, Ind. Children:

826.   I.   Thomas Palin, b. April 7, 1828; d. s. p. Oct. 10, 1830.

827.   II.   Henry Palin, b. Sept. 18, 1829.

828.   III.   Julia Ann Palin, b. April 2, 1831, in Henry Co., Ind.

829.   IV.   Sylvester Palin, b. Jan. 21, 1833.

830.   V.   Mary Jane Palin, b. April 13, 1835.

831.   VI.   Hiram H. Palin, b. Jan. 10, 1837.

832.   VII.   Jesse M. Palin, b. Jan. 6, 1839.

833. VIII.   Exum Nuby Palin, b. Sept. 28, 1841; d. Sept., 1842, inft.

219.   JESSE BOND (Thomas-Samuel-Joseph), son of Thomas and Mary (Nation) Bond, born near Westfield, Surry County, N. C., Oct. 4, 1808; died April 21, 1881, at Spiceland, Ind.; married June 18, 1829: Anna Cook, born July 4, 1811, daughter of Joseph and Lydia Cook; she died Dec. 6, 1846. He married second 1848: Delana Stanley, daughter of John and Elizabeth Stanley, born May 2, 1810, and died March 11, 1883. Children of Jesse and Anna:

834.   I.   Calvin, b. April 22, 1830.

835.   II.   Mahala, b. July 31, 1832; d. 1870; m. Seth Cloud.

836.   III.   William, b. Oct. 13, 1834.

837.   IV.   Lydia, b. Sept. 1, 1837; d. Oct. 19, 1858; did not m.

838.   V.   Oliver, b. Jan. 23, 1840; d. Sept. 3, 1847.

839.   VI.   Emily, b. Nov. 25, 1842; d. July 10, 1847.

840. VII.   Rhoda, b. Sept. 14, 1845; d. Aug. 15, 1847.

220. THOMAS BOND (Thomas-Samuel-Joseph), son of Thomas and Mary (Nation) Bond, born in Surry County, N. C., March 4, 1811; married in Wayne County, Ind., 1834: Ann Hawkins, born Dec. 17, 1816, daughter of Nathan and Rebecca (Roberts) Hawkins. Residence, near Webster, Wayne County. Ch:

841.   I.   Cornelius Bond, b. Dec. 2, 1834.
842.   II.   Matilda, b. Dec. 18, 1836; d. s. p.
843.   III. Jehu, b. Feb. 21, 1839; d. s. p.
844.   IV.   Jonathan, b. June 27, 1841; d. s. p.
845.   V.   Rebecca, b. Nov. 20, 1842.
846.   VI.   Lindley H., b. June 27, 1845.
847.   VII. Louise, b. May 6, 1848; d. s. p.
848.   VIII. Julia A., b. Jan. 10, 1851.
849.   IX.   Albert, b. July 23, 1853; m. Lida Barnes; he d. s.p.
850.   X.   Emily, b. July 5, 1856; d. inft.

221. HIRAM BOND (Thomas-Samuel-Joseph), born Jan. 7, 1814, probably in Indiana; married 1836: Lydia Peele, born Sept. 5, 1818; she died Jan. 17, 1890; he died Dec. 5, 1892, both in Oregon. He moved overland across the plains and settled in Linn County, Oregon, in 1847, three miles east of Corvallis, at which place his family was raised. Children:

851.   I.   Lucinda, b. Jan. 28, 1838.
852.   II.   Henry, b. Feb. 20, 1839; d. s. p. Nov. 17, 1887.
853.   III. Elam, b. Dec. 15, 1840.
854.   IV.   Milton, b. Dec. 7, 1844; not m. 1902.
855.   V.   Mary, b. Dec. 14, 1847.
856.   VI.   Hannah, b. May 1, 1849.
857.   VII. Joel, b. Feb. 20, 1851.
858.   VIII. Silas M., b. Feb. 21, 1853.
859.   IX.   Owen, b. Oct. 10, 1856.
860.   X.   Dayton, b. May 19, 1859.

222. PLEASANT BOND (Thomas-Samuel-Joseph), son of Thomas and Mary (Nation) Bond, born March 4, 1817, in Wayne County, Ind.; married Sally Hawkins, born April 28, 1818, in Wayne County, Ind., daughter of Nathan and Rebecca (Roberts) Hawkins. He died in Iowa Dec. 2, 1862. He moved to Warren County, Iowa, in 1859. Children:

861.   I.   Phebe A., b. April 21, 1838.
862.   II.   Eli, b. April 1, 1840; d. Aug. 9, 1841, inft.
863.   III. Exum N., b. Nov. 3, 1842.

864.   IV.   Hiram H., b. Nov. 14, 1844.

865.   V.   Thomas, b. Sept. 2, 1846.

866.   VI.   Elam L., b. Oct. 30, 1848, in Indiana.

867.   VII.   Anna J., b. March 15, 1853, in Iowa.

868.   VIII.   Alpheus, b. July 12, 1855.

224. PHEBE BOND (Thomas-Samuel-Joseph), born July 30, 1821, in Wayne County, Ind.; married in same county: David Roberts, born June 20, 1817, in Wayne County, son of Walter and Hannah (Johnson) Roberts, of Webster, Ind. They moved to Iowa where they made their home. N. f. k.

226. AMASA BOND (Samuel - Samuel - Joseph), son of Samuel and Charity (Beeson) Bond, born Dec. 26, 1809, in Surry County, N. C.; moved following year with his parents to Indiana, Wayne County; married Dec. 5, 1832: Sally Horton, born Jan. 2, 1809, daughter of Jacob and Phebe (Pierce) Horton. He lived in Indiana several years, then moved in 1856 to Montgomery County, Iowa. He died Oct. 31, 1857; she died March 29, 1885. Occupation, physician and farmer. Children:

869.   I.   Phebe, b. Sept. 4, 1833.

870.   II.   Milton, b. Jan. 6, 1835; d. s. p. in army while at Atlanta, Ga.

871.   III.   Jacob H., b. April 4, 1837.

872.   IV.   Samuel P., b. Jan. 28, 1839; d. s. p. Aug. 4, 1841.

873.   V.   Ellis, b. June 18, 1841.

874.   VI.   James Wilson, b. Nov. 23, 1843; d. May 17, 1863, while a soldier; killed at Black River Bridge.

875.   VII.   Amasa, b. June 2, 1847.

876.   VIII.   John William, b. March 23, 1852; d. Jan. 7, 1862, s. p.

227. SAMUEL BOND (Samuel - Samuel - Joseph), son of Samuel and Charity (Beeson) Bond, born Dec. 27, 1811; married Mary Harrold, daughter of Jonathan and Margaret (Schooley); residence, Wayne County and Hamilton County, Ind. He married second: Elizabeth Comer, widow of John Comer; no issue. He died in Hamilton County, Ind., March 4, 1863. Children by first wife:

877.   I.   Isaac, b. Jan. 9, 1833.

878.   II.   Ahijah, b. June 17, 1834.

879.   III.   Barclay, b. March 21, 1836.

880.   IV.   Margaret, b. Oct. 26, 1837.

881.	V.	Mahlon, b. Dec. 28, 1838; d. s. p.

228.	ELLIS BOND (Samuel-Samuel-Joseph), son of Samuel and Charity (Beeson) Bond, born Feb. 17, 1814, in Wayne County, Ind.; married Feb. 18, 1835: Elizà Bakehorn, born May 26, 1811; she died May 3, 1893; he died Feb. 16, 1859, in Douglass County, Kas.	He moved from Indiana to Kansas in 1854, and settled near Lawrence,where he was a pioneer and prominent citizen; farmed and built a mill.	It is said all descendants are temperate and good citizens.	Children:

882.	I.	Silas, b. Nov. 26; 1835.
883.	II.	Enos, b. Jan. 26, 1838.
884.	III.	Louise, b. Sept. 18, 1839.
885.	IV.	Sylvanus, b. Nov. 23, 1841; d. s. p. Nov. 12, 1900, at Coffeyville, Kas.
886.	V.	Luticia, b. April 29, 1845.
887.	VI.	Thomas, b. March 31, 1848.

229.	ANN BOND (Samuel-Samuel-Joseph), born Oct. 24, 1816, in Wayne County, Ind.; married Oct. 31, 1838: Jacob O. Davis.	They died when children were small.	Residence, Grant County, Ind.	Children:

888.	I.	Joel R. Davis, b. Nov. 6, 1839.
889.	II.	Jonathan Davis, b. Oct. 3, 1841.
890.	III.	Wilson Davis, b. Nov. 25, 1843.

230.	RUTH BOND (Samuel-Samuel-Joseph), b. ————; married Jan. 29, 1837, Edward Bakehorn.	They had six children, all deceased while young.	No living issue.

232.	RHODA BOND (Samuel-Samuel-Joseph), born April 8, 1824, in Wayne County, Ind., where she is yet living (1912); married March 26, 1845: Nathan Mendenhall, born in Stokes County, N. C., Oct. 4, 1820; he died June 9, 1897; he was the son of Jonathan and Ann (Phillips) Mendenhall.	Residence on farm one mile north of Webster, Ind.	Children:

891.	I.	Harvey Mendenhall, b. Feb. 22, 1846.
892.	II.	Samuel Bond Mendenhall, b. April 23, 1848.
893.	III.	Jonathan Mendenhall, b. June 15, 1850.
894.	IV.	Charity Mendenhall, b. May 21, 1855.
895.	V.	William Clayton Mendenhall, b. Jan. 25, 1857.
896.	VI.	Wilson D. Mendenhall, b. May 15, 1862; d. June 11, 1862, infant.
897.	VII.	Marietta Mendenhall, b. Dec. 25, 1863.

233. LYDIA BOND (Samuel-Samuel-Joseph), daughter of Samuel and Charity (Beeson) Bond, born Oct. 19, 1827; married Daniel Coggshall; had three children: Charity, Edward and Ruth Ann; all died without·issue. N. f. k.

234. JESSE BOND (Samuel-Samuel-Joseph), son and youngest child of Samuel and Charity (Beeson) Bond, born Jan. 9, 1832, near Webster, Wayne County, Ind.; m. Elizabeth Pitts, born May 17, 1834; she died Jan. 30, 1901. Residence, Marion, Ind. Children:

  898. -I. Lewis, b. Dec. 16, 1854.
  899. II. Mary Ann, b. Sept. 21, 1856.
  900. III. Ellis, b. Aug. 13, 1859.
  901. IV. Emma, b. Sept. 29, 1862.
  902. V. Clarkson, b. June 6, 1865.
  903. VI. Martha Ellen, b. April 8, 1869.
  904. VII. Etta, b. April 9, 1873.

235. JOEL BALDWIN (Dorcas-Samuel-Joseph), son of John and Dorcas (Bond) Baldwin; married Nancy Vincenhaler. Children:

  905. I. John Baldwin.
  906. II. George Baldwin.
  907. III. Benjamin Baldwin.
  908. IV. Douglas Baldwin.
  909. V. Effie Baldwin. N. f. k.

236. ELI BALDWIN (Dorcas-Samuel-Joseph), son of John and Dorcas (Bond) Baldwin; married Rachel Erickson. They had a daughter Rachel. N. f. k.

238. ANN BALDWIN (Dorcas-Samuel-Joseph), daughter of John and Dorcas (Bond) Baldwin; first married Levin Johnson. Two children:

  911. I. Eli Johnson.
  912. II. Rachel Johnson.

She married second John Pike. N. f. k.

239. ELIZA W. BALDWIN (Dorcas - Samuel - Joseph), daughter of John and Dorcas (Bond)·Baldwin; married John M. Hodson. Three children:

  913. I. Barclay Hodson, dec.
  914. II. Chalkley Hodson, of Pratt, Kas.
  915. III. Robert Hodson, a minister in M. E. Church. Residence in Missouri. N. f. k.

240. GEORGE BALDWIN (Dorcas-Samuel-Joseph), son of John and Dorcas (Bond) Baldwin, born in 1829; died Dec. 23, 1855; married Nov. 15, 1848: Rachel M. Hill; she died Nov. 30, 1859. Children:

916. I. Emma Baldwin, m. 1896: Charles Linscott.

917. II. Dr. George Baldwin, of Alexandria, Ind., a physician; he m. Nov. 10, 1878: Florence Belle Barnes, of Winchester.

249. NATHAN IRVIN BOND (Elizabeth-Samuel-Joseph), born Jan. 15, 1817, in Wayne County, Ind.; being brought up in a Bond family, he adopted that name and was known as Nathan I. Bond; occupation farmer and blacksmith; married first, June 13, 1839: Mary Ballenger, daughter of Joshua and Lucy; she died 1849; he died May 5, 1909. Residence Williamsburg, Ind. Children:

918. I. Dewitt Clinton, b. 1841.

919. II. James A., m. Aug. 26, 1871: Mary A. Davis; have no children; occupation blacksmith; Williamsburg, Ind.

920. III. John H.

921. IV. Sarah E.

922. V. Alvilida J.

He married second wife Feb. 2, 1851: Mary J. Cain, daughter of John and Rebecca (Neal) Cain. To this union was born:

923. VI. A daughter. N. f. k.

250. ELIZABETH BALDWIN (Elizabeth-Samuel-Joseph), daughter of Isaiah and Elizabeth (Bond) Baldwin, born Feb. 3, 1826; died April 15, 1907, age 83 years. She married David F. Wilson. Residence Spiceland, Ind. Children: .

924. I. A daughter; perhaps others. N. f. k.

250½. RILEY BOND (Ornon-Samuel-Joseph), son of Ornon and Anna (Hunt) Bond, born July 11, 1819; died April 25, 1882; married Sarah E. Risk; she died in Indianapolis, Ind., Dec. 11, 1902. Occupation millwright. Residence Indianapolis, Ind. N. f. k.

251. ELIZA BOND (Ornon-Samuel-Joseph), born Jan. 22, 1821; died Jan. 31, 1864, in Hamilton County, Ind.; married Jesse Small. Children:

925. I. Jesse Small and two others. N. f. k.

252. JANE BOND (Ornon-Samuel-Joseph), born Nov. 18, 1827; died in Hamilton County, Ind., March 23, 1863; married

Jacob Burnsides.   After her death he married again and moved to Muscatine, Ia.   N. f. k.

253.   NATHAN BOND (Ornon-Samuel-Joseph), born October .27, 1829, in Hamilton County, Ind.; died in Montgomery County, Kas., March 4, 1899; married Sarah Ann Smith.   He married second, Rhoda Bond, nee Stanbro, widow of his brother John.   Children of first marriage:

926.   I.   Lucina, b. Nov. 17, 1849.
927.   II.   Sylvester W., b. April 26, 1853.
928.   III.   Melvina, b. Dec. 3, 1854.

254.   JOHN BOND (Ornon-Samuel-Joseph), born in Indiana, Nov. 30, 1832; died Sept. 21, 1871, in Kansas; married Rhoda Stanbro, of Hamilton County, Ind.   Moved to Kansas 1874; farmer.   Children:

929.   I.   Asher, d. infancy.
930.   II.   Ellen.
931.   III.   William Wesley.
932.   IV.   Clovesta J., b. Feb. 26, 1856.
933.   V.   Nathan Milton, b. April 7, 1861.
934.   VI.   Elizabeth Ann.
935.   VII.   Elzena.
936. VIII.   Rhoda Wilkinson.
937.   IX.   Rachel M., b. Oct. 11, 1869.

255.   JESSE BOND (Ornon-Samuel-Joseph), born Jan. 5, 1835, in Hamilton County, Ind.; married Jan. 12, 1853: Emily Randall, daughter of Joseph and Keziah (Johnson) Randall; she died Nov. 21, 1871; he died.   He married second, 1872, Jane Stanley.   Children:

938.   I.   James G., b. May 9, 1854.
939.   II.   Martha Jane, b. Oct. 15, 1855; d. July 8, 1856, infant.
940.   III.   Lindley A., b. Sept. 14, 1857.
941.   IV.   Viola, b. Nov. 1, 1860.
942.   V.   Ovid, b. Feb. 1, 1863; d. Oct. 4, 1865, childhood.
943.   VI.   John M., b. April 18, 1865.
944.   VII.   William W., b. June 8, 1867.
945. VIII.   Flora Ellen, b. Dec. 4, 1869.
946.   IX.   Son; d. inft.
Children of second marriage:
947.   X.   Lillie A., b. Dec. 15, 1873.

948. XI. Charles A., b. March 13, 1875.

949. XII. Jesse R., b. May 3, 1877.

256. JOEL BOND (Ornon-Samuel-Joseph), son of Ornon and Anna (Hunt) Bond, born in Hamilton County, Ind., Jan. 17, 1838; died in Indianapolis, July 16, 1876; married June 12, 1856: Lavina Willett, born April 10, 1839, daughter of Joseph and Rachel Willett. Occupation stock dealer and livery. Children:

950. I. William Milton, b. Aug. 6, 1857; d. Sept. 30, 1857.

951. II. Eliza Ellen, b. Oct. 16, 1858; d. April 24, 1862; child.

952. III. Clara Etta, b. April 9, 1861.

953. IV. Franklin Ornon, b. July 20, 1863.

954. V. Emma Jane, b. Jan. 18, 1867; d. s. p. Nov. 15, 1886.

955. VI. Rachel Anne May, b. June 22, 1870.

956. VII. Rosa Estella, b. July 25, 1872.

957. VIII. Edna, b. Aug. 19, 1876; d. Sept. 21, 1876, infant.

257. MARTHA BOND (Ornon-Samuel-Joseph), born Dec. 9, 1842; died Jan. 27, 1877; married March 31, 1864: Allen Hanson, born Feb. 28, 1840; son of Borden and Rachel Hanson, nee Cox. He was a minister and member of Friends. He died June 17, 1894. Children:

958. I. Elmer Hanson, b. June 14, 1865; d. March 27, 1893; did not m.

959. II. Elisha Newton Hanson, b. Jan. 26, 1867.

960. III. Lida Hanson, b. May 13, 1869.

961. IV. Ervin Riley Hanson, b. Feb. 7, 1871.

962. V. Ornon Hanson, b. Dec. 12, 1872; d. Oct. 15, 1873, in Kansas; inft.

259. ELIZABETH TEAGLE (Ruth-Samuel-Joseph), daughter of Joseph and Ruth (Bond) Teagle, born Oct. 12, 1822, in Wayne County, Ind.; married June 27, 1838: Henry Roberts, born Aug. 8, 1814, son of Walter and Mary (Hawkins) Roberts, of Webster, Ind.; he died in Hamilton County, Ind.; she died Dec. 12, 1854, near Carmel. Occupation farmer. Residence Hamilton County, Ind. Children:

963. I. Matilda Roberts.

964. II. Mary Roberts.

965. III. Thomas Roberts.

966. IV. Joseph Roberts, atty-at-law, Noblesville, Ind.

967. V. Lizzie Roberts.

260. MARTHA ANN TEAGLE (Ruth-Samuel-Joseph), daughter of Joseph and Ruth (Bond) Teagle, born Nov. 3, 1824; died May 11, 1845; married Samuel Pitts. Children:

968. I. A daughter. N. f. k.

261. ALLEN TEAGLE (Ruth-Samuel-Joseph), son of Joseph and Ruth (Bond) Teagle, born Jan. 19, 1827; died May 26, 1854; married Mary Ann Harris. Children:

969. I. Emily Jane Teagle.

970. II. Leander Teagle.

262. AGATHA TEAGLE (Ruth-Samuel-Joseph), daughter of Joseph and Ruth (Bond) Teagle, born Dec. 29, 1830, in Wayne County, Ind.; married Aug. 5, 1857: Aaron Snider; he died Jan. 12, 1872. She married second Feb. 12, 1878: William Laflin. She had several children by first husband. Residence Richmond, Ind. N. f. k.

263. ELI TEAGLE (Ruth-Samuel-Joseph), son of Joseph and Ruth (Bond) Teagle, born May 19, 1833, in Wayne County, Ind.; married 1854: Martha Williams; moved to Kansas. Residence Medicine Lodge. Children:

971. I. Ruth Ann Teagle, b. April 29, 1855; d. Jan. 14, 1857·

972. II. Allen W. Teagle, b. Sept. 16, 1856.

973. III. Minnie Teagle, ·b. June 15, 1858.

974. IV. Elizabeth Teagle, b. April 6, 1860; d. Aug. 29, 1882.

975. V. Clayton C. Teagle, b. Feb. 28, 1862.

976. VI. Charles Teagle, b. Feb. 1, 1864.

977. VII. Franklin Teagle, b. Jan. 12, 1867; d. Dec. 15, 1872.

978. VIII. Flora Teagle, b. Dec. 30, 1868.

979. IX. Edward Eli Teagle, b. May 4, 1871·

980. X. Lela Teagle, b. Nov. 4, 1875.

264. MARY HAISLEY (Ruth-Samuel-Joseph), daughter of Ezekiel and Ruth (Bond-Teagle) Haisley, born May 11, 1843; married Nov. 17, 1864: Jesse H. Brooks, of Richmond, Ind. Children:

981. I. William E. Brooks.

982. II. Ruth Anna Brooks.

983. III. Huldah Elizabeth Brooks.
984. IV. Effie May Brooks.
985. V. John Henry Brooks.
986. VI. Mary Brooks.

265. JOEL BOND (Joseph-John-Joseph), son of Joseph and Abigail (Hinds) Bond, born Aug. 13, 1798, in Wayne County, Ky.; died by accident in felling a tree March 17, 1837; married in Wayne County, Ky.: Rebecca Molen, born March 11, 1807, daughter of Aquilla and Dozia Ann Molen; she died Oct. 3, 1887. To them were born four children:

987. I. Lewis Jackson, b. Oct. 5, 1828.
988. II. Miranda Jane, b. Feb. 17, 1830.
989. III. William Shelby, b. Dec. 4, 1831.
990. IV. John Wesley, b. May 20, 1833.

266. SARAH BOND (Joseph-John-Joseph), daughter of Joseph and Abigail (Hinds) Bond, born Dec. 13, 1799, in Wayne County, Ky.; died Nov. 25, 1858; married Oct. 31, 1822: William Davis, born Jan. 15, 1792, died Oct. 3, 1873. He was a native of Buncome County, N. C. Residence, near Monticello, Wayne County, Ky. Children:

991. I. Zerelda Jane Davis, b. Aug. 12, 1823.
992. II. James Perry Davis, b. Feb. 21, 1825.
993. III. Angaletta Matilda Davis, b. Jan. 13, 1826.
994. IV. Artema Davis, b. Dec.. 23, 1828.
995. V. Joseph Hinds Davis, b. Jan. 22, 1831.
996. VI. John William Davis, b. July 6, 1833.
997. VII. Martha Abigail Davis, b. Sept. 18, 1835.
998. VIII. Sarah Malinda Davis, b. Dec. 3, 1837.
999. IX. Susan Elizabeth Davis, b· Feb. 1, 1840.
1000. X. Margaret Louisa Davis, b. Aug. 31, 1843.
1001. XI. Mary Frances Davis, b. Nov. 14, 1845.

267. JOHN BOND (Joseph-John-Joseph), son of Joseph and Abigail (Hinds) Bond, born in Wayne County, Ky., about 1801; married Marian Brady. Their children, born in Wayne County, Ky.:

1002. I. Martin D.
1003. II. Isaac R.
1004. III. William H.
1005. IV. Joseph H., and four that died in infancy or childhood.

He married second: Polly Ann Barker, of Wayne County, Ky., and about the year 1838 moved to Cole County, Mo. Children by second marriage:

1006.   IX.   Berry C., b. Dec. 6, 1838.
1007.   X.   Joel J.
1008.   XI.   Charity J.
1009.   XII. John S.
1010.   XIII. James S.
1011.   XIV. Louis J.

268. JANE BOND (Joseph-John-Joseph), born Sept. 7, 1803, in Wayne County, Ky.; married June 24, 1822: Hamilton Wray, a native of Virginia, born Feb. 29, 1788; died Nov. 26, 1859, son of John Wray, who came from Ireland. She died April 3, 1870. Residence, Wayne County, Ky. Children:

1012.   I.   Angelo Ferguson Wray, b. May 9, 1823; d. s. p. Sept. 17, 1832.

1013.   II.   Margaret Malinda Wray, b. Dec. 2, 1824; d. Nov., 1903.

1014.   III.   Sallie Brown Wray, b. Feb. 2, 1828; d. Oct. 22, 1863.

1015.   IV.   Mariam Jane Wray, b. April 20, 1835; d. April 23, 1836.

1016.   V.   James William Wray, b. May 21, 1837; living 1905. Address, Paisley, Ky.

269. SAMUEL BOND (Joseph-John-Joseph), son of Joseph and Abigail, born in Wayne County, Ky. Married Nancy Wilboite, daughter of Elias. Children:

1017.   I.   Jane.
1018.   II.   E. Thompson.
1019.   III.   Minerva, did not m., and
1020.   IV.   Eliza, twins.
1021.   V.   Frances.
1022.   VI.   Granville, d. s. p.
1023.   VII.   Emily.
1024.   VIII. Marshall and
1025.   IX.   Perry, twins.
1026.   X.   John; d. s. p. when young man.

270. MALINDA BOND (Joseph - John - Joseph), born in Wayne County, Ky.; married Jacob Molen; she died March 6, 1862. Residence, Wayne County, Ky. N. f. k.

271. MATILDA BOND (Joseph-John-Joseph), daughter of Joseph and Abigail Bond; married James Molen and resided in Wayne County, Ky. N. f. k.

272. JOSEPH BOND (Joseph-John-Joseph), son of Joseph and Abigail Bond, born in Wayne County, Ky.; married in same county: Charity Hinds; she died in Missouri about 1860. He moved to Miller County, Mo., 1838. Twelve children:

1027.	I.	Simon H., b. Jan. 11, 1830.
1028.	II.	Micajah D., b. March 30, 1832.
1029.	III.	Elkanah D., b. Jan. 25, 1834.
1030.	IV.	Shelby Coffee, b. Feb. 20, 1836.
1031.	V.	Angelo F., b. Feb. 27, 1838, in Kentucky.
1032.	VI.	Marium G., b. Feb. 26, 1840, in Missouri.
1033.	VII.	Malinda A., b. Jan. 29, 1842.
1034.	VIII.	Martha A., b. Dec. 4, 1843.
1035.	IX.	Elizabeth M., b. May 25, 1845.
1036.	X.	Sarelda M., b. July 16, 1847.
1037.	XI.	Charity Melissa, b. Sept. 1, 1851.
1038.	XII.	Joseph Dixon, b. Oct. 3, 1854.

273. ELIZABETH BOND (Joseph-John-Joseph), born in Wayne County, Ky., March 29, 1815; married Alfred Carrender, and moved to Miller County, Mo. Children:

1039.	I.	Eliza Jane Carrender, b. June 29, 1837.
1040.	II.	George W. Carrender, b. June 28, 1839.
1041.	III.	Sarah A. Carrender, b. June 25, 1841.
1042.	IV.	Emily E. Carrender, b. July 19, 1843.
1043.	V.	Martha A. Carrender, b. Nov. 24, 1848.
1044.	VI.	John J. Carrender, b. 1851; d. inft.
1045.	VII.	James M. Carrender, b. Nov. 18, 1853.
1046.	VIII.	Mary L. Carrender, b. Nov. 18, 1856.

274. MARTHA BOND (Joseph-John-Joseph), born Sept. 24, 1817, in Wayne County, Ky.; married April 10, 1835: Solomon Mercer, born Aug. 20, 1813, son of Nicholas and Sina Mercer, of Grayson County, Ky.; residence, Grayson County, and about 1848 moved to Breckenridge County. He died Jan. 6, 1883. Children:

1047.   I.   John W. Mercer, b. Feb. 22, 1836; d. March 27, 1864.

1048.   II.   Joseph N. Mercer, b. June 5, 1838; d. Nov. 30, 1888.

1049.   III.   George W. Mercer, b. Dec. 20, 1840; d. March 6, 1862, while in army; served in Co. I, 3rd Ky. Cavalry.

1050.   IV.   Nathaniel Marshall Mercer, b. Aug. 18, 1842; served four years in Co. I, 3rd Reg. Ky. Cavalry. P. O. 1905, Eveleigh, Ky.

1051.   V.   Nancy C. Mercer, b. Feb. 22, 1844.

1052.   VI.   Harvey S. Mercer, b. Jan. 16, 1846; d. Dec. 18, 1870.

1053.   VII.   Amanda J. Mercer, b. March 6, 1848.

1054.   VIII.   Sina A. Mercer, b. May 18, 1850; d. inft.

1055.   IX.   Anna E. Mercer, b. June 9, 1852; d. inft.

1056.   Robert Board Mercer, b. Oct. 7, 1854; res., 1905, Plainview, Tex.

1057.   XI.   Susan J. Mercer, b. Aug. 9, 1856; d. 1862, childhood.

1058.   XII.   Ira D. Mercer, b. Jan. 6, 1859.

275.   HANNAH BOND (Joseph-John-Joseph), born Sept. 22, 1819, in Wayne County, Ky.; died July 30, 1877; married Isaac McCown, born May 15, 1818, died Jan. 15, 1864. He was son of John and Elizabeth McCown, also of Wayne County, Ky. Children:

1059.   I.   Malinda McCown, b. March 6, 1843.

1060.   II.   Joseph Bond McCown, b. Aug. 28, 1844.

1061.   III.   Elizabeth Ann McCown, b. Dec. 17, 1845.

1062.   IV.   Nancy Abigail McCown, b. Oct. 30, 1847; d. Dec. 28, 1863, s. p.

1063.   V.   Lucinda Matilda McCown, b. June 6, 1850.

1064.   VI.   John Ayres McCown, b. Oct. 23, 1852.

1065.   VII.   Martha Mercer McCown, b. Feb. 22, 1854.

1066.   VIII.   James William McCown, b. July 31, 1855.

1067.   IX.   Isaac Jackson McCown, b. Jan. 21, 1858.

1068.   X.   Hanna Eliza McCown, b. July 29, 1860.

278.   WILLIAM BOND (Benjamin-John-Joseph), son of Benjamin Bond, of Tennessee and Kentucky, and a grandson of John and Jane (Beeson) Bond. He was called "Whig" Billy Bond. He married his cousin Clara Bond, daughter of Isaac Bond. They moved to Arkansas before the war. Four children:

1069.   I.   James.

1070.   II.   Benjamin.

1071.   III.   William.

1072. IV. Josie, who married a man named Thomas. Did live at Downey, Calif. N. f. k.

279. WILLIAM MAYBERRY BOND (Joel-John-Joseph), son of Joel and Jane (Hinds) Bond, born in Wayne County, Ky. Oct. 2, 1815; died in Cole County, Mo., Jan. 9, 1874 (?). Married in Miller County, Mo.: Sarah Matilda Sullins, born Jan. 28, 1820, daughter of Peter and Elizabeth (Cox) Sullins; she died Nov. 2, 1868. Residence, twelve miles from Jefferson City, Cole County, Mo., on Tuscumbia road. He was buried in Bethel graveyard at Hickory Hill, Mo. Children:

  1073. I. Peter Jackson, b. Oct. 5, 1838, in Cole Co., Mo.
  1074. II. Joel Jefferson, b. Feb. 1, 1841·
  1075. III. William Monroe, b. 1849.
  1076. IV. Elizabeth.
  1077. V. James Asbury.

280. STEPHEN WASHINGTON BOND (Joel-John-Joseph), son of Joel and Jane (Hinds) Bond, born in Wayne County, Ky., 1820; died in Grayson County, Ky., Dec. 21, 1896. At the age of 16 he was apprenticed out to learn the tailors' trade in Danville, Ky., after which he worked at the trade in Monticello and Hardinsburg, Ky., Louisville, then located at Leitchfield, Ky., where he carried on a successful business. He then went to Versailles, Mo., and worked at his trade in that place and other towns in that state. Returning to Leitchfield, Ky., where he married Feb. 28, 1841: Nancy Berry Cunningham Ross, daughter of James and Margaret Ross. He then settled in Caneyville, Ky., where he engaged in merchandising and carried on flat-boating to New Orleans, and trade in tobacco, and became quite successful in business. She was living 1905. Children:

  1078. I. John Rodney, b. Feb. 7, 1842.
  1079. II. Thomas M., b. Feb. 2, 1844.
  1080. III. James Ross, b. Sept. 6, 1846; d. Feb. 2, 1892, s.p.
  1081. IV. Melissa, b. Feb. 15, 1856.
  1082. V. Louis Joel, b. March 18, 1858.
  1083. VI. Ulysses G., b. March 17, 1863.
  1084. VII. Mahala Jane, b. Oct. 13, 1867.

282. JOEL BOND, JR. (Joel-John-Joseph), son of Joel and Jane (Hinds) Bond, born in Wayne County, Ky.; died in Missouri; m.; n. f. k.

283. LEWIS G. BOND (Joel-John-Joseph), born in Wayne

County, Ky.; moved to Miller County, Mo.; married. N. f. k.

284. MARGARET BOND (Joel-John-Joseph), daughter of Joel and Jane (Hinds) Bond, born in Wayne County, Ky., moved in 1835 to Miller County, Mo.; married Philip Coats. Children:

1085. I. Sylvia Coats; m. Pink Jones.
1086. II. Thomas Coats; n. f. k.

285. ELIZABETH BOND (Joel - John - Joseph), born in Wayne County, Ky.; moved to Miller County, Mo.; married Mortimore McKinney. Children:

1087. I. Thomas McKinney.
1088. II. Franklin McKinney.
1089. III. James McKinney.
1090. IV. Margaret McKinney.
1091. V. Jane McKinney. N. f. k.

286. JANE BOND (Isaac-John-Joseph), eldest child of Isaac and Anna (Holmes) Bond, born in Wayne County, Ky., in 1807; died Dec. 25, 1878, in Miller County, Mo.; married in Kentucky, Feb. 7, 1827: Benjamin Hinds, born March 17, 1803, died July, 1858. Children:

1092. I. Polly Jane Hinds, b. Oct. 25, 1828.
1093. II. Mahala Hinds, b. Aug. 29, 1830.
1094. III. Andrew Hinds, b. Aug. 22, 1832.
1095. IV. Archibald Hinds, b. Feb. 9, 1843.
1096. V. Martha Hinds, b. June 8, 1844.
1097. VI. Sarah Hinds, b. Feb. 26, 1846.
1098. VII. Benjamin Hinds, Jr., b. Dec. 29, 1849.
1099. VIII. Isaac Hinds, b. Dec. 28, 1859.
1100. IX. Joseph D. Hinds.
1101. X. Mariah Hinds.
1102. XI. Ann Hinds.
1103. XII. Malinda Hinds.
1104. XIII. Marguerite Hinds.
1105. XIV. Rhoda Hinds. Names are not given in the order of their age. Joseph D. was old enough to be a soldier and served in an Illinois regiment.

289. BARTON S. BOND (Isaac-John-Joseph), son of Isaac and Anna (Holmes) Bond, born in Wayne County, Ky., 1827 (?); died in Miller County, Mo., Aug. 20, 1880; married. Children:

1106.   I.   Anna.
1107.   II.   Addie.
1108.   III.   Arthur D.
1109.   IV.   Drewry L.
1110.   V.   Perry O.
1111.   VI.   John B.
1112.   VII.   Effie.
1113.   VIII.   Linda.   N. f. k.

293. AMNER BEESON BOND (Isaac - John - Joseph), youngest daughter of Isaac and Anna (Holmes) Bond, born in Wayne County, Ky., in 1823; died in same county, July 28, 1887; married in 1840: James Hutchison, born 1820; he was living 1905. Children:

1114.   I.   Parmelia Hutchison, b. June 3, 1841; d. Aug. 4, 1902; married Benjamin Cannaday.

1115.   II.   Frances Ann Hutchison, b. Jan. 8, 1844; married Benjamin Roberts.

1116.   III.   James Hutchison, b. 1846.
1117.   IV.   Mary Jane Hutchison, b. Oct. 4, 1848.
1118.   V.   Isaac Bond Hutchison, b. July 29, 1850.
1119   VI.   Robert H. Hutchison, b. Jan. 9, 1852.
1120.   VII.   Ephraim Perry Hutchison, b. 1854.
1121.   VIII.   Henry Hutchison, b. 1856.
1122.   IX.   George Hutchison, b. 1858.
1123.   X.   Balzora Hutchison, b. 1860; did not m.; d. s. p.

294. MARGARET ANN BOND (William-John-Joseph), daughter and eldest child of William and Charity (Hinds) Bond, born Sept. 18, 1816, in Wayne County, Ky.; moved about 1836 to Cole County, Mo.; married Daniel Duncan. They raised several children. N. f. k.:

1124.   I.   James M. Duncan, Bass, Mo.   Others not reported.

295. JOHN WASHINGTON BOND (William-John-Joseph), born March 24, 1821, in Wayne County, Ky.; moved to Missouri about 1836; settled near Hickory Hill, Cole County; married Margaret Hinds (?); two children deceased. N. f. k.

296. ISAAC BEESON BOND (William-John-Joseph), son of William and Charity (Hinds) Bond; born in Wayne County, Ky., June 5, 1826; died in Missouri, Feb. 9, 1861; moved with his parents to Cole County, Mo., 1836; married Lydia Reece, born Nov. 22, 1825; she died March 13, 1862. Children:

1125.   I.   John William, b. Aug. 28' 1849.__
1126.   II.   Martin Samuel, b. Feb. 15, 1851.
1127.   III.   Charity Ann, b. Sept. 16, 1852.
1128.   IV.   Margaret Jane, b. April 22, 1854.
1129.   V..   Thomas Warren, b. June 4, 1855; d. s. p. childhood.
1130.   VI.   Mary Elizabeth, b. Dec. 13, 1856.
1131.   VII.   Isaac Daniel, b. Oct. 6, 1858.
1132.   VIII.   Lewis Benjamin, b. April 9, 1860.

297. WILLIAM SHELBY BOND (William-John-Joseph), son of William and Charity (Hinds) Bond, born in Wayne County, Ky., March 22, 1829; moved with his parents to Cole County, Mo., 1836; he died Dec. 20, 1904; married 1853; Mary Rebecca Stephens, born Aug. 13, 1836; she died July 8, 1896. Residence near Hickory Hill, Cole County, Mo. Children:

1133.   I.   John William, b. Oct. 14, 1855.
1134.   II.   Charity Jane, b. Nov. 18, 1858; d. s. p. Dec. 25, 1892.
1135.   III.   Margaret Ann, b. May 3, 1861; d. s. p. May 24, 1867.
1136.   IV.   Cordelia Frances, b. Jan. 11, 1866.
1137.   V.   Mary Price, b. Feb. 18, 1867; d. s. p. April 21, 18—.
1136.   VI.   Sarah Miranda, b. Dec. 4, 1871; d. s. p. April 25, 1898.
1139.   VII.   Ida Elizabeth, b. April 10, 1874; d. s. p. July 8, 1905.
1140.   VIII.   Noah Lee, b. Jan. 17, 1876; d. s. p. Jan. 29, 1884.
1141.   IX.   Alonzo Tilden, b. Oct. 5, 1880.
          (End of the Fifth Generation.)

CHAPTER VI.

SIXTH GENERATION.

300. ATHALINDA A. BOND (Edward-Benjamin-Edward-Joseph), daughter of Edward and Nancy Ann (Hayworth) Bond, born June 6, 1830, in Indiana; moved to Iowa with her parents; married Oct. 20, 1846: Havilah Thornburg; he died Dec. 25, 1892; she married second a Mr. Seamons. Her address 1905, Salem, Ia. Children:

1142. I. Lucinda Thornburg, b. March 7, 1848; d. Sept. 14, 1900.

1143. II. Abner E. Thornburg, b. April 19, 1859. P. O. address 1905, Salem, Ia.

301. JEDEDIAH BOND (Edward-Benjamin-Edward-Joseph), son of Edward and Nancy Ann (Hayworth) Bond, born in Henry County, Ind., April 16, 1832; married Feb. 23, 1856: Rachel Guyer, daughter of Joseph F. Guyer; residence Iowa and Missouri. He died Jan. 2, 1885; she died Oct. 25, 1904, at Schofield, Mo. Children:

1144. I. William Edward, b. Dec. 2, 1856.

1145. II. Ida Jane, b. Jan. 1, 1858.

1146. III. Benjamin F., b. April 11, 1860; d. s. p. 1876.

1147. IV. Amos Martin, b. July 19, 1863.

1148. V. Effie, b. Oct. 15, 1865; m. Dec. 17, 1903, George Montgomery; no issue.

1149. VI. Joseph Alfred, b. Oct. 1, 1867; d. s. p. 1891.

304. LUZENA S. BOND (Jedidiah-Benjamin-Edward-Josseph), daughter and eldest child of Jedidiah and Elmina (Stanley) Bond, b. June 10, 1833, in Wayne County, Ind.; married Feb. 26, 1852, in Henry County, Ind.: Prof. William P. Hastings, born in Henry County, July 12, 1833. He is a teacher and educator and has been connected with a number of educational institutions. Resided Indiana, Iowa, Tennessee, New York City, California. Address 1909, Springfield, Mass. Children:

1150. I. Elmina Jane Hastings, b. June 25, 1853.

1151. II. Nathan L. Hastings, b. Sept. 23, 1855.

1152. III. Letitia Angeline Hastings, b. June 29, 1858.

*1153. IV. William Hastings, b. May 12, 1861; d. s. p. July 24, 1862.

1153. V. William Walter Hastings, b. Nov. 1, 1865.

1154.   VI.   Edwin Hastings, b. July 1, 1869; d. Aug. 26, 1870.

1155.   VII.   Ernest Edwin Hastings, b. Sept. 5, 1872.

306.   MARTHA JANE BOND (Jedidiah-Benjamin-Edward-Joseph), born in Lee County, Ia., July 14, 1839; died Dec. 2, 1896; married Henry County, Ind., Feb. 1859: William L. Foreman, born July 9, 1834, in Wayne County, Ind.   In 1860 they moved to Pleasant Ridge, Lee County, Ia.   His residence Winterset, Ia.   Children:

1156.   I.   Charles L. Foreman, b. June 12, 1862.

1157.   II.   Alice L. Foreman, b. July 6, 1864.

1158.   III.   Lennie R. Foreman, b. Sept. 27, 1867.

1159.   IV.   Effie B. Foreman, b. Sept. 26, 1871.

308.   ANGELINA G. BOND (Jedidiah-Benjamin-Edward-Joseph), born in Lee County, Ia., June 15, 1843; moved with her parents to Henry County, Ind., when an infant; married Feb. 8, 1872: John Lowery, of same county; occupation farmer. Address 1909, New Castle, Ind.   Children:

1160.   I.   Eva Lowery.

309.   ELMINA BOND (Jedidiah-Benjamin-Edward-Joseph), born in Henry County, Ind., Aug 13, 1846; married Sept. 7, 1867: John Burk, farmer.   Address 1909, New Castle, Ind.   Children:

1161.   I.   Lula Burk.

310.   MARY ELIZABETH BOND (Jedidiah-Benjamin-Edward-Joseph), daughter of Jedidiah and Dinah Bond, born Jan. 30, 1854, in Henry County, Ind.; married Jan. 18, 1887: Robert Pope, born March 21, 1854, son of Edward and Mary K. Pope.   Residence 1909, Indianapolis, Ind. 903 Broadway.   No children:

311.   ELIZA NEWBY (Tabitha-Benjamin-Edward-Joseph), daughter of Elias and Tabitha (Bond) Newby, born in Henry County, Ind., Feb. 14, 1841; married John W. Payne; occupation, farmer and dealer in stock and grain.   Residence Spiceland, Ind.   Children:

1162.   I.   Emma Florence Payne, and

1163.   II.   Mary Etta Payne, twins.

1164.   III.   Lizzie Viletta, d. infancy.

1165.   IV.   Jessie Fremont Payne.

1166.   V.   Mary Lizzie Payne.

1167.   VI.   Olen Elsworth Payne.

312.   ELIZABETH   NEWBY   (Tabitha-Benjamin-Edward

Joseph), daughter of Elias and Tabitha (Bond) Newby, born Feb. 14, 1841; married first Frederick Phelps; he died March 7, 1863. Children:

1167.　I.　Charles A. Phelps, b. Aug. 3, 1862.

She married second, Jan. 1, 1865: Peter Shaffer, born Oct. 17, 1825; he died Aug. 20, 1903. Occupation, farmer. Residence near New Castle, Ind. Children:

1168.　I.　Ruth A. Shaffer, b. Oct. 11, 1865.

1169.　II.　Dora T. Shaffer, b. Jan. 3. 1872.

1170.　III.　Milton L. Shaffer, b. Dec. 15, 1876.

313. MARY ETTA BOND (Nathan H.-Benjamin-Edward-Joseph), daughter of Nathan Hunt and Abigail (Beard) Bond, born in Fountain City, then Newport, Ind., Dec. 16, 1837; moved with her parents to Lee County, Ia., when a child; married in Lee County, Oct. 12, 1856: Orson Case. She died 1887; he died June 30, 1888. Children:

1171.　I.　Nathan Bond Case, b. Dec. 22, 1859.

1172.　II.　John Chauncy Case, b. Jan. 7, 1861.

1173.　III.　William Ellsworth Case, b. May 19, 1864.

1174.　IV.　Benjamin Ellwood Case, b. June 12, 1866.

a-1174.　V.　Minnie Abigail Case, b. Sept. 29, 1875; now, 1910, Minnie Westerfield; P. O. Wahoo, Neb.

314. RACHEL ANN BOND (Nathan H.-Benjamin-Edward-Joseph), born in Lee County, Ia., Sept. 24, 1840; married March 20, 1859: Thomas Osborn. Children:

1175.　I.　Sylvester Osborn, b. March 18, 1860; P. O. 1903, Silverton, Colo.

1176.　II.　Lillie A. Osborn, b. March 21, 1864; m. Aug. 10, 1887, Lee Cooper; m. second, E. W. Sarber. Address Joy, Mo.

1177.　III.　Loda Lucretia Osborn, b. March 29, 1869; m. O. H. Mills; m. second, Mr. Lienbarger. Address Dallas City, Ill.

1178.　IV.　Oliver Osborn, and

1179.　V.　Olive Osborn, twins, b. March 9, 1874. Olive, address Guthrie, Okla.

315. WILLIAM PENN BOND (Nathan H.-Benjamin-Edward-Joseph), son of Nathan H. and Abigail (Beard) Bond, born in Lee County, Iowa, March 12, 1843; married Aug. 20, 1864: Emeline Binford, daughter of Benajah and Ann (Moon) Binford. Residence, Iowa and Colorado. Address, Denver, Col. Ch:

1181.　I.　Elmer Carroll, d. inft.

1182. II. Charles Ellsworth.
1183. III. Lydia Jasper, d. inft.
1184. IV. Clark Watson, b. Feb. 12, 1874.
1185. V. Harry Bertie, b. Dec. 25, 1872.
1186. VI. William Delbert.
1187. VII. Pearl Castor, d. inft.

317. HANNAH J. BOND (Nathan H.-Benjamin-Edward-Joseph), born May 15, 1848, in Union County, Ind.; married in Lee County, Iowa, Feb. 11, 1869: Eli Denny, born 1846, in Preble County, Ohio, son of John and Sarah. Residence, 1906, Western, Neb. Children:

1188. I. Alfred J. Denny, b. Dec. 9, 1871.
1189. II. Cora M. Denny, b. May 21, 1874.
1190. III. Luther L. Denny, b. May 1, 1877.
1191. IV. Orra D. Denny, b. Feb. 2, 1883.

318. ELIHU B. BOND (Nathan H.-Benjamin-Edward-Joseph), born in Lee County, Iowa, April 1, 1852; married in same county, Oct. 1, 1874: Experience Sheldon. Residence, Iowa, Nebraska, Idaho. Address, Myrtle Creek, Oregon. Children:

1192. I. Abbie, b. April 5, 1878, in Ringold Co., Ia.
1194. II. Bessie, b. April 20, 1891, in Sheridan Co., Neb.

319. JOHN BOND (William-John-Edward-Joseph), son and eldest child of William and Elizabeth (Wiles) Bond, born Nov. 3, 1820, in Surry County, N. C.; moved with parents to Henry County, Ind., when a child; married Lucinda Adams, born July 4, 1822. He died April 18, 1869. Occupation, farmer. Residence, Henry County, Ind. Eleven children:

1195. I. Enos, b. Oct. 26, 1842; d. s. p. April 26, 1863.
1196. II. Levi, b. Sept. 29, 1844.
1197. III. Mary, b. Sept. 27, 1846.
1198. IV. William, b. March 8, 1849; d. s. p. March 21, 1864.
1199. V. Semira, b. June 21, 1851; d. s. p. July 26, 1875.
1200. VI. Anna, b. Aug. 4, 1853; d. inft.
1201. VII. Gulielma, twin, b. Aug. 4, 1853; d. s. p. Aug. 17, 1855.
1202. VIII. John A., b. Jan. 3, 1856.
1203. IX. Joel E., b. July 17, 1858.
1204. X. Alvin P., b. Dec. 20, 1863; d. s. p. April 7, 1883.
1205. XI. Sarah E., b. Jan. 2, 1867.

320. AMELIA BOND (William-John-Edward-Joseph), born Nov. 19, 1822; died Sept. 14, 1864, in Henry County, Ind.; married Spencer Davis, born June 17, 1816, son of John and Ruth (Hadley) Davis; he died Sept. 14, 1864. Children:

1206.   I.   William Davis.
1207.   II.   John Davis, a soldier; d. during war.
1208. III.   Amos Davis.   •
1209. IV.   Eli Davis, d. s. p. in army.
1210.   V.   Miles Davis, of Mooreland, Ind.
1211. VI.   Joseph Davis, of Messick, Ind.
1212. VII.   Elizabeth Davis.
1213. VIII.   Marcus Davis, d. in childhood.

321. GULIELMA BOND (William-John-Edward-Joseph), born July 15, 1824; married Oct. 21, 1841: Evan Marshall, born May 25, 1821; she died Dec. 9, 1846, in Henry County, Ind.;- he died June 1, 1901, in Lee County, Iowa. Children:

1214.   I.   Elizabeth Marshall, b. Dec. 18, 1842.
1215.   II.   Anna Jane Marshall, b. Nov. 4, 1844.

322. FRANCES BOND (William-John-Edward-Joseph), born Jan. 12, 1826; married John Hutchens; she died Feb. 11, 1845. Children:

1216.   I.   Son, name unknown; Union soldier, d. during war.

323. MARY ANN BOND (William-John-Edward-Joseph), born in Henry County, Ind., Dec. 23, 1827; married Dec. 23, 1847: Joel Healton, born in North Carolina, son of John and Sarah (Adams) Healton, born June 19, 1828. She was many years a widow; died Aug. 26, 1909. Resided near Messick, Henry County, Ind. Children:

1217.   I.   Emeline Healton, b. Dec. 22, 1848.
1218.   II.   William B. Healton, b. April 17, 1851.
1219. III.   John A. Healton, b. Jan. 21, 1854.
1220. IV.   Albert M. Healton, b. Jan. 27, 1856.
1221.   V.   Thomas D. Healton, b. Aug. 24, 1858; d. s. p. Aug. 19, 1860.
1222. VI.   Sarah Elizabeth Healton, b. Dec. 5, 1860.
1223. VII.   Orilla Healton, b. April 13, 1863; d. s. p. March 25, 1866.
1224. VIII.   Nathan Marcus Healton, b. March 25, 1866.
1225. IX.   Mary Ellen Healton, b. Dec. 28, 1868.

324. ASENATH BOND (William - John - Edward - Joseph), born Jan. 6, 1830, in Henry County, Ind.; married Joel Adams.

son of Ebenezer and Rebecca (Davis) Adams. She died Aug. 26, 1855. Children:

1226. I. Preston Adams.

1227. II. Son.

333. JOHN KEYS (Elizabeth-John-Edward-Joseph), son of Benjamin P. and Elizabeth (Bond) Keys, born in Surry County, N. C., Dec. 27, 1827; moved with his father to Randolph County, Ind., 1835; married 1854: Lydia Hiatt; he died Sept. 23, 1892. Residence, Winchester, Ind. Children:

1228. I. Elizabeth Keys.

1229. II. Charlotte Keys.

1230. III. Simeon Keys.

1231. IV. Roseline Keys.

1232. V. Mary Keys.

1233. VI. Walter Keys.

334. JOSEPH KEYS (Elizabeth-John-Edward-Joseph), son of Benjamin P. and Elizabeth (Bond) Keys, born in Surry County, N. C., April 30, 1830; died in Randolph County, Ind., Feb., 1906; moved to Indiana 1835; married Aug. 20, 1853: Betsey V. Coats; she died May 8, 1901. Occupation, farmer. Resided east of Winchester, Ind. Children:

1234. I. Eli W. Keys; m. Mattie Davis; 2 ch.

1235. II. Lindo Keys; m. Mary E. Bond, daughter of Eli and Sarah (Lamb) Bond; 5 ch.

1236. III. Martin Keys; m. Lillie Blanton; 8 ch.

1237. IV. Elva J. Keys; m. Jesse Allen; 3 ch.

1238. V. Anna E. Keys; m. Vestal Haisley; 1 ch.

1239. VI. John L. Keys; m. Maud Wilson; 3 ch.

1240. VII. Elwood Keys; m. Ella McElvane; 2 ch.

335. MARY KEYS (Elizabeth - John - Edward - Joseph), daughter of Benjamin P. and Elizabeth (Bond) Keys, born Sept. 17, 1831; married John Gray. They had two sons, both deceased. She died Feb. 10, 1869; he died Nov. 2, 1860. One granddaughter, Grace Gray, the only survivor of this family. Residence, Winchester, Ind.

336. DANIEL H. KEYS (Elizabeth-John-Edward-Joseph), born in Surry County, N. C., May 23, 1833; died in Randolph County, Ind., Oct. 30, 1895; married first, Susannah Coffin; she died March 8, 1874. Children:

1241. I. Levi Keys, dec.

1242. II. Mary Jane Keys, dec.
1243. III. Washington Keys, of Crestline, Ohio.
1244. IV. Coffin Keys.
1245. V. Effie Keys, dec.

He married second, Mrs. Margaret Randall, nee Clark. Residence, Winchester, Ind. Children:

1246. VI. Naomi Keys.
1247. VII. Frances Keys.
1248. VIII. Ruth Keys.
1249. IX. Orpha Keys. Address, 1909, Winchester, Ind. N. f. k.

337. GEORGE BOND (Jesse-John-Edward-Joseph), son of Jesse and Rachel (Hobson) Bond, born Jan. 25, 1837; married; died in California. Had three children. Son named Frederick. N. f. k.

1250. I. Frederick.
1251. II.
1252. III.

339. JOHN BOND (Jesse-John-Edward-Joseph), son of Jesse and Rachel (Hobson) Bond, born Aug. 6, 1840; married Oct. 24, 1872: Rachel Minerva King, born March 9, 1855, daughter of Dr. King, formerly of Cass County, Ind. Residence, Holt County, Mo. Address, 1903, Oregon, Mo. He was a soldier, Co. G, 43rd Reg. Mo. Vol. Inft. Children:

1253. I. Robert Earl, b. Feb. 14, 1876.
1254. II. Wilmer O'Neil, b. Feb. 8 1878.
1255. III. Leigh King, b. Aug. 13, 1887.

340. STEPHEN BOND (Jesse-John-Edward-Joseph), son of Jesse and Rachel (Hobson) Bond, born Sept. 8, 1843; married April 2, 1862: Elizabeth Brinson, born Aug. 24, 1839; address, Maitland, Holt County, Mo. Children:

1256. I. Emma, b. Feb. 5, 1863; d. same day.
1257. II. Edward Alfred, b. March 19, 1864; d. inft.
1258. III. Anna Mary, b. March 20, 1865.
1259. IV. Nancy Frances, b. Oct. 19, 1866.
1260. V. William Sedley, b. May 8, 1868.
1261. VI. Rebecca Luella, b. July 22, 1870.
1262. VII. Lucinda May, b. May 1, 1873.
1263. VIII. Elva Retta, b. Oct. 22, 1875.
1264. IX. Julia Viola, b. Oct. 10, 1879; d. March 19, 1881.

341. ABEL BOND (Joshua-John-Edward-Joseph), son of Joshua and Rachel (Davis) Bond, born in Surry County, N. C., Dec. 22, 1825, being the eldest child of his parents; married March 28, 1844: Sarah Ann Sizemore, born May 7, 1825. He died near Stafford, Kas., Oct. 22, 1893; buried in Pleasant Valley cemetery. He moved from North Carolina in 1850; soon after settled in Iowa, but moved to Kansas in 1859. Occupation, farmer and colporteur, and spent a great deal of his time in delivering religious tracts, traveling all over the country and across the plains to California. Children:

   1265.   I.   Isom Robert, b. Feb. 10, 1845.

   1266.   II. Nancy Jane, b. Feb. 7, 1847; d. s. p. Aug. 19, 1861.

   1267. III. Rachel, b. Dec. 29, 1849.

   1268. IV. Martha Sylvira, b. July 9, 1852.

   1269.   V. Abel Joshua, b. Jan. 7, 1855.

   1270. VI. Mary Keziah, b. Oct. 11, 1857.

   1271. VII. Henry Worthington, b. May 1, 1860; d. s. p. April 14, 1881, at Emporia, Kas.

   1272. VIII. John S., b. Nov. 15, 1863.

   1273. IX. Cardelia, b. Oct. 22, 1868.

342. ENOS BOND (Joshua-John-Edward-Joseph), son of Joshua and Rachel (Davis) Bond, born in Surry County, N. C., Sept. 18, 1827; died at Mt. Pleasant, Henry County, Iowa; married Rachel Macy, daughter of William and Mary Macy. Occupation, farmer. She married again. Children:

   1274.   I.   John P.

   1275. II. William J.

   1276. III. Augustus.

   1277. IV. Name unknown. N. f. k.

343. WILLIAM BOND (Joshua-John-Edward-Joseph), born Oct. 17, 1829, in Surry County, N. C.; married Rebecca Hobson, born Oct. 15, 1830; she died April 1, 1857, in Surry County, N. C. He moved to Lee County, Iowa, in 1860, and to Hardin County, Iowa, 1861; moved to Kansas in 1886, where he was in 1905, near Stafford. He married second in North Carolina in 1859: Elizabeth Hutchens, daughter of Thomas and Sarah (Philips) Hutchens. No children last marriage; three by first:

   1278.   I.   Elbert B., b. June 10, 1850.

   1279. II. Selena, b. Aug. 27, 1851.

1280. III. Elzena, b. June 5, 1853.

344. JOHN BOND (Joshua-John-Edward-Joseph), son of Joshua and Rachel (Davis) Bond, born in Surry County, N. C., July 23, 1832; married April 29, 1856: Lydia Smith. Moved from North Carolina to Iowa in 1860 and to Kansas, 1862. Residence, Americus, Kas. Children:

1281. I. Philander Caswell, b. Feb. 26, 1857.
1282. II. Flora Angeline, b. May 9, 1859; d.
1283. III. Julia Ann, b. April 24, 1861.
1284. IV. Calista Irene, b. Dec. 3, 1864.
1285. V. Eli Smith, b. April 7, 1871.
1286. VI. Lydia May, b. May 14, 1873.
1287. VII. John Henry, b. Feb. 19, 1876.

345. SIMPSON BOND (Joshua-John-Edward-Joseph), son of Joshua and Rachel (Davis) Bond, born in Surry County, N. C., July 17, 1834; died in Kansas City, Mo., July 31, 1897; married Martha Reed. He moved from North Carolina to Iowa about 1860, and a few years later moved to Kansas; lived also at Kearney, Clay County, Mo. Then moved to Kansas City, where he died. Children:

1290. I. Priscilla.
1291. II. Virgil, dec.
1292. III. Anna, m. Mr. H. Ford, of Kansas City, Mo.
1293. IV. Cyrus, dec.
1294. V. Nathan.
1295. VI. William.
1296. VII. Cora.
1297. VIII. Charles.
1298. IX. Daughter, name unknown. N. f. k.

346. MARY BOND (Joshua-John-Edward-Joseph), born in Surry County, N. C., May 4, 1839; moved with her mother in 1860 to Hardin County, Ia., and in 1862 moved to Kansas, where she married May 26, 1868: Ebenezer Doan; moved in 1869 with mother to Hardin County, Ia., later settled near Laton, Rooks County, Kas. Children:

1299. I. Emma C. Doan, b. Aug. 15, 1869.
1300. II. Abner H. Doan, b. May 11, 1871; d. June 3, 1872, inft.
1301. III. Orlena Doan, b. Feb. 22, 1874.
1302. IV. Henrietta Doan, b. March 8, 1875.

1303. V. Alfred L. Doan, b. April 7, 1879.

1304. VI. Clayton Doan, b. Jan. 16, 1882.

348. MATILDA BOND (Joseph-John-Edward-Joseph), eldest child of Joseph and Naomi (Cox) Bond, born June 1, 1834, in Henry County, Ind., moving with her parents a year later to Parke County, Ind.; she died April 28, 1880; married first, Robert Heilman; had no issue from this marriage; married second, William Heilman. One child:

1305. I. Justus Heilman. N. f. k.

351. ANNA BOND (Joseph-John-Edward-Joseph), born April 26, 1840, in Parke County, Ind.; married Oct. 16, 1865: James Shaw, born June 22, 1827, in Kentucky, son of Jesse and Sarah (Davis) Shaw; he died Feb. 3, 1890. Her address 1910, Anna Shaw, North Platte, Neb. Children:

1306. I. Infant son, b. April 18, 1867; d. inft.

1307. II. Naomi Shaw, b. July 13, 1869; d. July 4, 1870, infant.

1308. III. Thomas B. Shaw, b. March 11, 1871.

1309. IV. Mary F. Shaw, b. Sept. 16, 1873; m.; d. March 5, 1899; no issue.

1310. V. James A. Shaw, b. Jan. 4, 1876.

352. NATHAN BOND (Joseph-John-Edward-Joseph), born in Parke County, Ind., March 1, 1843; died in Tippecanoe County, Dec. 14, 1879. Was soldier during war of rebellion. Married 1868: Nancy A. Patterson, born Aug. 25, 1844, daughter of Alexander and Clementine Patterson; she died Nov. 19, 1876. Children:

1311. I. Infant, d.

1312. II. E. Florence.

1313. III. Anna B., who was adopted into a family named Burgett and name changed to Anna B. Burgett.

1314. IV.

1315. V. Two d. in childhood, names unknown.

353. MARY BOND (Joseph-John-Edward-Joseph), born July 23, 1845; died March 20, 1878; married William Ward. Residence Parke County, Ind. Children:

1316. I. Naomi Ward, d. childhood.

1317. II. Joseph Ward, d. aged 16 years.

1318. III. Infant, d.

Parents and children all deceased.

354. MAHLON BOND (Joseph-John-Edward-Joseph), son of Joseph and Naomi (Cox) Bond, born in Parke County, Ind., Nov. 24, 1847: married Nov. 21, 1872: Caroline Ratliff, daughter of Thomas and Amaretta. Residence Veedersburg, Ind. Children:

    1319.   I.   John, b. March 19, 1879.
    1320.   II.   Lillie, b. Sept. 11, 1873.
    1321.   III.   Rosa, b. Sept. 30, 1883.

355. DANIEL HUFF BOND (Joseph - John - Edward - Joseph), son of Joseph and Naomi (Cox) Bond, born in Parke County, Ind., Jan. 10, 1850; married March 27, 1872: Margaret Ann Rector, born Dec. 24, 1853. Occupation, farmer. Address, 1910, Tangier, Ind. Children:

    1322.   I.   Rachel Alice, born Feb. 18, 1873.
    1323·   II.   Caroline Ellen, b. July 18, 1875.
    1324.   III.   Laura Frances, b. Dec. 4, 1878.
    1325.   IV.   Martha Jane, b. March 31, 1881.
    1326.   V.   Anna May. b. May 2, 1884.
    1327.   VI.   Adam Edward, b. Aug. 28, 1887.
    1328.   VII.   Ira Lane, b. July 7, 1889.
    1329.   VIII.   Charles Williams, b. April 4, 1893; d. s. p. Aug. 4, 1893.
    1330.   IX.   Ada Merl, b. March 8, 1895.

358. ADAM BOND (Joseph-John-Edward-Joseph), son and youngest child of Joseph and Naomi (Cox) Bond, born in Parke County, Ind., Feb. 16, 1856; married March 9, 1893: Elizabeth Bradford, born Aug. 9, 1867. She died at Carrington, N. D. His residence Jan., 1910, Sevenpersons, Alberta, Can. Children:

    1331.   I.   Alfred D., b. Jan. 28, 1894.
    1332.   II.   Ida May, b. Sept. 1, 1896.
    1333.   III.   Infant, b. Feb. 1898; d. 1898.
    1334.   IV.   Maurice and
    1335.   V.   Minnie, twins, b. Nov. 14, 1900.

367. JESSE WASSON (Lydia - William - Edward - Joseph), eldest son of Jehiel and Lydia (Bond) Wasson, born Oct. 22, 1821; died May 15, 1889, in Laporte, Ind.; married Jan. 1, 1840: Mary Cadwallader. Children:

    1336.   I.   Henry Wasson.
    1337.   II.   Elenora Wasson.

1338.   III.   Alice Wasson.

1339.   IV.   Augusta Wasson.

1340.   V.   Josephine Wasson.

1341.   VI.   Ami W. Wasson.

Jesse Wasson married second, March 31, 1855: — Haughan. Children:

1342.   VII.   Adaline Wasson.

1343.   VIII.   Buran Wasson.

1344.   IX.   Jesse Wasson, Jr.

1345.   X.   George Wasson.

1346.   XI.   Maud Wasson.

368. CHARLOTTE WASSON (Lydia-William-Edward-Joseph), daughter of Jehiel and Lydia (Bond) Wasson, born Nov. 28, 1823; married 1855: William Cox. · Children:

1347.   I.   William Wasson Cox.

1348.   II.   Ella Cox.

369. NANCY WASSON (Lydia-William-Edward-Joseph), daughter of Jehiel and Lydia (Bond) Wasson, born Sept. 30, 1825; died Sept. 7, 1854; married John Fosdick.   Children:

1349.   I.   Lydia Jane Fosdick.

1350.   II.   Timothy Jehiel Fosdick.

370. ASENATH WASSON (Lydia-William-Edward-Joseph), daughter of Jehiel and Lydia (Bond) Wasson, born March 8, 1828; died April, 1858; marries James P. Wasson.   Children:

1351.   I.   Franklin Wasson.

372. SARAH WASSON (Lydia-William-Edward-Joseph), daughter of Jehiel and Lydia (Bond) Wasson, born Jan. 17, 1834; died Feb. 25, 1902; married George H. Andrews, born Dec. 4, 1826.   Residence Chicago.   Children:

1352.   I.   Mary Jane Andrews.

1353.   II.   Lydia Ellen Andrews.

1354.   III.   Jehiel Andrews, and

1355.   IV.   James Andrews, twins.

1356.   V.   Sarah Ida Andrews.

375. MARTHA A. WASSON (Lydia-William-Edward-Joseph), daughter of Jehiel and Lydia (Bond) Wasson, born Aug. 23, 1840; married Howard J. Mason.   Children:

1357.   I.   Annie Hamilton Mason.

1358.   II.   Charles Howard Mason.

1359.   III.   Sarah Ella Mason.

1360. IV. Audra Hamilton Mason.

1361. V. Clarice Mason.

1362. VI. Wesley Sherman Mason.

1363. VII. Martha Mason.

1364. VIII. Oliver Carr Mason.

376. LYDIA ELLEN WASSON (Lydia-William-Edward-Joseph), daughter of Jehiel and Lydia (Bond) Wasson, born Aug. 23, 1840; died March 1, 1899; married Oliver Kinsey Carr. Children:

1365. I. Rachel Carr.

1366. II. John Carr.

1366. III. Jesse Carr.

1367. IV. Ruth Ann Carr.

1368. V. Clarence Carr.

1369. VI. Isaac Kinsey Carr.

1370. VII. Oliver K. Carr.

377. ELIZA WASSON (Lydia - William - Edward - Joseph), daughter of Jehiel and Lydia (Bond) Wasson, born July 21, 1843; married May 25, 1865: Eli Morris. Residence, Richmond, Ind. Children:

1371. I. Jehiel Wasson Morris.

1372. II. William Edwin Morris.

1373. III. Anna Elizabeth Morris; married John E. Woodhurst.

1374. IV. Martha Ellen Morris; m. Charles Sheidler.

378. LYDIA BOND (Jesse-William-Edward-Joseph), daughter of Jesse and Mary (Vore) Bond, born Jan. 21, 1823; died Aug. 31, 1862; married at Laporte, Ind., Dec. 7, 1848: Anslem Jones. Children:

1375. I. Sarah Eliza Jones.

1376. II. Lydia Ellen Jones.

380. ISAAC VORE BOND (Jesse-William-Edward-Joseph), born Dec. 2, 1825; died May 24, 1896; married Mary E. Rogers; she died Oct. 19, 1875. Residence Laporte, Ind. Children:

1377. I. William Andrew, b. May 17, 1854.

1378. II. Frank Arnold, b. July 22, 1862.

He married second. Children:

1379. III. Jesse Ira, b. Jan. 26, 1878.

382. SILAS BOND (Jesse-William-Edward-Joseph), son of Jesse and Mary (Vore) Bond, born Sept. 17, 1828, at Flat Rock,

Henry County, Ind.; m. Mary Jane Young, born Adrian, Mich.; she died Oct. 19, 1875. Residence Santa Barbara, Cal. Children:

1380.   I.   Leslie Judson, b. Dec. 3, 1873; d. Dec. 23, 1876.

1381. . II.   Carrie Louisa, b. April 11, 1877.

383. WILLIAM BOND (Jesse–William–Edward–Joseph), born May 13, 1830; died April 25, 1859; married Sarah Ann Giles. Children:

1382.   I.   Walter Silas.

1383.   II.   Willetta Josephine.

385. LOUISA ELVIRA STANTON (Charlotte (Bond)-William-Edward-Joseph), born Nov. 30, 1841; married July 8, 1866: Orin Lee Abbott, born April 1, 1834. Residence California. Children:

1384.   I.   Stanton Bond Abbott, b. Nov. 4, 1867, in Indiana.

1385.   II.   Milton Orin Abbott, b. Feb. 21, 1869, in California.

1386.   III.   William Abbott, b. March 8, 1871; d. 1871.

1387.   IV.   Myron Abbott, b. Dec. 22, 1872; d. Sept. 10, 1881.

387. WILLIAM HENRY BOND (William-William-Edward-Joseph), son of William and Mary (Hitchcock) Bond, born July 19, 1840; married April 21, 1862: Josephine Fisher, daughter of James and Mary Fisher, of St. Louis, Mo.; she died March 6, 1907. Residence Leavenworth, Kas. Children:

1388.   I.   Ada, b. May, 1864; m. Nov. 27, 1909: Thomas Quigley. Residence El Paso, Texas.

1389.   II.   William Quincy, b. June 11, 1867; d. Dec. 31, 1872.

1390.   III.   Estella May, b. June, 1869; married Herbert Nunn; no issue.

1391.   IV.   Lee, b. March 31, 1873; attorney-at-law. Residence Leavenworth, Kas.

389. PHILIP QUINCY BOND (William-William-Edward-Joseph), born Sept. 15, 1846, in Greenwood, Caddo Parish, La.; married Feb. 15, 1873: Sarah Ann Underwood, born in Wilmington, Ohio, May 11, 1854, daughter of Charles and Mary (Jones) Underwood. Children:

1392.   I.   Charles Leonidas, b. Aug. 14, 1875, at Salina, Kas.

1393.   II.   William Quincy, b. Aug. 21, 1877.

390. THOMAS LEONIDAS BOND (William-William-Edward-Joseph), born Dec. 22, 1849; married Dec. 22, 1874: Alice S. Garver, daughter of Samuel and Sarah Garver, of Chambersburg, Pa. Residence, Salina, Kas. Attorney at law. Children:

1394.   I.   Florence Emma, b. Feb. 10, 1876.
1395.   II.   Fannie May, b. Dec. 28, 1878; d. inft.
1396.   III.   Sarah Helen, b. Jan. 16, 1880; d. s. p. April 1, 1901.
1397.   IV.   Harry Austin, b. Feb. 18, 1882.
1398.   V.   Frank Garver, b. April 7, 1886.
1399.   VI.   Samuel Marion, b. Jan. 18, 1888.

391. IRENE BOND (John-William-Edward-Joseph), daughter of John and Nancy (Kennedy) Bond, born 1837; she died 1869; married first her second cousin: (425) Annet Underwood, born May 17, 1831, son of Lewis and Keziah (Bond) Underwood. Children:

1400.   I.   Charles M. Underwood, b. May 3, 1855.
1401.   II.   Matilda Underwood, b. July 4, 1859.

She and Mr. Underwood were divorced. She married second, a Mr. Griswold. Three children, all d. s. p. N. f. k.

392. MELISSA BOND (John - William - Edward - Joseph), daughter of John and Nancy (Kennedy) Bond, born 1839; married McClintock Milhollen. Residence. Bellingham, Wash. Ch:

1403.   I.   Mary Millhollen.
1404.   II.   Anna Millhollen.
1405.   III.   Thomas Millhollen. N. f. k.

393. JESSE R. BOND (John-William-Edward-Joseph), son of John and Nancy (Barnett) Bond, born Sept. 5, 1847; died 1874; married Belle Wise. Five children. Residence, Indiana, Texas. N. f. k. Children:

1406.
1407.
1408.
1409.
1410.

394. LORENZO D. BOND (John-William-Edward-Joseph), son of John and Nancy (Barnett) Bond, born April 22, 1849; died June, 1880, in California. One or more children:

1411.   I.   Daughter. Elizabeth. N. f. k.

395. CHARLOTTE BOND (John-William-Edward-Joseph),

daughter of John and Nancy (Barnett) Bond, born Aug. 18, 1851; married 1874: John B. Fuller, born Aug. 28, 1843. Residence, Chesterton, Ind. Children:

1412. I. John William Fuller, b. Aug. 31, 1876.
1413. II. Emily Fuller.
1414. III. Henry Fuller.
1415. IV. Charles C. Fuller.
1416. V. Della E. Fuller.

396. ALFRED P. BOND (John-William-Edward-Joseph), son of John and Nancy (Barnett) Bond, born Dec. 22, 1852; died in Oklahoma. Was attorney-at-law. Residence, Pella, Iowa. Children:

1417. I. Madge.
1418. II. William.

397. EMILY BOND (John-William-Edward-Joseph), born Feb. 11, 1855; died Jan. 25, 1878; married Edward Evans; he died about 1891. Children:

1419. I. Clara Evans.
1420. II. David Evans.
1421. III. George Evans.

401. CHRISTOPHER BOND (Daniel-Edward-Edward-Joseph), son of Daniel and Mary (Hussey) Bond, born in Wayne County, Ind., June 28, 1821; moved with his parents to Randolph County, Ind., about 1835; married Sarah Rinard (or Reynard), daughter of Solomon and Rachel (Green) Rinard, born 1826. Moved to Mahaska County, Iowa, about 1850, where he died July 7, 1858. Six children, four born before moving to Iowa. After his decease she moved back to Indiana; some years later moved to Missouri. Children:

1422. I. Moses; d. s. p.
1423. II. Phoebe.
1424. III. Catherine; d. s. p.
1425. IV. Henry, b. in Randolph Co., Ind.; d. s. p.
1426. V. Cyrus,.b. in Mahaska Co., Ia.; d. s. p.
1427. VI. Martha, b. Dec. 31, 1854, in Mahaska Co., Ia.

402. LAVINA BOND (Daniel - Edward - Edward - Joseph), born in Wayne County, Ind., March 11, 1824; died July 16, 1897, in Nebraska; married in Randolph County, Ind., Sept. 15, 1841: John Hull, born Feb. 6, 1819, son of Solomon and Elizabeth Hull. Moved to Mahaska County, Iowa, about 1845 or 1846,

where they resided many years, near Oskaloosa. He died.
Children:

1428.   I.   Mary Hull, b. Dec. 9, 1843, in Indiana.
1429.   II.   Tiddeman Hull, b. Jan. 22, 1845.
1430.   III.   Anna Hull, b. Jan. 28, 1847, in Iowa.
1431.   IV.   Sarah Hull, b. Dec. 9, 1848.
1432.   V.   Elizabeth Hull, b. Nov. 10, 1851.
1433.   VI.   Solomon Hull,. b. April 2, 1853.
1434.   VII.   George Hull, b. April 8, 1855.
1435.   VIII.   Daniel Hull, b. March 26, 1857.
1436.   IX.   Charles Hull, b. Nov. 28, 1858.
1437.   X.   Eunice Hull, b. May 14, 1861; d. s. p. Nov. 25,
1880.
1438.   XI.   John Franklin Hull, b. Nov. 9, 1862.
1439.   XII.   William W. Hull, b. May 13, 1867.

403. SARAH BOND (Daniel - Edward - Edward - Joseph),
born May 31, 1826; died Nov. 1, 1889; married Zimri Hollingsworth. Resided Ohio, Richmond, Chicago. Children:
1440.   I.   Mary Hollingsworth; m. Milton R. Shrock; res.
Chicago, Ill.; ch., 2 sons.
1441.   II.   Allen Hollingsworth, dec.
1442.   III.   Anna Hollingsworth; m. Newton Tracy; ch.,
Russell Tracy. Res. Indianapolis, Ind.

404. CYRUS BOND (Daniel - Edward - Edward - Joseph),
born Aug. 8, 1828; died 1888; he was physician and practiced
medicine in Mahaska County, Iowa; married Jan. 29, 1863:
Mary D. West, born Oct. 25, 1838; she died May 30, 1879.
Children:
1443.   I.   Charles Lewis, b. Aug. 1, 1864; d. Aug. 7, 1866.
1444.   II.   William, b. Nov. 21, 1872; d. Nov. 6, 1874.
1445.   III.   Minnie, b. July 27, 1867; m. a Mr. Sheppard;
she d. s. p.

405. EUNICE BOND (Daniel - Edward - Edward - Joseph),
born June 28, 1830, in Wayne County, Ind.; married May 22,
1865: Henry Nugent, born June 23, 1822. Address Jan., 1910,
Dayton, O., where they have resided many years. Children:
1446.   I.   Arthur Bond Nugent, b. July 22, 1867; d. Oct. 14,
1890, soon after graduating as physician; m.; one ch.; it d.

406. SIMON BOND (Daniel - Edward - Edward - Joseph),
born Oct. 21, 1832, in Wayne County, Ind.; married Susannah

Harris, daughter of Benjamin and Lydia (Hiatt) Harris. Merchant, Webster, Ind. He died in California, Jan. 17, 1898. Children:

1447.   I.   Mary Elmetta.
1448. II.   Charles Sumner.
1449. III.   Minerva Ella.
1450. IV.   Martha Emma.
1451.   V.   Susan Myrtle, dec.

407. PLEASANT BOND (Daniel-Edward-Edward-Joseph), son of Daniel and Mary (Hussey) Bond, born June 29, 1835; eductated at Earlham College and the University of Michigan at Ann Arbor. Residence Indianapolis, Ind. Special Agent Penn Mutual Life Insurance Co. m. Martha Wilson. Children:

1452.   I.   Nina.
1453. II.   Gertrude, dec.
1454. III.   Walter W.

410. SAMSON BOND (Benjamin-Edward-Edward-Joseph), son of Benjamin and Ellen (Goldsmith) Bond, born Jan. 7, 1830, near Newport, now Fountain City, Wayne County, Ind.; married May 21, 1847: Ann Jackson; moved to Minnesota 1855. He and five brothers were soldiers during the Civil War. He died June 18, 1871, in Minnesota. Children:

1455.   I.   Reuben, b. Jan., 1848; d. inft., age 5 years, and
1455-a. II.   Laban, twins, b. Jan., 1848; d. inft.
1455-b. III.   Ellen, b. 1849; d. childhood.
1455-c. IV.   William A., b. Jan. 18, 1851; d. s. p. about 1868.
1456.   V.   Nathan, b. July 1, 1852.
1457.   VI.   Floretta, b. Oct. 29, 1853.
1458. VII.   Caleb, b. May 21, 1855.
1459. VIII.   Sarah Ellen, b. May 14, 1857; d. s. p. Jan., 1869.
1460.   IX.   Samson, b. July 14, 1859; res. Brainerd, Minn.;
blacksmith by trade.
1461.   X.   Sebitha, b. Feb. 2, 1861.
1462.   XI.   Rebecca, b. Oct. 24, 1862.
1462-a. XII.   Benjamin, b. July, 1864; d. 1864, inft.
1463. XIII.   Jane, b. April 24, 1866.
1464. XIV.   Cornelia, b. Dec. 16, 1867.

412. PELATIAH BOND (Benjamin-Edward-Edward-Joseph), son of Benjamin and Ellen (Goldsmith) Bond, born in Wayne County, Ind., Feb. 8, 1834; married Aug. 12, 1862: Cornelia Edwards, born April 12, 1842, daughter of William and Sarah (Bolton) Edwards, of Hamilton County, Ind. In 1854 he moved with his parents to Minnesota. Some years later returned to Indiana and educated himself for a teacher. When the war came on he enlisted in April 15, 1861, in Eighth Reg. Vol. Inft. for three months. In 1862 he entered the service in the Second Ind. Cavalry, where he served three years. After the war he resided in Minnesota, Kansas, Indian Territory, Indiana and California. Occupation, teacher, merchant and farmer. Residence and address 1912, Sawtelle, Cal. Children:

1465. I. Myrtilla Leona, b. Dec. 8, 1863.

1466. II. Iona Luella, b. May 13, 1866; m. Robert L. Daily; she d. s. p. Jan. 23, 1884.

1467. III. Katie Cornelia, b. Dec. 16, 1870.

1468. IV. Myrlea Rebina, b. Aug. 28, 1872, in Neosha Co., Kas.; m. 1892: Palmer Ashton; she died at Pomona, Cal., Sept. 22, 1901, s. p.

413. HEZEKIAH BOND (Benjamin-Edward-Edward-Joseph), born Aug. 29, 1836, in Indiana; moved to Hennepin Co., Minn., 1854; married April 17, 1858: Ann Poalton, nee Hough, born May 18, 1829, daughter of John and Mary (Coggshall) Hough; John, son of John Hough, Sr. When Abraham Lincoln called for volunteers to put down the rebellion Hezekiah Bond entered the service in the First Minn. Reg. and participated in the Battle of Gettysburg and other engagements. He died Oct. 26, 1866, a prisoner of war at Salisbury, N. C. Children:

1469. I. Scipio, b. Aug. 28, 1859.

1470. II. Caroline, b. Jan. 16, 1861.

416. DANIEL BOND (Benjamin-Edward-Edward-Joseph), son of Benjamin and Ellen (Goldsmith) Bond, born April 2, 1842, in Randolph County, Ind.; moved with his parents to Hennepin County, Minn., in 1854. He enlisted and served in First Regiment Minnesota Vol. Inft. He took part in many hard-fought battles, Gettysburg being one of them. He was captured near Petersburg and remained a prisoner until near the close of the war. At the close of the war he returned to Indiana and attended different educational institutions for several years, then engaged in teaching and farming. Residence Indiana, Kentucky, California. Address, Dec., 1912, Los Angeles, Cal. Married first March 15, 1872: Lizzie C. Smith; she died s. p. Jan. 16, 1876; married second, Alice M. Bowman, of Hamilton County, Ind., daughter of Edmund and Sarah; she died May 5, 1895. Children:

1471.   I.   Edmund Bowman, b. June 15, 1879.
1472.   II.   John Brown, b. May 29, 1889.

Married third Sept. 5, 1896: Martha Taylor, nee Conlee. Ch.:

1473.   III.   Florence Vola.

417. EDWARD BOND (Benjamin-Edward-Edward-Joseph), youngest son of Benjamin and Ellen (Goldsmith) Bond, born near Lynn, Randolph County, Ind., May 3, 1845; moved with parents to Minnesota in 1854. In time of the rebellion served as soldier in Co. E, First Minn. Heavy Artillery. After his return from the army he engaged in farming in Randolph County, Ind. Married Oct. 24, 1869: Mary E. Knight, nee Ruble, daughter of Samuel and Ravenna (Mendenhall) Ruble; she died Aug. 18, 1900. His address in Sept., 1912, Sawtelle, Los Angeles County, Cal. Children:

1474.   I.   James D., b. Dec. 9, 1870.
1475.   II.   Emma Myrtle, b. Sept. 2, 1872.
1476.   III.   Milton W., b. Jan. 18, 1878; d. March 25, 1878, infant.
1477.   IV.   Samuel R., b. May 28, 1879.

418. ANDREW UNDERWOOD (Keziah-Edward-Edward-Joseph), eldest son of Lewis and Keziah (Bond) Underwood, born in Wayne County, Ind., Dec. 28, 1818; died in Indian Territory, now Oklahoma, near the city of Vinita, Feb. 11, 1904; married Jan. 28, 1839: Agatha Hutchins, born about 1822; she died Jan. 23, 1889. Occupation, farmer. Residence, Indiana, Iowa, Kansas, Arkansas, Indian Territory. Children:

1478.   I.   Henry H. Underwood, b. Dec. 16, 1840.
1479.   II.   Susannah E. Underwood, b. March 31, 1842.
1480.   III.   Anderson L. Underwood, b. Jan. 26, 1844.
1481.   IV.   George Underwood, b. 1846; d. inft.
1482.   V.   Wesley Underwood, b. 1848; d. inft.
1483.   VI.   Stacy J. Underwood, b. Sept. 5, 1852.
1484.   VII.   Andrew W. Underwood, b. June 12, 1854; d. s. p.

420. SUSANNAH UNDERWOOD (Keziah (Bond)-Edward-Edward-Joseph), born Jan. 28, 1823; died 1846; married Raford Kean. Two children:

1485.   I.   Emily Jane Kean, b. Oct. 29, 1842; m. Leander P.

Garrett. For further history see under name of Garrett in this volume.

1486. II. Martha M. Kean.

421. EXUM UNDERWOOD (Keziah-Edward-Edward-Joseph), son of Lewis and Keziah (Bond) Underwood, born May 12, 1825; married June 5, 1846: Jane M. Hutchins, born April 19, 1829, daughter of Dr. Johnson and Susannah (Adams) Hutchins. Occupation, farmer. Residence, Randolph County, Ind., and Adair County, Iowa. He died Oct. 28, 1861. Children:

1487. I. Samuel L. Underwood, b. Sept. 10, 1848; d. s. p. Feb. 17, 1849.

1488. II. Arthur S. Underwood, b. Dec. 29, 1850; d. s. p.

1489. III. Annet Wesley Underwood, b. Feb. 8, 1853. Res., Iowa and Kansas.

1490. IV. Martitia L. Underwood, b. May 6, 1855; m. (938) James G. Bond, son of Jesse and Emily (Randall) Bond, which see.

422. LUCINDA UNDERWOOD (Keziah (Bond) -Edward-Edward-Joseph), born Aug. 4, 1827; died Feb. 2, 1859; married in Randolph County, Ind., 1850: Jeremiah Rinard. Moved about 1858 to Adair County, Ia. Occupation, farmer. Address, 1903, Meridian, Idaho. He died April 16, 1911. Children:

1491. I. Alonzo Harvey Rinard, b. July 28, 1851, in Randolph Co., Ind.

1492. II. Amarian Larkin Rinard, b. March 8, 1853; m. Jan. 21, 1879: (1427) Martha Bond, dau. of Christopher, which see.

425. ANNET UNDERWOOD (Keziah (Bond) - Edward-Edward-Joseph), born May 17, 1831; married (391) Irene Bond, born 1837, daughter of John and Nancy (Kennedy) Bond. They were second cousins. Children:

1493. I. Charles Underwood, b. May 3, 1855.

1494. II. Matilda Underwood, b. July 4, 1859.

He and wife separated. Married second wife, Harriet Goodwin. He died 1862 (?). Children:

1496. IV. Alvena Underwood.

1497. V. Madison S. Underwood.

After his decease she moved with the two children to Kansas. N. f. k.

426. HULDAH MATILDA UNDERWOOD (Keziah (Bond)-

Edward-Edward-Joseph), born Oct. 10, 1833; died Sept. 24, 1877; married Nathan Mendenhall, of Randolph County, Ind. Residence, Indiana, Illinois. Children:

1498.   I.   Amos Armona Mendenhall, b. Aug. 12, 1851; m. Emma G. Simmons. Res., Winchester, Ind. R. F. D.

1499.   II.   Rose D. Mendenhall, b. Jan. 3, 1856.

1500.   III.   Mary E. Mendenhall, b. Feb. 17, 1860.

1501.   IV.   Jacob B. Mendenhall, b. June 1, 1867; d. s. p. June 16, 1880.

428.   ELIZABETH LURANA UNDERWOOD (K e z i a h (Bond) -Edward-Edward-Joseph), born July 29, 1837; married Stover Rinard, of Randolph County, Ind. Moved to Adair County, Ia., where their children were brought up. She died near Menlo, Ia. He died in Kansas. Children:

1502.   I.   Fremont Rinard, b. Jan. 31, 1858.

1503.   II.   Mary Etta Rinard, b. July 29, 1860.

1504.   III.   Ulysses G. Rinard, b. May 4, 1863.

1505.   IV.   Alonzo S. Rinard, b. Sept. 7, 1865.

433.   THOMAS W. ROBERTS (Elizabeth-Edward-Edward-Joseph), son of Solomon Whitson and Elizabeth (Bond) Roberts, born Dec. 16, 1822, near Richmond, Wayne County, Ind.; m. Lucinda Lough. He was a contractor and builder. Residence, Richmond, Ind. He died June, 1908, aged 86 years. Her address, Richmond, Ind. Children:

1506.   I.   Barton Roberts, d. childhood.

1507.   II.   Charles Roberts. Residence, Richmond, Ind.

434.   DR. DANIEL HUFF ROBERTS (Elizabeth (Bond)-Edward-Edward-Joseph), born Nov. 10, 1824, in Wayne County, Ind.; married in same county: Lizzie Austin, daughter of James Austin. For a few years he followed teaching, after which he engaged in the practice of medicine. Residence, Wayne and Madison Counties, Ind., Owatonna, Minn., Escondido, Calif. She died in California. He died Jan. 4, 1911, in Los Angeles, Calif. Children:

1508.   I.   James Austin Roberts; left his parents' home in 1869. N. f. k.

1509.   II.   Oliver Nixon Roberts; m. Mary Drew; he d. Sept., 1908; two ch:

(a)   Caroline Roberts.

(b)   Eugene Roberts.

1510.   III.   Milton Roberts; m. Nancy Beville.

1511.   IV.   Dr. Walter Roberts; m. Carrie Jones; res., St. Paul, Minn.   Moved to San Diego, Calif., Sept., 1912.

1512.   V.   Solomon Roberts;   m. Elizabeth Whipple; two children:

> (a)   Alice; m., has two ch.
> (b)   Daniel H. Roberts; m. Ida ————; he d.; had son: Daniel H. Roberts.

1513.   VI.   Esther Roberts; m. Frank Chapin; res., Escoudido, Calif.   Three ch:

> (a)   Roy Chapin.
> (b)   Bessie Chapin.
> (c)   Melville Chapin.

1514.   VII.   Alice Roberts; m. J. L. Andrew.   Res., 1910, Los Angeles, Calif.   Three ch:

> (a)   Paul Andrew.
> (b)   Thomas Andrew.
> (c)   Milton Andrew.

1515.   VIII.   Edward Roberts; m. Carolyn Parry.   Address, Minneapolis, Minn.   One ch:

> (a)   Henry Roberts.

443.   ARTEMAS ROBERTS (Elizabeth (Bond) - Edward - Edward-Joseph), born Oct. 28, 1841.   Educated at the University of Michigan, Ann Arbor.   Married Elizabeth Bellangee. They settled on a farm near Lincoln, Neb.   Occupation, civil engineer, architect, farmer.   Children:

1516.   I.   Dr. William Colfax Roberts, b. Sept., 1868, at Owatona, Minn.

1517.   II.   Artemas C. Roberts, b. March 7, 1871; orchardist; Paonia, Colo.

He married second: Mary Bellangee, sister of his first wife, dec.   Address, 1910, Dade City, Fla.   Six Children:

1518.   III.   John Milton Roberts, b. Oct. 3, 1873; civil engineer; address, 103 Park Ave., New York City.

1519.   IV.   James Russel Roberts, b. May 29, 1876; dairyman, Lincoln, Neb.

1520.   V.   Daniel Edward Roberts, general store, R. F. D. No. 1, Mead, Wn.

1521.   VI.   Charles Whitson Roberts, b. Oct. 11, 1880; civil engineer, Lincoln, Neb.

1522. VII. Barton Bellangee Roberts, b. Dec. 2, 1883; farmer, Lincoln, Neb.

1523. VIII. Mary Louisa Roberts, b. March 17, 1886; d. Feb. 4, 1887.

445. ELIAS PAYNE (Huldah-Edward-Edward-Joseph), son of Barnabas and Huldah (Bond) Payne, born June 20, 1841; married Margaret Louisa Eckman, born March 30, 1848; she died Jan. 21, 1888; he died Jan. 12, 1874. Residence, North Manchester, Wabash County, Ind. Children:

1524.   I. Laura Payne, b. Jan. 19, 1867; d. s. p. Feb. 5, 1867.

1525.   II. Rawley Payne, b. July 3, 1868; d. s. p. Aug. 24, 1868.

1526. III. Ithiel Payne, b. Aug. 1, 1869; res., Lincoln, Neb.

1527.   IV. Marshall Payne, b. Sept. 7, 1871. Dentist, Wabash, Ind.

447. LUZENA PAYNE (Huldah (Bond)-Edward-Edward-Joseph), born May 12, 1845; married William Brindle, born March 20, 1835; farmer; resided near North Manchester, Ind. Children:

1528.   I. Stacy Brindle, b. 1863 (?); m. Laura E. Crull; res., near Pennville, Blackford Co., Ind. Six children.

1529.   II. Alice Melissa Brindle; m.; d., no living issue.

1530. III. Anna Theresa Brindle, b. March 3, 1867; m. Rev. Samuel Frantz, son of Henry and Lizzie (Mills) Frantz. Address, 1905, North Manchester, Ind. One child:

  (a) Lela May Frantz.

1531.   IV. Asa Sylvester Brindle, b. Feb. 20, 1870, in Wabash Co., Ind.; m. Jan. 26, 1895: Lorena Ann Slusher, b. Sept. 24, 1873; she died March 23. 1905. Five children.

1532.   V. Arnie Lillian Brindle, b. about 1874; m. Lawrence Baker. Res., 1905, Laketon, Ind. One child.

1533.   VI. Albert Riley Brindle, b. March 25, 1876; d. s. p. May 12, 1887.

1534. VII. Mamie L. Brindle, b. 1882; m. Hays West, son of Harvey West. Res., 1905, North Manchester, Ind. Two ch.

449. ANNA PAYNE (Huldah (Bond) - Edward - Edward - Joseph), born April 12, 1848; married Levi Walters, a farmer. Residence, North Manchester, Ind. Children:

1535.   I.   Jesse Armory Walters, born 1870; m. Clara Bowers, dau. of John Bowers.   Four children.

1536.   II.   Clara Bertha Walters, b. 1873 (?); m. F. A. Sharp. Two children.

1537.   III.   Myrtle Belle Walters, b. 1878.

1538.   IV.   Grace Mabell Walters, b. 1884.

451.   MAHLON PAYNE (Huldah (Bond) -Edward-Edward-Joseph), born in Wabash County, Ind., Sept. 25, 1852; m. Feb. 15, 1877: Amanda Garretson, born Dec. 16, 1851, daughter of Talbot and Mary Ann Garretson.   Residence in 1912, Bakersfield, Calif.   Children: ·

1539.   I.   Clarence C. Payne, b. Dec. 13, 1877, in Kansas.

1540.   II.   Elmer A. Payne, b. May 3, 1879, in Kansas; m. at Seward, Neb., June 20, 1900: Emma L. Bick.

1541.   III.   Earnest M. Payne, b. Oct. 16, 1881, in Nebraska.

1542.   IV.   Orville D. Payne, b. July 19, 1883, in Nebraska.

1543.   V.   Irene D. Payne, b. July 24, 1885, in Nebraska.

452.   LEANDER P. GARRETT (Anna (Bond) - Edward - Edward-Joseph),eldest son of Jonathan and Anna(Bond) Garrett, born in Wayne County, Ind., Nov. 27, 1835; died at Indianapolis, Dec. 6, 1894; buried at·Westfield, Ind.   He moved to Guthrie County, Ia., 1856, where he married, July 2, 1858: Emily Jane Kean, daughter of Dr. Raford and Susannah (Underwood) Kean. Children:

1544.   I.   William Garrett, b. Oct. 11, 1859; d. inft.

1545.   II.   Charles Salathiel Garrett, b. Oct. 12, 1860; res., Casey, Ia.

He and his wife separated; he returned to Indiana and married Jan. 11, 1866: Mrs. Mary Early, nee Harold, of Howard County, Ind.   Children:

1546.   III.   Ulysses Grant Garrett, b. Nov. 3, 1867; m. Aug., 1889: Dora Pearch, of Howard Co., Ind.   Address, 1910, Kokomo, Ind., R. F. D. No. 1.   Children:

        (a)   Fern Garrett, b. Aug. 13, 1890.

        (b)   Victor Garrett, b. Oct. 20, 1893.

        (c)   Beulah Garrett, b. Aug. 29, 1896.

        (d)   Grace Garrett, b. Aug. 6, 1898.

        (e)   Eva Garrett, b. April 22, 1901.

1547.   IV.   Ida May Garrett, b. April 27, 1869; m. Joel Henry Brower.   Address, 1912, Sioux Falls, South Dakota.   Children:

      (a) Delilah Alice Brower, b. Dec. 22, 1887.

      (b) Roy Earl Brower, b. April 24, 1889.

1548.   V. Lulu Bertha Garrett, b. May 11, 1871; m. Feb. 9, 1890: Frank Ehrman. Address. 1912, Forest, Ind. Ch:

      (a) Vina Alta Ehrman, b. March 4, 1891.

      (b) Lester Ray Ehrman, b, Feb. 27, 1894.

      (c) George L. Ehrman, b. May 10, 1901.

      (d) Marion J. Ehrman, and

      (e) Mary May Ehrman, twins, b. June 9, 1905.

      (f) Nellie Ehrman, and

      (g) Lillie Ehrman, twins, b. Nov. 29, 1906.

454. VILENA GARRETT (Anna (Bond)-Edward-Edward-Joseph), daughter of (202) Jonathan and (98) Anna (Bond) Garrett, born in Hamilton County, Ind., Jan. 15, 1839; married in Wayne County, Ind., Jan. 29, 1857: Mahlon Harvey, born April 28, 1825, son of William and Sarah Harvey; he died August 10, 1864. She married second, Sept. 19, 1865: James C. Walker, born August 27, 1842, son of John and Sarah (Clawson) Walker, of Richmond, Ind. Address, 1912, Richmond, Ind. Children of first marriage:

1549.   I. William Harvey, b. April 30, 1858; d. s. p. Nov. 27, 1865.

1550.   II. Mary Alice Harvey, b. July 11, 1859; m. Aug. 28, 1878: Edward Lindorph Commons, b. June 11, 1856. Occupatiou, dairyman. Residence, Richmond, Ind. Children:

      (a) Arthur B. Commons, b. Nov. 17, 1879; m. June 19, 1902: Olive Wesler.

      (b) Robert Harvey Commons, b. March 28, 1882; m. April 4, 1901: Lethe Cooper.

      (c) Carlton Allen Commons, b. Nov. 29, 1894.

1551.   III. Frank Harvey, b. May 18, 1861; d. s. p. July 31, 1864.

1552.   IV. Eva Harvey, b. June 22, 1863; d. s. p. Aug. 8, 1864.

The children of second husband, James C. Walker:

1553.   V. Anna Belle Walker, b. Aug. 7, 1866; m. May 14, 1884: John Henry Studt, b. Sept. 28, 1861, son of Adolph and Sophia Studt; she died March, 1894. Children:

      (a) Howard Studt, b. Dec. 18, 1885.

      (b) Minnie Ethel Studt, b. Sept. 9, 1890.

(c)   Myree Eva Studt, b. Nov. 23, 1892.   Residence, Richmond, Ind.

1554.   VI.   Arthur Walker, b. Dec. 2, 1867; d. s. p. March 23, 1877.

1555.   VII.   Frankie Walker, b. Jan. 19, 1869; d. s. p. Feb. 9, 1869.

1556.   VIII.   Nettie May Walker, b. April 2, 1870; m. Dec. 24, 1889: Jesse L. Parshall, b. March 20, 1861, son of Henry and Nancy Parshall, of Richmond, Ind.; he died June 27, 1895.   Ch:

      (a)   Herbert E. Parshall, b. Feb. 14, 1894.

      (b)   Jesse Parshall, b. Dec. 1, 1895; d. April 1, 1907.

She (Nettie Parshall), married second, Dec. 17, 1896: Edward W. Carman, born March 4, 1868, son of George and Sarah (Hagg) Carman.   Children:

      (c)   George Everet Carman, b. Sept. 20, 1897.

      (d)   Ernest Leslie Carman, b. Oct. 16, 1899.

      (e)   Raymond Carman, b. Nov. 1, 1905.   Res., Wayne Co., Ind.

1557.   IX.   Bertha Pearl Walker, b. May 25, 1877; m. Jan. 29, 1896: Stephen M. Parish, b. Oct. 10, 1874, in Wayne Co., Ind., son of James and Nancy Ann (Phillips) Parish.   Occupation, farmer.   Children:

      (a)   Royce Raymond Parish, b. Dec. 12, 1896.

      (b)   Florence Alice Parish, b. Oct. 30, 1898; d. Aug. 31, 1903.

      (c)   Vilena Parish, b. April 16, 1900; d. Sept. 10, 1900; inft.

      (d)   Emmet Walker Parish, b. Aug. 23, 1901.

      (e)   Joseph C. Parish, b. June 7, 1904.

1558.   X.   Josie Elma Walker, b. Dec. 7, 1878; m. March 21, 1901: Frederick William Fetta, b. Oct. 30, 1870, son of George H. and Hannah (Awe) Fetta.   Res., Richmond, Ind.   Ch:

      (a)   Clarence Alden Fetta, b. March 27, 1902.

1559.   XI.   George Wayne Walker, b. Dec. 5, 1880; m. Nov. 24, 1909: Minerva Decker.   Res., Richmond, Ind.   R. F. D.

457.   SAMUEL BOND GARRETT (Anna-Edward-Edward-Joseph), son of Jonathan and Anna (Bond) Garrett, born Nov. 21, 1844, in Wayne County, Ind.; married Oct. 15, 1874: Annie L. Heath, born April 29, 1855, daughter of John W. and Mary

(Kendall) Heath, then of Madison County, Ind. At the time of his marriage he was engaged in the drug trade at Daleville, Ind., and was postmaster of the town for eleven years. Moved to Muncie in 1890 and engaged in real estate business. Spent much of his spare time for twenty-five years in genealogical work and in 1909 published a history of Welcome Garrett and his descendants. The collection of data for this and also for a history of the Bond family was begun in 1884. He was a member of Co. I, 153d Ind. Vol. Inft., is a Mason, Odd Fellow, Red Man and a member of the Grand Army of the Republic. She, Annie L. (Heath) Garrett, is a member of the Daughters of the American Revolution, being a great-granddaughter of Jacob Heath, who served in Captain Seth Murray's company, Col. Benjamin Ruggles Woodbridge (25th Reg.) Massachusetts Volunteers, in the year 1775. Children:

1560.   I.   Mark D. Garrett, b. Jan. 20, 1877, in Daleville, Ind.; a printer by trade and foreman in composing department of the Muncie (Ind.) Morning Star.

458. SOLOMON R. BOND (Elias-Edward-Edward-Joseph), born May 31, 1843; married Sept. 13, 1866: Sarah Jane Stanbro. He was a soldier in Co. A, 16th Reg. Ind. Vol. Inft. Moved to Iowa in 1867, settled on a farm in Grundy County. A few years later moved to Washington and still later to Oregon. Residence, 1912, Salem, Ore. Children:

1561.   I.   William Artemas.
1562.   II. Elias Austin.
1563.   III. Harry Domell.
1564.   IV. Osborn Penn.

460. SARAH ELIZABETH BOND (Elias-Edward-Edward-Joseph), born May 23, 1847; married Oct. 17, 1867: Charles C. Gurley, born Nov. 16, 1845, in Guilford County, N. C., son of Charles and Elmina (Hoskins) Gurley. He is a carpenter and contractor. Residence, Westfield, Ind. Children:

1565.   I.   Roland Hoskins Gurley, b. Aug. 13, 1869; d. s. p. Aug. 6, 1887.

1566.   II. Edward Artemas Gurley, b. Feb. 9, 1871.

1567.   III. Mary Avinelle Gurley, b. Feb. 9, 1873; d. s. p. Aug. 8, 1879.

1568.   IV. Anna Maud Gurley, b. Dec. 5, 1876.

1569.   V.   Melissa Myrtle Gurley, b. March 19, 1880; d. Dec. 25, 1881, inft.

1570.   VI.   Paul Charles Gurley, b. Jan. 28, 1890.

462.   ANNA JANE BOND (Elias-Edward-Edward-Joseph), born Sept. 6, 1851; married Whitford Shaul, son of Fletcher and Sarah (George) Shaul, of Pendleton, Ind.; she died Sept. 13, 1882; he died ——. Children:

1571.   I.   Melvin Shaul, b. June 13, 1877.

1572.   II.   Ora Shaul.

463.   JEREMIAH AUSTIN BOND (Elias-Edward-Edward-Joseph), born Aug. 22, 1854, in Wayne County, Ind.; moved to Madison County with his parents when a child; married Oct. 7, 1877: Melzena Kuhns, born March 22, 1854, daughter of Henry and Nancy Kuhns, of Madison County, Ind.   Residence, 1910, Pendleton, Ind.   Children:

1573.   I.   Francis Austin, b. July 13, 1878.

1574.   II.   Mary Etta, b. Oct. 2, 1880.

1575.   III.   Elias H., b. Feb. 2, 1883.

1576.   IV.   Lyle M., b. April 10, 1885.

1577.   V.   Dora Lee, b. Aug. 12, 1888.

1578.   VI.   Clarence R., b. Nov. 28, 1893.

464.   MARY ETTA BOND (Elias-Edward-Edward-Joseph), born May 11, 1857; married Aug. 13, 1879: Frank Dawson; she died.   Occupation, farmer.   Residence, Westfield, Ind.   Ch:

1579.   I.   Addie Dawson, d. age 6 months.

1580.   II.   Pearl Dawson.

1581.   III.   Glenn Dawson.

465.   MARTHA ELLA BOND (Elias - Edward - Edward - Joseph), born Jan. 26, 1859, in Madison County, Ind.; married Aug. 23, 1881, in Hamilton County, Ind.: Winfield Scott Wheeler, born Oct. 18, 1858, son of Marshall and Louisa (Wheeler) Wheeler.   Residence, 1910, Centralia, Wash.   Children:

1582.   I.   Raymond Wheeler, b. Sept. 27, 1882.

1583.   II.   Fannie Fern Wheeler, b. Oct. 8, 1888.

1584.   III.   Edna Grace Wheeler, b. June 28, 1895.

1585.   IV.   John Leland Wheeler, b. Oct. 2, 1898.

467.   ELIAS EDWARD BOND (Elias-Edward-Edward-Joseph), born April 16, 1864, near Pendleton, Ind.; died Jan. 9, 1886; he married March 20, 1884: Sarah Kuhns, daughter of Henry and Nancy Kuhns.   Children:

1586.   I.   Iona Luella, b. June 13, 1885.

492.   JONATHAN K. BOND (Nathan - Jesse - Edward - Joseph), born May 3, 1827, in Wayne County, Ind.; married first Dec. 25, 1845: Martha Ann Albertson, born Jan. 3, 1827; died Jan. 8, 1875. Occupation, farmer. Residence, Henry County, Ind. Children:

1587.   I.   John Milton, b. Dec. 19, 1847.

1588.   II.   William Henry, b. Dec. 9, 1853.

He married second Nov. 29, 1885: Elizabeth Shaffer, nee Albertson, widow of Henry Shaffer; she was sister to his first wife; he died Aug., 1905.

493.   RUTH ANN BOND (Nathan-Jesse-Edward-Joseph), born Feb. 7, 1829; married Dec. 25, 1846: Peter Shaffer, born Oct. 17, 1825; she died July 23, 1863. Residence, Henry Co., Ind. Children.

1589.   I.   Mary E. Shaffer, b. Feb. 7, 1849.

1590.   II.   Nathan B. Shaffer, b. March 1, 1851.

1591. III.   Martha J. Shaffer, b. Oct. 25, 1853.

494.   MARY J. BOND (Nathan-Jesse-Edward-Joseph), born in Wayne County, Ind.; married Oliver Draper. She died June 17, 1863. Residence, Henry County, Ind. Children:

1592.   I.   Leeburn (?) Draper.

1593.   II.   Laura Draper.

495.   HENRY THORNBURG BOND (Robert - Jesse -Edward-Joseph), born Feb. 10, 1827, in Clay township, Wayne Co., Ind.; married Sept. 4, 1860: Mary A. Boyd, b. 1833; she died Jan. 25, 1896. Residence, near Greensfork, Wayne County, Ind. Ch:

1594.   I.   Robert B., b. Nov. 4, 1861.

1595.   II.   Emma T., b. March 30. 1867; address, Greensfork, Ind.

1596. III.   James E., b. May 9, 1869.

496.   JOHN BOND (Robert-Jesse-Edward-Joseph), born March 8, 1828; died Feb. 13, 1895, near Greensfork, Ind.; married Oct. 11, 1855: Thornzy Ann Cheesman; she died Sept. 15, 1873; he married second Oct. 5, 1875: Melissa A. Stigleman. Five children were born to each of these, ten in all. Occupation, farmer, Greensfork, Ind. Children:

1597.   I.   Louisa C., b. March 10, 1859.

1597-a.   II.   Arthur D., b. Oct. 1, 1860.

1597-b. III.   Aretta, b. Nov. 5, 1863.

1597-c. IV. Oliver G., b. Sept. 17, 1869.

1597-d. V. Eva, b. April 8, 1873.

Children by second wife:

1597-e. VI. Claudia Ethel, b. Sept. 11, 1876.

1597-f. VII. Laurence C., b. Sept. 14, 1878.

1597-g. VIII. Myrtle Estella, b. Nov. 15, 1880; d. s. p. June 11, 1901.

1597-h. IX. Jesse Lee, b. March 22, 1884.

1597-i. X. Marie, b. Oct. 22, 1891.

497. LEWIS T. BOND (Robert-Jesse-Edward-Joseph), born near Greensfork, Ind.; married Melissa Boyd. Residence, 1910, Cambridge City, Ind. Children:

    I. Robert, b. ——; d. in childhood.

498. EMILY BOND (Robert-Jesse-Edward-Joseph), born June 22, 1830; married Feb. 7, 1854: George Julian. Residence, Wayne County, Ind. She died April 19, 1855. Children:

    I. Emma Julian, d. in childhood.

499. MILTON BOND (Robert-Jesse-Edward-Joseph), born ——; married Lavina Holderman, of North Manchester, Wabash County, Ind. Children:

1597-k. I. Ella.

1597-l. II. Morton Allen, res., unknown. Probably not living.

1597-m. III. Alberta.

1597-n. IV. Adele.

500. ABNER D. BOND (Robert-Jesse-Edward-Joseph), born April 19, 1836, near Greensfork, Ind.; married Rebecca Long; she died. Children:

1598. I. Emma C., b. Sept. 24, 1861.

1599. II. S. Maud, b. March 16, 1865.

He married second Feb. 27, 1867: Mary E. Scott, daughter of John and Martha J. (Willetts) Scott; she died Jan. 13, 1894. Ch:

1600. III. Virginia Blanche, b. April 14, 1878; d. Feb. 4, 1879, inft.

1601. IV. Edith A., b. May 20, 1882.

501. LYDIA E. BOND (Robert-Jesse-Edward-Joseph), born July 10, 1842; married March 8, 1866: Caleb W. King; she died April 8, 1879; residence, Wayne County, Ind. Children:

1601-a. I. Walter S. King, b. Dec. 6, 1866; m. Sept. 5, 1903: Evelyn Jeffries.

1601-b.   II.   Lewis E. King, b. Aug. 5, 1870; res., Richmond, Ind.

502.   LARKIN BOND (Robert-Jesse-Edward-Joseph), born March 16, 1847; married Sept. 30, 1869: Emma Celeste Scott; residence, Wayne County, Ind.; occupation, farmer.   He died July 27, 1882.   Children:

1602.   I.   Georgia, b. May 10, 1876.
1602-a.   II.   Lora, b. Dec. 18, 1877.
1602-b.   III.   Fred Scott, b. April 25, 1879; not m.

503.   MARGARET BOND (John - Jesse - Edward - Joseph), born Nov. 22, 1828, in Wayne County, Ind.; married Andrew J. Bell, born Nov. 1, 1812; died Jan. 6, 1883; she died 1904.   Residence Richmond. Ind.   Children:

1603.   I.   Frank Bell, b. Jan. 6, 1853.
1604.   II.   Charles E. Bell, b. June 9, 1855.

504.   WILLIAM HARLAN BOND (John-Jesse-Edward-Joseph), son of John and Mary (Barnard) Bond; born near Greensfork, Wayne County, Ind., July 23, 1840; married Aug. 27, 1868: Ellen Ebersole.   Residence Greensfork, Ind.   Children:

1604-a.   I.   Phebe C., b. Oct. 3, 1870.
1604-b.   II.   John W., b. Jan. 17, 1872.
1604-c. III.   Charles H., b. Aug. 25, 1877.

506.   PHEBE J. BOND (John-Jesse-Edward-Joseph), born ———; married: Marshall McMeans; n. f. k.

507.   OLIVER S. BOND (William-Jesse-Edward-Joseph), born near Greensfork, Wayne County, Ind., June 29, 1831; married Dec. 23, 1863: Clara A. Raymond, daughter of Hon. John Raymond.   For a number of years Mr. Bond has been engaged in business in Toledo, O., as merchant and broker, being president of the Merchants and Clerks Savings Bank of that city. Children:

1605.   I.   William, d. inft.
1606.   II.   Harry A.
1607.   III.   Eva.
1608.   IV.   Florence, d. inft.
1609.   V.   Mabel.
1610.   VI.   Walter.

508.   DAMARIS BOND (William - Jesse - Edward - Joseph), born Sept. 29, 1833; married Feb. 22, 1850: Elias H. Wright. Children:

1611. I. William Wright; m. Lillie Bush. Res. Fremont, O.
1612. II. Francenia Wright.

509. LARKIN T. BOND (William-Jesse-Edward-Joseph),
· born Dec. 6, 1835; married June 6, 1866: Nannie Lewis, daughter
of Allen W. and Lucy T. Lewis. Residence Wayne County, Ind.
Occupation, farmer. Residence, Richmond, Ind. Children:
1613. I. Gertrude, b. Sept. 16, 1867.
1614. II. Allen W., b. Jan. 4, 1869; d. s. p. Dec. 17, 1893.
1615. III. Leona L.

510. FRANCENIA BOND (William-Jesse-Edward-Joseph),
born Dec. 10, 1837; married Jan. 16, 1856: Samuel G. Snider.
Occupation, contractor. Residence 1909, Lafayette, Ind. Children:
1616. I. Charles Snider.
1617. II. Oliver Snider.
1618. III. Martha Snider.
1619. IV. Frederick B. Snider.
1620. V. Walter Snider. N. f. k.

511. ELIZA J. BOND (William-Jesse-Edward-Joseph), born
April 24, 1848; married William Cannaday. N. f. k.

512. MATTIE E. BOND (William-Jesse-Edward-Joseph),
born Aug. 4, 1853; died Dec. 11, 1897; married James C. Harrold. Children:
1621. I. Francenia Harrold.

513. CALVIN BOND (Enos-Jesse-Edward-Joseph), eldest
son of Enos and Susannah (Hoover) Bond, born Dec. 23, 1831;
died March 21, 1897; married Sept. 5, 1855: Mary M. Murphy,
daughter of Clement and Huldah Murphy. Residence, New
Castle, Ind. Children:
1622. I. Clara Florence, b. May 7, 1857.
1623. II. William Clement, b. June 14, 1858.
1624. III. Eddie Norris, b. Oct. 13, 1860; d. s. p. Nov. 15,
1870.

514. MARY ANN BOND (Enos - Jesse - Edward - Joseph),
born Nov. 25, 1833; married Aug. 14, 1851: Jesse G. Wickersham,
born Aug. 8, 1828. Children:
1625. I. Lee W. Wickersham.
1626. II. Carrie Wickersham.
She married second, Joel Garretson, of Madison County, Ind.;
he died. Her residence 1910, New Castle, Ind.

516. HANNAH BOND (Enos-Jesse-Edward-Joseph), born Jan. 4, 1838; married Aug. 1, 1855: Edward Strattan, born April 19, 1830, son of Joseph and Rebecca (Harvey) Strattan. Occupation, farmer. Address, New Castle, Ind. Children:

1627. I. Albert Strattan, b. July 15, 1856.

1628. II. William E. Strattan, b. Dec. 9, 1850; d. s. p. Sept. 13, 1859.

1629. III. Jesse A. Strattan, b. Aug. 7, 1860; d. s. p. Jan. 22, 1882.

1630. IV. Ella Strattan, b. Oct. 28, 1864.

1631. V. Benjamin Strattan, b. Jan. 6, 1866.

1632. VI. Minnie B. Strattan, b. April 4, 1879.

517. ISOM BOND (Enos-Jesse-Edward-Joseph), born April 21, 1840; died July 30, 1908, in New Castle, Ind.; married Sept. 25, 1862: Lydia Ann Wickersham, born Dec. 5, 1843, daughter of Oliver and Sarah J. Wickersham. Occupation, farmer. Residence, New Castle, Ind. Children:

1633. I. Oliver; d.

1634. II. Etta.

1635. III. Susannah.

1635a. IV. Lottie.

1636. V. Ernest.

1637. VI. Olive.

518. CATHERINE BOND (Enos-Jesse-Edward-Joseph), born Sept. 1, 1842; died April 30, 1897; married March 17, 1869: Edwin Hiatt, of Henry County, Ind. Occupation, farmer. Children:

1638. I. Claudius Hiatt.

1639. II. Ida Hiatt.

1640. III. Elmer Hiatt.

1640-a. IV. Enos Hiatt.

520. JESSE BOND (Enos-Jesse-Edward-Joseph), born July 30, 1846; married March 12, 1874: Mary E. Byers, born Aug. 31, 1841; died Jan. 11, 1910. Occupation, farmer, teacher. Residence, New Castle, Ind. Children:

1641. I. Nellie, b. June 4, 1876.

521. PHEBE BOND (Enos-Jesse-Edward-Joseph), born Aug. 20, 1849; married April 4, 1876: Rev. John Henry Hewit, a Universalist minister of some note, born Jan. 25, 1850, son of

Thomas and Mary Jane (Odom) Hewit. Residence, Henry County, Ind. Children:

1642. I. Carrie Hewit, b. June 16, 1877.

1643. II. Bertha Hewit, b. Oct. 11, 1882.

522. REBECCA ANN BOND (Isom-Jesse-Edward-Joseph), born June 6, 1837; died Oct. 7, 1892; married Nov. 25, 1852: Robert Butler, born March 29, 1827, died May 3, 1882. Residence, Henry County, Ind. Children:

1644. I. Eva Butler, b. Nov. 8, 1853.

1645. II. Albert Butler.

1646. III. Isom Leeburn Butler.

1647. IV. Nettie Butler.

1648. V. Leona Butler.

523. JESSE NICHOLSON (Ruth-Jesse-Edward-Joseph), son of Williams and Ruth (Bond) Nicholson, born March 22, 1835; married Mary McAfee. He died Aug. 4, 1896. Residence, Henry County, Ind. Have nine children.

524. MERRIT NICHOLSON (Ruth (Bond)-Jesse-Edward-Joseph), born Oct. 19, 1836; married Martha Ann Wisehart, daughter of Wilson and Tabitha Wisehart. Names of children not known to writer.

525. RACHEL NICHOLSON (Ruth (Bond)-Jesse-Edward-Joseph), daughter of Williams and Ruth (Bond) Nicholson, born Aug. 12, 1838; died Dec. 16, 1867; married John B. O'Hara, now deceased. Children:

1661. I. William O'Hara.

1662. II. Mark O'Hara.

526. REASON NICHOLSON (Ruth-Jesse-Edward-Joseph), son of Williams and Ruth (Bond) Nicholson, born May 27, 1841; died Nov. 12, 1901; married Ruth Ann Boyd, daughter of John; she died. Children:

1663. I. Nancy Nicholson.

1664. II. Ira Nicholson.

1665. III. Nathan Nicholson, and perhaps others.

527. NATHAN NICHOLSON (Ruth-Jesse-Edward-Joseph), son of Williams and Ruth (Bond) Nicholson, born March 24, 1843, in Henry County, Ind.; served thirty-seven months as soldier in 36th Reg. Ind. Vol. Inft.; was in all the battles in which the regiment participated: Shiloh, Perryville, Stone River, Lookout Mountain, Mission Ridge, and was wounded at Chicka-.

mauga. Married Sept., 1868: Lizzie Leonard; she died May 24, 1892. He married second, June 15, 1893: Almeda Donahoo. Children by first marriage:

1668.   I.   Pearl Nicholson, b. Dec. 1, 1870; m. James Keesling.

1669.   II.   Lawrence Nicholson, b. June 21, 1874.

528. MARTHA NICHOLSON (Ruth (Bond)-Jesse-Edward-Joseph), born Jan. 17, 1846; married May 12, 1892: Joseph M. Brown, attorney-at-law, New Castle, Ind. He was a soldier in 69th Reg. Ind. Vol. Inft. No children:

538. LEWIS BOND (Isaac-Jesse-Edward-Joseph), born Oct. 15, 1844; married Oct. 23, 1872: Ionia Scott, of Wayne County, Ind. Residence, Mexico, Miami County, Ind. Occupation, farmer. Children:

1670.   I.   Walter S., b. Aug. 23, 1873.

1671.   II.   Nellie J., b. Sept. 3, 1876.

1672.   III.   Blanche, b. June 23, 1880.

539. ARTHUR BOND (Isaac-Jesse-Edward-Joseph), born Dec. 10, 1846; married first, 1866: Elizabeth Collett; married second, 1880: Mary Englert, of New Castle, Ind. N. f. k.

543. ROBERT BOND (Jesse-Jesse-Edward-Joseph), son of Jesse and Jane (Cox) Bond, born ———; married Elizabeth Stroud, daughter of William Stroud; she died Dec. 14, 1872. Children:

1673.   I.   Hattie, b. Dec. 14, 1870.

He married second, Sept. 3, 1874: Lucretia M. Thomas, daughter of Lewis Thomas, of Madison County, Ind. Children:

1674.   II.   Oscar L., b. May 11, 1876.

545. DAVID BOND (Jesse-Jesse-Edward-Joseph), born July 25, 1849; died Dec. 29, 1905; married March 22, 1876, at Denver, Ind.: Addie Olds. Children:

1675.   I.   Gertrude, b. Sept. 18, 1877; m. Nov. 8, 1898: Dr. Jonathan Harvey Winterbotham, of Salina, Kas. No children:

1676.   II.   Jessie, b. April 29, 1886.

547. CHARLES BOND.

550. ALBERT BOND (Jesse-Jesse-Edward-Joseph), son of Jesse and Harriet (Hough) Bond, born Oct. 11, 1865; died May 12, 1897; married June 9, 1887: Margaret Jane Calvert, born Aug. 15, 1865. Residence, Mexico, Ind. Two children:

1677.   I.   Omer, b. March 30, 1894.

1678.   II.   Jesse, b. Oct. 31, 1897.

551. RUTH BOND (Jesse-Jesse-Edward-Joseph), daughter of Jesse and Harriet (Hough) Bond; born Jan. 6, 1868; died Nov. 18, 1898; married March 7, 1889: Deo Hood, born Oct. 9, 1868, son of John T. and Martha A. Hood. Children:

1679.   I.   Joseph L. Hood, b. July 5, 1890.
1680.   II.   Lyman Jesse Hood, b. Nov. 3, 1892.
1681.   III.   Clinton B. Hood, b. July 31, 1890.

551=A. BENJAMIN S. BOND (Jesse-Jesse-Edward-Joseph), born Dec. 27, 1871, in Miami County, Ind.; married July 16, 1900: Bessie Hood, daughter of John T. and Martha, born July 23, 1880; died Nov. 22, 1904. He married second, Nov. 11, 1906: Ethel June Whisler, born June 29, 1882, daughter of William A. and Polly Ann Whisler. Residence, McCoysburg, Ind. Children:

1682.   I.   Ruth Ann, b. Nov. 5, 1909.

553. JESSE MENDENHALL (Lydia (Bond)-Jesse-Edward-Joseph), born Nov. 11, 1846; married Aug. 14, 1873: Clarissa Jane Leonard. Occupation, farmer. Residence, New Castle, Ind., R. F. D. Children:

I.   Alice C. Mendenhall, b. July 14, 1874; married Clinton Hosier. Two children: Josephine and Carrol Hosier.

II.   Horace W. Mendenhall, b. —; m. April 11, 1899: Lola A. Wood. Four children: (a) Maurine, (b) Leonard, (c) Harrold, (d) Leslie.

554. WILLIAM MENDENHALL (Lydia (Bond)-Jesse-Edward-Joseph), born June 23, 1850; married Emma Shirk. Residence, New Castle, Ind. Children:

I.   Frederick Mendenhall.
II.   Walter Mendenhall.
III.   Verne Mendenhall.
IV.   India Mendenhall.
V.   Katie Mendenhall.
VI.   Edith Mendenhall.

555. MARTHA MENDENHALL (Lydia (Bond)-Jesse-Edward-Joseph), born Dec. 4, 1857, in Henry County, Ind.; married Oct. 22, 1881: Frank P. Modlin, born Aug. 2, 1853, in Iowa. Residence, 1910, New Castle, Ind., R. F. D. Children:

I.   Ethel Modlin, b. Oct. 24, 1882; m. Aug. 30, 1907: Roscoe D. Edwards.

II.   Harry Modlin, b. July 12, 1885.

III.   Mark Modlin, b. June 11, 1887.

IV.   Everett Modlin, b. Aug. 6,.1890.

V.   John Modlin, b. Sept. 2, 1894.

VI.   Olive Frances Modlin, b. June 8, 1898.

VII.   Georgia Lois Modlin, b. July 2, 1900.

557. LUTHER MENDENHALL (Lydia (Bond)-Jesse-Edward-Joseph), born ——; married Grace Munden. Residence, New Castle, Ind. Children:

I.   George Mendenhall.

560. LYDIA E. BOND (Abijah-Joshua-Edward-Joseph), born Feb. 21, 1851; married Nov. 7, 1873: Charles C. Bailey, born Feb. 10, 1845. Occupation, watchman. Residence 1912, Muncie, Ind. Children:

1700.   I.   Edward Bailey, b. June 25, 1874; d. March 9, 1882, in childhood.

1701.   II.   Hannah Ruth Bailey, and

1702.   III.   John William Bailey, twins, b. July 3, 1877.

1703.   IV.   Cora Luella Bailey, b. July 14, 1880; d. Feb. 9, 1881, inft.

1704.   V.   Almoretta Bailey, b. Jan. 19, 1882.

1705.   VI.   Susan Pauline Bailey, b. April 22, 1884.

1706.   VII.   James Lilburn Bailey, b. July 25, 1886.

1707.   VIII.   Sarah Jane Bailey, b. May 3, 1888.

1708.   IX.   Rex Clifton Bailey, b. May 24, 1890.

1709.   X.   Florence Pearl Bailey, b. April 2, 1893.

561. JOHN JOSHUA BOND (Abijah-Joshua-Edward-Joseph), born in Jay County, Ind., Sept. 12, 1853; married July 16, 1881: Mary E. Bone, born Jan. 2, 1864, daughter of Fetta and Mary (Paling) Bone. Address 1910, Pennville, Ind. Children:

1710.   I.   William H., b. June 6, 1882.

1711.   II.   Goldie W., b. Jan. 20, 1884.

1712.   III.   Bertie E., b. Jan. 27, 1886.

1713.   IV.   Daisy E., b. May 28, 1888.

1714.   V.   Lelia M., b. July 30, 1890.

1715.   VI.   John E., b. July 24, 1892.

1716.   VII.   Jesse A., b. July 19, 1895.

1717.   VIII.   Mary O., b. Dec. 31, 1897.

1718.   IX.   Infant, b. April 17, 1900; d.

1719.   X.   Tunis E., b. April 1, 1901.

1720.   XI.   Verda Olive, b. Jan. 17, 1903; d. June 3, 1903, infant.

1721. XII.   Harold, and

1722. XIII.   Gerald, twins, b. Oct. 3, 1905.

1723. XIV.   Freda, b. Aug. 9, 1908.

563.   SUSAN PALENA BOND (Abijah-Joshua-Edward-Joseph), born April 23, 1858; married Sept. 2, 1876: James Lilburn Rigby, a farmer.   Residence, Balbec, Jay County, Ind.   No children.

564.   SARAH ELIZABETH BOND (Abjah-Joshua-Edward-Joseph), born Jan. 7, 1861; married Aug. 11, 1877: William C. Bunker.   Residence 1910, Robinson, Ill.   Children:

1724.   I.   Ira L. Bunker, b. May 15, 1878; d. Aug. 18, 1878, infant.

1725.   II.   Iva M. Bunker, b. May 8, 1880.

1726.   III.   William E. Bunker, b. Dec. 28, 1882.

1727.   IV.   Retta R. Bunker, b. Sept. 17, 1886.

1728.   V.   Burl O. Bunker, b. March 11, 1890.

1729.   VI.   Bertie A. Bunker, b. April 8, 1892.

1730.   VII.   Gold E. Bunker, b. July 26, 1894.

1731. VIII.   Baby, b. 1896; d. inft.

575.   MARY ELIZABETH BOND (William-Joshua-Edward-Joseph), born March 16, 1851, in Indiana; married in Missouri, Nov. 27, 1870: George W. Ransdell, a farmer.   Residence, Eldorado Springs, R. F. D., Cedar County, Mo.   Children:

1732.   I.   Louis Wilmer Ransdell, b. March 3, 1872.   Residence, Kansas City, Mo.   He graduated from State Normal, at Warrensburg, Mo.

1733.   II.   Frank E. Bond Ransdell, b. Jan. 13, 1874; attorney-at-law, Gage, Okla.   He has twice been elected representative to the State Legislature on the Democratic ticket, first in 1899, again in 1901.

577.   LOUISA BOND (Aaron-Joseph-Edward-Joseph), born July 2, 1836; died Dec. 28, 1863; married May 17, 1857: Lawrence G. Bantham.   Children:

1734.   I.   Samuel Aaron Bantham, b. Aug. 8, 1858; d. s. p. Sept. 30, 1858.

1735.   II.   Charles W. Bantham, b. Aug. 7, 1859.   Residence, Grant Co., Ind.

1736. III. Joseph I. Bantham, b. May 28, 1861; m. Myrtle Jackson. Residence, Dora, Wabash Co., Ind.

579. ZILPHA ANN BOND (Aaron-Joseph-Edward-Joseph), born Dec. 24, 1841; died Feb. 23, 1898; married Feb. 5, 1863: William Henry Barnhart, died 1870; she married second, Dec. 23, 1874: Christian Markey; he died Dec. 18, 1878. She died Feb. 23, 1898. Children first marriage:

1737. I. Ida Barnhart, b. Feb. 1, 1865; m. Orange Markey. Res., Eaton, O., R. F. D.

1738. II. Florence Barnhart, b. Nov. 5, 1867; m. Feb. 11, 1896: Charles Zehring, of West Alexandria, O.

Children of second marriage:

1739. III. Infant.

1740. IV. Edward B. Markey.

1741. V. Amos Markey.

582. URSULA HARRIET BOND (Aaron-Joseph-Edward-Joseph), born March 7, 1848; married Nov. 1, 1866: Edward A. Kelley, born June 25, 1845; he died April 29, 1887. Occupation, farmer, and he was a soldier during war of the rebellion. To this union there was seven children:

1742. I. Infant.

1743. II. Edward Austin Kelley, b. Jan. 2, 1869; m.; d. April 22, 1899, in Texas.

1744. III. Henry B. Kelley, b. Sept. 17, 1870.

1745. IV. Matthew Kelley, b. Oct. 7, 1872.

1746. V. Albert T. Kelley, and

1747. VI. Alfred W. Kelley, twins, b. Oct. 17, 1874; Alfred d. infant.

1748. VII. Amy Ann Kelley, b. Oct. 26, 1876; d. Oct. 7, 1877, s. p.

She married second, Aug. 27, 1884: Henley James, born April 11, 1840. Residence, Huntington County, Ind. Children:

1749. VIII. Grant James.

587. LYDIA BOND (Isaac-Joseph-Edward-Joseph), born June 29, 1839; married April 17, 1878: John Holloway, now deceased. Residence, Lincolnville, Ind. No children.

590. ROSANNA BOND (Isaac -Joseph -Edward -Joseph), born Sept. 14, 1845; married April 29, 1866: Levin Wright, born Nov. 8, 1842, son of Peter and Catherine Wright. Residence, Huntington, Ind. Children:

1750.   I.   Flora E. Wright, b. Aug. 6, 1867.
1751.   II.   Laura G. Wright, b. June 23, 1870.
1752.   III.   John Frank Wright, b. Sept. 5, 1872.
1753.   IV.   Isola G. Wright, b. June 16, 1875.
1754.   V.   Lillie V. Wright, b. Aug. 12, 1877.
1755.   VI.   Louie F. Wright, b. Sept. 1, 1879.
1756.   VII.   Clara W. Wright, b. Aug. 9, 1882.

592. JOSEPH JONES (Achsah -Joseph -Edward -Joseph), son of Sylvanus and Achsah (Bond) Jones, born Sept. 6, 1833; married May 18, 1859: Sarah Kindley. P. O., 1910, Webster, Ind. Children:

I.   William H. Jones, b. Nov. 21, 1860.
II.   Mary A. Jones, b. Feb. 12, 1862.
III.   Emma J. Jones, b. April 19, 1864.
IV.   Charles E. Jones, b. Nov. 21, 1866; d. June 14, 1869.
V.   Eva S. Jones, b. May 3, 1870.
VI.   Ellwood Jones, b. Nov. 17, 1874; d. Nov. 2, 1882.
VII.   Edwin A. Jones, b. Dec. 28, 1881.

594. ELIZABETH JONES (Achsah (Bond) -Joseph-Edward-Joseph), born Feb. 11, 1837; married in Randolph County, Nov. 3, 1859: Caleb K. Farrington. Residence, Indiana, Iowa and Kansas. Children:

I.   William Sylvanus Farrington, b. Aug. 25, 1860, in Warren Co., Iowa.
II.   Mary J. Farrington, b. May 4, 1863, in Jay Co., Ind.; m. Seth D. Warren, P. O., Lynn, Okla.
III.   Charles Farrington, b. July 28, 1865.
IV.   Albert Farrington, b. May 2, 1870, in Warren Co., Iowa.
V.   Arthur Farrington, b. July 23, 1873, in Des Moines, Ia. Address, Lynn, Okla.
VI.   Minnie Farrington, b. June 26, 1876; d. inft., 1876.

She married second: William G. Mullen. Address, 1905, Atwood, Kas.

607. AMANDA ELVIRA HIATT (Dinah (Bond) -Joseph-Edward-Joseph), born Feb. 8, 1841; married Jan. 12, 1860: William O'Brien, born March 17, 1834; he died Sept. 19, 1899. Ch:

I.   Robert O'Brien, b. Sept. 3, 1860.
II.   Mary Jane O'Brien, b. Aug. 7, 1862.
III.   Eliza O'Brien, b. Sept. 12, 1864.
IV.   Ella O'Brien, b. July 26, 1868.

V.   Mary Jane O'Brien, b. Jan. 10, 1885.

VI.   Eliza O'Brien, b July 12, 1888.

VII.   Ella O'Brien, b. May 9, 1890.

611.   SARAH A. HIATT (Dinah (Bond) -Joseph-Edward-Joseph), born Oct. 14, 1847; married Rev. Daniel Coats.   He was a private soldier in Co. B, Seventh Ind. Cavalry.   Address, 1903, Vilas, Kas.   Children:

I.   Frederick N. Coats, b. 1869; d. 1871, inft.

II.   Rosella Coats, b. Jan. 7, 1872; m. March 13, 1892: Andrew J. Hull.

III.   Roscoe Coats, b. March 21, 1874; m. Oct. 7, 1900: Viola Moreign.

IV.   Martha Coats, b. April 9, 1876; m. May 8, 1894: John Babcock.

614.   EZRA BOND (Mahlon-Joseph-Edward-Joseph), born in Wayne County, Ind., May 15, 1840.   Served his country during the war in Co. H, 84th Reg. Ind. Vol. Inft., his father being in same regiment.   Residence, Girard, Kas.   Children as reported:

1800.   I.   Frank, d. in youth.

1801.   II.   Curtis.

1802.   III.   Leonora.

1803.   IV.   Otis.

615.   MARY A. BOND (Mahlon - Joseph - Edward - Joseph), born Aug. 12, 1842, in Wayne County, Ind.; married Dec. 21, 1863: Josiah Mullin, born Sept. 16, 1816, son of William and Christine (Jones) Mullin; he died Nov. 1, 1894.   Residence, Liberty, Ind.   R. F. D.   Children:

1805.   I.   Mollie M. Mullin, b. Oct. 21, 1864.

1806.   II.   Harry J. D. Mullin, b. Dec. 31, 1873; of River Vale, Ind.

1807.   III.   Tamer N. Mullin, b. Dec. 2, 1875.

1808.   IV.   Isaac T. Mullin, b. Nov. 22, 1878.

1809.   V.   Susan I. Mullin, b. Dec. 16, 1884; m. Sept. 29, 1900: William A. Stanton, of Lotus, Union Co., Ind.

616.   ESTHER D. BOND (Mahlon-Joseph-Edward-Joseph), born Sept. 1, 1844, in Wayne County, Ind.; died Jan. 28, 1896, in Iowa; married Clayton Lewelling.   Children:

1810.   I.   Emma Lewelling, b. July 5, 1864; m. Oct. 15, 1884: ——— Biddinger.   One son:

(a) Raymond Henry Biddinger, b. Feb. 16, 1886.

1811. II. Elva Lewelling, b. Jan. 28, 1866; m. July 16, 1885: W. J. Gray. Children:

(a) Lee Leroy Gray.

(b) Mabel Leane Gray. Res., Norton, Kas.

622. MAHLON C. PERRY BOND (Mahlon-Joseph-Edward-Joseph), born March 4, 1854, in Wayne County, Ind.; married Aug. 16, 1876, in Kosciusko County, Ind.: Sarah E. Heagy, born July 10, 1857, in Wayne County, Ind., daughter of Theodore and Mary E. Heagy. Residence, Harriman, Tenn. Children:

1812. I. Albert S., b. Jan. 14, 1879, in Indiana.

1813. II. Jesse E., b. June 26, 1881; m. Nov. 13, 1909: Miss Cora May Spurrier, of Liberty, Ind.

1814. III. Willard E., b. June 20, 1883.

1815. IV. Mary A., b. Jan. 18, 1885.

1816. V. Leonard H., b. Dec. 12, 1886; d. accident Nov. 12, 1903.

1817. VI. Mahlon Harold, b. March 4, 1891, in Tennessee.

1818. VII. E. Walter, b. Nov. 3, 1892.

623. ANNA P. BOND (Mahlon - Joseph - Edward - Joseph), born Nov. 25, 1855; married Oct. 4, 1874: Joseph B. Marshall. Residence, Wayne County, Ind. Address, Richmond. R. F. D. Children:

1819. I. Daughter, d. inft.

1820. II. William P. Marshall, b. Aug. 29, 1884.

631. CHARLES WRIGHT (Ann (Bond) -Joseph-Edward-Joseph), born Nov. 1, 1860; married Dec. 10, 1881: Ada A. Throckmorton, born June 6, 1861; she died May 10, 1884. Residence, Wayne County, Ind. Children:

I. Harry A. Wright, b. Nov. 3, 1882.

He married Aug. 18, 1888: Mary E. Davis, born Nov. 2, 1871. Children:

1821. II. Russell W. Wright, b. May 3, 1889.

1822. III. Crystal Wright, b. Jan. 19, 1891.

633. ERASTUS BOND (Peter-Joseph-Edward-Joseph), born Oct. 21, 1851; married May 31, 1871: Mary Hortense Murray, born Oct. 5, 1852, daughter of John B. and Rachel Murray. Residence, Richmond, Ind. Children:

1823. I. Louisa G., dec., aged 20 years.

1824. II.   Wilbur C., d. inft.

1825. III. Edna J.

1826. IV.   Laura G., dec.

1827. V.   Charles W.

1828. VI.   J. Elmer.

636. CHARLES FRANCIS BOND (Peter-Joseph-Edward-Joseph), born April 18, 1860; m.   Residence, last report, Beaver Falls, Pa. N. f. k.

635. MARIANNA BOND (Peter-Joseph-Edward-Joseph), born Jan. 4, 1866; married Nov. 1, 1883: William J. Hippard, of Richmond, Ind. Children:

1829. I.   Inez M. Hippard, d. inft.

1830. II.   Vera Hippard.

1831. III. Mariam L. Hippard.

1832. IV.   Wilbur Hippard.

639. SARAH MENDENHALL BOND (Peter-Joseph-Edward-Joseph), born Oct. 27, 1870; married June 20, 1892: Joseph Froggatt, born May 18, 1867, son of Joseph and Elizabeth Ann Froggatt, who came from Whitewood, near Normantown, Yorkshire, England. Residence, Orange, N. J. Children:

1833. I.   Joseph Bond Froggatt, b July 27, 1895.

1834. II.   Dorothea M. Froggatt, b. Aug. 30, 1900.

647. MARTHA BOND (Benjamin-Silas-Benjamin-Joseph), born Feb. 2, 1833; married May 29, 1851: Enos Baldwin, son of William H. and Elizabeth (Hunt) Baldwin; he died about 1870. She resides in Zanesfield, O. Children:

1835. I.   William H. Baldwin, of Mt. Victory, O.

1836. II.   J. Howard Baldwin, of Coldwater, Mich.

1837. III. Benjamin F. Baldwin, of Baraboo, Wis.

649. SARAH BOND (Benjamin - Silas - Benjamin - Joseph), born Dec. 16, 1837; died May 31, 1886, at Spiceland, Ind.; married Sept. 11, 1861: Elgar Brown, born Nov. 16, 1836, son of Elgar and Mary (Huff) Brown; he died April 20, 1889. Residence, Henry County, Ind. Children:

1838. I.   Emma L. Brown, b. Jan. 11, 1862; m. John M. Busby, of Anderson, Ind.

1839. II.   Mary L. Brown, b. April 4, 1865; m. Levi T. Pennington, of Spiceland, Ind.

1840. III. Martha E. Brown, b. Sept. 17, 1867.

1841. IV.   Sarah Brown, b. Aug. 23, 1870; d. inft.

1842.   V.   Joseph A. Brown, b. Feb. 13, 1872; d. 1881, child-hood.

1843.   VI.   Bessie Brown, b. Aug. 21, 1876.

These and all their ancestors for generations past are and were Friends or Quakers.

650.   ELIZABETH BOND (Benjamin - Silas - Benjamin - Joseph), born Feb. 7, 1839, in Union County, Ind.; died Feb. 3, 1901, in Barclay, Kas.; married Sept. 13, 1866: Josiah Butler, son of John and Elizabeth T. Butler, of Mahoning County, Ohio. They moved to Kansas in 1885. She, Elizabeth (Bond) Butler, was a teacher, missionary and minister of the Gospel among Friends. Children:

1844.   I.   Frank J. Butler, b. Oct. 9, 1867. Res., West Branch, Iowa.

1845.   II.   Mary E. Butler, b. June 6, 1869; d. s. p. Oct. 16, 1889.

1846.   III.   Emma L. Butler, b. Feb. 7, 1874.

1847.   IV.   William H. Butler, b. Feb. 29, 1876, of Quincy, Ill.

652.   WILLIAM BOND (Benjamin-Silas-Benjamin-Joseph), born Oct. 9, 1844, in Indiana; died in Pomona, Cal., Jan. 28, 1894. During the Civil War he served in the Second Battery of the Chicago Board of Trade. Married, 1866: Phebe Cadwallader, born Aug. 31, 1845. Her address, 1910, Long Beach, Cal. Ch:

1848.   I.   Benjamin Franklin, b. Oct. 15, 1868.

1849.   II.   Minnie, b. Nov. 20, 1870.

1850.   III.   Elizabeth, b. Feb. 10, 1873.

1851.   IV.   Alice, b. Jan. 31, 1875.

1852.   V.   Josephine, b. April 5, 1877.

1853.   VI.   Emma, b. April 5, 1881.

1854.   VII.   Bessie, b. May 14, 1884.

1855.   VIII.   Leota, b. April 14, 1886.

654.   ESTHER BOND (Benjamin-Silas-Benjamin-Joseph), born Feb. 2, 1850; married 1868: Rev. Ira C. Johnson, a Friends minister. Residence, Lynn, Ind. Children:

1856.   I.   Edith Johnson, b. May 27, 1873; m. May 30, 1896: Albert Winslow.

·1857·   II.   Grace Johnson, b. April 11, 1878; d. March 19, 1879.

1857.   III.   Mary Lydia Johnson, b. Sept. 9, 1880.

1858. IV. Cyrus E. Johnson, b. Oct. 14, 1885.

1859. V. Harvey Bain Johnson, b. Jan. 19, 1888.

656. SILAS WALTER BOND (Eli-Silas-Benjamin-Joseph), born April 2, 1852; married at Iowa Falls, Iowa, May 16, 1876: Flora E. Boughton. Residence, 1904, Estherville, Iowa. Ch:

1860. I. Ernest Clifford, b. April 26, 1877, at Iowa Falls, Iowa.

1861. II. Walter Winfield, b. 1879.

1862. III. Arthur Howard, b. Jan. 9, 1881.

1863. IV. William Eli, b. Nov. 25, 1882.

1864. V. Raymond Leslie, b. April 21, 1885.

1865. VI. Hattie Leona, b. June 24, 1888.

1866. VII. Kenneth Boughton, b. May 2, 1895.

657. REV. DANIEL WILLIAMS BOND (Silas W.-Silas-Benjamin-Joseph), born Nov. 28, 1835; married Dec. 25, 1860: Matilda Shaw, born April 8, 1842. He is a Wesleyan minister, also farmer. Residence, Stockton, Ill. Children:

1867. I. John Wesley, b. Oct. 22, 1861.

1868. II. Silas Walter, b. Jan. 13, 1864.

1869. III. George W., Oct. 20, 1865.

1870. IV. Alvin Shelly, b. Aug. 26, 1868.

1871. V. Nellie May, b. April 8, 1878.

1872. VI. Henry Phippen, b. May 22, 1880. Residence, Reno, Nev.

658. JOSIAH H. BOND (Silas W.-Silas-Benjamin-Joseph), born June 10, 1838; married Sept. 4, 1863: Mary A. Smith, born Feb. 2, 1842. Residence, 1910, Marshalltown, Ia. Children:

1873. I. Maggie Luella, b. Oct. 26, 1865. d. Jan. 17, 1876.

1874. II. Charles Austin, b. Nov. 29, 1869.

1875. III. Eunice Adeline, b. Aug. 16, 1872.

1876. IV. Lewis Franklin, b. Sept. 26, 1874.

1877. V. Mary Ethel, b. April 2, 1880.

1878. VI. Frederick Silas, b. Dec. 9, 1882.

659. MARY BOND (Silas W.-Silas-Benjamin-Joseph), born 1842; married Jan. 5, 1862: Clinton A. Bamber, born 1841, son of John and Mary (Eckerson) Bamber. Residence 1910, Iowa Falls, Iowa. Occupation, contractor and builder. Children:

1879. I. Clara R. Bamber, b. 1862.

1880. II. Lulu B. Bamber, b. 1866.

1881. III. Roy C. Bamber, b. 1879.

660. MARTHA E. BOND (Silas W.-Silas-Benjamin-Joseph), born Nov. 20, 1844; married April 2, 1868: James I. Bogenrief, a farmer. Residence 1910, Iowa Falls, Iowa. Children:

1882. I. Clyde Bogenrief, b. Feb. 25, 1869; m. Morthy Boddy. Res., Swea City, Iowa.

1883. II. Effie Bogenrief, b. March 4, 1873: m. 1891: Albert Russ.

1884. III. Edna Bogenrief, b. Dec. 25, 1876; m. 1900: William Cunningham.

1885. IV. Mary Bogenrief, b. March 22, 1880.

1886. V. Lisle Bogenrief, a son, b. April 15, 1884.

661. ADALINE BOND (Silas W.-Silas-Benjamin-Joseph), born Dec. 24, 1848, in Illinois; married in Iowa, June 29, 1867: A. M. Caldwell. Residence, Shawnee, Okla. She moved with her parents to Hardin County, Iowa, in 1865. He was a soldier in Co. F, 32d Reg. Iowa Vol.; wounded April 19, 1864, in Louisiana, and a prisoner at Tyler, Tex., during the next fifteen months, when the war closed. Children:

1887. I. Willard E. Caldwell, b. April 7, 1870; m.

1888. II. Everet B. Caldwell, b. Feb. 18, 1880.

662. EMMA J. BOND (Silas W.-Silas-Benjamin-Joseph), born April 4, 1859, in Joe Daviess County, Ill.; married in Iowa Falls, Iowa, July 9, 1875: Columbus L. Haworth, born May 1, 1857, son of James Riley and Melissa J. (Fisher) Haworth. Residence, Iowa, Idaho. He is a merchant. Address 1910, 859 Jefferson street, Boise, Idaho. Children:

1889. I. Bessie Rebecca Haworth, b. Jan. 13, 1879.

1890. II. Luella E. Haworth, b. Dec. 3, 1886.

663. JOHN W. BOND (Milton-Silas-Benjamin-Joseph), born Sept. 28, 1839, in Huntington County, Ind.; married Jan. 21, 1858: Ellen J. Morrow, born Dec. 12, 1836. Residence, Grant County, Ind. Children:

1891. I. Sylvester, b. Dec. 11, 1858.

1892. II. Mary L., b. Feb. 21, 1861.

1893. III. Sarah Alice, b. Feb. 14, 1863; m. Feb. 27, 1892: Barnabas P. Bogue.

1894. IV. Leah Florence, b. July 10, 1869.

1895. V. Malinda, b. June 15, 1874.

664. LUCINDA BOND (Milton-Silas-Benjamin-Joseph), born Oct. 21, 1841, in Huntington County, Ind.; married Jan.

24, 1861: James H. Morrow, born Oct. 21, 1838, in Highland County, O.; he died May 23, 1902. Her address, River, Ind. Children:

1896.   I.   Sarah Ellen Morrow, b. Oct. 29, 1861; m. Andrew Wright.

1897.   II.   Florence Morrow, b. Sept. 14, 1863; m. Levi L. Ulrich, of Huntington, Ind.

1898. III.   Dessie Morrow, b. June 6, 1874.

671.   JOHN BOND (Stephen-Silas-Benjamin-Joseph), born Feb. 22, 1848; died Jan. 9, 1883; married Mary Magee. Children:

1899.   I.   Clara May, b. July 13, 1875; m. —— Abrems. Residence 1904, Missoula, Mont.

1900.   II.   Ella Myrtle, b. Feb. 25, 1879; m. W. F. Morris. Residence 1904, New Castle, Ind.

672.   JESSE BOND (Stephen-Silas-Benjamin-Joseph), born June 2, 1850; married Vienna Thornburg. Residence, Parker City, Ind. Children:

1901.   I.   Luella.

1902.   II.   Carl.

1903.   III.   Xenia Myrtle.

1904.   IV.   Carrie, b. June, 1885.

1905.   V.   Edgar.

1906.   VI.   Jennie.

1907.   VII.   Arthur.

1908. VIII.   Marie.

673.   BENJAMIN FRANKLIN BOND (Stephen-Silas-Benjamin-Joseph), born Dec. 19, 1852; married Aug. 26, 1882: Viretta Fetters, born Oct. 20, 1863, daughter of John and Catherine (Reece) Fetters. His father died when he was a small boy; he was raised near Farmland by Matthew Clevenger. Residence 1910, Muncie, Ind. Children:

1909.   I.   Prentice Albert, b. Sept. 18, 1883.

1910.   II.   Blanche, b. Jan. 8, 1886.

1911. III.   John, b. April 6, 1888.

1912.   IV.   Gladys Bessie, b. June 26, 1892.

1913.   V.   Fay, b. Sept. 15, 1895.

677.   REV. WILLIS H. BOND (Solomon-Silas-Benjamin-Joseph), born Aug. 11, 1854, in Wayne County, Ind.; married Dec. 11, 1879: Mira Thornburg, d. 1888. Children:

1914.   I.   Archie A., b. Nov. 19,. 1880; a physician. Res., Westfield, Ind.

1915.   II.   Hershel H., b. Sept. 27, 1883.

1916.   III.   Mira F., b. Aug. 29, 1888; d. May 17. 1892. ·

He married second: Ella Pegg, daughter of David and Lydia (Woodard) Pegg. He married third: Lelia Hoskins. Residence 1910, Carmel, Ind.

679. MARY E. BOND (Solomon-Silas-Benjamin-Joseph), born Oct. 11, 1859; died May 10, 1890; married Sept. 16, 1880: Charles Dixon, born May 2, 1859, son of Riley Dixon; he died May 9, 1902. Children:

1917.   I.   Opha Dixon, b. June 26, 1882; m. May 3, 1902: O.. Butler.

1918.   II.   Wilna E. Dixon, b. Jan. 1887.

680. LYDIA E. BOND (Solomon-Silas-Benjamin-Joseph), born March 7, 1868; married Nov. 2, 1893: George Warren Teter, born Feb. 20, 1867, son of George and Helen (Abbott) Teter. Residence, Boxley, Ind. Children:

1919.   I.   Infant, b. July 14, 1894; d. 1894.

682. ALICE BOND (Jesse-Silas-Benjamin-Joseph), born Nov. 2, 1851; married July 11, 1867: Robert Ruggles. Residence Huntington County, Ind. Children:

1920.   I.   Chloe Ruggles, b. July 15, 1868; m. Isaiah Garwood, b. ——. Children:

    (a) Mattie Garwood, b. 1886.

    (b) Laura Garwood.

    (c) Eva Garwood, b. May 15, 1894.

1921.   II.   Anna Ruggles, b. May 16, 1876; m. in 1892: Chester Burris. Children:

    (a) Loren Burris, b. 1893.

    (b) Chloe Burris, b. 1895.

683. LYDIA BOND (Jesse-Silas-Benjamin-Joseph), born July 23, 1853; married Ellis Bowman. Residence, Mount Etna, Ind. Children:

1922.   I.   Estella Bowman, b. May 20, 1871; d. s. p.

1923.   II.   Samuel Bowman, b. Jan. 23, 1874.

1924.   III.   Anna Jane Bowman, b. Feb. 28, 1877.

1925.   IV.   William Ellis Bowman, b. March 11, 1880.

1926.   V.   Dious Ellsworth Bowman, b. June 19, 1883.

1927.   VI.   Alice L. Bowman, b. Jan. 5, 1886.

1928.   VII.   Mattie Bowman, b. Aug. 1, 1892.

685.   ANNA BOND (Jesse-Silas-Benjamin-Joseph), born Jan. 19, 1866; married Joseph Roberson, born March 17, 1863; he died Feb. 27, 1889.   Children:

1929.   I.   Eva Roberson, b. July 28, 1885.

1930.   II.   Jennie Roberson, b. May 16, 1887.

She married second: Elliot Roberson, born Oct. 22, 1866.   Residence, Mount Etna, Ind.   Children:

1931.   III.   Ethel Roberson, b. Jan. 27, 1890.

1932.   IV.   Frank Roberson, b. May 20, 1892.

1933.   V.   Marie Roberson, b. Aug. 30, 1900.

702.   CALVIN T. BOND (William A.-Eli-Benjamin-Joseph), born April 9, 1855, in Salem, Iowa; married April 9, 1885: Mary E. Cammack, born Aug. 20, 1856; died June 4, 1905, daughter of Levi Cammack.   Children:

I.   William L., b. Feb. 18, 1886.

II.   Edna B., b. Sept. 1, 1887.

III.   Edward A., b. Feb. 3, 1892.

IV.   Edith C., b. Oct. 16, 1897.

703.   SARAH ELIZABETH (called Lizzie) BOND (William A.-Eli-Benjamin-Joseph), born June 18, 1856; married Nov. 14, 1877: John H. Steinmetz.   Children:

I.   Y. Estal Steinmetz, b. Oct. 10, 1878.

II.   R. Cecil Steinmetz, b. Nov. 26, 1879; m. Nov. 7, 1903: A. T. Jones.   Residence, Seattle, Wash.

III.   Catherine Steinmetz, b. May 11, 1882; m. March 20, 1908: A. D. Butler.   Res. 1910, Oklahoma City, Okla.

IV.   William H. Steinmetz, b. March 4, 1884.

V.   Clarence Steinmetz, b. Feb. 26, 1886.

VI.   Abby A. Steinmetz, b. Oct. 10, 1889; m. Sept. 10, 1907: R. R. Morey.

VII.   S. Elizabeth Steinmetz, b. Dec. 13, 1894.

VIII.   John B. Steinmetz, b. Jan. 27, 1896.

IX.   Merton Steinmetz, b. Sept. 28, 1897.

X.   Thelma Steinmetz, b. Aug. 27, 1898.

XI.   L. Virgil Steinmetz, b. April 5, 1900.

704.   FLORENCE BOND (William-Eli-Benjamin-Joseph), born June 13, 1860; married April 7, 1881: Charles L. Weeks; he died April, 1885.   Children:

I.   Forest L. Weeks.

II. Eva C. Weeks, m. 1904: William B. Newman; he d. 1908. She married second: Thomas E. Weeks, a brother to her former husband. They moved to Oklahoma, 1893. She died Oct. 8, 1905; he died Jan. 7, 1907. The children reside in Cherokee, Okla. To this later union was born six children:

708. ADA BOND (Benjamin-Eli-Benjamin-Joseph), born ——; married —— Boucher.

709. MARY ADEL BOND (Benjamin-Eli-Benjamin-Joseph), born ——; married —— Murray.

710. BELLE BOND (Benjamin-Eli-Benjamin-Joseph), born ——; married —— Sturdevant; residence, Corvallis, Mont.

711. MINNIE BOND (Benjamin - Eli - Benjamin - Joseph), born, ——; married Philip O'Donnel.

766. REV. JOHN S. BOND (Darius-Joseph S.-Samuel-Joseph), born May 23, 1828; he is a Quaker preacher. Residence, Indiana, Iowa, California. Address, Villa Park, Calif. Married Elizabeth Calborne. Children:

2000.   I.   Sabina Ann.
2001. II.   Mary Jane, d. aged 14 years.
2003. III.   Anna Betsey.
2004. IV.   Hannah Matilda.
2005.   V.   Amanda Mariah.
2006. VI.   Emma.
2007. VII.   Eunice.

He married second: Mary J. Hammer, nee Mills, widow of Hiram Hammer. Children:

2008. VIII. Elizabeth.
2009. IX.   Sarah L.
2010.   X.   Esther.

768. REUBEN BOND (Darius-Joseph S.-Samuel-Joseph), born in Randolph County, Ind., July 16, 1831; died at Chico, Calif., June 21, 1903; married Nov. 4, 1856: Nancy Herring, born March 13, 1838, in Hamilton County, Ind.; she died Nov. 15, 1900. He moved to Iowa in 1838, and moved to California in 1852. Was a soldier in Co. B, 11th Reg. Iowa Inft. Occupation, carpenter, farmer and fruit grower. Children:

2011.   I.   Anna, b. Oct. 19, 1857; married John Davis; d. s. p. July 4, 1879.
2012. II.   William Henry, b. Dec. 14, 1859; d. Nov. 16, 1860.
2013. III.   Lydia Jane, b. Aug. 2, 1861.

2014.   IV.   Albert W., b. Feb. 21, 1863.
2015.   V.   Etta, b. Oct. 5, 1867.
2016.   VI.   Mary, b. April 10, 1869.
2017.   VII.   Lon. b. Sept. 13, 1876.

769.· EUNICE BOND (Darius-Joseph S.-Samuel-Joseph), born 1833; died 1896; married Charles Davis.   Children:
2018.   I.   Mary E. Davis.
2019.   II.   Hannah Davis.
2020.   III.   Nancy Davis.
2021.   IV.   Joseph Davis.
2022.   V.   Clara Davis.
2023.   VI.   Reuben Davis.
2024.   VII.   Ethlene Davis.

770.   MATILDA BOND (Darius-Joseph S.-Samuel-Joseph), born 1837; married Jonathan Cox.   Residence, Chico, Calif.   N. f. k.

771.   ASA BOND (John-Joseph S.-Samuel-Joseph), born Nov.- 13, 1829; married April 22, 1852: Abigail Hodgen, born Dec. 22, 1833, daughter of Nathan and Mourning (Coffin) Hodgen.   Residence, Jonesboro, Ind.   Children:
2025.   I.   Lindley, b. April, 1853; d. July 25, 1853, inft.·
2026.   II.   Wilson H., b. Oct. 17, 1854.
2027.   III.   Ruth A., b. Nov. 19, 1856; d. Aug. 18, 1860.
2028.   IV.   Nathan A., b. June 26, 1861.
2029.   V.   William, b. March 26, 1863; d. April, 1863.
2030.   VI.   Emma Dora, b. June 27, 1866.
2031.   VII.   John H., b. May 1, 1870; d. Aug. 24, 1870.

772.   ELI BOND (John-Joseph S.-Samuel-Joseph), born Oct. 27, 1831; died 1897 (?) in Randolph County, Ind.; married March 24, 1853: Sarah Lamb, born Sept. 29, 1832, died April 23, 1906, daughter of Hosea and Mary Lamb.   Children:
2032.   I.   John A., b. Jan. 24, 1855.
2033.   II.   Mary E., b. Dec. 26, 1858.
2034.   III.   Lydia E., b. Feb. 8, 1862.

773.   LEVI BOND (John-Joseph S.-Samuel-Joseph), born Oct. 24, 1833; married July 20, 1854: Sarah Elizabeth Feagans, born Nov. 12, 1838, daughter of James H. and Rebecca Feagans, of Randolph County, Ind.   Residence, near Farmland, Ind.   Ch:
2035.   I.   Rebecca Jane, b. Oct. 25, 1855.
2036.   II.   Lavina Ann, b. Aug. 25, 1857.

2037. III. James Albert, b. April 24, 1859.
2038. IV. Susannah D., b. Oct. 17, 1861.
2039. V. Mary Elizabeth, b. May 28, 1864.
2040. VI. Mark W., b. Aug. 16, 1867.
2041. VII. John W., b. Sept. 9, 1869.
2042. VIII. Benjamin E., b. July 21, 1871.
2043. IX. Goldie Emma E., b. June 15, 1875.

774. LYDIA BOND (John-Joseph S.-Samuel-Joseph), born Jan. 8, 1836; married James Jessup. N. f. k.

775. HIRAM BOND (John-Joseph S.-Samuel-Joseph), born Jan. 3, 1839; married Feb. 16, 1865: Pauline M. Albright, born Aug. 24, 1836, daughter of Philip and Catherine (Straden) Albright, of Arcanum, O. Residence, 1909, Toledo, O. Children:
2044. I. Luella D., b. Aug. 24, 1866, in Arcanum, Ohio.
2045. II. John Edgar, b. Nov. 12, 1869, at Farmland, Ind.
2046. III. Philip Albert, and
2047. IV. Elizabeth C., twins, b. Sept. 13, 1871; both dec.
2048. V. Hettie A., b. July 27, 1876, in Toledo, Ohio.

776. DARIUS BOND (John-Joseph S.-Samuel-Joseph), born Aug. 29, 1841; married Jan. 14, 1864: Hannah Hunt, born July 12, 1843, daughter of Pleasant and Ann (Williams) Hunt. Ch:
2049. I. Pleasant A., b. Oct. 11, 1865.
2050. II. Loretta A., b. Nov. 18, 1866.
2051. III. Alistus J., b. Oct. 25, 1868.
2052. IV. Oliver E., b. Feb. 15, 1873.
2053. V. Nelson E., b. Nov. 25, 1875; d. Oct. 18, 1892.
2054. VI. Leonora E., b. July 3, 1878.
2055. VII. Parvin W., b. Nov. 25, 1880.

778. RHODA BOND (John-Joseph S.-Samuel-Joseph), born Oct. 14, 1849; died July 23, 1893; married March 21, 1866: Joab Lamb, born April 11, 1845, son of Restor and Betsey (Thornburg) Lamb. Children:
2056. I. Irvin R. Lamb, b. Feb. 15, 1868.
2057. II. Orla J. Lamb, b. June 25, 1870.
2058. III. Clinton E. Lamb, b. July 27, 1875.
2059. IV. Luther E. Lamb, b. Aug. 27, 1879.
2060. V. Otto W. Lamb, b. Oct. 21, 1882.

779. IRENE BOND (John-Joseph S.-Samuel-Joseph), born Jan. 3, 1854; married March 2, 1872: Clarkson Whitaker. Children:

2061.   I.   Clara L. Whitaker, b. Dec. 20, 1872.

2062.   II.   Clarence E. Whitaker, b. Jan. 17, 1877; d. s. p. Oct. 29, 1902; a member of 158th Reg. Ind. Vol. Inft.

She married second: March 13, 1880: John Addington.   Ch:

2063.   III.   Mabel G. Addington, b. April 13, 1886.

782.   LAVINA BOND (Mordecai-Joseph S.-Samuel-Joseph), born Oct. 21, 1834; married Aug. 27, 1854: William J. Rhynolds, both deceased.   Children:

2064.   I.   John B. Rhynolds, of Oxford, Neb.

2065.   II.   Jesse M. Rhynolds, d.

2066.   III.   Malinda Rhynolds.

2067.   IV.   Irilla J. Rhynolds, d.

2068.   V.   Eva Rhynolds.

2069.   VI.   Mary E. Rhynolds.

2070.   VII.   Jasper M. Rhynolds.

2071.   VIII.   William A. Rhynolds.

2072.   IX.   Charles E. Rhynolds.

2073.   X.   Eliza A. Rhynolds.

786.   EUNICE BOND (Mordecai-Joseph S.-Samuel-Joseph), born Dec. 26, 1843; married Ezra Hockett.   Residence, 1903, Spencer, Ia.   Children:

2074.   I.   Sarah A. Hockett.

2075.   II.   Amanda Hockett, dec.

2076.   III.   Rachel Etta Hockett.

2077.   IV.   James D. Hockett.

2078.   V.   Eunice Hockett.

787.   JOSHUA M. BOND (Mordecai-Joseph S.-Samuel-Joseph), born Jan. 16, 1846; married Anna Arnett; he died June 13, 1868.   Children:

2069.   I.   A daughter residing in California.   N. f. k.

788.   WILLIAM M. BOND (Mordecai-Joseph S.-Samuel-Joseph), born May 1, 1848; married Nov. 17, 1869: Caroline E. Beeson.   Residence, Salem, Iowa.   Children:

2080.   I.   Lillie C., b. Aug. 7, 1870.

2081.   II.   William Albert, b. July 13, 1873.

He married second June 18, 1889: Elma Banker.

797.   REV. JEHIEL BOND (Levi-Joseph S.-Samuel-Joseph), born Jan. 30, 1842; married April 26, 1866: Anna J. Marshall, born Nov. 4, 1844, daughter of Evan and Gulielma (Bond) Marshall, of Henry County, Ind.   Residence, Webster, Ind.   He has for many years been interested in family history and reunions of the Bond family. Children:

2082. I. Clara E., b. Nov. 7, 1868.

2083. II. S. Edgar, b. Aug. 1, 1876.

2084. III. Jennie, b. Oct. 24, 1878.

800. ELIZABETH E. BOND (Zimri-Joseph S.-Samuel-Joseph), born Nov. 3, 1859; married Aug. 27, 1881: William Diggs Parker. Residence, Farmland, Ind. N. f. k.

802. REV. ALBERT BOND (Zimri-Joseph S.-Samuel-Joseph), born Jan. 17, 1863; married March 10, 1895: Arrilda Marshall, daughter of Dr. Evan and Margaret (Newby) Marshall, of Salem, Ia. He is a minister in Friends church, also farmer. Residence, 1904, Hartford, Kas. Children:

2085. I. Merritt Zimri, and

2086. II. Earlington Evan, twins, b. Aug. 30, 1898.

2087. III. Margaret, b. June, 1901.

804. LINETTA BOND (Zimri-Joseph S.-Samuel-Joseph), born March 20, 1866; married July 2, 1892: Oliver T. Randall, Residence, Alexandria, Ind. N. f. k.

805. FREDERICK BOND (Zimri-Joseph S.-Samuel-Joseph), born Dec. 13, 1867; married Feb. 3, 1892: Margaret R. Valentine, born March 9, 1872, daughter of James and Catherine (Smith) Valentine, of Iowa. Residence, 1904, Columbia, Wn. The family spend much time in Alaska, where he is interested in mining. Children:

2088. I. Katherine J., b. June 21, 1893.

2089. II. Charles A., b. Feb. 20, 1895; d. Dec. 8, 1897.

2090. III. Marguerite, b. Nov. 11, 1903 (?).

811. MARY MELISSA HARROLD (Lavina (Bond)-Joseph S.-Samuel-Joseph), born May 30, 1852; died May 7, 1875; married William Jessop; he died; married second: Oliver P. Hammond. One child:

(a) Blanche, b. April 4, 1875; m. John Smith, of Downs, Kas.

814. EUNICE LEAH HARROLD (Lavina (Bond) -Joseph S.-Samuel-Joseph), born April 30, 1860; married Oliver P. Hammond. Address, Roseburg, Ore.

816. OLIVER OSCAR HARROLD (Lavina (Bond) -Joseph S.-Samuel-Joseph), born April 21, 1869; m.; P. O., 1910, Mt. Ayer, Iowa. Two children:

(a) Raymond O. Harrold.

(b)   Georgia Alice Harrold.   N. f. k.

817.   PRISCILLA BOND (Amer-Thomas-Samuel-Joseph), born Nov. 1, 1828; married Caleb Hodson; moved to Yamhill County, Oregon, where they lived many years.   Both now deceased.   N. f. k.

819.   THOMAS BOND (Amer-Thomas-Samuel-Joseph), born May 12, 1834, in Indiana; married Oct. 30, 1856: Martha Ann Hosier, born Jan. 27, 1834, daughter of Nathan and Alice Hosier, of Greensboro, Henry County, Ind.   Residence, 1912, Birmingham, Ala.   Children:

2191.   I.   Carrie E. Bond, b. Feb. 14, 1858.

820.   DR. CALEB BOND (Amer-Thomas-Samuel-Joseph), born Oct. 3, 1836; died Sept. 21, 1892; married Matilda J. Julian, born May 5, 1844, died March 9, 1885, daughter of Peter and Adeline.   He was a physician and druggist.   Residence, Cadiz, Ind. Children:

2092.   I.   Otis R., b. Nov. 15, 1864.

2093.   II.   George J., b. Aug. 27, 1867.

2094.   III.   Vera Estella, b. April 8, 1869; died July 3, 1890.

2095.   IV.   Waldo E., b. Feb. 25, 1871.

He married second: Levisa Tuttle, of Delaware County, Ind. Children:

2096.   V.   Llano Bond. b. May 23, 1891.

824.   MAHLON BOND (Amer - Thomas - Samuel - Joseph), born Nov. 30, 1850; married Feb. 13, 1873: Eunice E. Hunt, daughter of Ammiel and Abigail (Cox) Hunt.   Residence, Wayne County, Ind., Muncie, Ind.   Children:

2097.   I.   Leona.

2098.   II.   Rev. Leslie.

2099.   III.   Lillian, b. Nov. 10, 1877; d. Oct. 8, 1886.

827.   HENRY PALIN (Betsey (Bond) -Thomas-Samuel-Joseph), born Sept. 18, 1829; married first: Mary Ann Hays.   Residence, Wingate, Ind.   Children:

2100.   I.   Winfield C. Palin.

He married second: Keziah Boord.   Seven children:

2101.   II.   Mary Palin.

2102.   III.   Julia Palin; m. Dr. Robert Claypool.

2103.   IV.   Emma Palin; m. Frederick Wales.

2104.   V.   Ella Palin; m. John Winnie.

2105.   VI.   Charles Palin.

2106.   VII.   Lillie Palin; m. Frank Royalty.

2107. VIII.   Maude Palin.

2108.   IX.   Glella Palin, dec.

828. JULIA ANN PALIN (Betsey (Bond) -Thomas-Samuel-Joseph), born April 22, 1831, in Henry County, Ind.; married Feb. 13, 1856, in Fountain County, Ind.: Richard Henry; he died Oct. 14, 1892.   Residence, Potomac, Ill., R. F. D. 3.   Ch:

2109.   I.   Frank H. Henry, b. Dec. 3, 1856.

2110.   II.   Hiram A. Henry, b. Feb. 27, 1858.

2111. III.   Clara Jane Henry, b. July 8, 1862.

2112.   IV.   Joseph P. Henry, b. Sept. 12, 1864.

829. SYLVESTER PALIN (Betsey (Bond) -Thomas-Samuel-Joseph), born Jan. 21, 1833; died Nov. 29, 1880; married Feb. 21, 1854: Susannah Tracy, born July 20, 1836.   Children:

2113.   I.   Aura Alice Palin, b. Nov. 29, 1855.

2114.   II.   Arlistes E. Palin, b. April 7, 1858.

2115. III.   Jennie Louisa Palin, b. Aug. 11, 1862.

2116.   IV.   Julia Ann Palin, b. Dec. 18, 1864.

830. MARY JANE PALIN (Betsey (Bond) -Thomas-Samuel-Joseph), born April 13, 1835; married George Applegate. Residence, Sutherland, Neb.   Children:

2117.   I.   Melissa Applegate.

2118.   II.   Exum Applegate.

2119. III.   Lincoln Applegate.

2120.   IV.   Byron Applegate.

2121.   V.   Grant Applegate.

2122.   VI.   Dora Applegate.

2123. VII.   Nellie Applegate.

2124. VIII.   Lafayette Applegate.

831. HIRAM PALIN (Betsey (Bond) -Thomas-Samuel-Joseph), born Jan. 10, 1837; married Louisa Jones.   Residence, Fountain County, Ind.   She died.   Three children:

2125.   I.   Urah Palin.

2126.   II.   Alvessa Palin.

2127. III.   Homer Palin, d. inft.

He married second: Lottie Scott.   Children:

2128.   IV.   Helen Palin.

2129.   V.   Scott Palin.

2130.   VI.   Benjamin Palin.

2131. VII.   Harry Palin.

2132. VIII. Inez Palin.

832. JESSE M. PALIN (Betsey (Bond) -Thomas-Samuel-Joseph), born Jan. 6, 1839; married Aug. 28, 1860: Mary Fry, born 1838. Residence, Mallott, Fountain County, Ind. ·Ch:

2133.   I.   Fred Palin, b. 1863.
2134.   II. Minnie Palin, b. 1865.
2135.   III. Austin Palin, b. 1869.
2136.   IV. Edward Palin, b. 1873.
2137.   V.   Myrtle Palin, b. 1875; m. 1903: S. Edgar Bond.
2138.   VI. Mabel, d. inft.
2139.   VII. Harry, d. inft.

834· CALVIN BOND (Jesse-Thomas-Samuel-Joseph), born April 22, 1830; married 1853: Margaret Ann Murphy, born 1835. Occupation, cabinet maker and undertaker. Residence, Carmel, Ind. Children:

2140.   I.   Wesley.
2141.   II. Artalissa.
2142.   III. William C., b. 1860.
2143.   IV. Clara L.
2144.   V.   Jesse.
2145.   VI. Oliver P. M.
2146.   VII. Austin.

835. MAHALA BOND (Jesse-Thomas-Samuel-Joseph), born July 31, 1832; died 1870; married 1853: Seth Cloud. Children:

2147.   I.   Evaline Cloud.
2148.   II. Lydia Cloud, dec.
2149.   III. Josephine Cloud.
2150.   IV. Sidney Cloud. Res., Kansas. N. f. k.

836. WILLIAM BOND (Jesse-Thomas-Samuel-Joseph), born Oct. 3, 1834; married 1855: Sarah A. Jessop, born May 1, 1837, daughter of Thomas and Rebecca Jessop. Residence, Webster, Ind. Children:

2151.   I.   Emily Ann, b. Aug. 12, 1856; died Nov. 16, 1856, inft.
2152.   II. Thomas J., b. Aug. 27, 1857.
2153.   III. Franklin W., b. Sept. 17, 1860.
2154.   IV. Jesse L, b. Oct. 7, 1862; d. May 15, 1864.
2155.   V.   Micajah John, b. July 27, 1865.
2156.   VI. Charles E., b. Nov. 15, 1867.
2157.   VII. William Penn, and

2158. VIII. Robert Barclay, twins, b. Nov. 5, 1871.

2159. IX. Rebecca A., b. March 21, 1876.

841. CORNELIUS BOND (Thomas - Thomas - Samuel - Joseph), born in Wayne County, Ind., Dec. 2, 1834; died March 21, 1897; married Oct. 13, 1853: Anna E. Eigenbrodt, born in Franklin County, Penn., Nov. 6, 1832; she died April, 1907, in Richmond, Ind. Children:

2160. I. Adaline V. M., b. Aug. 17, 1854.

2161. II. Anna Josephine, b. May 6, 1856; d. March 18, 1895.

2162. III. Louisa Emma, b. Sept. 8, 1858.

2163. IV. William Albert, b. Aug. 31, 1860.

2164. V. Charles Thomas Hartman, b. Aug. 24, 1862.

2165. VI. Rebecca Caddie, b. Nov. 1, 1869; d. April, 1906.

2166. VII. Jeannette M., b. Jan. 19, 1872.

845. REBECCA BOND (Thomas-Thomas-Samuel-Joseph), born Nov. 20, 1842; died Sept., 1901; married Dec. 25, 1882: David Baldwin. Residence, Wayne County, Ind. Children:

2167. I. Almeda Baldwin.

846. LINDLEY H. BOND (Thomas-Thomas-Samuel-Joseph), born June 27, 1845; married Sept. 14, 1865: Sarah Jay, born May 16, 1847, daughter of Henry H. and Sarah (Strawbridge) Jay. Residence, Webster, Ind. Children:

2168. I. Rosetta, b. Nov. 5, 1866; d. July 15, 1867, inft.

2169. II. Luella, b. Aug. 29, 1868.

2170. III. William Albert Henry, b. Dec. 18, 1869.

2171. IV. Emma L., b. Oct. 12, 1875.

2172. V. DeWitt Clifton, b. 1878; d. Sept. 19, 1893.

848. JULIA A. BOND (Thomas-Thomas-Samuel-Joseph), born Jan. 10, 1851; married Aug. 22, 1883: John Barnes. Residence, Webster, Ind. Children:

2173. I. Harold Barnes.

2174. II. Elmer Barnes.

851. LUCINDA BOND (Hiram-Thomas-Samuel-Joseph), born Jan. 28, 1838; died Dec. 31, 1901; married June 28, 1855: Perry G. Earl, born Feb. 7, 1825; died Oct. 26, 1883. Residence, Oregon. Children:

2175. I. Hiram Jasper Earl, b. Aug. 6, 1856.

2176. II. Melissa J. Earl, b. March 1, 1858.

2177. III. Philip E. Earl, b. 1859; d. inft.

2178.   IV.   Harvey Chase Earl, b. Nov. 28, 1860.

2179.   V.   Hannah M. Earl, b. Oct. 2, 1862.

2180.   VI.   Thomas P. Earl, b. Oct. 2, 1864;- P. O., 1903, Waha, Idaho.

2181.   VII.   Mary N. Earl, b. April 14, 1870.

2182.   VIII.   George W. Earl, b. Feb. 22, 1873.

852. ELAM BOND (Hiram-Thomas-Samuel-Joseph), born Dec. 15, 1840, in Oregon; married Dec. 2, 1873: Elizabeth Cook. Residence, Oregon, Idaho. P. O., 1903, Waha, Idaho. Children:

2183.   I.   Rose R., b. Jan. 14, 1875.

2184.   II.   Oliver E., b. Nov. 21, 1876. .

2185.   III.   Clara A., b. Sept. 14, 1879.

2186.   IV.   Josephine, b. June 29, 1883.

2187.   V.   Louisa, b. Feb. 17, 1886.

2188.   VI.   Robert Owen, b. Sept. 5, 1888.

2189.   VII.   Jennie Laura, b. Sept. 12, 1890.

2190.   VIII.   Florence, b. Feb. 17, 1892.

2191.   IX.   Angeline, b. Oct. 6, 1895.

855. MARY BOND (Hiram-Thomas-Samuel-Joseph), born Dec. 14, 1847; married George E. Knowlton. N. f. k.

856. HANNAH BOND (Hiram - Thomas - Samuel - Joseph), born May 1, 1849, in Linn County, Ore.; married Oct. 26, 1865: Berryman Cummings, son of Ruth and Beulah. Residence, Halsey, Ore. Children:

2192.   I.   Lillie Belle Cummings, b. Oct. 25, 1866.

2193.   II.   Hiram Newton Cummings, b. Oct. 3, 1868.

2194.   III.   Inez Valedia Cummings, b. July 3, 1870.

2195.   IV.   William Arley Cummings, b. Jan. 23, 1874.

2196.   V.   Nellie Cummings, b. March 22, 1876.

2197.   VI.   Lydia May Cummings, b. May 7, 1878.

2198.   VII.   Martin E. Cummings, b. Sept. 24, 1880.

2199.   VIII.   Lewis B. Cummings, b. April 7, 1883.

2200.   IX.   Margaret Elizabeth Cummings, b. March 16, 1891.

857. JOEL BOND (Hiram-Thomas-Samuel-Joseph), born Feb. 20, 1851. Residence, Port Orford, Oregon. N. f. k.

858. SILAS M. BOND (Hiram - Thomas - Samuel - Joseph), born Feb. 21, 1853; married and has five children. N. f. k.

859. OWEN R. BOND (Hiram - Thomas - Samuel - Joseph),

born Oct. 10, 1856; married Jan. 25, 1899: Jane Morgan. Residence, Halsey, Ore. N. f. k.

861. PHEBE ANN BOND (Pleasant-Thomas-Samuel-Joseph), born April 21, 1838; married Dec. 15, 1859: John Adamson, born June 1, 1833, died Aug. 1, 1878, son of Mordecai and Susannah Adamson. Residence, Warren County, Ia. Ch:

2201. I. Nathaniel B. Adamson, b. Feb. 25, 1861.

2202. II. Alpheus T. Adamson, b. April 16, 1863; d. May 18, 1864.

2203. III. Drucilla W. Adamson, b. April 27, 1866.

2204. IV. William E. Adamson, b. Feb. 17, 1868.

2205. V. Tillman P. Adamson, b. May 14, 1870.

2206. VI. Mary Alice Adamson, b. Oct. 20, 1872.

2207. VII. Eli Elza Adamson, b. Dec. 17, 1874; d. March 15, 1876.

863. EXUM BOND (Pleasant - Thomas - Samuel - Joseph), born Oct. 3, 1842, in Indiana; married Oct. 28, 1864: Margaret Barnett, born August 17, 1846. Residence, Redfield, Iowa. Children:

2208. I. Eva M., b. Aug. 31, 1865.

2209. II. Luella M., b. April 2, 1868.

2210. III. Jesse, b. March 1, 1872.

2211. IV. Lizzie J., b. April 10, 1876; d. Jan. 29, 1878.

2212. V. Leroy, b. Aug. 2, 1880.

864. HIRAM BOND (Pleasant - Thomas - Samuel - Joseph), born Nov. 14, 1844; married Mary E. Laid, daughter of Thomas Jefferson and Mary E. Laid. Residence, Winterset, Ia. Ch:

2213. I. Flora M., b. Aug. 31, 1873.

865. THOMAS BOND (Pleasant-Thomas-Samuel-Joseph), born in Indiana, Sept. 3, 1846; married Dec., 1868: Nancy E. Fard. Moved in 1875 to Nebraska. Address, 1904, Bloomington, Neb. Children:

2214. I. Nettie Ann, b. June 10, 1870.

2215. II. Rosetta, b. Sept. 27, 1873.

He married second Jan. 21, 1881: Florence H. Bower, born in Ohio Nov. 12, 1860.

2216. III. Mollie S., b. March 12, 1882.

2217. IV. Effie Augusta, b. Dec. 3, 1884.

2218. V. Nora May, b. Dec. 23, 1890.

2219. VI. Esther, b. Jan. 8, 1895.

2220. VII. Allen James, b. June 18, 1900; d. June, 1901.

2221. VIII. Baby, born 1904.

866. ELAM L. BOND (Pleasant-Thomas-Samuel-Joseph), born in Indiana, Oct. 30, 1848; married 1882: Sarah A. Williams, daughter of Isaac N. and Amanda Williams. Residence, Bloomington, Neb. She died Feb. 11, 1900. Children:

2222. I. Edith May, b. Oct. 26, 1883.

2223. II. Morick, b. June 1, 1885.

2224. III. Isaac Newton, b. Oct. 11, 1888.

867. ANNA J. BOND (Pleasant-Thomas-Samuel-Joseph), born March 15, 1853; married Nov. 23, 1876: George Simon, born Oct. 24, 1848, son of Christian R. and Harriet (Anthony) Simon. Residence, 1904, Soldier, Kas. Children:

2225. I. Lavera Simon, b. Oct. 20, 1877, in Iowa.

2226. II. Ward Simon, b. Oct. 3, 1879.

2227. III. Florence N. Simon, b. Sept. 17, 1881; d. Sept. 5, 1886.

2228. IV. Roxy Simon, b. Nov. 10, 1883, in Iowa.

2229. V. Roscoe Simon, b. Feb. 7, 1885, in Nemaha Co., Kas.

2230. VI. Clarence Simon, b. Aug. 21, 1887; d. March 27, 1889.

2231. VII. Viola May Simon, b. May 15, 1889.

868. ALPHEUS BOND (Pleasant-Thomas-Samuel-Joseph), born in Wayne County, Ind., July 12, 1855; married Julia E. Maxwell, daughter of Dillon and Elizabeth Maxwell, of Warren County, Ia. He moved with his parents to Iowa in 1859. Residence, Winterset, Ia. Children:

2232. I. Otho C., b. June 14, 1879.

2233. II. Ira E., b. Feb. 21, 1882; d. Jan. 31, 1885.

2234. III. Desford D., b. Jan. 3, 1884; d. June, 1884, inft.

2235. IV. Lester M., b. July 16, 1886.

2236. V. Clair A., b. June 14, 1892.

2237. VI. Pearl M. (a dau.) b. Aug. 19, 1896.

869. PHEBE BOND (Amasa-Samuel-Samuel-Joseph), born in Wayne County, Ind., Sept. 4, 1833; moved to Iowa 1856; married Oct., 1858: Armstead Milner, born Aug. 19, 1829, in Highland County, Ohio, son of Oliver and Nancy (Garrett) Milner. Occupation, farmer. Residence, Red Oak, Ia. Children:

2238. I. Cornelia L. Milner, b. July 14, 1859.

2239. II. Mary Milner, and

2240. III. Anna Milner, twins, b. May 10, 1861.

2241. IV. Oliver Amasa Milner, b. Feb. 20, 1863.

2242. V. Alice N. Milner, b. Jan. 21, 1865.

2243. VI. Sadie L. Milner, b. Oct. 25, 1868.

2244. VII. Harvey E. Milner, b. Sept. 11, 1870.

2245. VIII. Emma R. Milner, b. Oct. 30, 1872.

2246. IX. Quinnette Milner, b. April 21, 1877.

2247. X. Clyde Milner, b. Oct. 22, 1881; d. Oct. 14, 1882, inft.

871. JACOB H. BOND (Amasa-Samuel-Samuel-Joseph), born April 4, 1837; married April 1, 1862: Phebe Horton, born April 12, 1840, daughter of Ira Horton. Residence, Red Oak, Ia. He died Feb. 1, 1906. Children:

2248. I. Oscar William, b. May 8, 1863; d. April 30, 1864.

2249. II. Minnie A., b. Jan. 8, 1865; d. Aug. 1, 1866.

2250. III. Amasa T., b. Sept. 20, 1867.

875. AMASA BOND (Amasa-Samuel-Samuel-Joseph), born in Indiana, June 2, 1847; moved with his parents to Montgomery County, Ia., in 1856; married Feb. 25, 1869: Laura E. Murray, born June 29, 1849; she died April 20, 1885. Residence, Red Oak, Ia. Children:

2251. I. Maude L., b. Jan. 24, 1870.

2252. II. Clarence B., b. Dec. 6, 1871.

2253. III. Effie B., b. Feb. 18, 1874.

2254. IV. Earl J., b. Aug. 24, 1881.

877. ISAAC BOND (Samuel-Samuel-Samuel-Joseph), born Jan. 9, 1833; married March, 1865: Louisa Randall, both deceased. Residence, Carmel, Ind. Children:

2255. I. Mary, b. July 7, 1867.

2256. II. Abbie I., b. Aug. 7, 1869.

2257. III. Laura E., b. April 22, 1872.

2258. IV. Ethel, b. Jan. 22, 1874.

2259. V. Clara B., b. Dec. 4, 1876.

2260. VI. Ida May, b. Feb. 13, 1878.

2261. VII. Aletha C., b. June 16, 1881.

878. AHIJAH BOND (Samuel-Samuel-Samuel-Joseph), born June 17, 1834; married Nov. 8, 1855: Maria M. Carey, born March 10, 1836, died Sept. 16, 1868; she was daughter of Sylvanns and Sarah Carey, of Carmel, Ind. He married second,

Feb. 22, 1872: Sarah Jane Winslow. Residence, Indiana, Kas.
Children:
2262. I. Ira M., b. Oct. 31, 1857.
2263. II. Daniel C., b. June 26, 1860; d. Sept. 9, 1861, inft.
2264. III. Samuel S., b. Aug. 22, 1863.
Children of second marriage:
2265. IV. John C., b. March 28, 1873.
2266. V. George W., b. Feb. 8, 1875.
2267. VI. William A., b. Feb. 28, 1877; d. March 10, 1877.
2268. VII. Odena D., b. June 4, 1878; d. March 30, 1882.

879. BARCLAY BOND (Samuel-Samuel-Samuel-Joseph),
born March 21, 1836; died Jan. 1, 1898, in Cherokee County,
Kas.; married first Dec. 8, 1859: Sarah A. Lancaster, of Carmel,
Ind. He moved to Illinois in 1868 and to Kansas in 1879. Ch:
2269. I. Albert L., b. Oct. 30, 1860.
2270. II. Mahlon D., b. Dec. 29, 1861.
2271. III. Ruth A., b. Dec. 22, 1862.
2272. IV. Robert B., b. Feb. 22, 1864.
He married second March 31, 1869: Elizabeth Thornton, born
Jan. 12, 1846. Children:
2273. V. Flora E., b. Feb. 22, 1870.
2274. VI. Miles H., b. March 14, 1872.
2275. VII. Minnie C., twin sister; d. in infancy.
2276. VIII. Samantha J., b. Oct. 17, 1876.
2277. IX. Samuel B., b. Sept. 12, 1878.
2278. X. Sarah Ettie, b. April 28, 1880.
2279. XI. Charles, b. Jan. 2, 1882.
2280. XII. Otis Lee, b. Nov. 15, 1883.

880. MARGARET BOND (Samuel-Samuel-Samuel-Joseph),
born Oct. 26, 1837, in Hamilton County, Ind.; married Ira C.
Mendenhall, son of James and Rebecca, of Hamilton County,
Ind. Residence, Lacygne, Kas. Children:
2280-a. I. Albert R. Mendenhall, b. Feb. 1, 1857; d. Sept.
15, 1875, s. p.
2280-b. II. Samuel D. Mendenhall, b. Feb. 7, 1859; d.
Dec. 6, 1862, s. p.
2280-c. III. Mary E. Mendenhall, b. April 20, 1861.
2280-d. IV. Boswell Ward Mendenhall, b. July 8, 1863.
2280-e. V. Almedia Mendenhall, b. Jan. 17, 1866.
2280-f. VI. I. Warren Mendenhall, b. July 22, 1868.

2280–g. VII.   Charles A. Mendenhall, b. Sept. 15, 1870.
2280–h. VIII. James W. Mendenhall, b. Sept. 1, 1874.
2280–i. IX.   Margaret Mendenhall, b. March 6, 1877.

882. SILAS BOND (Ellis-Samuel-Samuel-Joseph), born in
Wayne County, Ind., Jan. 26, 1835; married in Douglas County,
Kas., March 13, 1859: Sarah Rohrer, born May 14, 1840, in
Holmes County, Ohio, daughter of Daniel and Jane Rohrer.
Residence, Osage County, Kas. He died Jan. 8, 1902. Children:

2281.   I.   Eliza Jane, b. Feb. 24, 1860.
2282.   II.   Harvey Thompson, b. March 31, 1862.
2283.   III.   Milton Elmore, b. Sept. 2, 1864.
2284.   IV.   Mary Etta, b. July 3, 1867.
2285.   V.   Horace Greely, b. Sept. 19, 1870.
2286.   VI.   Dora Ellen, b. Jan. 26, 1872.
2287.   VII.   Rachel Anna, b. Oct. 25, 1875.
2288.   VIII.   Daniel Bert, b. July 18, 1878.
2289.   IX.   Thomas Alva, and
2290.   X.   Rosa Elva, b. Oct. 10, 1882.

883. ENOS BOND (Ellis-Samuel-Samuel-Joseph), born Jan.
26, 1838, in Indiana; died May 24, 1909; moved to Lawrence
County, Kas., 1854; married March 31, 1859: Emily Rohrer,
daughter of Daniel and Jane. Residence, Lawrence County,
Kas. Children:

2291.   I.   Alice, b. Jan. 24, 1860.
2292.   II.   Adaline, b. Jan. 5, 1862.
2293.   III.   Ellis, b. Dec. 12, 1863.
2294.   IV.   Clara, b. Oct. 1, 1866.
2295.   V.   Metta, b. Dec. 8, 1868.
2296.   VI.   Lena, b. Dec. 20, 1868.
2297.   VII.   Minnie, b. Dec. 29, 1868. Triplets; all dec.
2298.   VIII.   Calvin, b. May 16, 1870.
2299.   IX.   Herbert, b. Aug. 21, 1872; d. June 6, 1888.
2300.   X.   Demming, b. Nov. 22, 1874.
2301.   XI.   Porter, b. Jan. 28, 1877, and
2302.   XII.   Rosa, twins, b. Jan. 28, 1877; d. Feb. 1, 1877.
2303.   XIII.   Chester, b. Dec. 4, 1880.

884. LOUISA BOND (Ellis-Samuel-Samuel-Joseph), born
Sept. 18, 1839, in Wayne County, Ind.; married in Kansas, Nov.
11, 1857: Jesse Whitson, born in Wayne County, Ind., March 2,

1830; he died Aug. 23, 1902.   Her address 1904, Tappenish, Wn.
Children:

·2304.   I.   George W. Whitson, b. Oct. 5, 1858.

2305.   II.   Owen B. Whitson, b. April 16, 1861, in Kansas.

2306.   III.   Willis Elsworth Whitson, b. Aug. 16, 1863, in
Grant Co., Ind.; d. 1863, inft.

2307.   IV.   Elmer Augustine Whitson, b. Sept. 20, 1864; d.
age 4.

2308.   V.   Ellis John Whitson, b. Jan. 17, 1870.   Res. 1908,
Leavitt, Neb.

2309.   VI.   Orange Judd Whitson, b. Aug. 23, 1873.   Address Bates, Mich.

2310.   VII.   Herbert Gleason Whitson, b. Feb. 10, 1876; d.
1880.

2311.   VIII.   Lawrence Whitson, b. Oct. 16, 1879.   Res. 1908,
Harriman, Tenn.

887.   THOMAS BOND (Ellis-Samuel-Samuel-Joseph), born
March 31, 1848; married April 28, 1871: Rachel E. Vancil, daughter of Daniel and Amelia (Byers) Vancil.   Address 1904, Lakeside, Wn.   Children:

2312.   I.   Amelia V., b. Nov. 17, 1873, in Kansas.

2313.   II.   Celia, b. Sept. 3, 1876.

2314.   III.   Ralph, b. April 3, 1879.

2315.   IV.   Mabel, b. April 2, 1882.

2316.   V.   Abbie, b. Jan. 10, 1885.

891.   HARVEY MENDENHALL (Rhoda (Bond)-Samuel-
Samuel-Joseph), born Feb. 22, 1846; died June 7, 1901; married
Nov. 17, 1867: Sarah E. Quigg; issue four children.   Residence,
Wayne County, Ind.   N. f. k.

892.   SAMUEL BOND MENDENHALL (Rhoda (Bond)-
Samuel-Samuel-Joseph), born April 23, 1848, in Wayne County,
Ind.; died Dec. 3, 1892; married Sept. 26, 1872: Mary Amanda
Borton, daughter of Eber and Cynthia (Roberts) Borton; she
was born June 23, 1852.   Residence, Wayne County, Ind.   Chil-
dren:

2322.   I.   Mark C. Mendenhall, b. Nov. 7, 1873; m. 1898:
Pearl C. Moore.   Address Richmond, Ind.

2323.   II.   Blanche E. Mendenhall, b. March 31, 1877; m.
Oct. 1, 1902: Lawrence J. Grace.

2324.   III.   Inez C. Mendenhall, b. April 11, 1888.

893. JONATHAN MENDENHALL (Rhoda (Bond)-Samuel-Samuel-Joseph), born June 15, 1850; married Martha J. Caty; issue, 4 children, 2 living. Residence, Webster, Wayne County, Ind.

894. CHARITY MENDENHALL (Rhoda (Bond)-Samuel-Samuel-Joseph), born Feb. 21, 1855; married Dec. 24, 1874: Henry Atkins, of Webster, Ind. Issue, 3 children, 1 living. N. f. k.

895. WILLIAM CLAYTON MENDENHALL (Rhoda (Bond)-Samuel-Samuel-Joseph), born Jan. 25, 1857; died Jan. 25, 1907; married Sept. 10, 1878: Annie R. Newby. Issue, 4 children, 3 living. N. f. k.

897. MARIETTA MENDENHALL (Rhoda (Bond)-Samuel-Samuel-Joseph), born Dec. 25, 1863; married Dec. 25, 1886: Charles Marine; he died Sept. 3, 1891; issue, 2 sons. She married second: Nathan E. Overman. Residence, Richmond, Ind. N. f. k.

898. LEWIS BOND (Jesse-Samuel-Samuel-Joseph), born Dec. 16, 1854; married Lucretia Green. Residence, Marion, Ind. No issue. N. f. k.

899. MARY ANN BOND (Jesse-Samuel-Samuel-Joseph), born Sept. 21, 1856; married Jacob Quickell. Residence, Davenport, Ia. No issue.

900. ELLIS BOND (Jesse-Samuel-Samuel-Joseph), born Aug. 13, 1859; married Oct. 8, 1882: Francelia M. Tripp. Residence, Richmond, Ind. Children:

2337.   I.   Marie, b. Dec. 18, 1885.

2338.   II.   Hazel.

918. DE WITT CLINTON BOND (Nathan-Elizabeth-Samuel-Joseph), born 1841; died Oct. 9, 1901; married July 30, 1863: Lucy L. Ball. Residence, Williamsburg, Ind. Children:

o2338.   I.   Mary Ellen, b. March 1, 1865.

2339.   II.   William A., b. Aug. 19, 1866.

2340.   III.   Martha F., b. July 18, 1887.

926. LUCINDA BOND (Nathan-Ornon-Samuel-Joseph), born Nov. 17, 1849, in Hamilton County, Ind.; married March 6, 1870, in Kansas: William Mesenhimer; she died March 10, 1892. Children:

2341.   I.   Schuyler C. Mesenhimer, b. Jan. 8, 1872.

2342.   II.   Alwilda Mesenhimer, b. Jan. 3, 1875.

927. SYLVESTER W. BOND (Nathan-Ornon-Samuel-Joseph), born April 26, 1853, in Hamilton County, Ind.; married first, Jan., 1875: Elizabeth Jane Metsker, of Douglas County, Kas. Children:

2343.   I.   Tena, b. Nov., 1875.

He married second, Oct. 12, 1884: Luella Brown, a native of Cherokee Nation, one-eighth Indian blood. · Residence, Vinita, Okla. Children:

2344.   II.   Carrie L., b. Aug. 25, 1885; d. Aug. 2, 1886.

2345.   III.   Eddie Sanders, b. March 24, 1887.

2346.   IV.   William Penn, b. July 2, 1892.

2347.   V.   Albert Harland, b. April 28, 1896.

She died. He married third.

928. MELVINA BOND (Nathan-Ornon-Samuel-Joseph), born Dec. 3, 1853, in Hamilton County, Ind.; married Jan. 1, 1873, in Douglas County, Kas.: Anson Wellington Fisher, a farmer, born in Ohio, March 16, 1848, son of Henry C. and Mary Fisher. Residence, Overbrook, Kas. Children:

2348.   I.   Jennie Belle Fisher, b. Oct. 30, 1873.

2349.   II.   Albert Wilbur Fisher, b. March 15, 1876.

2350.   III.   Harry Wellington Fisher, b. Feb. 27, 1879.

2351.   IV.   Gertrude Mildred Fisher, b. May 2, 1884.

930. ELLEN BOND (John-Ornon-Samuel-Joseph), born in Indiana; married in Kansas, April 2, 1871: William Henderson; she died June 1, 1898. Resided Indiana, Missouri, Kansas. Children:

2352.   I.   Frank Henderson, b. March 19, 1872.

2353.   II.   Henry Henderson, b. Feb. 16, 1874.

2354.   III.   Ora Henderson, b. Oct. 29, 1875.

2355.   IV.   Odessa Henderson, b. Nov. 19, 1877.

2356.   V.   Letitia Henderson, b. May 16, 1879.

2357.   VI.   William Henderson, b. April 2, 1882; d. inft.

2358.   VII.   Charles Henderson, b. Aug. 21, 1884.

2359.   VIII.   Virgie Henderson, b. Feb. 7, 1887.

932. CLOVESTA J. BOND (John-Ornon-Samuel-Joseph), born Feb. 26, 1856, in Indiana; married in Iroquois County, Ill., March 19, 1874: Sarah Ann Caulkins, born Oct. 14, 1855. Residence 1905, Keokuk Falls, Okla. Children:

2360.   I.   William Henry, b. Dec. 7, 1874.

2361.   II.   Mary Malinda, b. Dec. 18, 1876; d. inft.

2362. III. Estella, b. Oct. 26, 1878; d. 1879.

2363. IV. Eliza, b. April 10, 1880.

2364. V. Clovesta H., b. Jan. 26, 1882.

933. NATHAN MILTON BOND (John-Ornon-Samuel-Joseph), born April 7, 1861, in Hamilton County, Ind.; married in Franklin County, Kas., Nov. 30, 1882: Eva J. Yockey, born May 1, 1857, daughter of Milton and Sarah Yockey. Residence 1904, Dearing, Kas. Children:

2365. I. John Henry, b. Nov. 29, 1883; d. Sept. 11, 1885.

2366. II. Bertha May, b. July 1, 1885.

2367. III. Milton Leroy, b. April 5, 1889.

2368. IV. Mina Pearl, b. Feb. 8, 1892.

2369. V. Ruth Grace, b. April 22, 1895.

2370. VI. Nellie Nora, b. Oct. 18, 1899.

934. ELIZABETH ANN BOND (John-Ornon-Samuel-Joseph), born in Indiana; married, in Kansas: James J. Hanby. Residence 1904, Coffeyville, Kas. N. f. k.

935. ELZENA BOND (John-Ornon-Samuel-Joseph), writes her name Ella, born March 23, 1865; married first, in Kansas, Feb. 12, 1890: Alvin E. Martin, born May 6, 1863; died Nov. 5, 1898. Children:

2371. I. James Dunlavy Martin, b. April 6, 1891.

2372. II. Clarence Bond Martin, b. Oct. 13, 1894.

She married second, Nov. 28, 1901: James Robert Berry, a native of Kentucky, born March 7, 1869. Residence 1904, Brandenburg, Ky.

936. RHODA ROSELLA BOND (John-Ornon-Samuel-Joseph), married Deo Wilkerson. Residence, Coffeyville, Kas. N. f. k.

937. RACHEL M. BOND (John-Ornon-Samuel-Joseph), born Oct. 11, 1869; married March 7, 1885: George Miller, born April 10, 1861. Residence 1903, Flora, Oregon. Children:

2375. I. David Miller, b. Dec. 16, 1885; died childhood.

2376. II. Cora Miller, b. April 9, 1888.

2377. III. Walter Miller, b. Jan. 9, 1891.

2378. IV. Ollie Miller, b. Dec. 20, 1893; d. Oct. 30, 1894.

2379. V. Elsie Miller, b. Feb. 1, 1896.

2380. VI. George A. Miller, b. July 12, 1898; d. May 11, 1899.

2381. VII. Florence Miller, b. March 30, 1900.

2382. VIII.   John Miller, b. Aug. 3, 1903.

938.   JAMES G. BOND (Jesse-Ornon-Samuel-Joseph), born May 9, 1854, in Hamilton County, Ind.; married in Iowa, Martitia Underwood, born May 6, 1855, daughter of Exum and Jane M. (Hutchins) Underwood.   Children:

2383.   I.   Grace, b. June 28, 1878; d. Oct., 1885.   N. f. k.

940.   LINDLEY A. BOND (Jesse-Ornon-Samuel-Joseph), born Sept. 14, 1857; married Aug. 23, 1871: Rosella Randall. Children:

2384.   I.   Pierre Alice, b. Dec. 19, 1872.   N. f. k.

941.   VIOLA A. BOND (Jesse-Ornon-Samuel-Joseph), born in Hamilton County, Ind., Nov. 1, 1860; married Aug. 29, 1880: William Allen, born Dec. 4, 1856, in Indiana.   Residence 1904, Otego, Jewel County, Kas.   Children:

2385.   I.   Lydia Allen, b. Sept. 7, 1883.

2386.   II.   Jesse Allen, b. Nov. 21, 1885.

2387.   III.   Albert Allen, b. Sept. 4, 1887.

2388.   IV.   Bertha Allen, b. Sept. 28, 1891.

2389.   V.   Lillie Allen, b. April 9, 1893.

2390.   VI.   Bessie Allen, b. Oct. 29, 1898.

952.   CLARA ETTA BOND (Joel-Ornon-Samuel-Joseph), born April 9, 1861; married May 24, 1883: Forrest Augustus Tanner, born Dec. 15, 1858, in New York.   Occupation, farmer. Residence 1905, Fort Collins, Colo.   Children:

2500.   I.   Lloyd L. Tanner, b. Feb. 21, 1884.

2501.   II.   Mabel M. Tanner, b. March 14, 1885.

2502.   III.   Chauncey Earl Tanner, b. Nov. 15, 1886.

2503.   IV.   Joel Marion Tanner, b. Aug. 21, 1888; d. inft.

2504.   V.   Charles Glenn Tanner, b. Nov. 25, 1890.

2505.   VI.   Della Blanche Tanner, b. Aug. 12, 1892.

2506.   VII.   Hazel Mary Tanner, b. Nov. 14, 1893.

2507. VIII.   Alma Almeda Tanner, b. Nov. 21, 1898.

953.   FRANKLIN ORNON BOND (Joel-Ornon-Samuel-Joseph), born July 20, 1863, in Indiana; died June 24, 1900; married Oct. 30, 1886: Jessie Sheard, born Dec. 4, 1866, daughter of Percival and Cecilia Sheard, of Jewel Co., Kas.   They separated July 13, 1894.   Residence, Esbon, Jewel County, Kas.   Children:

2508.   I.   Myrtle, b. Aug. 20, 1887.

2509.   II.   Florence E., b. Oct. 7, 1888.

2510. III. Joel, b. Feb. 9, 1890; d. inft.

2511. IV. Raymond, b. March 10, 1891.

2512. V. Golda, b. Feb. 1, 1893.

2513. VI. Mabel, b. Feb. 22, 1895.

955. RACHEL ANNE MAY BOND (Joel-Ornon-Samuel-Joseph), born June 22, 1870; married Aug. 28, 1892: John O. Stevenson. Residence, Stuart, Ia. Children:

2514. I. Abeula Stevenson, b. Oct. 12, 1893.

2515. II. Eva May Stevenson, b. Jan. 23, 1895.

2516. III. Margaret Lavina Stevenson, b. March 4, 1903.

957. ROSA ESTELLA BOND (Joel-Ornon-Samuel-Joseph), born July 25, 1872; married Feb. 22, 1893: Charles Beck. Residence, 1905, Des Moines, Ia. Children:

2517. I. Bessie V. Beck, b. March 21, 1894.

2518. II. Bertie Beck, b. May 16, 1898; d. March, 1901.

959. ELISHA NEWTON HANSON (Martha (Bond)-Ornon-Samuel-Joseph), son of Allen and Martha (Bond) Hanson, born Jan. 26, 1867, in Indiana; married April 14, 1897: Mary J. Claybaugh, born Aug. 3, 1875. Reisdence, North Branch, Kansas. Children:

2519. I. Verl William Hanson, b. May 2, 1900.

961. ELVIN RILEY HANSON (Martha (Bond) - Ornon-Samuel-Joseph), born Feb. 7, 1871; married Feb. 24, 1895: Clara A. Davis, daughter of Caleb and Mary Ann Davis. Residence, Haviland, Kas. Children:

2520. I. Lela Esther Hanson, b. Jan. 1, 1896.

2521. II. Melvin Allen Hanson, b. Sept. 14, 1899.

987. LEWIS JACKSON BOND (Joel-Joseph-John-Joseph), born Oct. 5, 1828, in Wayne County, Ky.; died Oct., 1856, accident in Missouri; married Nancy Baker. Children:

2600. I. Daughter; m. a Mr. Walters.

2601. II. N. f. k.

988. MIRANDA JANE BOND (Joel-Joseph-John-Joseph), born Feb. 17, 1830; married Oct. 10, 1850: Thomas Etter, born Feb. 17, 1831; died June 12, 1874. Residence, Girard, Ill. Ch:

2602. I. Mary Jane Etter, b. 1851; d. inft.

2603. II. Martha E. Etter, b. June 8, 1853; d. s. p. March 4, 1870.

2604. III. Malinda M. Etter, b. April 24, 1856.

2605.   IV.   William H. Etter, b. May 20, 1858; d. May 11, 1860.

2606.   V.   Lucinda Caroline Etter, b. May 11, 1863.

2607.   VI.   Thomas Marion Etter, b. Jan. 5, 1866.

2608.   VII.   Robert Etter, b. April 24, 1873; d. inft.

989.   WILLIAM SHELBY BOND (Joel-Joseph-John-Joseph), born Dec. 4, 1831, in Wayne County, Ky.; died Jan. 18, 1905, in McCoupin County, Ill.; married Dec. 24, 1859: Nancy England.   Residence, Girard, Ill.   Children:

2609.   I.   Russell, b. April 17, 1861; d. July 1, 1863, inft.

2610.   II.   James M., b. April 27, 1862.

2611.   III.   Thomas Franklin, b. Feb. 3, 1871.

1002.   MARTIN D. BOND (John-Joseph-John-Joseph), born in Wayne County, Ky.; died in Miller County, Mo.; married Charlotte Newton.   Her residence, 1905, in Oklahoma.   Ch:

2612.   I.   Simeon S.

2613.   II.   Martha Matilda; m. Malone.

2614.   III.   James P.

2615.   IV.   Catherine, d. s. p.

2616.   V.   Julia.

2617.   VI.   Isabelle; m. Henry Smith.   N. f. k.

1003.   ISAAC R. BOND (John-Joseph-John-Joseph), born in Wayne County, Ky.; died in Miller County, Mo.; married in Miller County, Mo.: Mary Tracy.   Children:

2618.   I.   Mary, d. s. p.

2619.   II.   Melvina.

2620.   III.   Thomas.   N. f. k.

1004.   WILLIAM H. BOND (John-Joseph-John-Joseph), born in Wayne County, Ky.; died in California; married Elizabeth McHenry.   Children:

2621.   I.   Jane.

2622.   II.   Joseph B.   N. f. k.

1005.   JOSEPH H. BOND (John-Joseph-John-Joseph), born 1842, in Wayne County, Ky.; died 1867 in same county; married Fannie Conley.   He was farmer, stock dealer, distiller and lieutenant in Southern army during the Civil War.   Children:

2623.   I.   John William, b. 1867.

1006.   BERRY C. BOND (John-Joseph-John-Joseph), son of John and second wife, Polly Ann Bond; born Dec. 6, 1838; married March 17, 1861: Jane Enloe, of Cole County, Mo.; she died Oct. 10, 1886. His residence, Enon, Mo. Children:

2624. I. John J., b. Aug. 15, 1862.
2625. II. Joseph C., b. Feb. 10, 1864.
2626. III. Rebecca C., b. Aug. 17, 1866; d. inft.
2627. IV. Mary L., b. July 19, 1868.
2628. V. James P., b. Nov. 18, 1870.
2629. VI. Leona F., b. Jan. 22, 1875.
2630. VII. Louis S., b. Oct. 9, 1877.
2631. VIII. Ada A., b. Aug. 11, 1881.
2632. IX. Edwin S., b. Aug. 10, 1884.

He married second March 12, 1887: Rachel R. Hays.

1024. MARSHALL BOND (Samuel-Joseph-John-Joseph), son of Samuel and Nancy (Wilhoite) Bond, born in Pickett Co., Tenn.; married in same county, Mary E. Holden. Six children, three living:

2633. I. Martha E., b. July 25, 1887; m. James M. Stephens, of Moodyville, Tenn.
2634. II. Margaret.
2635. III. Samuel Garton, b. 1885.

1027. SIMEON H. BOND (Joseph-Joseph-John-Joseph), born Jan. 11, 1830; married; had several children, two living:

2636. I. Albert.
2637. II. Elizabeth.

1028. MICAJAH BOND (Joseph-Joseph-John-Joseph), born March 30, 1832; m. Children:

2640. I. William.
2641. II. James.

1037. CHARITY MELISSA BOND (Joseph-Joseph-John-Joseph), born Sept. 1, 1851; married 1867: John M. Hill. Residence, Grandview, Mo. Children:

2642. I. William J. Hill, b. Sept. 2, 1868.
2643. II. Lucretia J. Hill, b. May 20, 1870.
2644. III. Belle Hill, b. Sept. 20, 1871.
2645. IV. Jessie Hill, b. June 20, 1874.
2646. V. Nora Hill, b. Feb. 28, 1877.
2647. VI. John S. Hill, b. Nov. 17, 1879.

1073. PETER JACKSON BOND (William-Joel-John-Joseph), born Oct. 5, 1838; married in Polk County, Mo., June 26, 1859: Mary E. McLain, born June 7, 1839. He served in Confederate army in Captain McQuiddy's company, Col. McFarland's regiment, Confederate States of America. Residence, 1905, Peel, Ore. Moved to Oregon 1889. Children:

2701.   I.   William Houston, b. May 19, 1860.
2702.   II.   Peter Guy, b. Feb. 10, 1862; d. inft.
2703.   III.   Maggie Belle, b. Dec. 24, 1863.
2704.   IV.   Howell Lenair, b. Dec. 27, 1866.
2705.   V.   May Florence, b. Aug. 2, 1870.

1074. JOEL JEFFERSON BOND (William-Joel-John-Joseph), born Feb. 1, 1841; married Betty Baker, of Columbia, Mo., daughter of Baptist preacher who came from England. Residence, 1905, Victor, Mont. Occupation, civil engineer. Served in Union army and was commissioned captain. Was also teacher, school superintendent and legislator. Had five children, one named Anna. N. f. k.

1075. WILLIAM MONROE BOND (William-Joel-John-Joseph), born 1849; married 1872: Leona Scott, daughter of Thomas J. Scott. Children:

2711.   I.   Emmet Scott.
2712.   II.   Barcia May.
2713.   III.   Arthur Jefferson.

1076. ELIZABETH BOND (William - Joel - John - Joseph), married about 1860: Dick Watson. Two children:

2714.   I.   James Watson.
2715.   II.   Sally Watson, m. N. f. k.

She married second: William Wylis. Children:

2716. III.   Nellie Wylis.
2717. IV.   Bernice. N. f. k.

1077. JAMES ASBURY BOND (William-Joel-John-Joseph), born May 14, 1856; married Nov. 6, 1876: Miss Missouri Isabelle Larkins; she died Jan. 2, 1878; was daughter of Thomas J. and Marietta (Ross) Larkins, Miss Ross being a sister to Chief Ross of the Cherokee Indians at the time of their removal from Tennessee. Residence, in 1911, Spokane, Wn. Occupation, contractor of brick and stone work. Children:

02715.   I.   Alma, b. Oct. 23, 1877. Address, Little Rock, Ark.

He married second July 3, 1880: Melissa Addie Hildreth, widow of James, and daughter of James Swinney. Children:

02716. II.   May, b. March 21, 1885.

02717. III. William Edward, b. April 20, 1888.

2718. IV. Minnie, b. Jan. 18, 1891.

1078. JOHN RODNEY BOND (Stephen-Joel-John-Joseph), born Feb. 7, 1842; married Jan. 27, 1870: America Hudson, born May 1, 1850, daughter of James and Mary Hudson. Residence, Caneyville, Ky. Children:

2719. I. William Thomas, b. Aug. 6, 1871.

2720. II. Mary Frances, b. Aug. 7, 1873.

2721. III. John R., b. Sept. 9, 1882; d. inft., 1882.

1079. THOMAS M. BOND (Stephen - Joel - John - Joseph), born Feb. 2, 1844; married Amanda E. Wilson. Residence, Caneyville, Ky. Children:

2722. I. Oscar Stephen, b. Dec. 15, 1876.

2723. II. James Ross, b.

2724. III. George William.

2725. IV. Susan H.

1081. MELISSA BOND (Stephen-Joel-John-Joseph), born Feb. 15, 1856; married William Jasper Wilson. Residence, Caneyville, Ky. They have a duaghter, Carrie W., wife of Thomas Spurrier, of Caneyville, Ky. N. f. k.

1083. ULYSSES G. BOND (Stephen - Joel - John - Joseph), born March 17, 1863; married Rebecca Parish. Residence, Clarkson, Ky. History wanted.

1084. MAHALA JANE BOND (Stephen-Joel-John-Joseph), born Oct. 13, 1867; married John M. Jones. N. f. k.

1100. JOSEPH D. HINDS (Jane (Bond)-Isaac-John-Joseph), son of Benjamin and Jane (Hinds) Bond; married Martha J. Johnson. He was a soldier in an Illinois regiment during the Civil War. Children, so far as known:

2801. I. Isaac B. Hinds, of Aubrey, Texas.

2802. II. Mathew Hinds.

2803. III. John B. Hinds, of Kidder, Mo.

2804. IV. Henry L. Hinds, of Spring Garden, Mo. N. f. k.

1117. MARY JANE HUTCHISON (Amner (Bond)-Isaac John-Joseph), daughter of James M. and Amner Beeson (Bond) Hutchison; born Oct. 4, 1848; married Leander Fulton. Residence, Rankin, Wayne County, Ky. Children:

2805. I. George Fulton, b. Jan. 29, 1876.

2806. II. Charles Fulton, b. Aug. 15, 1877.

2807. III. Vada Fulton, b. Jan. 25, 1881.

2808.   IV.   Clarence Fulton, b. Sept. 5, 1885.   N. f. k.

1118.   ISAAC BOND HUTCHISON (Amner (Bond)-Isaac-John-Joseph), born July 29, 1850; married Feb. 6, 1877: Angeline Kelly, born March 17, 1855; she died July 25, 1887.   Residence, Slick Rock, Barren Co., Ky.   Children:

2809.   I.   James Grant Hutchison, b. Jan. 25, 1878; physician.

2810.   II.   John Kelly Hutchison, b. April 11, 1879.

These two sons served in Cuban war; also in Philippines.

1125.   JOHN WILLIAM BOND (Isaac-William-John-Joseph), born Aug. 28, 1849; married.   Residence, Russellville, Mo.   Has children.   N. f. k.

1126.   MARTIN SAMUEL BOND (Isaac-William-John-Joseph), born Feb. 18, 1851; died Feb. 14, 1902; married Aug. 13, 1871: Eliza Simpson, born Jan. 10, 1853.   Residence, Cole Co. Mo.   Children:

2900.   I.   Maud, b. July 6, 1872.
2901.   II.   Annie, b. Nov. 1, 1875.
2902.   III.   Emma Leona, b. Jan. 14, 1880.
2903.   IV.   Alvan Louis, b. Feb. 27, 1883.
2904.   V.   Estella Luella, b. Dec. 9, 1885.
2905.   VI.   Dora Jordan, b. May 18, 1889.
2906.   VII.   John Thomas, b. Feb. 9, 1894.

1127.   CHARITY ANN BOND (Isaac-William-John-Joseph), born Sept. 16, 1852; married first Jan. 2, 1870: John Blank, born June 27, 1853; died Aug. 1, 1875.   Children:

2907.   I.   Henry Blank, b. Nov. 9, 1874.

Married second Jan. 17, 1878: Turner Wilkerson Cliburn. Residence, Cole County, Mo.   Children:

2908.   II.   Jennie Cliburn, b. Jan. 11, 1879; d. s. p. Oct. 11, 1882.

2909.   III.   Hattie Cliburn, b. July 29, 1882.
2910.   IV.   Lucy Cliburn, b. Oct. 26, 1884; d. Oct. 29, 1888.
2911.   V.   Daniel Harrison Cliborn, b. April 25, 1889.
2912.   VI.   Birdette Cliburn, b. May 20, 1892.

1130.   MARY ELIZABETH BOND (Isaac-William-John-Joseph), born Dec. 13, 1856; married John Conway Odell, born July 27, 1840; died Nov. 12, 1891, a soldier in Co. E, Fifth (?) Missouri Cavalry.   Children:

2913.   I.   Edward L. Odell, b. Sept. 2, 1876.

2914. II. Elias A. Odell, b. Sept. 16, 1878.

2915. III. Samuel Odell, b. Dec. 13, 1881; d. inft.

2916. IV. John N. Odell, b. Nov. 25.

2917. V. Evaline Odell.

She married second Aug. 17, 1898: Franklin M. Tribett. Residence, Russellville, Cole Co., Mo.

1131. ISAAC DANIEL BOND (Isaac-William-John-Joseph), born Oct. 6, 1858; married Nov. 10, 1876: Lena E. Steenbarger; she died May 20, 1883. He is a carpenter and contractor and Judge of the Court. Residence, Russellville, Cole County, Mo. Children:

2918. I. William A.

2919. II. Minnie.

2920. III. Leona.

He married second Nov. 6, 1886: Jennie G. Jordon, daughter of Dr. W. D. Jordon, of Hickory Hill, Mo.

1132. LEWIS BENJAMIN BOND (Isaac-William-John-Joseph), born April 9, 1860; married Jan. 20, 1884: Emma Jane Vaughan, born Aug. 4, 1866. Residence, Hickory Hill, Cole County, Mo. Farmer. He died July, 1909. Children:

2921. I. Anna Lee, b. Nov. 3, 1884.

2922. II. Virginia Maud, b. Jan. 8, 1887.

2923. III. Charles Fountain, b. Dec. 16, 1889.

2924. IV. Daniel Ward, b. Feb. 24, 1892.

2925. V. Dee Nolen, b. July 16, 1894.

2926. VI. Melvin Grant, b. Dec. 20, 1889.

2927. VII. Benjamin Paul, b. May 20, 1903.

1133. JOHN WILLIAM BOND (William S.-William-John-Joseph), born Oct. 14, 1855; married April 17, 1891: Cora M. Rowe, daughter of John and Nancy Rowe. Reside near Eugene, Cole County, Mo. Occupation, farmer. Children:

2928. I. Dollie Myrtle, b. Feb. 19, 1893; d. March 1, 1895.

2929. II. Bertha May, b. Feb. 22, 1894.

2930. III. Grace Maud, b. Feb. 20, 1895.

2931. IV. John Wesley, b. Dec. 11, 1896.

2932. V. Ivy Dewey, b. Oct. 10, 1898.

2933. VI. Lydia Bell, b. Jan. 14, 1900.

2934. VII. Edna Pearl, b. March 13, 1902.

2935. VIII. Emmet Lee, b. Oct. 5, 1905.

END OF SIXTH GENERATION.

CHAPTER VII.

SEVENTH GENERATION.

1142. LUCINDA THORNBURG (Athalinda (Bond) - Edward-Benjamin-Edward-Joseph), born March 7, 1848; died Sept. 14, 1900, in Lee County, Ia.; married ————. N. f. k.

1143. ABNER EDWARD THORNBURG (Athalinda (Bond)-Edward-Benjamin-Edward-Joseph), born in Lee County, Iowa; married. P. O. address, 1910, Salem, Iowa.

1144. WILLIAM EDWARD BOND (Jedidiah - Edward - Benjamin-Edward-Joseph), born Dec. 2, 1856, in Lee County, Ia.; moved with his parents to Polk County, Mo., 1866; married April 24, 1885: Susie A. Wilcher. Address, 1910, Violet, Mo. Children:

3000.	I.	Effie, b. Sept. 29, 1886.
3001.	II.	Ida May, b. Jan. 19, 1888.
3002.	III.	Lydia Rachel, b. Nov. 25, 1889.
3003.	IV.	Lula Viola, b. Nov. 11, 1891.
3004.	V.	Nellie, b. Feb. 10, 1893.
3005.	VI.	Exonia, b. April 6, 1894.
3006.	VII.	Jasper A., b. Oct. 20, 1895.
3007.	VIII.	Oscar B., b. Jan. 20, 1897.
3008.	IX.	Lottie D., b. April 7, 1900.
3009.	X.	Lizzie, b. Aug. 15, 1902.

1145. IDA JANE BOND (Jedidiah-Edward-Benjamin-Edward-Joseph), born Jan. 1, 1858, in Iowa; married Sept. 2, 1879: John Thornton Wynkoop. Residence, 1910, Eudora, Polk Co., Mo. Children:

3010.	I.	Daisy A. Wynkoop, b. Oct. 14, 1880.
3011.	II.	William J. Wynkoop, b. Jan. 30, 1882.
3012.	III.	Laura L. Wynkoop, b. July 13, 1884.
3013.	IV.	Adelbert M. Wynkoop, b. July 21, 1886.
3014.	V.	Susie M. Wynkoop, b. Jan. 7, 1888.
3015.	VI.	Maud L. Wynkoop, b. April 15, 1890.
3016.	VII.	Amos A. Wynkoop, b. June 18, 1892.
3017.	VIII.	Martha B. Wynkoop, b. Feb. 23, 1894.
3018.	IX.	Anna R. Wynkoop, b. Jan. 17, 1896.
3019.	X.	Ida B. Wynkoop, b. March 9, 1897; d. Feb. 10, 1898.
3020.	XI.	John M. Wynkoop, and

3021. XII. James M. Wynkoop, twins, b. May 16, 1900.

3022. XIII. Ingra Wynkoop, b. Nov. 19, 1903.

1147. AMOS MARTIN BOND (Jedidiah-Edward-Benja-min-Edward-Joseph), born July 19, 1863, in Lee County, Iowa. Moved with his parents in 1866 to Missouri; married May 24, 1886: Laura Catherine Young; she died June 15, 1907. His address, 1910, Slater, Mo. R. F. D. 1. Children:

3023. I. Raymond Jedediah, b. March.11, 1887, at Miami, Mo.; m. July 24, 1907: Minnie Jackson. Res., Miami, Mo.

3024. II. Ruby Mae, b. July 8, 1889, at Ash Grove, Mo.; m. Oct. 22, 1906: William C. Harris. Res., Slater, Mo.

3025. III. Gertrude Augusta, b. Jan. 18, 1892; m. Jan. 12, 1910, Marvin W. Lawler. Res., Slater, Mo. R. F. D. 2.

3026. IV. Florence Riva, b. Dec. 14, 1893.

3027. V. Coin Allen, b. Feb. 28, 1896.

3028. VI. Morris Benjamin, b. Oct. 10, 1898, at Miami, Mo.

3029. VII. Ralph Amos, b. Jan. 22, 1901.

VIII. Katheline Oriana, b. Dec. 26, 1904.

IX. Laura Catherine, b. June 6, 1907.

1150. ELMINA JANE HASTINGS (Luzena (Bond)-Jedidiah-Benjamin-Edward-Joseph), born June 25, 1853; married March 23, 1871: D. Sylvester Patty. Residence, 1910, Redfield, Iowa. Children:

3030. I. William Patty, b. Aug. 25, 1872; d. Dec. 10, 1874.

3031. II. Lillian Patty, b. Oct. 11, 1874; d. Oct. 14, 1874.

3032. III. Mary L. Patty, b. Aug. 14, 1876.

3033. IV. Carl Patty, b. Dec. 5, 1878.

3034. V. Luzena D. Patty, b. Feb. 13, 1882.

3035. VI. Laura Patty, b. ——.

3036. VII. Willard Patty, b. March 9, 1892.

1151. NATHAN L. HASTINGS (Luzena (Bond)-Jedidiah-Benjamin-Edward-Joseph), born Sept. 23, 1855; married Feb. 18, 1876: Rhoda Huldah Grinnell, daughter of J. A. and Martha. Residence, 1910, Maryville, Tenn. Children:

3037. I. Mary Lena Hastings, b. April 17, 1877.

3038. II. Linneaus Roy Hastings, b. Sept. 21, 1879.

3039. III. Ellen Pearl Hastings, b. May 11, 1882.

3040. IV. Kittie Hastings, b. Aug. 5, 1886, d. June 8, 1887.

3041. V. Rosa Evalyn Hastings, b. Oct. 29, 1889.

3042. VI. Faith Hastings, b. Feb. 7, 1898; d. Feb. 11, 1898.

1152. LETITIA ANGELINE HASTINGS (Luzena (Bond) Jedidiah-Benjamin-Edward-Joseph), born June 29, 1858; married Oct. 6, 1879: William O. Garner. Residence, 1910, Cleremont, Cal. Children:

3043. I. Herman Garner.
3044. II. Karl Garner, b. Nov. 12, 1890.

1153. DR. WILLIAM WALTER HASTINGS (Luzena (Bond)-Jedidiah-Benjamin-Edward-Joseph), born Nov. 1, 1865;, married June 22, 1897: Elizabeth Fairbank. Residence 1910, Springfield, Mass. Children:

3045. I. William Hastings, b. Aug. 6, 1898.
3046. II. Allen Wood Hastings, b. Jan. 17, 1900.
3047. III. Stanley Bond Hastings, b. Dec. 7, 1901.

1155. ERNEST EDWIN HASTINGS (Luzena (Bond)-Jedidiah-Benjamin-Edward-Joseph), born Sept. 5, 1872; married July 27, 1896: Helen Patterson Kirkwood. Residence 1910, Kerman, Cal. Children:

3048. I. Helen Hastings, b. June 12, 1897.
3049. II. Mildred Hastings, b. Oct. 2, 1898.
3050. III. Ernest Hastings, b. Dec. 26, 1900; d. July 7, 1902.
3051. IV. Charles Hastings, b. Oct. 4, 1902.

1182. CHARLES ELLSWORTH BOND (William P.-Nathan-Benjamin-Edward-Joseph), born June 25, 1866; married Alice A. Black. Children:

3052. I. Wallace Binford.
3053. II. Dorothy R.
3054. III. Irene.

1184. CLARK WATSON BOND (William P.-Nathan-Benjamin-Edward-Joseph), born Feb. 12, 1874; married Oct. 17, 1894: Elsie Effie Purdy, born Oct. 17, 1876. Residence, Denver, Colo. Children:

3055. I. Orville Ernest, b. Oct. 23, 1895.
3056. II. Russell Gilbert, b. Aug. 22, 1897.
3057. III. Gladys Lanore, b. June 10, 1900.
3058. IV. Everett Roy, b. Oct. 1, 1902.
3059. V. Marjorie May, b. Oct. 29, 1904.

1185. HARRY BERTIE BOND (William P.-Nathan-Benjamin-Edward-Joseph), born Dec. 25, 1872; married Jessie Templeton, born Aug. 17, 1876. Occupation, merchant. Residence 1910, Burnham, Neb. Children:

3060. I. Dick Greenwood, b. March 22, 1897.
3061. II. Happy, b. Aug. 22, 1899.
3062. III. Ona, b. May 4, 1901.
3063. IV. Penn Marcus, b. Dec. 23, 1903.

1186. WILLIAM DELBERT BOND (William P.-Nathan-Benjamin-Edward-Joseph), born March 12, 1877; married Sept. 9, 1902: Bertha Belle Caswell. Children:

3064. I. Theodore, b. Oct. 28, 1903.

1192. ABBIE BOND (Elihu-Nathan-Benjamin-Edward-Joseph), born April 5, 1878, in Ringold County, Iowa.

1194. BESSIE BOND (Elihu-Nathan-Benjamin-Edward-Joseph), born April 20, 1891, at Hay Spring, Sheridan County, Neb.

1196. LEVI BOND (John-William-John-Edward-Joseph), born Sept. 29, 1849; married Mary Ellen Fouts; after his decease she married James Mower. Residence 1905, Indianapolis, Ind. Children:

3065. I. Lalah.
3066. II. Nellie.

1197. MARY BOND (John-William-John-Edward-Joseph), born Sept. 23, 1846; married Dec. 25, 1884: Emanuel Sears; he died. Children:

3067. I. Earnest Sears, b. Aug., 1888.

She married second, Jan. 12, 1899: John Hawkins. Residence, near Mooreland, Henry County, Ind.

1202. JOHN A. BOND (John-William-John-Edward-Joseph), born Jan. 3, 1856; died Jan. 27, 1900; married Jane, daughter of Moses and Adelpha Brown. Residence, Mooreland, Ind. Children:

3068. I. Minnie, and
3069. II. Clara, twins.
3070. III. Amy.
3071. IV. Clifford.

1203. JOEL E. BOND (John-William-John-Edward-Joseph), born July 17, 1858, in Henry County, Ind.; married Dec. 14, 1884: Susan Yauky, born Jan. 31, 1862, daughter of Jacob and Katherine (Hannenger) Yauky. Residence, New Castle, Ind., R. F. D., No. 6. Occupation, farmer. Children:

3072. I. Loring, b. May 8, 1886.

1205. SARAH ELIZABETH BOND (John-William-John-Edward-Joseph), born Jan. 25, 1867; married Nelson Allen. Residence, near Messick, Henry County, Ind. Children:

3073. · I. Nellie Allen.
3074. II. Murray Allen.
3075. III. Dexter Allen.

1206. WILLIAM DAVIS (Amelia (Bond)-William-John-Edward-Joseph), son of Spencer and Amelia (Bond) Davis, born ——; married Mattie Remington; he died Dec. 13, 1902. Residence, Henry County, Ind. Five children. N. f. k.

1208. AMOS DAVIS (Amelia (Bond)-William-John-Edward-Joseph), born in Henry County, Ind.; married Esther Ann Hill; he died 1902. Residence, Henry County, Ind. Had seven children, five living. N. f. k.

1210. MILES DAVIS (Amelia (Bond)-William-John-Edward-Joseph), born in Henry County, Ind.; married Nancy J. Carey. Residence, Mooreland, Ind. Three children. N. f. k.

1211. JOSEPH DAVIS (Amelia (Bond)-William-John-Edward-Joseph), born in Henry County, Ind.; married —— Wilkinson. Residence, Messick, Ind. N. f. k.

1212. ELIZABETH DAVIS (Amelia (Bond)-William-John-Edward-Joseph), born in Henry County, Ind.; married Mordecai Lundy. Residence, Losantville, Ind. N. f. k.

1214. ELIZABETH MARSHALL (Gulielma (Bond)-William-John-Edward-Joseph), born Dec. 18, 1842; married Aug. 25, 1859: Allen Compton, born Feb. 5, 1830, son of Nathan and Nancy (Wayne) Compton, of Henry County, Ind. Residence, Killduff, Jasper County, Iowa. Children:

3076. I. Nathan A. Compton, b. July 10, 1861.
3077. II. William E. Compton, b. July 25, 1864; d. Dec. 10, 1865.
3078. III. Sylvester M. Compton, b. Nov. 18, 1866.
3079. IV. Dora A. Compton, b. July 24, 1869.
3080. V. Lennie M. Compton, b. Dec. 29, 1871.
3081. VI. Albert A. Compton, b. Jan. 22, 1875.

1215. ANNA JANE MARSHALL (Gulielma (Bond)-William-John-Edward-Joseph), born Nov. 4, 1844; married April 26, 1866: Jehiel Bond, for history see No. 797, Jehiel Bond. Children:

3082.   I.   Clara.   (See 2082.)

3083.   II.   S. Edgar.   (See 2083.)

3084.   III.   Jennie.   (See 2084.)

1217.   EMELINE HEALTON (Mary A. (Bond)-William-John-Edward-Joseph), born Dec. 22, 1848, in Henry County, Ind.; died Aug. 21, 1884; married Levi Beals, son of Joseph. Residence, near Messick, Ind.   Children:

3085.   I.   Son, deceased.

3086.   II.   Lillie Beals, m. Omer Davis, son of Amos and Esther.

1218.   WILLIAM B. HEALTON (Mary A. (Bond)-William-John-Edward-Joseph), born April 17, 1851; married Mary E. Millican.   Residence, Henry County, Ind.   Three children. N. f. k.

1219.   JOHN A. HEALTON (Mary A. (Bond)-William-John-Edward-Joseph), born Jan. 21, 1854; married Ella Koons, daughter of Peter and Catherine.   Residence, near Messick, Ind.   Five children.   N. f. k.

1220.   ALBERT M. HEALTON (Mary A. (Bond)-William-John-Edward-Joseph), born Jan. 27, 1856; married Hannah Wilkinson.   Residence, Henry County, Ind.   N. f. k.

1224.   NATHAN MARCUS HEALTON (Mary A. (Bond)-William-John-Edward-Joseph), born March 25, 1866, in Henry County, Ind.; married Grace Beals, daughter of Aaron.   Residence, Mooreland, Ind.   Children:

3087.   I.   Edward Healton.

3088.   II.   Wilbur Healton.

1225.   MARY ELLEN HEALTON (Mary A. (Bond)-William-John-Edward-Joseph), born Dec. 28, 1868; married Lewis Wilkinson.   N. f. k.

1253.   ROBERT EARL BOND (John-Jesse-John-Edward-Joseph), born Feb. 14, 1876; married Julia May Abel.   Residence, Oregon, Holt County, Mo.   Children:

3089.   I.   Viola Charline.

3090.   II.   Mildred Minerva.

3091.   III.   Andrew Gerald.

1254.   WILBUR O'NEIL BOND (John-Jesse-John-Edward-Joseph), born Feb. 8, 1878; married Anna Laura Bimberger. Residence, Holt County, Mo.   Children:

3092.   I.   Lillian Pearl.

3093. II. Earl.

3094. III. John Franklin.

3095. IV. Stella.

1258. ANNA MARY BOND (Stephen-Jesse-John-Edward-Joseph), born March 20, 1865; married April 8, 1885: Albert Stafford, born in Nebraska, May 20, 1860, son of Lemuel and Nancy. Occupation, carpenter and contractor. Residence 1910, 553 Elizabeth street, San Francisco, Cal. Children:

3096. I. Mabel Moss Stafford, b. Aug. 14, 1886, in Holt County, Mo.

3097. II. Nellie Madge Stafford, b. Oct. 30, 1888.

3098. III. Stephen Sedley Stafford, b. Aug. 16, 1892, in Butte Co., Cal.

3099 IV. Stella May Stafford, b. Dec. 23, 1894, in Holt Co., Mo.

3100. V. Albert H. and

3101. VI. Anita Hester Stafford, twins, b. Sept. 23, 1902.

1259. NANCY FRANCES BOND (Stephen-Jesse-John-Edward-Joseph), born Oct. 19, 1866; married March 23, 1884: Joel David Hildebrand; he died Oct. 21, 1903. She resides at Mound City, Mo. Children:

3102. I. Lula May Hildebrand, b. Feb. 6, 1885.

3103. II. Goldie Elizabeth Hildebrand, b. July 8, 1886; died Sept. 19, 1887, inft.

3104. III. Myrtle Salome Hildebrand, b. May 29, 1889.

3105. IV. Mary Gertrude Hildebrand, b. March 23, 1895.

1260. WILLIAM SEDLEY BOND (Stephen-Jesse-John-Edward-Joseph), born May 8, 1868; married May 26, 1901: Ada Belle West, born Nov. 14, 1880. Residence 1910; Maitland, Holt County, Mo. Children:

3106. I. Edgar Earl Bond, b. Sept. 23, 1902.

1261. REBECCA LUELLA BOND (Stephen-Jesse-John-Edward-Joseph), born July 22, 1870; married John Merrell Norvell, born Sept. 4, 1858. Residence 1910, Lookeba, Okla. Children:

3107. I. Velva Floy Norvell, b. Dec. 2, 1892.

3108. II. Jessie Elva Norvell, b. Aug. 28, 1895.

3109. III. Inez Josie Norvell, b. Sept. 24, 1897.

1265. ISOM ROBERT BOND (Abel-Joshua-John-Edward-Joseph), born in what is now Yadkin County, N. C., Feb. 10,

1845; married May 30, 1864: in Emporia, Kas.: Elizabeth Hunt, daughter of Joel and Mary; she died Sept. 15, 1866; he married second, Feb. 14, 1869: Alma Pearson, born in Clinton County, O., Aug. 20, 1850, daughter of Lewis and Mary Ann (Hunt) Pearson. Occupation, stone mason. Residence, Roosevelt, Okla. Children:

3110.   I.   Almeda, b. Jan. 29, 1870.
3111.   II.   Irva Hillyard, b. Jan. 22, 1872.
3112.   III. Ida, b. Dec. 29, 1873.
3113.   IV.   Arzella, b. Feb. 6, 1876; d. lnft.
3114.   V.   Ardella, b. Feb. 9, 1878; d. inft.
3115.   VI.   Earl, b. Feb. 23, 1880.
3116.   VII. Myrtle, b. May 11, 1883.
3117.   VIII. Ethel and
3118.   IX.   Mabel, twins, b. June 8, 1887.
3119.   X.   Beatrice, b. Feb. 11, 1891.

1267. RACHEL BOND (Abel-Joshua-John-Edward-Joseph), born in Surry County, N. C., Dec. 29, 1849; died Emporia, Kas., March, 1872; married Jan. 26, 1868: Solomon A. Stout, born Oct. 31, 1844, in Chatham County, N. C.; died 1871, in Kansas. His residence, Kansas. Children:

3120.   I.   William M. Stout, b. April 4, 1869.
3120a.   II.   Solomon S. Stout, b. Aug. 28, 1871; d. 1872, inft.

1268. MARTHA SYLVIRA BOND (Abel-Joshua-John-Edward-Joseph), born July 9, 1852, in Hardin County, Iowa; married Feb. 18, 1868: Aquilla Cope, born April 24, 1848. Residence, 1910, Mullinville, Kas. Children:

3121.   I.   Sarah E. Cope, b. March 12, 1870; d. April, 1870.
3122.   II.   Anna M. Cope, b. July 15, 1871; d. Dec. 27, 1874.
3123.   III. William Arthur Cope, b. March 10, 1874.
3124.   IV.   Lucinda Cope, b. May 5, 1876; d. lnft.
3125.   V.   Oscar D. Cope, b. July 14, 1877; d. 1877.
3127.   VII. David Nathan Cope, b. Aug. 9, 1878.

1269. ABEL JOSHUA BOND (Abel-Joshua-John-Edward-Joseph), born Jan. 7, 1855, in Hardin County, Ia.; married Feb. 6, 1873, in Barry County, Mo.: Permelia Lydia Hutchins, born in Surry County, N. C., daughter of Charles and Mary D. Hutchins. Children:

3128.   I.   James H., b. Dec. 25, 1873, in Barry Co., Mo.
3129.   II.   Mary Christina, b. Sept. 28, 1875.

3130. III.   Lowell M., b. July 4, 1877; d. s. p., 1893.

3131. IV.   William H., b. Aug. 26, 1881.

3132. V.   Bertha Almeda, b. Aug. 15, 1883.--

3133. VI.   Anna Pearl, b. Nov. 18, 1885.

3134. VII.   Orville Aquilla, b. Dec. 4, 1892.

1270. MARY KEZIAH BOND (Abel-Joshua-John-Edward-Joseph), born Oct. 11, 1857; married Aug. 5, 1875: David Raleigh Hall, born May 31, 1847. Residence, Cunningham, Kas. Ch:

3135.   I.   Minnie Jane Hall, b. June 26, 1876; m. Nov. 28, 1901: W. A. Sutton. Res., Mullinville, Kas.

3136.   II.   Daisy Myrtle Hall, b. Feb. 1, 1879; m. March 8, 1899: J. A. Sutton. Address, Cunningham, Kas.

3137.   III.   Pearl Cecil Hall, b. April 15, 1881; m. April 22, 1903: James Weir. Res., Alva, Okla.

3138.   IV.   Effie Maud Hall, b. March 10, 1883; m. May 22, 1905: William Price. Res., Mullinville, Kas.

3139.   V.   Archie Cornelius Hall, b. March 23, 1885; m. Sept. 30, 1905: Estella Ingram. Res., Cunningham, Kas.

3140.   VI.   William Abel Hall, b. March 8, 1887.

3141. VII.   Elsie May Hall, b. June 15, 1889.

3142. VIII.   Frederick Raleigh Hall, b. Sept. 25, 1891.

3143.   IX.   Leo John Hall, b. April 7, 1898.

3144.   X.   Blanche Inez Hall, b. July 24, 1900.

1272. JOHN S. BOND (Abel-Joshua-John-Edward-Joseph), born Nov. 15, 1863, in Lyon County, Kas.; married Nov. 15, 1885: Jennie Emma Blood, born Sept. 10, 1869, Marinet, Wis. Residence, 1910, Stafford, Kas. Children:

3145.   I.   Amy Lorena, b. Oct. 16, 1886, in Cherokee Nation, Ind. Ter.; m. Rev. J. B. Hoskinson. Residence, Liberal, Seward Co., Kas.

3146.   II.   Nellie T., b. Aug. 21, 1891, in Stafford, Kas.

3147.   III.   Lucy A., b. Nov. 10, 1894.

3148.   IV.   Hiram H. M., b. Feb. 26, 1897.

3149.   V.   Fred W., b. July 30, 1902; d. Aug. 22, 1902.

3150.   VI.   Harold Cornelius, b. Sept. 24, 1903.

1273. CORDELIA L. BOND (Abel-Joshua-John-Edward-Joseph), born Oct. 22, 1868; married 1899: William May. Residence, 1910, Moberly, Mo. N. f. k.

1278. ELBERT B. BOND (William-Joshua-John-Edward-Joseph), born June 10, 1850; died Aug. 27, 1886, in Wyoming,

Ill.; married June 23, 1881, in Hardin County, Iowa: Ida Ellis. Children:

3161. I. Rebecca Caroline, b. July 16, 1883.

3162. II. Essie Elizabeth, b. Aug. 18, 1885.

1279. SELENA BOND (William-Joshua-John-Edward-Joseph), born Aug. 27, 1851; married July 15, 1866: Solomon Stanley, born Oct. 22, 1842, son of Joseph and Naomi. Residence, 1910, Elmore, Minn. Children:

3163. I. Levi Robert Stanley, b. Sept. 12, 1867; m. May 29, 1900: Arcelia Wing. Res., Pinto, North Dakota.

3164. II. Clinton Minor Stanley, b. Feb. 27, 1875.

3165. III. Amanda Ellen Stanley, b. April 18, 1878; m. Sept. 9, 1902: Elder S. Jackson. Res. (1909), Centura, Wis.

3166. IV. Ida Loretta Stanley, b. Feb. 3, 1880; m. Feb. 26, 1902: Lewis Edward Slyter. Res. (1909), Crookston, Minn.

3167. V. Calvin Henry Stanley, b. Feb. 7, 1883.

3168. VI. Theodore Riley Stanley, b. July 6, 1884.

3169. VII. Sarah Mabel Stanley, b. July 4, 1890.

3170. VIII. Eva May Stanley, b. Sept. 16, 1892.

1280. ELZENA BOND (William-Joshua-John-Edward-Joseph), born June 5, 1853, in Yadkin County, N. C.; married Abraham Hutchens, born Oct. 1, 1843; he died April 18, 1896; he was son of Thompson and Sarah C. (Phillips) Hutchens. Residence, New Providence, Hardin County, Ia. Children:

3171. I. Albert A. Hutchens, b. Aug. 9, 1871.

3172. II. Frank E. Hutchens, b. April 15, 1873; d. Jan. 1, 1890, s. p.

3173. III. Samuel R. Hutchens, b. July 9, 1875.

3174. IV. Cora E. Hutchens, b. Oct. 2, 1877.

3175. V. William Arthur Hutchens, b. Nov. 13, 1880.

3176. VI. Sarah Rebecca Hutchens, b. June 19, 1888.

1281. PHILANDER CASWELL BOND (John-Joshua-John-Edward-Joseph), born Feb. 26, 1857, in North Carolina; moved with his parents to Iowa in 1860 and to Kansas in 1862; married Sarah J. Brattain, born March 8, 1869. Residence and post-office (1910) Poncha Springs, Colo. Children:

3177. I. Esther, b. Jan. 2, 1891.

3178. II. Lydia, b. Oct. 12, 1893.

3179. III. Christian, b. Oct. 29, 1896.

1283. JULIA ANN BOND (John-Joshua-John-Edward-Jo-

seph), born April 24, 1861; died March 31, 1898, in Garfield Co.;
Okla.; married Feb. 14, 1879: William Henry Ingmire, born Nov.
13, 1853, in Ohio. Residence (1910), Garber, Okla. Children:

3180. I. Mary Ethel Ingmire, b. Oct. 21, 1880; m. I. L.
Haskins. Res. (1910), Manitou, Okla.

3182. II. Frankie Ingmire, b. July 6, 1882; d. 1883.

3183. III. Ross John Ingmire, b. Nov. 25, 1884.

3184. IV. Thomas Arthur Ingmire, b. Jan. 28, 1886.

3185. V. Charles Hamilton Ingmire, b. Dec. 25, 1888.

3186. VI. Lydia C. Ingmire, b. Jan. 4, 1890; d. July 1,
1895.

3187. VII. Earl William Ingmire, b. Oct. 21, 1891.

3188. VIII. Harry Edward Ingmire, b. Dec. 5, 1894.

3189. IX. David Sanford Ingmire, b. Dec. 13, 1896; d.
1897, inft.

3190. X. Floyd Bond Ingmire, b. March 20, 1898.

1284. CALISTA IRENE BOND (John-Joshua-John-Edward-Joseph), born Dec. 3, 1864, in Lyon County, Kas.; married
Feb. 11, 1891: Vinson Clarkson Lamb, born Sept. 29, 1868, in
Morgan County, Ind. Res. (1910), Dunlap, Kas. Children:

3191. I. Roy C. Lamb, and

3192. II. Toy C. Lamb, twins, b. Oct. 6, 1898.

1286. LYDIA MAY BOND (John-Joshua-John-Edward-Joseph), born May 14, 1873; married Ed Wiley. Residence,
Dunlap, Kas. Children:

3193. I. Frederick Dale Wiley.

1287. JOHN HENRY BOND (John-Joshua-John-Edward-Joseph), born Feb. 19, 1876; married Rosa Murdock. Residence,
(1910) Americus, Kas. No children.

1312. ELIZABETH FLORENCE BOND (Nathan-Joseph-John-Edward-Joseph), born April 3, 1870, in Indiana; married
April 3, 1888: Albert R. Mahin. Residence, LaFayette, Ind.
Children:

3200. I. Charles Roscoe Mahin, b. July 24, 1889.

1319. JOHN BOND (Mahlon-Joseph-John-Edward-Joseph),
born March 19, 1879; married Lula Wood. Residence, Veedersburg, Ind. Children:

3201. I. Letha, b. Feb. 8, 1902.

3202. II. Lelah, b. Feb. 2, 1903.

3203. III. Carl, b. May 9, 1905.

3204. IV. Helen, b. May 15, 1909.

1320. LILLIE BOND (Mahlon - Joseph - John - Edward-Joseph), born Sept. 11, 1873; married Jacob Bradford.

1322. RACHEL ALICE BOND (Daniel-Joseph-John-Edward-Joseph), born Feb. 18, 1873, in Parke County, Ind.; married Aug. 26, 1894: William Baxter Little, born May 3, 1875, son of Joseph and Nancy. Residence (1910), Kingman, Ind. Ch:

3205. I. Raymond G. Little, b. June 24, 1895; d. inft.

3206. II. Audrey Glenn Little, a dau., b. Oct. 8, 1896.

1323. CAROLINE ELLEN BOND (Daniel-Joseph-John-Edward-Joseph), born. July 18, 1875; married Simon Teague.

1324. LAURA FRANCIS BOND. (Daniel-Joseph-John-Edward-Joseph), born Dec. 4, 1878; married John Griffin. Residence, Catlin, Ind. N. f. k.

1325. MARTHA JANE BOND (Daniel-Joseph-John-Edward-Joseph), born March 31, 1881, in Parke County, Ind.; married Newton Lewis. Residence, Catlin, Ind. N. f. k.

1326. ANNA MAY BOND (Daniel-Joseph-John-Edward-Joseph), born May 2, 1884, in Parke County, Ind.; married William Woodrow. Residence (1910), Kingman, Ind. N. f. k.

1381. CAROLYN LOUISA BOND (Silas-Jesse-William-Edward-Joseph), born April 11, 1877, in Santa Barbara, Cal.; married Oct. 16, 1891: Walter H. Jones. Residence (1903), Denver, Col. Children:

3207. I. Walter B. Jones, b. Aug. 7, 1902.

1382. WALTER SILAS BOND (William-Jesse-William-Edward-Joseph), born ————. Married May Randolph, of Elkhart, Ind.

1383. WILLETTA JOSEPHINE BOND (William - Jesse - William-Edward-Joseph), married Birthday Cone, of Elkhart, Ind. Children:

3208. I. Leroy Cone, b. Sept. 8, 1885, in Elkhart, Ind.

1394. FLORENCE EMMA BOND (Thomas L.-William-William-Edward-Joseph), born Feb. 10, 1876; married Herbert D. Crosby. Residence, Wichita, Kas. N. f. k.

1400. CHARLES M. UNDERWOOD (Irene (Bond)-John-William-Edward-Joseph), born May 3, 1855, in Porter County, Ind.; married Nov. 27, 1878: Lettie A. Barrett, born April 13, 1858, daughter of John. Residence, Anoka, Minn. Children:

3210.   I.   Jessie Irene Underwood, b. Feb. 15, 1880; d. Jan. 26, 1888.

3211.   II.   Gertrude E. Underwood, b. Nov. 19, 1881; d. Sept. 22, 1909; m. L. Tronson; had two children.

3212.   III.   Rosa Edna Underwood, b. Nov. 21, 1883.

3213.   IV.   Dora E. Underwood, b. Dec. 4, 1885; m. June 24, 1909: Linn French.

3214.   V.   Roy M. Underwood, b. Dec. 12, 1888.

3215.   VI.   Ralph Sylvester Underwood, b. Oct. 3, 1891.

3216. VII.   William Bond Underwood, b. June 25, 1895.

3217. VIII.   Vernon Leroy Underwood, b. Oct. 14, 1899.

1401. MATILDA JANE UNDERWOOD (Irene (Bond)-John-William-Edward-Joseph), born July 4, 1859, in Porter County, Ind.; married 1874: Lemuel A. Gowan, born Sept. 18, 1851, in Madison County, Ill., son of George and Catherine. Residence, Desoto, Mo.   Children:

3218.   I.   Malcom L. Gowan, b. Jan. 11, 1875.

3219.   II.   Bayard Gowan, b. May 15, 1878; d. inft.

3220.   III.   Archie Ford Gowan, b. Oct. 14, 1884; d. March 21, 1897.

3221.   IV.   Bertha K. Gowan, b. Feb. 10, 1887.

3222.   V.   Norman Gowan, b. Oct. 19, 1891.

3223.   VI.   G. Donald Gowan, b. July 16, 1893.

3224. VII.   Virgil Warren Gowan, b. Jan. 8, 1897.

1412. JOHN WILLIAM FULLER (Charlotte (Bond)-John-William-Edward-Joseph), born Aug. 31, 1876, in Porter County, Ind.; married Alice McHenry.   Residence 1910, Whiting, Ind. Five children:

    I.   Georgiana Fuller.

   II.   Eva Fuller.

  III.   Irene Fuller.

  IV.   Birdie Fuller.

   V.   John Fuller, Jr.

1413. EMILY FULLER (Charlotte (Bond)-John-William-Edward-Joseph), married Roy Sherwood. Children: Roy, Raymond and Howard. Residence, Chesterton, Ind. N. f. k.

1423. PHOEBE BOND (Christopher-Daniel-Edward-Edward-Joseph), born in Randolph County, Ind.; moved in 1866 with her mother to Missouri, where she married W. P. Rynard

(?) and had two children. She died by being drowned and was buried in Pettis County, Mo. N. f. k.

1427. MARTHA BOND (Christopher-Daniel-Edward-Edward-Joseph), born Dec. 31, 1854, in Mahaska County, Iowa; married Jan. 21, 1879: Amerian Larkin Rinard, born March 8, 1853, in Adair County, Iowa, son of Jerry and Lucinda. Residence 1903, Meridian, Idaho. Children:

3225. I. Hugh Vernon Rinard, b. Feb. 3, 1880; d. Feb. 22, 1890.

3226. II. Cora E. Rinard, b. July 18, 1883; d. 1893.

3227. III. Roy L. Rinard, b. May 18, 1886.

3228. IV. Myrtle May Rinard, b. March 31, 1889; d. Feb. 15, 1900.

3229. V. Elma L. Rinard, b. Jan. 4, 1891.

1428. MARY HULL (Lavina (Bond)-Daniel-Edward-Edward-Joseph), born Dec. 9, 1843, in Indiana; died June, 1877; married John Frederick Hanson. Residence, Indiana-Iowa. Children:

3230. I. Endre Dahl Hanson, b. ——; m. Hockett.

3231. II. Margaret Lavina Hanson; d. s. p.

3233. III. Elias Hanson; m. Res., Garretson, S. D.

3234. IV. Casper W. Hanson, Stickney, S. D.

3235. V. Sibyl J. Hanson; m. —— Thompson. Res., Seattle, Wash.

3236. VI. Florence N. Hanson.

3237. VII. Marie Estella Hanson; m. Henry Watland. Res. Athol, S. D.

3238. VIII. Olive Anna Hanson; m. F. C. Upton. Res., Mahaska, Kas.

3239. IX. Bertha L. Hanson; m. John Earl. Res., Stickney, S. D.

1430. ANNA HULL (Lavina (Bond)-Daniel-Edward-Edward-Joseph), born Jan. 23, 1847; married Addison J. Thomas. Residence, Central City, Neb. Children:

3240. I. Lillian Thomas; d. s. p.

3241. II. Charles Alonzo Thomas; m. Maude Morris. Res., Clarks, Neb.

3242. III. Luetta Thomas; m. Harry Davis. Res., Geneva, Neb.

3243. IV. Luella Thomas; m. William Hogue. Res., Friend, - Neb.

3244. V. Ross Harlan Thomas; m. Nellie Sheets. Res., Central City, Neb.

1431· SARAH HULL (Lavina (Bond)-Daniel-Edward-Edward-Joseph), born Dec. 19, 1848; married Joseph D. Wilson. Residence, Tobias, Neb.· Children:

3245. I. May Wilson; d. s. p. age 17 years.

3246. II. Elmer W. Wilson; m. Alice Hogue. Res., Tobias, Neb.

3247. III. Robert B. Wilson; m. Kate Sutfin. Res., McCook, Neb.

·3248· IV.· Carrie Lavina Wilson; m. Bert Crouch. Res., Tobias, Neb.

3249. V. Frank Wilson; m. Maude Sutfin. Res., Tobias, Neb.

3250. VI. Benjamin Harrison Wilson.

1423. ELIZABETH HULL (Lavina (Bond)-Daniel-Edward-Edward-Joseph), born Nov. 10, 1851; died May 8, 1807; married John A. Wilson. Residence, Tobias, Neb. Children:

3251. I. George Arthur Wilson; m. Cora Cummings. Res., Tobias, Neb.

⁻3252. II. Cora Lavina Wilson; m. Edward Mort. Res., Tobias, Neb.

3253. III. Leslie Wllson. Res., Tobias, Neb. .

1433. DR. SOLOMON L. HULL (Lavina (Bond)-Daniel-. Edward-Edward-Joseph), born April 2, 1853; married Susie Shaw; she died May 3, 1903. Res., Central City, Neb. Children: ·

·3254. I. Charles Ezra Hull, d. 1903.

3255. II. Howard Ernest Hull; Central City, Neb.

3256. III. Eunice Ruth Hull.

He married second, Dec. 11, 1906: Ada Baker. ·

1435. DANIEL HULL (Lavina (Bond)-Daniel-Edward-Edward-Joseph), born March 26, 1857; married Effie Glasscock. Residence, Oskaloosa, Ia. Children: ·

3257. I. Ethel Hull; m. John Alden. Res., Oskaloosa, Ia.

3258. II. Clifford Hull, Oskaloosa, Ia.

3259. III. Grace Hull.

   IV. Mary Hull.

   V. Iola (?).

1436. CHARLES HULL (Lavina (Bond)-Daniel-Edward-Edward-Joseph), born Nov. 28, 1858; married Mary Wilson. Residence, Lacey, Ia. Children:

3260. I. Homer Hull; m. —— Plank. Res., Lacey, Ia.
3261. II. Chester Hull.
3262. III. Charlotte Hull; m. —— Upton. Res., Lacey, Ia.

1438. JOHN FRANKLIN HULL (Lavina (Bond)-Daniel-Edward-Edward-Joseph), born Nov. 9, 1863; died Sept. 18, 1896; married Elsie Delong. She married second, a Mr. Head. Residence, Denver, Colo. Children:

3263.. I. Ruby Hull.
3264. II. Maude Hull. Res., Denver, Colo.

1439. WILLIAM WALTER HULL (Lavina (Bond)-Daniel-Edward-Edward-Joseph), born May 13, 1867; married Ada Upton. Residence, Exeter, Neb. Children:

3265. I. Fern Hull.
3266. II. Walter Hull.
     III. Leroy Hull.
     IV. Ilah Hull.

1447. MARY ELMETTA BOND (Simon-Daniel-Edward-Edward-Joseph), born in Wayne County, Ind.; married Cornelius Harris. Residence, Mecca, Cal. One child: Everett Harris.

1448. DR. CHARLES SUMNER BOND (Simon-Daniel-Edward-Edward-Joseph), born in Wayne County, Ind.; married Julia Boyd, daughter of Dr. Samuel S. Boyd, of Dublin, Ind. Physician and surgeon, Richmond, Ind. Children:

3267. I. George.
3268. II. Florence.
3269. III. Alice.
a3269. IV. Juliet.

1449. MINERVA ELLA BOND (Simon-Daniel-Edward-Edward-Joseph), born Wayne County, Ind.; married Dr. Melville F. Johnston. Residence, Richmond, Ind. Has son Donald.

1452. NINA BOND (Pleasant-Daniel-Edward-Edward-Joseph), born ——; married Charles B. Campbell. judge of Circuit Court, Kankakee, Ill. Children:

I. Charles Bond Campbell.
II. Pleasant Whipple Campbell, b. Jan. 23, 1910.

1454. WALTER W. BOND (Pleasant-Daniel-Edward-Edward-Joseph), born Jan. 1, 1881, in Indiana; graduate Princeton University, 1902; automobile business Indianapolis, 1912; residence, 610 E. Thirty-first street, Indianapolis; married Alice Howland, daughter Hiram B. and Caroline Green, of Marion County, Ind. Children:

3270.   I.   Walter W., Jr., b. July 2, 1903.
3271.   II.   Charles Howland, b. Feb. 27, 1905.
          III.   Henry Sale, b. Nov. 10, 1911.

1456. NATHAN BOND (Samson-Benjamin-Edward-Edward-Joseph), born July 1, 1852; married Mary Smith. Children:

3272.   I.   Flora Etta.
3273.   II.   William.
3274.   III.   Cornelia.
3275.   IV.

1457. FLORA ETTA BOND (Samson-Benjamin-Edward-Edward-Joseph), born Oct. 29, 1853; married Feb. 23, 1874: Russell T. Varney; d. s. p. about 1875.

1458. CALEB BOND (Samson-Benjamin-Edward-Edward-Joseph), born May 21, 1855; married 1887: Mrs. Anna Russell, nee Dennis, widow of William Russell. Residence 1910, Brainerd, Minn. No children:

1461. SEBITHA BOND (Samson-Benjamin-Edward-Edward-Joseph), born Feb. 2, 1861; married Feb. 1, 1879: James Deering. Residence, Anoka, Minn. Children:

3276.   I.   Nellie Deering, b. July 27, 1881.
3277.   II.   Celia Deering, b. April 27, 1883.
3278.   III.   Sarah Deering, b. Nov. 8, 1886.
3279.   IV.   Agnes Deering, b. April 24, 1889; d. railroad accident Oct. 9, 1904.
3280.   V.   Charles Deering, b. Sept. 8, 1891.
3281.   VI.   Edna Deering, b. May 25, 1893.
3282.   VII.   Lucile Deering, b. June 1, 1896; d. Jan. 8, 1899.
3283.   VIII.   Irene Deering, b. Oct. 30, 1898.
3284.   IX.   Arthur Deering, b. June 1, 1901.
3285.   X.   Harriet Deering, b. May 3, 1904.
3286.   XI.   Edward Deering, b. May 29, 1906.

1462. REBECCA BOND (Samson-Benjamin-Edward-Edward-Joseph), born Oct. 24, 1862; married Richard Henry Staples (?). She died. Children:

3287. I. Carrie (?), b. Dec. 18, 1888; m. Frank Emery. N. f. k.

1463. JANE BOND (Samson-Benjamin-Edward-Edward-Joseph), born April 24, 1866, in Minnesota; married Aug. 26, 1883: Russell T. Varney, by trade a blacksmith. She was his second wife, he having previously been married to her sister, Flora Etta. Children:

3287–a. I. Huldah Varney, b. Nov. 11, 1884.

3287–b. II. Betsey Varney, b. April 15, 1886.

3287–c. III. Richard T. Varney, b. June 8, 1888.

1464. CORNELIA ANN BOND (Samson-Benjamin-Edward-Edward-Joseph), born Dec. 16, 1867; married Sept. 23, 1888: William Obed Russell, born Jan. 28, 1867. Residence, Hinckley, Minn. Children:

3288. I. Gertrude Lillian Russell, b. April 16, 1889.

3289. II. William Goldsmith Russell, b. Oct. 11, 1891.

3290. III. Flora Mae Russell, b. March 20, 1893.

3291. IV. Myrtle Belle Russell, b. June 12, 1894.

3292. V. Rainie Alfred Russell, b. Feb. 3, 1896.

3293. VI. Mildred Violet Russell, b. Dec. 13, 1897.

3294. VII. Martha Ann Russell, b. Nov. 25, 1899.

3295. VIII. Earl Stephen Russell, b. April 23, 1901.

3296. IX. Clara Phoebe Russell, b. Jan. 29, 1904.

3297. X. Alta Helen Russell, b. Oct. 30, 1906.

3298. XI. Douglas Paul Russell, b. Aug. 30, 1908.

1465. MYRTILLA LEONA BOND (Pelatiah-Benjamin-Edward-Edward-Joseph), born Dec. 8, 1863, in Hamilton County, Ind.; married March 28, 1883: William Franklin Hunt, son of Benjamin and Sarah (Ross) Hunt. Residence, Modoc, Ind. Children:

3300. I. Mary Iona Hunt, b. March 5, 1884: m. 1906: Roy Keever.

3301. II. Katie G. Hunt, b. May 21, 1892; d. April 8, 1901.

3202. III. Bonnie Myrlea Hunt, b. July 10, 1894; d. April 15, 1901.

1467. CORNELIA KATHERINE BOND (Pelatiah-Benjamin-Edward-Edward-Joseph), born Dec. 16, 1870, in Minneapolis, Minn.; married 1892: Alfred Pascoe, of Pomona, Cal.; married second, Clinton White. Residence, 1910, Riverside, Cal. Children:

3303.　I.　Corinne, b. 1893.

3304.　II.　Walter, b. 1895.

1469. DR. SCIPIO BOND (Hezekiah-Benjamin-Edward-Edward-Joseph), born Aug. 28, 1859, in Minnesota; married Dec. 2, 1886: Laura A. Burrill. Residence, Anoka, Minn. Dentist and member City Council. Children:

3305.　I.　Dorothy, b. Nov. 11, 1900.

1470. CAROLINE BOND (Hezekiah - Benjamin - Edward - Edward-Joseph), born Jan. 16, 1861, in Minnesota; married July 21, 1889: Elijah Madison Adams, born March 25, 1862, son of Joel and Sarah (Stanfield) Adams, of Brown Co., Ill. Residence, Blaine, Wn. Children:

3306.　I.　Victor Goldsmith Adams, b. July 7, 1890.

3307.　II.　Portia Anada Adams, b. March 25, 1898.

3308.　III.　Daphne Dale Adams, b. March 19, 1900.

1475. MYRTLE BOND (Edward - Benjamin - Edward - Edward-Joseph), born Sept. 2, 1872, in Randolph County, Ind.; married Feb. 11, 1898: Rev. Oren Wall, born Feb. 12, 1877, son of Edwin L. and Jane (Oren) Wall. Residence (1912), Yoncalla, Oregon. Minister in M. E. church. Children:

3309.　I.　Ellen Wall, b. May 30, 1899; d. Sept. 12, 1901.

3310.　II.　John Oren Wall, b. March 2, 1902.

3311.　III.　Esther Hughes Wall, b. May 13, 1904, in Greencastle, Ind.

3312.　IV.　Lawrence Lee Wall, b. June 13, 1907, in Heltonville, Ind.

1477. SAMUEL R. BOND (Edward-Benjamin-Edward-Edward-Joseph), born May 28, 1879, in Randolph County, Ind.; married June 12, 1899: Letitia M. Hinshaw, daughter of Elza and Mary E. Hinshaw, of Snowhill, Ind. He was a soldier in Co. F, 158th Reg. Ind. Vol. Inft. during the Cuban war. Residence (1910), Pellston, Mich. Children:

3313.　I.　Wilbur M., b. Feb. 25, 1902.

3314.　II.　Sidney, a dau., b. Feb. 29, 1904.

3315.　III.　Francis Raymond, b. Oct. 11, 1907.

1478. HENRY H. UNDERWOOD, born Dec. 16, 1840; married March 6, 1864, in Kosciusko County, Ind.: Eliza Noel, born Sept. 27, 1846. He was a soldier in Co. F, 48th Reg. Ind. Vol. Inft. Residence (1910), Warsaw, Ind. Children:

3316.　I.　Nancy L. Underwood, b. Nov. 14, 1866; d. 1884;

married Cyrus Quigley. One child: Anice Quigley, of Alton, Kas.

3317. II. Ina A. Underwood, b. April 28, 1869; m. John W. Noel. One child: Ermal Noel.

3318. III. Minnie I. Underwood, b. March 23, 1885; d. Aug. 9, 1897; m. Ed. G. Hinkley. Ch: Edna Lavina Hinkley. Residence, Warsaw, Ind.

1479. SUSANNAH UNDERWOOD, born March 31, 1842; died June 10, 1900; married July 21, 1859: Zenas L. Eaton, born Jan. 22, 1826. Children:

3319. I. Maud Eaton, b. March 18, 1869; m. July 9, 1900: William Devine. Res., Vinita, Okla.

3320. II. Kate Eaton, b. Aug. 29, 1871; m. William S. Ashton. Ch: John, Cyrus C., Charles M. and Eugene R. Ashton.

1561. WILLIAM ARTEMAS BOND (Solomon-Elias-Edward-Edward-Joseph), married ———. Residence (1912) Vesper, Clatsop County, Oregon.

1562. ELIAS AUSTIN BOND (Solomon-Elias-Edward-Edward-Joseph), married ———. Occupation, teacher. Residence, (1912), Bellingham, Wn.

1563. HARRY DOMELL BOND (Solomon-Elias-Edward-Edward-Joseph), married ———. Occupation, bridge contractor. Residence (1912), LaFayette, Yamhill Co., Ore.

1566. EDWARD ARTEMAS GURLEY (Lizzie (Bond)-Elias-Edward-Edward-Joseph), born Feb. 9, 1871; married Dec. 20, 1890: Bertha A. Denny, born Oct. 4, 1867, daughter of Eli. Residence, Westfield, Ind. No children.

1568. ANNA MAUD GURLEY (Lizzie (Bond)-Elias-Edward-Edward-Joseph), born Dec. 5, 1876, in Hamilton County, Ind.; married Feb. 22, 1905: Noah H. Vernon, son of Abner and Jemima (Haines) Vernon. Residence, Pendleton, Ind. Occupation, farmer. Children:

3330. I. Geneve Vernon, b. Aug. 10, 1907.

1571. MELVIN SHAUL (Anna J. (Bond)-Elias-Edward-Edward-Joseph), born June 13, 1877; married Aug. 10, 1897: Mabel Warriner, born March, 1878, daughter of Henry C. and Alvira (Brown) Warriner. Residence (1910), Pendleton, Ind. Children:

3331. I. Harold M. Shaul, b. March 28, 1898.
3332. II. Helen Anna Shaul, b. Dec. 9, 1901.

3333.   III.   Mildred Carrie Shaul, b. June 5, 1905.

1572.   ORA SHAUL (Anna J. (Bond)-Elias-Edward-Edward-Joseph), born ——; married Bert Davis, a farmer.   Residence, (1910), Lawrence, Ind. R. F. D.   Children:

3334.   I.   Everet Davis.

3335.   II.   Remona Davis.

1573.   FRANCIS AUSTIN BOND (Jerry-Elias-Edward-Edward-Joseph), born July 13, 1878, in Madison County, Ind.; married Dec. 30, 1908: Edna Towne, born Sept. 3, 1887, daughter of John and Effie Towne. Occupation, machinist.   Residence, Pendleton, Ind.

1574.   MARY ETTA BOND (Jerry-Elias-Edward-Edward-Joseph), born Oct. 2, 1880; married May 29, 1901: Joseph Putnam.   Residence, Olivia, Minn.

1576.   LYLE M. BOND (Jerry-Elias-Edward-Edward-Joseph), born April 10, 1885, in Madison County, Ind.; married Benjamin Lukens.   Children:

3336.   Horace Willard Lukens, b. Sept. 17, 1904.

She married second Sept. 13, 1908: Luther Green, a farmer. Address (1910), Pendleton, Ind.

1577.   DORA LEE BOND (Jerry-Elias-Edward-Edward-Joseph), born Aug. 12, 1888; married Aug. 8, 1909, at Pendleton, Ind.: William Walker. Occupation, draughtsman.   Residence, (1912), Muncie, Ind.   Children:

I.   Wilfred, b. ——, 1911.

II.   William Oral, b. Sept. —, 1912.

1580.   PEARL DAWSON (Mary E. (Bond)-Elias-Edward-Edward-Joseph), born ——; married John Ballard.   Residence, Westfield, Ind.   Children:

3337.   I.   Edith Ballard.

3338.   II.   Mary Olive Ballard.

3339.   III.   Thelma Ballard.

3340.   IV.   Geneve Etta Ballard.

1581.   GLENNA DAWSON (Mary E. (Bond)-Elias-Edward-Edward-Joseph), born ——; married Frank Ressler.   Residence, Westfield, Ind.   No children:

1586.   IONA LUELLA BOND (Elias E.-Elias-Edward-Edward-Joseph), born June 13, 1885; married April 23, 1905: Richard Ashby.   Residence, Pendleton, Ind.   Children:

3341. I. Laura Ashby.

3342. II. Donald Ashby.

1587. JOHN MILTON BOND (Jonathan K.-Nathan-Jesse-Edward-Joseph), born Dec. 19, 1847; married Emily Boland, of Henry County, Ind. Occupation, fármer. Residence, New Castle, Ind. R. F. D. Children:

3343. I. Jennie Tamer, b. Jan. 29, 1869.

3344. II. Merton.

3345. III. Blanche.

1588. WILLIAM HENRY BOND (Jonathan K.-Nathan-Jesse-Edward-Joseph), born Dec. 9, 1853; married Catherine Shrade; she died May 2, 1906. Residence, Henry County, Ind. Children:

3346. I. Lula Martha, b. April 4, 1875.

3347. II. Cecil.

1594. ROBERT B. BOND (Henry T.-Robert-Jesse-Edward-Joseph), born Nov. 4, 1864, in Wayne County, Ind.; married March 12, 1890: Nannie E. Roller, born Nov. 19, 1872. Residence, Greensfork, Ind. Children:

3348. I. Lewis Roller, b. Jan. 9, 1907.

1596. JAMES E. BOND (Henry T.-Robert-Jesse-Edward-Joseph), born May 9, 1869; married March 26, 1902: Lenora Harris, born Dec. 3, 1871. Children:

3349. I. Alice Virginia, b. March 18, 1905.

1597. LÓUISA C. BOND (John-Robert-Jesse-Edward-Joseph), born March 10, 1859, near Greensfork, Wayne County, Ind.; married Sept. 13, 1881: Arthur B. Palmer. Residence (1910), Webster, Ind. Children:

3350. I. Louis Clarent Palmer, b. May 7, 1886.

1597=B. ARETTA BOND (John-Robert-Jesse-Edward-Joseph), born Nov. 5, 1863; married Jan. 18, 1881: Calvin Davis; she died Sept. 7, 1888; he died Nov. 9, 1888. Children:

3351. I. Verlin T. Davis, b. Jan. 3, 1883. His residence, Greensfork, Ind.

1597=C. OLIVER G. BOND (John-Robert-Jesse-Edward-Joseph), born Sept. 17, 1869; married June, 1894: May Deck. Residence, Greensfork, Ind. Children:

3352. I. Robert Lewis, b. March 2, 1901.

1597=D. EVA BOND (John-Robert-Jesse-Edward-Joseph),

born April 8, 1873; married Feb. 29, 1896: George Nicholson. Address, ·Greensfork, Ind. Children:

3353.   I.   Hazel Nicholson, b. Jan. 6, 1907.

3354.   II.   Helen Nicholson, b. Feb. 5, 1909.

1597=E. CLAUDIA ETHEL BOND (John-Robert-Jesse-Edward-Joseph), born Sept. 11, 1876; married Oct. 17, 1903: Byram Pierce. Address, Economy, Ind. Children:

3355.   I.   Robert Lewis Pierce, b. April 5, 1907.

1598. EMMA C. BOND (Abner-Robert-Jesse-Edward-Joseph), born Sept. 24, 1861; died Nov. 4, 1889; married Albert R. Jones. Residence, Wayne County, Ind. Children:

.3356.   I.   Forrest B. Jones, b. April 8, 1876.

3357.   II.   Mary Lucile Jones, b. Oct. 24, 1889.

1599. S. MAUD BOND (Abner-Robert-Jesse-Edward-Joseph), born March 16, 1865; married June 12, 1889: William Woodruff; he died Jan. 28, 1902. She married second: Thomas B. Millikan, attorney at law, New Castle, Ind.

1601. EDITH A. BOND (Abner-Robert-Jesse-Edward-Joseph), born May 20, 1882, in Wayne County, Ind.; married June 24, 1908: Joseph Morgan, of Indianapolis, Ind.

1602. GEORGIA BOND (Larkin T.-Robert-Jesse-Edward-Joseph), born May 10, 1876, in Wayne County, Ind.; married Dec. 14, 1898: Joseph B. Hurst. Residence, .Cambridge City, Ind. Children:

3360.   I.   Marjorie Hurst, b. Sept. 29, 1899.

3361.   II.   Foster Scott Hurst, b. June 22, 1904.

3362.   III.   Emily, and

3363.   IV.   John Dickson Hurst, b. Jan. 30, 1910.

1602=A. LORA BOND (Larkin - Robert - Jesse - Edward-Joseph), born Dec. 18, 1887; married Sept. 30, 1905: Omer Guyton. Residence, Wayne County, Ind.

1603. FRANK BELL (Margaret (Bond)-John-Jesse-Edward-Joseph), born Jan. 6, 1853; married 1875: Catherine Louk. Residence, Richmond, Ind. Children:

3364.   I.   Cora Bell, b. July 22, 1879; m. 1901: Omer Chase.

3365.   II.   Maud Bell, b. Oct. 29, 1881; d. s. p. Jan. 6, 1902.

1604. CHARLES E. BELL (Margaret-John-Jesse-Edward-Joseph), born June 9, 1855; married Sept. 23, 1875: Elizabeth Paulus. Residence, Richmond, Ind. Children:

3366.   I.   Homer Frederick Bell, b. Sept. 9, 1876.

3367. II. Floyd Charles Bell, b. June 4, 1881.

1604=A. PHEBE C. BOND (William H.-John-Jesse-Edward-Joseph), born Oct. 3, 1870; married July 22, 1891: Robert H. McNeil, baggagemaster. Residence, Columbus, Ind. Children:

3368. I. Lillie McNeil, b. Aug. 19, 1892.

3369. II. Esther McNeil, b. March 2, 1896.

1604=C. CHARLES H. BOND (William H.-John-Jesse-Edward-Joseph), born Aug. 25, 1877; married April 21, 1897: Marie M. Kolling, of Richmond, Ind. Residence (1910), Greensfork, Ind. Children:

3370. I. Wilbur K., b. Jan. 15, 1898.

1606. HARRY A. BOND (Oliver S.-William-Jesse-Edward-Joseph), b. ——; married in England, Carrie Dalton. Residence, Toledo, O. Four children. N. f. k.

1613. GERTRUDE BOND (Larkin-William-Jesse-Edward-Joseph), born Sept. 16, 1867; died 1905; married first, William H. Eliason, born April 17, 1867; died Dec. 11, 1893, without children; she married second, June 25, 1902: Robert S. Ashe, born Sept. 29, 1866, son of Robert and Sarah, of Cambridge, Mass. Residence, Richmond, Ind. Children:

3401. I. Lewis Bond Ashe, b. Sept. 12, 1903.

1622. CLARA FLORENCE BOND (Calvin-Enos-Jesse-Edward-Joseph), born May 7, 1857, in New Castle, Ind.; died Oct. 21, 1900, in Dunkirk, Ind.; married Sept. 5, 1877: Barton Warren Stone Fairfield, born April 17, 1849. Children:

3402. I. Edith May Fairfield, b. Thursday morning, Sept. 6, 1883, in Fargo, N. D. Address 1903, Stanford University, Palo Alto, Cal.

3403. II. Earl Bond Fairfield, b. Feb. 14, 1887; d. July 30, 1887.

3404. III. Clarence Hubert Fairfield, b. Sept. 30, 1890; d. Nov. 22, 1891.

1623. WILLIAM CLEMENT BOND (Calvin-Enos-Jesse-Edward-Joseph), born June 15, 1858; married Mary Elliott, daughter of Stephen. Residence, New Castle, Ind. Occupation, merchant and manufacturer. Children:

3405. I. Jean.

1625. LEE W. WICKERSHAM (Mary A. (Bond)-Enos-Jesse-Edward-Joseph), born in Henry County, Ind.; married Ida Leonard. Residence, New Castle, Ind. Children:

3406. I. Bertha Wickersham.

1626. CARRIE WICKERSHAM (Mary A.-Enos-Jesse-Edward-Joseph), born in Henry County, Ind.; married Walter R. Cammack. Residence, New Castle, Ind. Children:

3407. I. Pearl May Cammack.

3408. II. Jessie Fern Cammack.

1627. ALBERT STRATTON (Hannah (Bond)-Enos-Jesse-Edward-Joseph), born July 15, 1856; married Feb. 28, 1884: Louisa Unthank. Residence, Henry County, Ind. Children:

3409. I. Anna May Stratton, b. May 10, 1885.

3410. II. Lois Stratton, b. Dec. 27, 1887.

3411. III. Myron Stratton, b. Aug. 17, 1895.

1630. ELLA STRATTON (Hannah (Bond)-Enos-Jesse-Edward-Joseph), born Oct. 26, 1864; married Feb. 15, 1893: Alonzo C. Hodson. Residence, Henry County, Ind. Children:

3412. I. Floyd Hodson, b. Dec. 29, 1893.

3413. II. Fern Hodson, b. Nov. 26, 1894.

3414. III. Mabel Hodson, b. Oct. 4, 1897.

3415. IV. Ivan Hodson, b. Oct. 17, 1899.

1631. BENJAMIN STRATTON (Hannah (Bond)-Enos-Jesse-Edward-Joseph), born Jan. 6, 1866; married Aug. 4, 1897: Ella Moore. Residence, Henry County, Ind. N. f. k.

1632. MINNIE B. STRATTON (Hannah (Bond)-Enos-Jesse-Edward-Joseph), born April 4, 1879; married Sept. 7, 1898: Milton Stafford, a farmer. Residence, Greensboro, Ind. Children:

3416. I. Loell Stafford, b. Jan. 3, 1901.

3417. II. Edith Stafford, and

3418. III. Edna Stafford, twins, b. Dec. 6, 1902.

1634. ETTA BOND (Isom-Enos-Jesse-Edward-Joseph), born ——; married Aug. 12, 1885: Edward Bland. Residence, New Castle, Ind. Children:

3419. I. Otis Bland, b. ——; m. Jan. 8, 1912: Annie Yeager.

1635. SUSANNAH BOND (Isom-Enos-Jesse-Edward-Joseph), born ——; married April 30, 1890: Mont Valandingham Milligan. Residence, New Castle, Ind. Children:

I. Martha, b. March 4, 1904.

II. George, b. Sept. 25, 1905.

1636. ERNEST BOND (Isom-Enos-Jesse-Edward-Joseph),

born ——; married Sept. 24, 1903: Dora Ethel Binford. Residence, Henry County, Ind. Children:

I. Olive Ruth, b. June 7, 1908.

II. Laura May, b. July 13, 1909.

III. Ernest Howard, b. Sept. 17, 1911.

1637. OLIVE BOND (Isom-Enos-Jesse-Edward-Joseph), born ——; married Oct. 28, 1903: Dr. C. U. Hall. Residence, New Castle, Ind. Children:

I. Marjorie Ella Hall, b. Sept. 21, 1910.

1641. NELLIE BOND (Jesse-Enos-Jesse-Edward-Joseph), born June 4, 1876, in Henry County, Ind.; married April 11, 1899: Stewart Runyan, born April 11, 1873, son of Andrew J. and Margaret. Residence 1910, Mansfield, O. Children:

3430. I. Margaret Runyan, b. Dec. 14, 1900.

3431. II. Robert Runyan, b. July 9, 1902.

3432. III. Mary Elizabeth Runyan, b. Dec. 22, 1909.

1642. CARRIE HEWIT (Phebe (Bond)-Enos-Jesse-Edward-Joseph), born Feb. 16, 1877; married June 8, 1898: Aldona Yauky, son of Jacob and Catherine (Henninger) Yanky. Residence, Henry County, Ind. Children:

3433. I. Rea Hewit Yauky, b. May 8, 1901.

3434. II. Madge Yauky, b. June 17, 1902.

1643. BERTHA HEWIT (Phebe (Bond)-Enos-Jesse-Edward-Joseph), daughter of Rev. John Henry and Phebe (Bond) Hewit, born Oct. 11, 1882; married Sept., 1906: Charles M. Miller. N. f. k.

1644. EVA BUTLER (Rebecca (Bond)-Isom-Jesse-Edward-Joseph), born Nov. 8, 1853; married Oct. 28, 1875: Robert Hall, born July 24, 1842, son of Phineas and Mary. Residence, Lewisville, Ind. No issue.

1645. ALLEN BUTLER (Rebecca (Bond)-Isom-Jesse-Edward-Joseph), born April 26, 1856; married Sept. 29, 1878: Martha Murphy, born July 7, 1860; died Jan. 16, 1889. Residence, Henry County, Ind. Children:

3435. I. Nola Butler.

He married second, April 22, 1891: Margaret Hanley. Children:

3437. II. Rebecca Butler.

3438. III. Addie Butler.

3439. IV. Mary Butler.

1646. ISOM LEEBUM BUTLER (Rebecca (Bond)-Isom-Jesse-Edward-Joseph), born June 25, 1858; married Jan. 3, 1889: Anna Raffensbarger. Residence, Lewisville, Ind. _Children:
  I. Vera Butler.
  II. Carl Butler.
  III. Deborah Butler.
  IV. Pauline Butler.

1647. NETTIE BUTLER (Rebecca (Bond)-Isom-Jesse-Edward-Joseph), born May 26, 1867; died Oct. 21, 1908; married Aug. 26, 1889: Otis Stubbs. Residence, Lewisville, Ind. Children:
  I. Mildred Stubbs.
  II. Celia Stubbs.
  III. Raymond Stubbs.
  IV. Marie Stubbs.
  V. Thelma Stubbs.

1648. LEONA BUTLER (Rebecca (Bond)-Isom-Jesse-Edward-Joseph), born Feb. 13, 1876; married Jan. 26, 1898: Marion Howe. Children:
  I. Helen Howe.
  II. Irene Howe.
  III. Eugene Howe.

1670. WALTER S. BOND (Lewis-Isaac-Jesse-Edward-Joseph), born Aug. 23, 1873; married April 15, 1899: Mary E. Fisher, of Denver, Ind. Residence, Miami County, Ind. Children:
  3451. I. Venice Marie.

1671. NELLIE J. BOND (Lewis-Isaac-Jesse-Edward-Joseph), born Sept. 3, 1876; married Feb. 23, 1899: Gilbert J. Hood. Residence, Peru, Ind. Children:
  3452. I. Margaret Iona Hood.

1672. BLANCHE BOND (Lewis-Isaac-Jesse-Edward-Joseph), born June 23, 1880; married Dr. Frederick E. Grafft, a dentist, of Wabash, Ind. Children:
  3453. I. Martha Bernice Grafft.

1673. HATTIE BOND (Robert-Jesse-Jesse-Edward-Joseph), born Dec. 14, 1870; married Jan. 23, 1890: Edwin Murphy, born Aug. 29, 1867, son of Jesse and Rebecca. Occupation, farmer. Residence, Peru, Ind., R. F. D. No. 5. Children:
  3454. I. Nellie J. Murphy, b. June 25, 1891.

3455. II. Robert H. Murphy, b. July 7, 1899.

1674. OSCAR L. BOND (Robert-Jesse-Jesse-Edward-Joseph), born May 11, 1876, in Miami County, Ind.; married Nov. 30, 1899: Cora E. Eikenberry. Residence, Chili, Ind. Children:

3456. I. Lyman H., b. Feb. 14, 1902.

1710. WILLIAM H. BOND (John J.-Abijah-Joshua-Edward-Joseph), born June 6, 1882; married July 16, 1904: Lora Snider, born Sept. 16, 1886. Residence, Pennville, Ind.

1711. GOLDIE W. BOND (John J.-Abijah-Joshua-Edward-Joseph), born Jan. 20, 1884, in Jay County, Ind.; married April 3, 1904: Elmer Batten, born April 2, 1885. P. O. 1910, Balbec, Ind.

1712. BERTIE E. BOND (John J.-Abijah-Joshua-Edward-Joseph), born Jan. 27, 1886, in Jay County, Ind.; married Aug. 8, 1906: Grace Hoskins, born Aug. 18, 1886. Residence, Pennville, Ind. Children:

3501. I. Arlo Bond, b. Sept. 1, 1907.

3502. II. Bernice, b. March 21, 1909.

1713. DAISY E. BOND (John J.-Abijah-Joshua-Edward-Joseph), born May 28, 1888; married Jan. 1, 1904: John Evans, born March 11, 1883. Residence, Portland, Ind. Children:

3503. I. Chester Evans, b. Oct. 24, 1904.

3504. II. Mildred Evans, b. Oct. 14, 1906; d. inft.

Homer Evans, b. Sept. 29, 1907; d. July 27, 1909.

1714. LELIA BOND (John J.-Abijah-Joshua-Edward-Joseph), born July 30, 1890; married Sept. 2, 1908: Albert Whitaker, born Jan. 24, 1890. Residence, Pennville, Ind.

1725. IVA BUNKER (Sarah E. (Bond)-Abijah-Joshua-Edward-Joseph), born May 8, 1880; married Dec. 26, 1900: Ethelbert Paxson. Children:

3505. I. Thessel, a dau., b. Oct. 11, 1901; d. Sept. 5, 1903.

3506. II. Thelma Garnet Paxson, b. June 30, 1903.

1726. WILLIAM E. BUNKER (Sarah E. (Bond)-Abijah-Joshua-Edward-Joseph), born Dec. 28, 1882; married Dec. 26, 1900: Lena Moore. Children:

I. Thomas Cecil Bunker, b. July 26, 1902.

1812. ALBERT S. BOND (Mahlon C. P.-Mahlon-Joseph-Edward-Joseph), born Jan. 14, 1879, in Indiana; married Oct.

26, 1903: Martha Dimmick, in Covert, N. Y., daughter of Jesse L. and Susan Dimmick. N. f. k.

1815. MARY A. BOND (Mahlon C. P.-Mahlon-Joseph-Edward-Joseph), born Jan. 18, 1885; married Oct. 26' 1902: J. Leonard Bicknell, son of Oscar and Elizabeth. N. f. k.

1838. EMMA L. BROWN (Sarah (Bond)-Benjamin-Silas-Benjamin-Joseph), born June 11, 1862; married Dec. 25, 1882: John M. Busby, born Jan. 13, 1858, son of Silas and Elizabeth (McCallister) Busby. Address, Anderson, Ind., R. F. D. Children:

> I. Lena M. Busby, b. Dec. 15, 1883.
> II. Charles E. Busby, b. June 6, 1885.
> III. Grattan A. Busby, b. Nov. 15, 1887.
> IV. Blanche A. Busby, b. Dec. 30, 1889.
> V. Edith Busby, b. April 17, 1892.
> VI. Earnest Busby, b. July 22, 1894.
> VII. Frederick Busby, b. Oct. 21, 1896.
> VIII. Loyd Busby, b. July 4, 1899.
> IX. Arthur Busby, b. Sept. 9, 1902.

1839. MARY L. BROWN (Sarah (Bond)-Benjamin-Silas-Benjamin-Joseph), born April 4, 1865; married Oct. 30, 1890: Levi T. Pennington, son of John and Elizabeth (Wiltsie) Pennington. Residence, Spiceland, Ind. Children:

3507. I. Elgar J. Pennington, b. Sept. 9, 1891.
3508. II. Everet L. Pennington, b. March 4, 1893.
3509. III. Agnes M. Pennington, b. March 11, 1896.
3510. IV. Irene Pennington, b. Aug. 30, 1897.
3511. V. Leslie Pennington, b. Oct. 30, 1899.

1846. EMMA L. BUTLER (Elizabeth (Bond)-Benjamin-Silas-Benjamin-Joseph), born Feb. 20, 1874; married Oct. 3, 1894: Samuel Benton, son of Samuel and Harriet Benton, of Barclay, Kas. Residence, Orland, Calif. Children:

3512. I. Esther M. Benton, b. Aug. 25, 1895.
3513. II. Christina M. Benton, b. June 26, 1897.
3514. III. Mildred M. Benton, b. Sept. 12, 1899.

1848. BENJAMIN F. BOND (William-Benjamin-Silas-Benjamin-Joseph), born Oct. 15, 1868, in Indiana; married April 17, 1894: Laura May Holliday. Occupation, real estate dealer. Residence (1912), Long Beach, Calif. Children:

3515. I. Julia, b. Feb. 25, 1895.

3516. II. Ruth E., b. July 18, 1896.

3517. III. Franklin Paul, b. Aug. 10, 1900.

1849. MINNIE BOND (William-Benjamin-Silas-Benjamin-Joseph), born Nov. 20, 1870; married Sept. 3, 1895: Dr. J. W. Goodwin.

1851. ALICE BOND (William-Benjamin-Silas-Benjamin-Joseph), born Jan. 31, 1875; married Feb. 27, 1900: Elmer Galley. Residence, 1910, Huntington Park, Calif. Children:

3518. I. William Galley, b. Jan. 6, 1902.

3519. II. Cyrus Galley.

1852. JOSEPHINE BOND (William-Benjamin-Silas-Benjamin-Joseph), born April 5, 1877; died Nov. 5, 1903; married May 18, 1902: Hugh Gerrard. Children:

3520. I. Thelma Gerrard, b. Aug. 20, 1903.

1853. EMMA BOND (William-Benjamin-Silas-Benjamin-Joseph), born April 5, 1881; married Oct. 9, 1902: Albert Gerrard. Residence, 1910, Santa Anna, Orange County, Calif.

1854. BESSIE BOND (William-Benjamin-Silas-Benjamin-Joseph), born April 14, 1884; married ——— White. Residence (1910), Columbus, N. M.

1860. ERNEST CLIFFORD BOND (Silas-Eli-Silas-Benjamin-Joseph), born April 26, 1877, at Iowa Falls, Ia.; married May 20, 1903: Sadie Myrick. Residence (1910) Milwaukee, Wis. Children:

3522. I. Clifford Myrick, b. March 27, 1904.

3523. II. Marjorie, b. March —, 1906.

1861. WALTER WINFIELD BOND (Silas-Eli-Silas-Benjamin-Joseph), born 1879, in Geneva, Ia.; married June 11, 1907: Mabel Weightman. Residence (1910), Kalispell, Mont. Ch:

3524. I. Lucile, b. March 27, 1908.

1864. RAYMOND LESLIE BOND (Silas-Eli-Silas-Benjamin-Joseph), born April 21, 1885; married Jan. 2, 1906: Mary Louise Barr. Present occupation, actor. Children:

3525. I. Geneva, b. July —, 1908.

1867. JOHN WESLEY BOND (Daniel-Silas-Silas-Benjamin-Joseph), born Oct. 22, 1861; married Sept. 24, 1884: Isabelle Price, born June 17, 1862. Residence, Ottawa, Kas. Children·

3526. I. Annie May, b. Dec. 5, 1885.

3527. II. Jessie Matilda, b. March 6, 1888.

3528. III. Effie Isabelle, b. Jan. 15, 1891.

3529. IV. Frances Winfiels, b. Aug. 14, 1893.

3530. V. Lois Irene, b. June 3, 1897.

3531. VI. Mildred Blanche, b. July 6, 1903.

1868. SILAS WALTER BOND, A. M. (Daniel-Silas-Silas-Benjamin-Joseph), born Jan. 13, 1864; married Aug. 11, 1896: Hattie West, born Feb. 17, 1863. He is now (1910) president of the Wesleyan College at Miltonvale, Kas. Graduated from Wheaton college. He is a Wesleyan preacher of the gospel. Children:

3532. I. Silas Walter, b. Dec. 5, 1899.

3533. II. John West, b. Nov. 7, 1902.

1869. GEORGE W. BOND, B. S. (Daniel-Silas-Silas-Benjamin-Joseph), born Nov. 20, 1865; married Sept. 3, 1895: Mary Katherine Dresser, born May 31, 1873. Residence (1910), Wheaton, Ill. He graduated from Wheaton college. Children:

3534. I. Walter Dresser Bond, b. July 27, 1896; d. Sept. 25, 1897.

3535. II. Anna Adaline, b. March 6, 1898.

3536. III. Daniel William, b. July 8, 1899.

3537. IV. George W., b. Sept. 21, 1900.

3538. V. Geraldine Guinness, b. April 25, 1903.

3539. VI. John W.

3540. VII. Ernest W.

1870. SHELLEY A. BOND (Daniel-Silas-Silas-Benjamin-Joseph), born Aug. 26, 1868; married Oct. 16, 1900: Jessie L. Ward, born Feb. 26, 1866. Residence (1910) Santa Paula, Ventura County, Calif.

1871. NELLIE MAY BOND (Daniel-Silas-Silas-Benjamin-Joseph), born April 8, 1878; married Sept. 24, 1899: Charles Hazelhurst. She is professor of ancient language in the Wesleyan college at Miltonville, Kas., at this time (1910). Children:

3541. I. Madeline.

1874. CHARLES AUSTIN BOND (Josiah-Silas-Silas-Benjamin-Joseph), born Nov. 29, 1869, in Hardin County, Ia.; married July 3, 1895: Clara N. Penny, daughter of Newton and Catherine Penny, of Iowa Falls, Ia. Residence (1910), Nevada, Ia. Children:

3542. I. Cleo Arthur, b. April 25, 1896.

3543. II. Hattie Belle, b. Aug. 19, 1897.

3544. III. Frank Luverne, b. June 15, 1899.

3545. IV. James Walter, b. Nov. 4, 1902.

3546. V. Margaret Nellie, b. March 8, 1904.

1875. EUNICE ADALINE BOND (Josiah-Silas-Silas-Benjamin-Joseph), born Aug. 16, 1872; married Sept. 10, 1909: R. V. Jones, of Boone, Ia.

1876. LEWIS FRANKLIN BOND (Josiah-Silas-Silas-Benjamin-Joseph), born Sept. 26, 1874; married April 10, 1907: Mary Eda Brice, born Dec. 1, 1873. Occupation, locomotive engineer. Residence, Eagle Grove, Ia.

1877. MARY ETHEL BOND (Josiah-Silas-Silas-Benjamin-Joseph), born April 2, 1880; married Oct. 22, 1902: Wesley James Beck, a blacksmith. Residence, Hampton, Franklin County, Ia. Children:

3547. I. Vivian Lucile Beck, b. Oct. 30, 1903, in Hampton, Ia.

3548. II. Wesley Everet Beck, b. Nov. 28, 1907; d. Sept. 25, 1908.

1891. SYLVESTER BOND (John-Milton-Silas-Benjamin-Joseph), born Dec. 11, 1858; married Alena Jay. Residence, Marion, Ind. Children:

3549. I. Ethel, b. Oct. 22, 1882; d. 1890.

3550. II. Wilbur E., b. Dec. 7, 1884.

3551. III. Oral, b. Nov. 21, 1889.

3552. IV. John Roscoe, b. July 7, 1891.

3553. V. Walter Milton, b. May 10, 1893.

3554. VI. Oscar V., b. Dec. 17, 1894.

1892. MARY L. BOND (John-Milton-Silas-Benjamin-Joseph), born Feb. 21, 1861; married 1879: Wilson Myers. Residence, Grant County, Ind. Children:

3555. I. Bertha Amanda Myers, b. June 17, 1880.

3556. II. Albert Myers, b. Feb. 6, 1884.

1901. LUELLA BOND (Jesse-Stephen-Silas-Benjamin-Joseph), born ——; married 1897: Hezekiah Guy Dickason. Residence (1910) Muncie, Ind. Children:

3557. I. Carl Dickason.

3558. II. Fern Dickason.

3559. III. Earl Bond Dickason.

1902. CARL BOND (Jesse-Stephen-Silas-Benjamin-Joseph), born ——; married 1904: Malinda Holliday. Residence, Parker, Ind. Children:

3560.   I.   Opal, b. about 1905.

1903. XENIA MYRTLE BOND (Jesse-Stephen-Silas-Benjamin-Joseph), born ——; married Edward Hoel. Residence, Parker, Ind. Children:

3561.   I.   Mildred Hoel, b. about 1905.

1905. EDGAR H. BOND (Jesse-Stephen-Silas-Benjamin-Joseph), born ——; married Fern C. Rawlins. Residence, Muncie, Ind.

1906. JENNIE BOND (Jesse-Stephen-Silas-Benjamin-Joseph), born ——; married Dec., 1909: Earl Bartow. Residence, Parker, Ind.

1909. PRENTICE ALBERT BOND (B. Frank-Stephen-Silas-Benjamin-Joseph), born Sept. 18, 1883; married July 27, 1907: Lula Dees. Residence, Muncie, Ind.

1910. BLANCHE BOND (B. Frank-Stephen-Silas-Benjamin-Joseph), born Jan. 8, 1886; married Matthew Kettlewood. Children:

3570.   I.   Virgil Kettlewood, b. July 23, 1902.

She married second Jan., 1906: Frank Zaph. Residence, Muncie, Ind.

2013. LYDIA JANE BOND (Reuben-Darius-Joseph-Samuel-Joseph), born Aug. 2, 1861, in Hardin County, Ia.; married Dec. 25, 1879: John H. Adamson, son of Aaron and Amy. Residence, Chico, Calif. Children:

3571.   I.   Berthe May Adamson, b. Oct. 19, 1880, in Iowa; m. Alvah F. Earl.

3572.   II.   Maude E. Adamson, b. Oct. 6, 1882; m. Hugh Fairman.

3573. III.   Guy Edgar Adamson, b. Nov. 7, 1884.

3574.   IV.   Pearl Adamson, b. July 26, 1893.

3575.   V.   Ruby Adamson, b. July 26, 1893; d. 1895.

3576.   VI.   Frank Adamson, b. May 8, 1895.

2014. ALBERT W. BOND (Reuben-Darius-Joseph-Samuel-Joseph), born Feb. 21, 1863; married first: Emma Johnson. Ch:

3577.   I.   E. Bert.

He married second: Elizabeth Thompson. His occupation, contractor and builder. Residence, Chico, Calif.

2015. ETTA BOND (Reuben - Darius - Joseph - Samuel - Joseph), born Oct. 5, 1867; married T. I. Robson. Married sec-

ond: Herbert J. Hinds, a farmer. Residence (1910) Spokane, Wash. Children:
3601. I. Ralph Hinds.
3602. II. Bessie Hinds, d. by drowning, aged two years.
3603. III. Mildred Hinds.
2016. MARY BOND (Reuben - Darius - Joseph - Samuel Joseph), born April 10, 1869; married June 13, 1888: Herbert F. Kyte, born July 17, 1864, in Wisconsin. Address, Lewiston, Nez Perces County, Ida. Railroad station agent. Children:
3604. I. Cecil Kyte, b. Jan. 28, 1890, in Iowa.
3605. II. Floyd Kyte, b. Aug. 17, 1892, in Iowa.
3606. III. Harold A. Kyte, b. July 13, 1900, in Idaho.
2017. LON BOND (Reuben-Darius-Joseph-Samuel-Joseph), born Sept. 13, 1876, in Iowa; married June 10, 1903: Helen Ivy Woods, a native of California. He is an attorney at law. Residence (1910) Chico, Calif. Children:
3607. I. Helen, b. 1906.
3608. II. Reuben, b. 1909.
2026. REV. WILSON H. BOND (Asa-John-Joseph-Samuel-Joseph), born Oct. 17, 1854; married March 20, 1879: Sarah M. Neal, daughter of Mahlon and Mariah. Residence, Jonesboro, Ind. He is a minister of the gospel in Friends church. Children:
3609. I. Elbert A., b. March 16, 1880.
3610. II. Leroy Elam, b. Jan. 27, 1883.
3611. III. Wayne Wilson, b. Jan. 14, 1885.
3612. IV. Brose H., b. Nov. 12, 1886.
3613. V. Charles Asa, b. Sept. 15, 1892.
3614. VI. Alice Luella, b. Jan. 10, 1896.
2028. NATHAN ALVA BOND (Asa-John-Joseph-Samuel-Joseph), born June 26, 1861; married Nov. 19, 1887: Mary Small, daughter of Benjamin and Rachel (Presnall) Small. Residence, Marion, Ind. Children:
3615. I. Everett A., b. Feb. 1890; d. Aug., 1890.
3616. II. Asa Earl, b. Aug. 11, 1896.
3617. III. Edgar Ross, b. Sept. 23, 1897; d. Jan. 16, 1898, inft.
3618. IV. Edwin Ralph, b. Sept. 23, 1897; d. Oct., 1897.
He married second: Fannie Smith. Children:
3619. V. Leland Francis, b. Dec. 21, 1900.
3620. VI. Alva Leon, b. Jan. 3, 1903.

3621. VII.   Mary Louise, b. June 29, 1908; d. 1908.

3622. VIII. Harry Leonard, twins, b. June 29, 1908.

He married third Feb. 25, 1910: Nora Fox, of Marion, Ind.

2030. EMMA DORA BOND (Asa-John-Joseph-Samuel-Joseph), born June 27, 1866; married Dec. 17, 1885: Charles Terree, born Nov. 14, 1864, son of John and Rebecca (Harvey) Terree.. Children:

3623. I.   Jessie Terree, b. March 23, 1887.

3624. II.   Lola Terree, b. June 22, 1892.

3625. III. Osha Terree, b. June 27, 1895.

3626. IV.   Pauline Terree, b. July 14, 1899.

3627. V.   Martelle Terree, b. July 14, 1903.

2032. JOHN A. BOND (Eli-John-Joseph-Samuel-Joseph), born Jan. 24, 1855; married Jan. 22, 1876: Fannie R. Wright, daughter of William and Rebecca. Occupation, farmer and merchant. Residence 1910, Farmland, Ind. Children:

3628. I.   Raymond, b. Sept. 15, 1888.

3629. II.   Marion D., b. 1893.

2033. MARY E. BOND (Eli-John-Joseph-Samuel-Joseph), born Dec. 26, 1858; died Sept. 2, 1895; married Jan. 23, 1879: Lindo Keys, son of Joseph and Betsey (Coats) Keys, of Winchester, Ind. Residence, Randolp County, Ind. Children:

3630. I.   Anala E. Keys, b. July 7, 1880.

3631. II.   Alice W. Keys, b. Nov. 13, 1881.

3632. III. Ethel L. Keys, b. Aug. 2, 1885.

3633. IV.   Edna M. Keys, b. May 5, 1887.

3634. V.   Donna M. Keys, b. Oct. 28, 1889; d. June 26, 1892.

3635. VI.   Clarence L. Keys, b. March 11, 1892.

2034. LYDIA E. BOND (Eli-John-Joseph-Samuel-Joseph), born Feb. 8, 1862; married Sept. 29, 1876: William H. Thornburg. Residence, Farmland, Ind. Children:

3636. I.   Chonie R. Thornburg, b. Aug. 29, 1878.

3637. II.   Chester M. Thornburg, b. July 6, 1882.

2035. REBECCA JENNIE BOND (Levi-John-Joseph-Samuel-Joseph), born Oct. 25, 1855, in Indiana; married Feb. 9, 1878: Charles T. Durkee, born April 1, 1853. Residence, Fremont, Neb. Children:

1638. I.   William Whitacre Durkee, b. Jan. 7, 1879.

2036. LAVINA ANN BOND (Levi-John-Joseph-Samuel-

Joseph), born Aug. 25, 1857; married Rev. John N. Ross, pastor of Avondale Christian Church, in Muncie, Ind. Children:

3639.　I.　Cyntha Ross.
3640.　II.　Elizabeth Ross.
3641.　III.　Charles Ross.
3642.　IV.　Earnest Ross.

2037. JAMES ALBERT BOND (Levi-John-Joseph-Samuel-Joseph), born April 24, 1859; married Rose Field. Five children:

3643.　I.　Walter. N. f. k.
　　　II.　Samuel.
　　　III.　Benjamin.
　　　IV.　Henry.
　　　V.　Amy.

2038. SUSANNAH D. BOND (Levi-John-Joseph-Samuel-Joseph), born Oct. 17, 1861; married March 20, 1879: Levi Jessup, son of James and Rebecca (Cox) Jessup, of Randolph County, Ind. Residence 1910, Avenue City, Mo. Children:

3644.　I.　Maggie Lillian Jessup, b. Jan. 26, 1882.
3645.　II.　James Earl Jessup, b. March 4, 1885; d. Feb. 22, 1887.
3646.　III.　Benjamin Earnest Jessup, b. March 4, 1887.
3647.　IV.　Carl Levi Jessup, b. Dec. 23, 1889.
o3647.　　　Frank Milford Jessup, b. Sept. 14, 1893.
3648.　V.　Nancy Blanche Jessup, b. Oct. 6, 1895.
3649.　VI.　Lula, and
3650.　VII.　Lola, twins, b. July 27, 1901; Lola d. Sept. 27, 1901.
　　　IX.　Martha Ruth, b. Aug. 24, 1904.

2039. MARY ELIZABETH BOND (Levi-John-Joseph-Samuel-Joseph), born May 28, 1864; married —— Potter; he died. Her residence, 1910, ———. Children:

Paskel, Tessa, Metta, Tena, Hazel, Willard, Erba, Ivy.

2040. MARK W. BOND (Levi-John-Joseph-Samuel-Joseph), born Aug. 16, 1867; married first, Ada Perdue; she died May, 1891. Married second, April 2, 1892: Caroline Kist, of St. Louis, Mo. He is contractor and builder. Residence 1910, St. Louis, Mo. No children:

2043. GOLDIE E. BOND (Levi-John-Joseph-Samuel-Joseph), born June 15, 1875; married John James. Residence, Farmland, Ind.

2044. LUELLA D. BOND (Hiram-John-Joseph-Samuel-Joseph), born Dec. 26, 1865, at Arcanum, O.; married June 3, 1890, in Toledo, O.: Wilbur Taylor, born July 10, 1867, son of John V. Residence 1910, Cleveland, O. Occupation, traveling salesman.

2045. JOHN EDGAR BOND (Hiram-John-Joseph-Samuel-Joseph), born Nov. 12, 1869, at Farmland, Ind.; married Jan. 1, 1896: Mary G. Hollingshead. Residence, Toledo, O. Children:

   3680.   I.   Edwin Nathan, b. May 5, 1897.

   3681.   II.   Lucy Evelyn, b. Feb. 28, 1903.

   3682.   III.   Wilbur Leslie, b. Jan. 25, 1905.

2048. HETTIE A. BOND (Hiram-John-Joseph-Samuel-Joseph), born July 27, 1876, in Toledo, O.; married Sept. 31, 1898: John J. Van Etten, born May 28, 1876, son of J. W. and Eliza. Residence 1910, 746 Illinois street, Detroit, Mich. Children:

2049. PLEASANT ALMA BOND (Darius - John - Joseph - Samuel-Joseph), born Oct. 11, 1865, in Randolph County, Ind.; married Oct. 12, 1882: Florence B. Cowgill, born Sept. 16, 1867, daughter of William and Ann (McMann) Cowgill. Residence, Wayne County, Ind. P. O. 1910, Centerville, Ind. Children:

   3683.   I.   Frederick E., b. May 22, 1884.

   3684.   II.   Elsie A., b. Oct. 30, 1887.

   3685.   III.   Olive L., b. Dec. 14, 1899.

2050. LORETTA A. BOND (Darius-John-Joseph-Samuel-Joseph), born Nov. 18, 1866; married Jan. 24, 1889: Alonzo A. Thornburg, son of Maurice and Matilda (Thornburg) Thornburg. She died May 11, 1906. Residence, Winchester, Ind. Children:

   3686.   I.   Novarrina Thornburg, b. June 28, 1890.

   3687.   II.   Maurice Thornburg, b. Jan. 23, 1892.

   3688.   III.   Sala Thornburg, b. Nov. 8, 1895.

   3689.   IV.   Ruby Thornburg, b. July 27, 1897.

   3690.   V.   Halsie Thornburg, b. Aug. 1, 1903.

2051. ALISTUS J. BOND (Darius-John-Joseph-Samuel-Joseph), born Oct. 25, 1868; married Feb. 27, 1891: Mary M. Cowgill, daughter of William and Ann. Residence, Webster, Ind.

2052. OLIVER E. BOND (Darius-John-Joseph-Samuel-Joseph), born Feb. 15, 1873; married May 29, 1897: Nellie Cecil, daughter of Z. W. and Mary (King) Cecil. Residence, Parker, Ind. Children:

3700.　I.　Naomi.
3701.　II.　Roger Cecil.
3702.　III.　Esther.
3703.　IV.　Chlorice.

2054. LEONÓRA BOND (Darius-John-Joseph-Samuel-Joseph), born July 30, 1878, in Randolph County, Ind.; married July 20, 1893: Roy L. Amburn, son of William and Alice. Residence, Parker City, Ind. Children:
3704.　I.　Oma Amburn.
3705.　II.　D. Cedrick Amburn.

2055. PARVIN W. BOND (Darius-John-Joseph-Samuel-Joseph), born ——; a minister. Home address, Farmland, Ind.

2061. CLARA L. WHITAKER (Irene (Bond)-John-Joseph-Samuel-Joseph), born Dec. 20, 1872; married Clarence Fuller. Residence 1904, Dayton, O. N. f. k.

2080. LILLIE C. BOND (William-Mordecai-Joseph-Samuel-Joseph), born Aug. 7, 1870; married March 13, 1894: John Thomas, born April 4, 1871. Residence, Hebron, Adair County, Iowa. Children:
3706.　I.　Charles Albert Thomas, b. July 17, 1898.
3707.　II.　Iva Odessa Thomas, b. July 31, 1902.

2081. WILLIAM ALBERT BOND (William-Mordecai-Joseph-Samuel-Joseph), born July 13, 1873; married April 4, 1900: Ollie Smith, born Feb. 10, 1881. Address, Hebron, Adair Co., Iowa. Children:
3708.　I.　Faith Rose, b. April 16, 1901.
3709.　II.　Olive Fern, b. Aug. 6, 1902.
3710.　III.　Lillian M., b. Dec. 20, 1906.

2082. CLARA E. BOND (Jehiel-Levi-Joseph-Samuel-Joseph), born Nov. 7, 1868, in Wayne County, Ind.; married Aug. 8, 1894: Rev. Richard Haworth, son of James P. Residence 1910, Wabash, Ind. Pastor of Friends Church, in South Wabash. Children:
3711.　I.　Lura Haworth, b. Dec. 10, 1896.
3712.　II.　Wilfred Haworth, b. Nov. 2, 1901.
3713.　III.　Clifford Haworth, b. Feb. 12, 1905.

2083. DR. S. EDGAR BOND (Jehiel-Levi-Joseph-Samuel-Joseph), born Aug. 1, 1876, in Wayne County, Ind.; married Myrtle J. Palin, born Aug. 3, 1875, daughter of Jesse and Mary (Fry) Palin, of Fountain County, Ind. He is a physician and surgeon. Secretary of the American Association for the study of Spondylotherapy. Residence, Richmond, Ind. Children:

3714.   I.   Byron Leland, b. May 8, 1906.

3715.   II. Finley Palin, b. Nov. 4, 1909.

2084. JENNIE BOND (Jehiel-Levi-Joseph-Samuel-Joseph), born Oct. 24, 1878; married Aug. 2, 1905: Walter S. Painter, superintendent of schools, Lowell, Ind. Children:

3716.   I.   Mildred Painter and

3717.   II. Lowell Painter, twins, b. Sept, 17, 1906.

2092. OTIS R. BOND (Dr. Caleb-Amer-Thomas-Samuel-Joseph), born Nov. 15, 1864; married Sept. 2, 1890: Emma L. Holmes, daughter of David and Mary F. Residence, New Castle, Ind. Children:

3718.   I.   Ralph Ardo, b. Sept. 3, 1892.

3719.   II. Lucy Marie, b. Sept. 6, 1897.

2097. LEONA BOND (Mahlon-Amer-Thomas-Samuel-Joseph), born Jan. 28, 1874; married Dec. 24, 1899: Rev. Zeno H. Doan, son of Ephraim and Jane (Hadley) Doan. Residence, New Providence, Hardin County, Iowa. Children:

3720.   I.   Kenneth Bond Doan, b. Aug. 9, 1901.

2098. REV. LESLIE BOND (Mahlon-Amer-Thomas-Samuel-Joseph), born Jan. 1, 1876. Minister Friends Church. Residence, Indiana-Iowa. Address 1912, Fountain City, Ind.

2140. WESLEY BOND (Calvin-Jesse-Thomas-Samuel-Joseph), born ——; married 1880: Mollie Conner. Occupation, farmer. Residence, Westfield, Ind. In 1895 he married second wife: Aletha Tomlinson. Children:

Names not reported.

2141. ARTALISSA BOND (Calvin-Jesse-Thomas-Samuel-Joseph), born ——; married William Hill. Residence, Hamilton County, Ind. Children:

3723.   I.   Emma Hill, b. ——.

3724.   II. Margaret Edith Hill.

2142. WILLIAM C. BOND (Calvin-Jesse-Thomas-Samuel-Joseph), born 1860; married May 25, 1892: Clara F. Siler, born 1872, daughter of Jeremiah H. and Eleanor. Residence, Fowler, Kas. Children:

3725.   I.   Frederick W., b. 1893.

3726.   II. Eleanor L., b. 1897.

3727.   III. Margaret A., b. 1902.

3728. IV. Sarah Catherine, b. March 24, 1904.

3729. V. Rufus Calvin, b. Jan. 16, 1907.

2143. CLARA S. BOND (Calvin-Jesse-Thomas-Samuel-Joseph), born ——; married Elbert B. Morris. Residence, Bloomingdale, Ind. Children:

3730. I. Freeda Morris.

3731. II. Byron Morris.

3732. III. Emery Morris.

2144. JESSE BOND (Calvin-Jesse-Thomas-Samuel-Joseph), born ——; married Dora Alvey. Residence, Carmel, Ind. Occupation, painter and paperhanger. Children:

3733. I. Haley.

He married second, 1908: Amelia Ortwine.

2145. OLIVER P. M. BOND (Calvin-Jesse-Thomas-Samuel-Joseph), born ——; married Grace Hall. Occupation, mail carrier. Residence, Indianapolis, Ind. Children: N. f. k.

2146. AUSTIN BOND (Calvin - Jesse - Thomas - Samuel - Joseph), born ——; married 1908: Lillian Sanders. Residence, Carmel, Ind.

2152. THOMAS J. BOND (William-Jesse-Thomas-Samuel-Joseph), born Aug. 27, 1857; married Aug. 1878: Elizabeth Sheppard; she died. Children:

3744. I. Urah E., b. Oct. 5, 1880.

He married second June 21, 1889: Catherine Black, daughter of Peter and Elizabeth. Residence, Wayne County, Ind. Address (1910) Richmond, Ind. Children:

3735. II. Sarah, b. May 13, 1890.

3736. III. William, b. May 23, 1891.

3737. IV. Phebe, b. Jan. 9, 1893; m. Nov. 20, 1909: Robert J. Paddock.

3738. V. Lula May, b. Feb. 15, 1895.

3739. VI. Roy Black, b. March 20, 1899.

2153. FRANKLIN W. BOND (William-Jesse-Thomas-Samuel-Joseph), born Sept. 17, 1860; married May 25, 1886: Anna Mary Emmons. Residence, Richmond, Ind. Children:

3740. I. Nellie R., b. July 3, 1887; married April 27, 1908: Thomas McAvoy.

3741. II. Hershel, b. May 24, 1889.

3742. III. Anna M., b. Sept. 1, 1891; m. Dec. 11, 1909: Walter B. Chapman.

2155. JOHN M. BOND (William-Jesse-Thomas-Samuel-Joseph), born July 27, 1865; married Feb. 3, 1887: Jennie S. Cheesman, born Oct. 6, 1864, daughter of Vernon and Catherine Cheesman. Residence, Wayne County, Ind. Address (1910), Richmond, Ind. R. F. D. No. 7. Children:

3743.   I.   Fannie Alice, b. Oct. 1, 1889; m. Oct. 28, 1908: William J. Feasel.

2156. CHARLES E. BOND (William-Jesse-Thomas-Samuel-Joseph), born Nov. 5, 1867; married Dec. 29, 1892: Caroline J. Wadkins; she died July 14, 1901. Residence, Richmond, Ind. Children:

3744.   I.   Harry, b. Oct. 10, 1893.
3745.   II.   Winifred, b. May 30, 1897; d. July 8, 1897.
3746.   III. Rosa A., b. Nov. 5, 1898.
3747.   IV.   Edith, b. March 18, 1901.

He married second Dec. 22, 1906: Anna Fraiser.

2157. WILLIAM PENN BOND (William-Jesse-Thomas-Samuel-Joseph), born Nov. 5, 1871; married May 16, 1896: Subina Miller, daughter of John and Margaret. Residence (1910), Williamsburg, Ind. Children:

3748.   I.   Carrie, b. March 8, 1891.
3749.   II.   Clifford, b. Nov. 26, 1892; d. Feb. 21, 1902.
3750.   III. Myrtle, b. Sept. 2, 1894.
3751.   IV.   Jessie, b. Dec. 8, 1896; d. Oct. 16, 1897.
3752.   V.   Della, b. May 8, 1904; d. Oct. 18, 1905.

2160. ADALINE V. BOND (Cornelius - Thomas - Thomas - Samuel-Joseph), born Aug. 17, 1854; married Oct. 16, 1884: DeWitt C. Jay, born Sept., 1851, son of Henry and Priscilla. Residence, Webster, Wayne County, Ind.

2162. LOUISA EMMA BOND (Cornelius-Thomas-Thomas-Samuel-Joseph), born Sept. 8, 1858; married Aug. 29, 1895: Everet Pickett, born Dec. 5, 1861, son of William and Ellen. Residence, Webster, Ind.

2163. WILLIAM ALBERT BOND (Cornelius - Thomas - Thomas-Samuel-Joseph), born Aug. 31, 1860; married Aug. 29, 1895: Estella S. Irvin, daughter of Henry M. and Amanda Irvin. Residence, Webster, Ind. Children:

3753.   I.   Marie Elizabeth, b. Oct. 3, 1896.

2164. CHARLES THOMAS HARTMAN BOND (Cornelius-

Thomas-Thomas-Samuel-Joseph). Residence, Richmond, Ind. N. f. k.

2166. JENNETTE BOND (Cornelius - Thomas - Thomas - Samuel-Joseph), born Jan. 19, 1872, in Wayne County, Ind.; married Feb. 22, 1899: Orlando Harry Little, born Nov. 28, 1865, in Randolph County, Ind., son of Nathan T. and Miriam. Residence, Richmond, Ind. Children:

3754. I. Lowell Cornelius Little, b. March 9, 1901.

3755. II. Miriam Elizabeth Little, b. Sept. 20, 1902.

2169. LUELLA BOND (Lindley-Thomas-Thomas-Samuel-Joseph), born Aug. 29, 1868; married James Thompson, son of William and Rohanna. Residence, Webster, Ind. Occupation, farmer. Children:

3756. I. Hazel Thompson, b. June 16, 1893; d. Nov. 11, 1894.

3757. II. Cora E. Thompson, b. Nov. 11, 1894.

2170. WILLIAM ALBERT BOND (Lindley-Thomas-Thomas-Samuel-Joseph), born Dec. 18, 1869; married March 18, 1893: Cora E. Thomas, daughter of Peter and Priscilla. Residence, Wayne County, Ind. In city fire department, Richmond, Ind.

2178. HARVEY CHASE EARL (Lucinda (Bond) - Hiram-Thomas-Samuel-Joseph), born Nov. 28, 1860, in Oregon; married Dora F. Boggs, born Dec. 30, 1874, daughter of William and Mary. Residence (1904) Steptoe, Wash. Children:

3758. I. Reefa Earl, b. July 5, 1894.

3759. II. Isa I. Earl, b. Feb. 23, 1899.

3760. III. Ivy Earl, b. June 28, 1900.

2183. ROSE R. BOND (Elam-Hiram-Thomas-Samuel-Joseph), born Jan. 14, 1875; married Sept. 1, 1896: Martin Boyer. Residence, Idaho. Children:

3761. I. Clara Ellen Boyer, b. Sept. 14, 1900.

2184. OLIVER E. BOND (Elam-Hiram-Thomas-Samuel-Joseph), born Nov. 21, 1876; married Dec. 25, 1900: Mary Stone.

2201. NATHANIEL B. ADAMSON (Phebe (Bond) -Pleasant-Thomas-Samuel-Joseph), born Feb. 25, 1861; married Feb. 25, 1883: Mary Belle Garn, born May 1, 1862. Occupation, farmer. Residence, Alberta, Canada. Children: .

3800. I. Leona May Adamson, b. May 3, 1884, in Iowa.

3801. II. John Adamson, b. Dec. 27, 1888.

3802. III. Oscar Irvin Adamson, b. Nov. 23, 1900.

3803. IV. Clara Adamson, b. July 11, 1903, in Alberta, Can.

2204. WILLIAM E. ADAMSON (Phebe (Bond)-Pleasant-Thomas-Samuel-Joseph), born Feb. 17, 1868; married May 3, 1894: Ada Florence Coles, born Nov. 1, 1861. Residence, Iowa. Children:

3804. I. Estella May Adamson, b. May 9, 1895.

3805. II. Tilman Arthur Adamson, b. July 24, 1896.

3806. III. Hannah Phebe Adamson, b. Dec. 22, 1897.

3807. IV. Frank Elsworth Adamson, b. Oct. 26, 1900.

2205. TILMAN P. ADAMSON (Phebe (Bond)-Pleasant-Thomas-Samuel-Joseph), born May 14, 1870; married May 16, 1891: Mary Rosetta Coles, born May 20, 1863; occupation, farmer. Residence, Warren County, Iowa. Children:

3808. I. Lorena Adamson, b. April 17, 1892; d. Aug. 31, 1892.

3809. II. William L. Adamson, b. March 28, 1894; d. Oct. 7, 1895.

3810. III. Loren Adamson, b. June 5, 1896.

3811. IV. Leo Adamson, b. July 25, 1897. ·

3812. V. Mabel Adamson, b. Jan. 8, 1899.

3813. VI. Bonnie Adamson, b. May —, 1900.

2206. MARY ALICE ADAMSON (Phebe (Bond)-Pleasant-Thomas-Samuel-Joseph), born Oct. 20, 1872; married June 28, 1899: Owen M. Crumley, born Sept. 7, 1868. Residence, Iowa.

2208. EVA M. BOND (Exum-Pleasant-Thomas-Samuel-Joseph), born Aug. 31, 1865, in Warren County, Ia.; married May 13, 1882, in Custer County, Neb.: Jesse E. Garringer, born June 20, 1850; he died March 11, 1895, in Cherry County, Neb. She married second Dec. 25, 1902: Erwin A. Hadley, born June 19, 1857, in Morgan County, Ind. Residence, Earlham, Iowa. Children of first marriage:

3814. I. Edward Garringer, b. March 3, 1884; d. 1884.

3815. II. Albert E. Garringer, b. June 15, 1885; d. April 11, 1886.

3816. III. Edith M. Garringer, b. March 10, 1887; d. April, 1887.

3817. IV. Harry B. Garringer, b. July 13, 1888, in Nebraska; d. May 25, 1900, in Earlham, Iowa.

3818. V. Noah A. Garringer, b. Dec. 11, 1890, in Nebraska.

3819. VI. Louisa Jane Garringer, b. June 7, 1894, in Custer Co., Neb.

2209. LUELLA M. BOND (Exum-Pleasant-Thomas-Samuel-Joseph), born April 2, 1868; married Dec. 19, 1891, in Custer County, Neb.: Francis M. Lively, born Jan. 7, 1868, in Randolph County, Ill. Occupation, carpenter. Residence, Linden, Iowa. Children:

3820. I. Estella Margaret Lively, b. Oct. 27, 1892.

3821. II. Dorothy C. Lively, b. June 19, 1897; d. 1898.

2210. JESSE BOND (Exum-Pleasant-Thomas-Samuel-Joseph), born March 1, 1872, in Dallas County, Ia.; married June 7, 1902: Cyrena Morgan, born Sept. 5, 1866. Residence, Goldfield, Colo.

2213. FLORA M. BOND (Hiram-Pleasant-Thomas-Samuel-Joseph), born Aug. 31, 1873; married Walter S. Smith, born June 1, 1867; died July 23, 1898. Children:

3822. I. Albert G. Smith, b. Nov. 11, 1893; d. Dec. 15, 1894.

3823. II. Alvin Bond Smith, b. Feb. 24, 1895.

She married second: S. Leroy Smith. Children:

3824. III. Bruce Leroy Smith, b. Oct. 30, 1901.

2214. NETTIE ANN BOND (Thomas-Pleasant-Thomas-Samuel-Joseph), born June 10' 1870; married Oct. 30, 1890: Frank Robertson, son of Levi and Eunice. Residence (1910) Bridgeport, Neb. Children:

3825. I. Ralph Robertson.

3826. II. Henry Robertson.

3827. III. Florence Robertson.

3828. IV. Olive Robertson.

3829. V. Laith Robertson.

3830. VI. Elnora Robertson.

2215. ROSETTA BOND (Thomas-Pleasant-Thomas-Samuel-Joseph), born Sept. 27, 1873; married Aug. 26, 1902: Gustaff Eckberg. Residence (1910) Chase, Neb.

2216. MOLLIE S. BOND (Thomas-Pleasant-Thomas-Samuel-Joseph), born March 15, 1882; married Dec. 14, 1898: Milton M. Cook, son of James and Emily. Residence (1910) Kolls, S. D. Children:

3831. I. Cora Cook.

3832. II. Floyd Cook.

3833. III. Otis Cook.

3834. IV. Esther Cook.

3835. V. Iva Cook.

2217. EFFIE AUGUSTA BOND (Thomas-Pleasant-Thomas-Samuel-Joseph), born Dec. 3, 1884; married George Thomas. Residence (1910) Cambridge, Neb. Children:

3836. I. Florence Thomas.

3837. II. Vernon Thomas.

3838. III. Earnest Thomas.

2222. EDITH MAY BOND (Elam-Pleasant-Thomas-Samuel-Joseph), born Oct. 26, 1883; married March 20, 1902: Wilbur A. League, a farmer. Residence, Bloomington, Neb. Children:

3839. I. Grace Violet League, b. Aug. 15, 1903.

2225. LAVERA SIMON (Anna (Bond)-Pleasant-Samuel-Joseph), born Oct. 20, 1877, in Iowa; married April 17, 1901, in Nemaha County, Kas.: Isaac Leroy Howe, born Sept. 6, 1878. Residence, Soldier, Jackson County, Kas. Children:

3840. I. Chester Orlow Howe, b. Aug. 14, 1902.

2238. CORNELIA L. MILNER (Phebe (Bond) - Amasa - Samuel-Samuel-Joseph), born July 14, 1859; married March 12, 1887: John Vetter, born July 16, 1857, son of Adam and Eve (Hughes) Vetter. Residence, Redoak, Iowa. Children:

3851. I. Maude Vetter, b. Feb. 22, 1888.

3852. II. Cornelia Vetter, b. Nov. 6, 1890.

3853. III. John Milner Vetter, b. Oct. 2, 1895.

2240. ANNA MILNER (Phebe (Bond) - Amasa - Samuel - Samuel-Joseph), born May 10, 1861, in Iowa; married in Omaha, Neb., Feb. 20, 1895: William Henry Emery, born 1865, son of John and Mattie (Scott) Emery. Residence, Omaha, Neb.

2241. OLIVER AMASA MILNER (Phebe (Bond)-Amasa-Samuel-Samuel-Joseph), born Feb. 20, 1863; married Jan. 27, 1892: Cornelia Merritt, born April 21, 1867, daughter of Hon. N. W. and Plumie (Johnson) Merritt. Residence, Redoak, Iowa.

2242. ALICE N. MILNER (Phebe (Bond)-Amasa-Samuel-Samuel-Joseph), born Jan. 21, 1865; married Oct. 15, 1890: John William Stacy, born Jan. 20, 1859, son of Horatio and Mary. Residence, Omaha, Neb. Children:

3854. I. Ruth Stacy, b. Dec. 3, 1891.

3855. II. Edna Stacy, b. Jan. 27, 1894.

2244. HARVEY E. MILNER (Phebe (Bond)-Amasa-Samuel-Samuel-Joseph), born Sept. 17, 1870; married April 30, 1896: Cedella Hite, born Aug. 30, 1874, in Princeton, Ill. Residence, Ogden, Utah. Children:

3856. I. Marion Olive Milner, b. June 18, 1899, in Redoak, Iowa.

3857. II. Ronald Milner, b. Nov. 3, 1902, in Boulder, Col.

2245. EMMA RHODA MILNER (Phebe (Bond)-Amasa-Samuel-Samuel-Joseph), born Oct. 30, 1872, in Redoak, Iowa; married Feb. 15, 1893: D. B. Lyon, son of J. N. and Sophia, born Oct. 7, 1867. Ranchman. Residence, Carbondale, Colo.

3858. I. Bernice Lyon, b. Dec. 12, 1893, in Belgrade, Neb.

3859. II. Florence Lyon, b. April 11, 1896.

3860. III. Lois Lyon, b. Dec. 9, 1897.

2251. MAUDE L. BOND (Amasa-Amasa-Samuel-Samuel-Joseph), born Jan. 24, 1870; married Sept. 23, 1897: Chris Kohli. Residence, Redoak, Iowa.

2252. CLARENCE B. BOND (Amasa-Amasa-Samuel-Samuel-Joseph), born Dec. 6, 1871; married Sept. 23, 1897: Adda Honey, born Nov. 21, 1871, daughter of William E. and Ellen. Residence, Iowa, Colorado. P. O. Victor, Colo. Children:

3861. I. Leroy Maxwell, b. in Colorado, July 24, 1903.

2253. EFFIE B. BOND (Amasa-Amasa-Samuel-Samuel-Joseph), born Dec. 5, 1871; married William Burgess Honey, born Jan. 21, 1870, son of William E. and Ellen (Fleety) Honey. Residence, Iowa Falls, Okla. P. O. Stillwater, Okla. Children:

3862. I. Jay Burgess Honey, b. Dec. 28,1891.

3863. II. Thane Ivory Honey, b. July, 1893.

2255. MARY ETTA BOND (Isaac-Samuel-Samuel-Samuel-Joseph), born July 7, 1867, in Hamilton County, Ind.; married Sept. 2, 1887: Ambrose Cox. Residence 1910, Maquoketa, Iowa. Children:

3864. I. Claude E. Cox, b. Sept. 6, 1890.

2257. LAURA EMMA BOND (Isaac-Samuel-Samuel-Samuel-Joseph), born July 22, 1872; died April 10, 1906; married Jan. 15, 1896: Jerome Thomas Wise. Residence, Hamilton County, Ind. Children:

3865. I. Ethel Irene Wise, b. June 26, 1902.

3866. II. Grace Muriel Wise, b. Aug. 25, 1904.

2260. IDA MAY BOND (Isaac-Samuel-Samuel-Samuel-Joseph), born Feb. 13, 1878; married April 2, 1896: Alvin Addison Cox. Address 1910, Noblesville, Ind., R. F. D. 8. Children:

3867.　I.　Isaac Darrel Cox, b. Jan. 7, 1897.

3868.　II.　Jesse Walter Cox, b. Oct. 18, 1899.

3869.　III.　Edna May Cox, b. May 4, 1903.

3870.　IV.　Dorothy Cox, b. April 9, 1906.

2261.　ALTHA CARRIE BOND (Isaac-Samuel-Samuel-Samuel-Joseph), born June 16, 1881; married Dec. 23, 1901: J. Walter Toye. Residence 1910, 48 Gladstone avenue, Indianapolis, Ind. Children:

3871.　I.　Margaret, and

3872.　II.　Louise Toye, twins, b. Dec. 9, 1902.

2262.　IRA M. BOND (Ahijah-Samuel-Samuel-Samuel-Joseph), born Oct. 31, 1857, in Indiana; married Dora Lamb. Residence, Wichita, Kas. Children:

3873.　I.　Estella O., b. Dec. 18, 1883.

3874.　II.　Milford E., b. July 5, 1889.

3875.　III.　Mabel, b. Dec. 18, 1890.

3876.　IV.　R. Opal, b. Jan. 4, 1894.

2264.　SAMUEL S. BOND (Ahijah-Samuel-Samuel-Samuel-Joseph), born Aug. 22, 1863; married March 21, 1894: Mary Louise Bartl, born Feb. 12, 1875, in Daber, Germany. Residence 1910, Stafford, Kas. Children:

3877.　I.　Charles Ahijah, b. Jan. 14, 1895.

3878.　II.　Roy Sylvanus, b. April 12, 1896; d. Nov. 27, 1896.

3879.　III.　Cyril Baveley, b. March 22, 1898.

3880.　IV.　Almeda Louise, b. April 10, 1901.

2265.　JOHN C. BOND (Ahijah-Samuel-Samuel-Samuel-Joseph), born March 28, 1873, in Tonganoxie, Leavenworth County, Kas.; married Dec. 30, 1896, in Rock Creek, Jefferson County, Kas.: Cora E. Fleming, born April 1, 1872, in Platte County, Mo., daughter of Jared and Indiana (Castetter) Fleming. Residence 1910, Ozawkie, Kas., R. F. D. 2. Children:

3881.　I.　Herbert A., b. Nov. 23, 1900.

2269.　ALBERT L. BOND (Barclay-Samuel-Samuel-Samuel-Joseph), born Oct. 30, 1860; married Sarah Alice Thornton, born Feb. 23, 1870, daughter of Enos and Rose Ann. Residence 1910, Rose Hill, Butler County, Kas. Children:

3882.　I.　Leroy, b. Sept. 14, 1890.

3883.　II.　Everett, b. April 10, 1892.

3884.　III.　Clarence J., b. March, 1894.
3885.　IV.　Nellie M., b. Aug. 2, 1895.
3886.　V.　Edith M., b. Jan. 10, 1898.
3887.　VI.　William F., b. Aug. 9, 1900.
3888.　VII.　Glenn L., and
. 3889.　VIII.　Gladys Bell, twins, b. Feb. 17, 1903; both d. 1903.
3890.　IX.　Herald, b. Nov. 26, 1905.
3891.　X.　Irene Alice, b. July 11, 1908.

2270. MAHLON D. BOND (Barclay-Samuel-Samuel-Samuel-Joseph), born Dec. 29, 1861; married Ora A. Johnson, born Aug. 8, 1868. Residence, Haviland, Kas. Children:

3891.　I.　Mary E., b. Feb. 21, 1890.
3892.　II.　Melva Nellie, b. March 2, 1892; d. Sept. 29, 1893.
3893.　III.　Bessie Roberta, b. June 8, 1894.
3894.　IV.　Mahlon Barclay, b. Nov. 26, 1896.
3895.　V.　Lillian L., b. Sept. 25, 1898.
3896.　VI.　Eddie L., b. Jan. 25, 1900.
3897.　VII.　Ruth M., b. Dec. 8, 1906.
3898.　VIII.　Louise, b. Nov. 27, 1909.

2271. RUTH A. BOND (Barclay-Samuel-Samuel-Samuel-Joseph), born Dec. 22, 1863; married 1883: Alpheus M. Cox, born April 26, 1857, in Randolph County, N. C. Residence 1910, Haviland, Kiowa County, Kas. Children:

3901.　I.　Alva G. Cox, b. 1884.
3902.　II.　Dora B. Cox, b. 1887.
3903.　III.　Melva R. Cox, b. 1889.
3904.　IV.　Nina O. Cox, b. 1894.
3905.　V.　Flora E. Cox, b. 1898.
3906.　VI.　Robert Barclay Cox, b. 1900.
3907.　VII.　Ira Alpheus Cox, b. 1902.

2272. ROBERT B. BOND (Barclay-Samuel-Samuel-Samuel-Joseph), born Feb. 22, 1864, in Indiana; married in Kansas: Martha Elizabeth Davis, born Nov. 25, 1865. Residence 1910, Rose Hill, Kas.

2273. FLORA E. BOND (Barclay-Samuel-Samuel-Samuel-Joseph), born Feb. 22, 1870; married Elias Baldwin, born Oct. 24, 1854, son of Jack Baldwin, of Marion, Ind. Children:

3908.　I.　Delight Baldwin, b. March 26, 1892.

3909.   II.   Anna Baldwin, b. Aug. 6, 1896.

3910.   III.   Ruth Baldwin, b. Nov. 9, 1901.

3911.   IV.   Catherine Baldwin, b. July 5, 1903.

3912.   V.   Grace Irene Baldwin, b. Sept. 1, 1907.

2274.   MILES H. BOND (Barclay-Samuel-Samuel-Samuel-Joseph), born March 14, 1872; married Jemima Jane Barker, born June 5, 1876. Residence 1910, Long Beach, Cal. Children:

3913.   I.   Oscar M., b. May 12, 1891.

3914.   II.   Faral E., b. Aug. 9, 1900.

2276.   SAMANTHA J. BOND (Barclay-Samuel-Samuel-Samuel-Joseph), born Oct. 17, 1876; married Oct. 9, 1898: William Osborn, born Dec. 2, 1874. Residence, Columbus, Kas. Children:

3915.   I.   Ralph Juston Osborn, b. Sept. 23, 1899.

3916.   II.   Robert Barclay Osborn, b. March 11, 1903.

3917.   III.   Paul Osborn, b. Dec. 7, 1908.

2277.   SAMUEL BOND (Barclay-Samuel-Samuel-Samuel-Joseph), born Sept. 12, 1878; married March 10, 1906: Daisy Mills, born Jan. 10, 1880. Residence, Kansas and California. Address 1912, Redlands, Cal. Children:

3918.   I.   Elvin Samuel, b. Jan. 9, 1904.

2280=C.   MARY E. MENDEHALL (Margaret (Bond)-Samuel-Samuel-Samuel-Joseph), born April 20, 1861; married John W. Bullard. Address 1910, Olney, Ill., R. F. D. 9. N. f.k.

2280=D.   BOSWELL WARD MENDENHALL (Margaret (Bond)-Samuel-Samuel-Samuel-Joseph), born July 8, 1863; married Ruhama Stainbrook. Residence, Lacygne, Kas.

2280=E.   ALMEDIA C. MENDENHALL (Margaret (Bond)-Samuel-Samuel-Samuel-Joseph), born Jan. 7, 1866; married John P. Boaz; she died. N. f. k.

2280=F.   J. WARREN MENDENHALL (Margaret (Bond)-Samuel-Samuel-Samuel-Joseph), born July 22, 1868; married Elizabeth Ratcliff; he died. N. f. k.

2280=G   CHARLES A. MENDENHALL (Margaret (Bond)-Samuel-Samuel-Samuel-Joseph), born Sept. 15, 1870; married Lillie Jones. Residence, Lacygne, Kas.

2280=H.   JAMES W. MENDENHALL (Margaret (Bond)-Samuel-Samuel-Samuel-Joseph), born Sept. 1, 1874; married Lucy Twinkle. Residence, Lacygne, Kas.

2280=I. MARGARET MENDENHALL (Margaret (Bond)-Samuel-Samuel-Samuel-Joseph), born March 6, 1877; married Aug. 24, 1898: Arthur E. Wells. Address 1910, Nora, Ind., R. F. D. 11. Children:

3919.   I.   Mary Florence Wells, b. Oct. 16, 1899.

2281. ELIZA JANE BOND (Silas-Ellis-Samuel-Samuel-Joseph), born Feb. 24, 1860; married Feb. 15,1882: Frank Mesenhimer, born July 17, 1858, son of Henry and Nancy. Residence, Overbrook, Kas. Children:

3920.   I.   Gertie Mesenhimer, b. July 20, 1883.

3912.   II.   Arthur Mesenhimer, b. March 9, 1885.

3922.   III.   Ethel Mesenhimer, b. Jan. 6, 1894.

2282. HARVEY THOMPSON BOND (Silas-Ellis-Samuel-Samuel-Joseph), born March 31, 1862; married March 4, 1884: Nannie Stratton, born April 22, 1868, daughter of John and Melva. Residence, Lawrence, Kas., R. F. D. Children:

3923.   I.   Eliza, b. Jan. 14, 1891.

3924.   II.   Helen, b. Sept. 5, 1893.

2283. MILTON ELMORE BOND (Silas-Ellis-Samuel-Samuel-Joseph), born Sept. 21, 1864; married March 19, 1889: Susie Catherman, born Dec. 18, 1869, daughter of Michael and Nellie. Residence, Lawrence, Kas., R. F. D.

2284. MARY ETTA BOND (Silas-Ellis-Samuel-Samuel-Joseph), born July 3, 1867; married Sept. 15, 1888: Frank Sauer, born Dec. 29, 1869, son of Frederick and Marguerite. Residence, Lawrence, Kas. Children:

3925.   I.   Bertha Sauer, b. July 10, 1890.

3926.   II.   Josephine Sauer, b. Dec. 9, 1893.

3927.   III.   Minnie Sauer, b. Dec. 21, 1900.

        IV.   Frederick Sauer, b. March 23, 1903.

2286. DORA ELLEN BOND (Silas-Ellis-Samuel-Samuel-Joseph), born Jan. 26, 1872; married Feb. 16, 1893: Silas Barton, son of Matthew and Minerva. Residence in Lawrence, Kas. Children:

3928.   I.   Leta Barton, b. Feb. 14, 1894.

3929.   II.   Gladys Barton, b. Aug. 29, 1895.

3930.   III.   Owen Barton, b. July 22, 1897.

3931.   IV.

2287. RACHEL ANNA BOND (Silas-Ellis-Samuel-Samuel-Joseph), born Oct. 25, 1875; married Nov. 20, 1895: Ezra Barnhart, born May 3, 1872, son of Daniel and Susie. Residence, Overbrook, Kas. Children:

3932.   I.   Oscar Barnhart, b. July 22, 1897.

3933.   II.   Amy Barnhart, b. Sept. 24, 1898.

3934. III.   Alda Barnhart, b. June 23, 1900.

2288. DANIEL 'BERT BOND (Silas-Ellis-Samuel-Samuel-Joseph), born July 18, 1878; married April 17, 1901: Lucy Barnhart, daughter of Daniel and Susie. Residence, Overbrook, Kas.

2291. ALICE BOND (Enos-Ellis-Samuel-Samuel-Joseph), born Jan. 24, 1860; married March 14, 1877: Peter Carlson, a native of Sweden. Residence, Kansas. Children:

3935.   I.   Sophia Carlson, b. Jan. 28, 1878; d. Jan. 29, 1898; married May 19, 1897: Myron Haner.

3936.   II.   Rosa Carlson, b. July 14, 1880; m. Oct. 4, 1899: Myron Haner.

3937. III.   Tena Carlson, b. Sept. 6, 1882; d. Sept. 1, 1901.

3938.   IV.   Clarence Carlson, b. Sept. 13, 1884.

3939.   V.   Arthur Carlson, b. Nov. 11, 1886; d. Sept. 21, 1897.

3940.   VI.   Henry Carlson, b. Feb. 4, 1889.

3941. VII.   Clara Carlson, b. June 6, 1891.

3942. VIII.   Enos Carlson, b. Jan. 12, 1894.

3943.   IX.   Nellie Carlson, b. Aug. 1, 1896.

2292. ADALINE BOND (Enos - Ellis - Samuel - Samuel-Joseph), born Jan. 5, 1862; married July 6, 1881: Gustaf Johnson, a native of Sweden; he died June 3, 1901. Residence, Lawrence, Kas., R. F. D. 8. No children:

2293. ELLIS BOND (Enos-Ellis-Samuel-Samuel-Joseph), born Dec. 4, 1863; married May 20, 1880: Mary Webber. Residence, Lawrence, Kas. Children:

3944.   I.   Maud, b. Sept. 29, 1889.

3945.   II.   Marvin, b. Nov. 12, 1891.

3946. III.   Alvin, b. April 16, 1893.

3947.   IV.   Lillie, b. Aug. 9, 1896.

3948.   V.   Ruth, b. Aug. 14, 1899.

2294. CLARA BOND (Enos-Ellis-Samuel-Samuel-Joseph), born Oct. 1, 1866; married March 17, 1886: Charles Longanecker, a farmer. Residence, Lawrence, Kas. Children:

3949.   I.   Clark Longanecker, b. Feb. 2, 1887.

3950.   II.   Leonard Longanecker, b. April 3, 1890.

2298. CALVIN S. BOND (Enos-Ellis-Samuel-Samuel-Joseph), born May 16, 1870; married Dec. 19, 1900: Lillian Shade. Residence, San Diego, Cal. Occupation, farmer. Children:

3951. I. Ross, b. Aug. 26, 1903.

2300. DEMMING BOND (Enos-Ellis-Samuel-Samuel-Joseph), born Nov. 22, 1874; married Dec. 23, 1897: Estella Darnell. Occupation, grocer. Address, Lawrence, Kas. Children:

3952. I. Roy, b. April 27, 1899.

3953. II. Clyde, b. March 8, 1904.

2301. PORTER BOND (Enos-Ellis-Samuel-Samuel-Joseph), born Jan. 28, 1877; married Dec. 12, 1900: Maud Flory. Residence, Douglas County, Kas. Children:

3954. I. Murray, b. Feb. 28, 1902.

2312. AMELIA BOND (Thomas-Ellis-Samuel-Samuel-Joseph), born Nov. 17, 1873; married Aug. 16, 1901: Emerson Downey. Residence, Lakeside, Chelan County, Wash. Occupation, farmer and fruit raiser. Children:

3955. I. Mary Eunice Downey, b. Aug. 19, 1903; d. Jan. 11, 1906.

3956. II. Milford Harold Downey, b. Sept. 13, 1905.

3957. III. Forest Parker Downey, b. Aug. 4, 1908.

2313. CELIA BOND (Thomas - Ellis - Samuel - Samuel - Joseph), born Sept. 3, 1876; married Sept. 19, 1894: John B. Higgins, a fruit and grain raiser. Residence 1910, Brays, Douglas County, Wash. Children:

3958. I. Walter Thomas Higgins, b. May 20, 1899.

3959. II. Arthur Clarence Higgins, b. Feb. 9, 1906.

2314. RALPH BOND (Thomas - Ellis - Samuel - Samuel - Joseph), born April 3, 1879. Residence, Brays, Wash. Farmer. Not married.

2315. MABEL EDNA BOND (Thomas-Ellis-Samuel-Samuel-Joseph), born April 2, 1882; married Sept. 3, 1901: Wesley M. Porter, a grain and fruit farmer. Residence, Lakeside, Wash. Children:

3960. I. Kenneth Vancie Porter, b. Sept. 19, 1903.

3961. II. Velma Porter, b. Aug. 28, 1905; d. March 14, 1906.

2339. WILLIAM A. BOND (DeWitt-Nathan-Elizabeth-Samuel-Joseph), born Aug. 19, 1866; married Nov. 7, 1894: Anna M. Jefferis, daughter of Abraham S. and Edith (Fellows) Jefferis, of Richmond, Ind. Educated at Earlham College;

graduated from the law department of DePauw University in the spring of 1890. Occupation, attorney-at-law. Served as prosecuting attorney from 1898 to 1903. Residence, Richmond, Ind.

2341. SCHUYLER C. MESENHIMER (Lucina (Bond)-Nathan-Ornon-Samuel-Joseph), born Jan. 8, 1872; married May 4, 1898: Clara M. Stake. Residence, Lawrence, Kas. Children:

3965. I. Harold S. Mesenhimer, b. Feb. 7, 1899; d. July 30, 1903.

3966. II. Orland Leslie Mesenhimer, b. Sept. 10, 1900.

2342. ALWILDA A. MESENHIMER (Lucina (Bond)-Nathan-Ornon-Samuel-Joseph), born Jan. 3, 1875; died Feb. 8, 1903; married June 30, 1897: Charles A. Griffith. Residence, Lawrence, Kas. Children:

3967. I. Leona Lavina Griffith, born Aug. 7, 1898.

3968. II. Edwin D. Griffith, b. June 26, 1900; d. Feb. 10, 1901.

2343. TENA BOND (Sylvester-Nathan-Ornon-Samuel-Joseph), born Nov. —, 1875; married Dec. 20, 1893: William A. Kinzie. Residence, Lone Star, Kas. He is a farmer and preacher Brethren Church. Children:

3969. I. Roy Clifford Kinzie, b. Oct. 10, 1895.

3970. II. Archie Raymond Kinzie, b. Aug. 26, 1899.

3971. III. Lila Fern Kinzie, b. Feb. 15, 1903.

3972. IV. Earl Christian Kinzie, b. May 31, 1907.

2352. FRANK HENDERSON (Ellen (Bond)-John-Ornon-Samuel-Joseph), born March 19, 1872; married Feb. 4, 1895: Ella Johnson, born June 26, 1878. Residence, Severy, Kas. Children:

3973. I. William Henderson, b. Nov. 2, 1895.

3974. II. Edith Henderson, b. Feb. 26, 1898.

3975. III. Cecil M. Henderson, b. Nov. 21, 1900.

3976. IV. Louis Franklin Henderson, b. June 8, 1903.

2610. JAMES M. BOND (William S.-Joel-Joseph-John-Joseph), born April 27, 1862; married Dec. 2, 1886: Emma V. Cowen, of Jerseyville, Ill. Occupation, conducting a restaurant. Residence 1912, Indianapolis, Ind. Children:

I. Lora Mae.

II. Lester M., d. Nov. 13, 1908, in Panama.

III. Mary Alma.

2624. JOHN J. BOND .(Berry-John-Joseph-John-Joseph), born March 15, 1862; married Nannie Moore, of Bates County, Mo. Residence 1910, Chandler, Okla. Children:

3980. I. Bertie.
3981. II. Carey.
3982. III. Delbert.

2625. JOSEPH C. BOND (Berry-John-Joseph-John-Joseph), born Feb. 10, 1864; married Eliza Berry. Residence, Henley, Cole County, Mo. Children:

3983. I. Oliver.
3984. II. George.

2627. MARY L. BOND (Berry-John-Joseph-John-Joseph), born July 19, 1868; married Barney Berry, a farmer. Residence, Kendree, Okla. Eight children.

2628. JAMES P. BOND (Berry-John-Joseph-John-Joseph), born Nov. 18, 1870; married first, Sophronia Amos; married second, Callie Campbell. Three children.

2629. LEONA F. BOND (Berry-John-Joseph-John-Joseph), born Jan. 2, 1875, in Miller County, Mo.; married Dec. 7, 1902: William Taylor, born April 17, 1856. Occupation, plumber and steamfitter. Residence, Oklahoma City.

2630. LOUIS S. BOND (Berry-John-Joseph-John-Joseph), born Oct. 9, 1877; married Elizabeth Scott. Residence, Stroud, Okla. Three children.

2631. ADA A. BOND (Berry-John-Joseph-John-Joseph), born Aug. 11, 1881; married Byron Scott. Residence, Russellville, Mo. One child.

2632. EDWIN S. BOND (Berry-John-Joseph-John-Joseph), born Aug. 2, 1884; married Mirtie Wais (?). Residence, Enon, Mo. One child.

2712. BARCIE MAY BOND (William-William-Joel-John-Joseph), born ———; married James Monroe Hill. Address, Latham, Mo.

2713. ARTHUR JEFFERSON BOND (William-William-Joel-John-Joseph), born ———; married Minnie Stevens. Address, Meta, Mo.

2715. A L M A B O N D (James-William-Joel-John-Joseph), born Oct. 23, 1877; married William Murphy; residence, Little Rock, Ark. No issue. They separated and in 1909 she assumed her former name of Alma Bond. Residence 1911, Little Rock, Ark.

2716. MAY BOND (James-William-Joel-John-Joseph), born ——; married B. B. Moad, an electrician. Residence, Los Angeles, Cal. Children:

    I.　Lewis Brooks Moad, b. Nov. 12, 1903, in St. Louis, Mo.

    II.　Edna May Moad, b. June 8, 1905.

Mr. and Mrs. Moad separated and she married second: Dr. G. T. Pool. Residence 1911, Grandview, Wn.

2718. MINNIE E. BOND (James-William-Joel-John-Joseph), born Jan. 18, 1891, in Van Buren, Ark.; married Sept. 28, 1908, in Spokane, Wash.: Lewis Gilbert Cameron. Children:

    I.　Eugene Gilbert Cameron, b. Sept. 19, 1909.

    II.　Berry (?) George Cameron, b. Jan. 3, 1911, in Spokane, Wash.

CHAPTER VIII.

EIGHTH GENERATION.

3000. EFFIE BOND (William-Jedidiah-Edward-Benjamin-Edward-Joseph), born Sept. 29, 1886; married Sept. 7, 1905: Volney Spellman. Residence 1150, State street, Springfield, Mo. Children:

4101.   I.　Gladys May Spellman, b. June 16, 1906.

4102.   II.　William Spellman, b. Nov. 30, 1907.

4103.   III.　Hazel Spellman, b. April 15, 1909.

3001. IDA MAY BOND (William-Jedidiah-Edward-Benjamin-Edward-Joseph), born Jan. 19, 1888; married Feb. 15, 1903: George Jester. Residence 1910, Kiowa, Barber Co., Kas. Children:

4104.   I.　William Eugene Jester, b. Sept. 1, 1905.

4105.   II.　Delphine Perleana Jester, b. Feb. 2, 1907.

3002. LYDIA RACHEL BOND (William-Jedidiah-Edward-Benjamin-Edward-Joseph), born Nov. 25, 1889; married Aug. 13, 1905: Archibald Boren. Residence, Polk County, Mo. Children:

4106.   I.　Muriel Boren.

3023. RAYMOND JEDIDIAH BOND (Amos-Jedidiah-Edward-Benjamin-Edward-Joseph), born March 11, 1887, in

Miami, Mo.; married July 24, 1907: Minnie Jackson. Address 1910, Miami, Mo.

3024. RUBY MAE BOND (Amos-Jedidiah-Edward-Benjamin-Edward-Joseph), born July 8, 1889, at Ash Grove, Mo.; married Oct. 22, 1906: Calvin Harris. Address 1910, Slater, Mo.

3025. GERTRUDE AUGUSTA BOND (Amos-Jedidiah-Edward-Benjamin-Edward-Joseph), born Jan. 8, 1892; married Jan. 12,1910: Marion W. Lawler, of Slater, Mo.

3072. LORING BOND (Joel-John-William-John-Edward-Joseph), born May 8, 1886; married. Residence, Henry County, Ind. Children:

4110. I. Carlos Francis, b. ——, 1909.

3110. ALMEDA BOND (Isom-Abel-Joshua-John-Edward-Joseph), born Jan. 29, 1870; married Dec. 8, 1885, in Rice County, Kas.: Edward Jones, a stone cutter. Residence 1910, Cooperton, Okla. Children:

4116. I. Evan Isom Jones, b. Oct. 5, 1886.
4117. II. Myrtle Jones, b. March 10, 1892.
4118. III. Robbin Jones, b. May 3, 1894.
4119. IV. Nellie Jones, b. Aug. 1, 1898.

3111. IRVA HILLYARD BOND (Isom-Abel-Joshua-John-Edward-Joseph), born Jan. 22, 1872; married Feb. 24, 1896, in Melrose, Kas.: Lillie Eagan, daughter of John. Occupation, stationary engineer. Residence, Chitwood, Mo. Children:

4120. I. Clara, b. Dec. 15, 1897.
4121. II. Beulah.
4122. III. Clarence Glen.

3112. IDA BOND (Isom-Abel-Joshua-John-Edward-Joseph), born Dec. 29, 1873; married Dec. 12, 1890: Logan L. Baxter. Residence, Butte, Mont. Children:

4123. I. Ervin Isom Baxter, b. Dec. 21, 1895.
4124. II. Mary Ann Baxter, b. Aug. 3, 1898.
4125. III. Logan Luther Baxter, b. April 5, 1903.

3120. WILLIAM M. STOUT (Rachel (nee Bond)-Abel-Joshua-John-Edward-Joseph), born April 4, 1869; married Oct. 16, 1897, at Hutchinson, Kas.: Lillian C. Smith, daughter of John W. and Hannah T. (Little) Smith. Occupation, farmer. Residence 1910, Cullison, Kas. Children:

I. Ima C. Stout, b. Nov. 27, 1905, at League City, Texas.

3128. JAMES HARVEY BOND (Abel-Abel-Joshua-John-

Edward-Joseph), born Dec. 25, 1873; married Maggie Barngrass. Children:

4126.   I.   Mabel L.
4127.   II.   Hazel Permelia.

He married second. N. f. k.

3129. MARY CHRISTINA BOND (Abel-Abel-Joshua-John-Edward-Joseph), born Sept. 28, 1875; married Theodore Kirkhart. Residence 1910, Gate, Okla. Children:

4128.   I.   Carl C. Kirkhart.
4129.   II.   Earl A. Kirkhart.
4130.   III.   Fay Kirkhart, a son.
4131.   IV.   Fern Kirkhart.

3131. WILLIAM H. BOND (Abel-Abel-Joshua-John-Edward-Joseph), born Aug. 26, 1881; married Carrie King, daughter of Charles and Ella. Residence 1910, Cullison, Pratt County. Kas. Children:

4132.   I.   William Oscar.
4133.   II.   Alvin Joshua.
4134.   III.   Irene Elizabeth.

3132. BERTHA ALMEDA BOND (Abel-Abel-Joshua-John-Edward-Joseph), born Aug. 15, 1883; married George King, son of Charles and Ella King. Residence 1910, Cullison, Pratt County, Kas. Children:

4135.   I.   Lorena May King.
4136.   II.   Verne Albert King.
4137.   III.   Mary King.

3145. AMY LORENA BOND (John S.-Abel-Joshua-John-Edward-Joseph), born Oct. 16, 1886, in Cherokee Nation; married Rev. J. B. Hoskinson. Residence 1910, Liberal, Seward County, Kas.:

3161. REBECCA CAROLINE BOND (Elbert-William-Joshua-John-Edward-Joseph), born July 16, 1883, in Hardin County, Iowa; married July 15, 1899: in Odell, Neb.: Ezra E. Bardwell. Address 1910, Sidney, Iowa. Children:

4138.   I.   Lester H. Bardwell, b. Nov. 30, 1901.
4139.   II.   Carl Elbert Bardwell, b. Sept. 4, 1903.
4140.   III.   Elsie Viola Bardwell, b. April 9, 1905.

3162. ELSIE ELIZABETH BOND (Elbert-William-Joshua-John-Edward-Joseph), born Aug. 18, 1885, in Stark County, Ill.;

married Dec. 24, 1901, in Sidney, Fremont County, Iowa: Wilson
Thompson. Residence 1910, Coburg, Iowa. Children:
    4141. I. Lewis Ancil Thompson, b. May 29, 1903.
    4142. II. Wayne Thompson, b. Sept. 25, 1904.
    3287=A. HULDAH VARNEY (Jane (Bond)-Samson-Benja-
min-Edward-Edward-Joseph), born Nov: 14, 1884; married April
4, 1904: August Frederick Johann Le Clair, born Dec. 28, 1869:
Children:
    4143. I. Alma Emma Bessie Le Clair, b. Feb. 3, 1905.
    4144. II. Albert Carl Johann Le Clair, b. Oct. 10, 1906.
    4145. III. Anna Fredrick Le Clair, b. Sept. 1, 1908.
    3287=B. BESSIE VARNEY (Jane (Bond)-Samson-Benja-
min-Edward-Edward-Joseph), born April 15, 1886; married Johann Peter Carl Tafelmeyer, born March 4, 1881. Children:
    4146. I. Henry Albert Tafelmeyer, b. Sept. 22, 1907.
    3609. ELBERT A. BOND (Wilson-Asa-John-Joseph-Sam-
uel-Joseph), born March 16, 1880; married May 18, 1904: Jessie Brooks. Residence, Jonesboro, Ind. Children:
    4147. I. ———, son, b. Jan. 31, 1908.
    3611. WAYNE WILSON BOND (Wilson-Asa-John-Joseph-
Samuel-Joseph), born Jan. 14, 1885; married May 6, 1908: Elva
Means. Residence, Grant County, Ind.
    3612. BROSE H. BOND (Wilson-Asa-John-Joseph-Samuel-
Joseph), born Nov. 12, 1886; married June 21, 1909: Ethel Thorn-
burg. Residence, Grant County, Ind.
    3623. JESSIE TEREE (Emma (Bond)-Asa-John-Joseph-
Samuel-Joseph), born March 23, 1887; married March 12, 1904:
Mart Trader. Residence 1909, Fairmount, Ind. Children:
    Three daughters.
    3683. FREDERICK E. BOND (Pleasant-Darius-John-Jo-
seph-Samuel-Joseph), born May 22, 1884; married Dec. 12, 1907:
Emma B. Clevenger. Residence, Wayne County, Ind.
    3684. ELSIE A. BOND (Pleasant-Darius-John-Joseph-Sam-
uel-Joseph), born Oct. 30, 1887; married Jonathan Bright Winters. Residence, Brownsville, Ind. Children:
    4161. I. Earl L. Winters, b. May 31, 1909.

CHAPTER IX.

JOHN BOND.

There is in my possession considerable data of the descendants of John Bond, whose name is mentioned early in the pages of this book; he was brother to Joseph and son of Benjamin and Ann (Paradise) Bond, of Bidestone, Wiltshire, England. John came over to Philadelphia in 1721, and married, 1724–5, Sarah Cadwallader, and settled within the limits of Byberry Monthly Meeting of Friends. He died in 1748. For other data of him the reader is referred to Chapter I. His children:

5001.   I.   Benjamin.
5002.   II.   Abraham.
5003.   III.   John.
5004.   IV.   Edward.
5005.   V.   Isaac.
5006.   VI.   Hannah.

5001. BENJAMIN BOND (John), born ——; Benjamin married in Christ's Church, Philadelphia, Oct. 13, 1755: Rosanna Miller, and moved to Goshen, Chester County, 1762, and became a member of Chester Monthly Meeting in 1787. Children:

5007.   I.   Abraham.
5008.   II.   Amos.
5009.   III.   Elizabeth, whose husband in the year 1798 was Adam Barton.

5002. ABRAHAM BOND (John), married Elizabeth Cadwallader (?). He died prior to 1797. Residence, Bucks County, Pennsylvania. Children:

5010.   I.   John; history wanted.
5011.   II.   Levi.
5012.   III.   Mary.

5003. JOHN BOND (John), born Feb. 14, 1735, O. S.; died 1775–8. He married, about 1758, Margaret Allen, and moved to Virginia in 1771. He and his wife were both eminent preachers among Friends. This I learned from their granddaughter, Leah George. Children:

5013.   I.   Allen.
5014.   II.   Hannah (O'Neil).
5015.   III.   Rebecca (Koontz).
5016.   IV.   Mary (Barr).

5017. V. John, b. Dec. 20, 1775.

5004. EDWARD BOND (John), born in Pennsylvania, Sept. 4, 1738; died May 23, 1826; he married June 7, 1765: Mary Fox; she died April 14, 1831, and it was thought she was 88 years old. They moved to Virginia in 1778, placing their church membership with Hopewell Monthly Meeting. They were living in Bedford County in 1793, and a few years later moved to Grayson County, Virginia. The copy of the family record in my possession is all written out in full without use of figures. Children:

5018. I. Susan Bond, "was born the 27th of 3d month in the year of our Lord 1766, near 3 o'clock in the morning."

5019. II. Sarah Bond, b. Oct. 5, 1767, 2 o'clock a. m.

5020. III. Mary Bond, b. Aug. 22, 1769, 9 o'clock a. m.

5021. IV. Benjamin Bond, b. May 26, 1771, 4 o'clock a. m.

5022. V. Alice, b. May 23, 1773, near 4 o'clock a. m.

5023. VI. Martha, b. (Sunday) May 28, 1775.

5024. VII. Elizabeth, b. May 23, 1778.

5025. VIII. Ruth, b. Feb. 22, 1781.

5026. IX. Hannah, b. Feb. 3, 1783.

5027. X. Levi Bond, b. Feb. 7, 1785. Levi must have died prior to 1793, for in the list of the children given by Edward's cousin, Edward (Joseph), no mention is made of Levi.

5005. ISAAC BOND (John), born in Pennsylvania; married first, Jane Williams, by whom he had two daughters:

5028. I. Rebecca.

5029. II. Mary.

He moved to Virginia, apparently without family. His second wife was Lydia. Residence, Goose Creek, Bedford County, Va. Children:

5030. III. Joshua, b. April 18, 1788.

5031. IV. Israel, b. Dec. 18, 1789.

5032. V. Abraham, b. April 1, 1792.

5033. VI. Susley, b. April 2, 1798.

5034. VII. Reuben, b. Sept. 5, 1801.

Nothing further known of any of these.

5007. ABRAHAM BOND (Benjamin-John). Abraham's wife was Elizabeth. They were living near Chestertown, Delaware County, Penn., in 1797, and at that time had four sons and two daughters. Children:

5035. I. Benjamin.

5036. II. Jonathan.
5037. III. Amos.
5038. IV. Adam.
5039. V. Deborah.
5040. VI. Ann.
No further history.

5008. AMOS BOND (Benjamin-John). In 1793 Amos Bond (wife Rachel) lived in Delaware County, Penn., and at that time had only one child:

5041. I. Isaac. N. f. k.

5011. LEVI BOND (Abraham-John). Nothing has been learned of his descendants except from the memoranda of his cousin Edward Bond (Joseph), who visited him in 1797. He says Levi and his wife (Hannah) have three sons and two daughters. Residence, Newtown, Bucks County, Pa. Children:

5042. I. Abraham.
5043. II. Robert.
5044. III. Thomas.
5045. IV. Elizabeth.
5046. V. Jane.

5013. ALLEN BOND (John-John). Allen married in Virginia, Sarah Dobbins, and moved to Belmont County, Ohio, a few years later, when his son was a small boy. Children:

5047. I. Allen Bond, Jr.
5048. II. Joseph.
5049. III. John, b. Oct. 15, 1791.
5050. IV. Abner Dobbins.
5051. V. Rebecca (Broomhall).
5052. VI. Elizabeth (Smith) had one daughetr, Elizabeth. N. f. k.
5053. VII. Margaret; had no issue.
5054. VIII. Thomas; d. probably without issue.

5014. HANNAH BOND (John-John) married John O'Neil in Virginia. John came to Virginia from Maryland. They had three children. John died and some years later Hannah and the children all died. I have in my possession a copy of a letter written by Hannah O'Neil dated March 20, 1802. They lived near New Market, Va.

5015. REBECCA BOND (John-John). Rebecca married , Philip Koontz, a jolly Dutchman who came from Maryland to

Rockingham, Va. He had a farm and a sawmill on James branch of the Shenandoah river. They had only one daughter named Hannah, who married a man named Martin Lower. After three children were born to the Lowers they moved to Ohio. N. f. k.

5016. MARY BOND (John-John). She married George Barr, a native of Ireland. He parted from his wife and visited his native country a few years after his marriage. Mary died about 1808; buried at New Market, Va. He married again and settled in Newport, Delaware. Their only son was reared in Virginia. Children:

5055. I. George Washington Barr, b. Feb. 24, 1804.

5017. JOHN BOND (John-John), born Dec. 20, 1775; died May 24, 1854; married in Frederick County, Va., Oct. 1, 1800: Rachel Lupton. He was born at Rude's Hill on north fork of the Shenandoah river near Steambarger's, now known as Meemsbottom, Shenandoah County, Va. He lived a while at Coldstream on Capron river, Hampshire County, Va., now West Virginia. Removed from there to Frederick County, Va., about 1805, where he lived a larger part of his life a few miles north of Winchester. He never saw his father, as the father died before John was born. On Oct. 14, 1841, he married a second wife: Lydia McClun. The children are all from his first marriage. Children:

5056. I. Abner, b. Oct. 10, 1801.

5057. II. Hannah (George), b. Sept. 10, 1804.

5058. III. Leah (George), b. Dec. 4, 1804.

5059. IV. Sarah L., b. March 20, 1810; m. 1854: Miller Johnson. She d. s. p.

5060. V. John, b. 1812; d. inft.

5061. VI. Margaret (Baker), b. July 27, 1813.

5021. BENJAMIN BOND (Edward-John). The record says "Benjamin Bond, son of Edward and Mary his wife, was born the twenty-sixth of the Fifth month in the year of our Lord one thousand seven hundred and seventy-one near four o'clock in the morning." He was born within the bounds of Abington Monthly Meeting in Pennsylvania; moved with his father to Virginia when seven or eight years old. Then to Bedford County and later to Grayson County, Va., and from there to Ohio. Then about the year 1835 settled in Grant County, Ind., where he lived the rest of his days. He died Dec. 31, 1857, and is buried on a farm graveyard north of the city of Marion, Ind. He married Susannah Allen. Children:

5062.   I.   Joseph, b. Oct. 16, 1795; history wanting.
5063.   II.   Mary, b. Nov. 2, 1797; m. Edward Gaines.
5064.   III.   Edward.
5065.   IV.   Ruth (m. Abraham Woolman).
5066.   V.   Elizabeth (m. Samuel Woolman or Wildman).
5067.   VI.   Hannah (m. Marshall, settled in Ohio).
5068. VII.   Moses, b. Dec. 7, 1807, near Lynchburg, Va.
5069. VIII.   Sally (m. James Hicks). N. f. k.
5070.   IX.   Susannah (m. Samuel McNairy).

5047. ALLEN BOND, JR. (Allen-John-John), born in Virginia; moved with his parents to Belmont County, Ohio, where he married; name of wife not known to the writer. He was living at Morristown, Ohio, as late as 1885. Children:

5071.   I.   Rebecca, did not m.
5072.   II.   Mary Ann.
5073.   III.   Sarah (Graves).
5074.   IV.   Elizabeth; deceased.
5075.   V.   John H.; deceased.
5076.   VI.   John A., residence, Morristown, Ohio.
5077. VII.   William.
5078. VIII.   Elizabeth Jane; deceased. N. f. k.

5048. JOSEPH BOND (Allen-John-John), married and lived and died in Belmont County, Ohio. Children:

A-5071.   I.   Eliza.
A-5072.   II.   Jonathan.
A-5073.   III.   William; m.; had son Joseph and daughters Eliza and Mary.
A-5074.   IV.   Esther. N. f. k.

5049. JOHN BOND (Allen-John-John), born in Belmont County, Ohio, Oct. 15, 1791; died at Dublin, Wayne County, Ind., April 7, 1876; married 1822: Elizabeth McMillan, born in Pennsylvania, Jan. 8, 1800; she died Sept. 5, 1887. They settled in Wayne County, Ind., in 1839. Children:

A-5075.   I.   Rebecca, b. Feb. 24, 1824; d. Nov. 15, 1911; m. Laban Holland; had two ch: Louisa and Elbridge Holland.
A-5076.   II.   Rachel, b. 1826; m. Rudolph Burkett. Ch: I. Alcinda (Bradway).
A-5077.   III.   Calvin, b. Dec. 28, 1829.

A–5078. IV. Leah, b. Dec. 29, 1830; m. Hervy Craven, attorney-at-law, of Pendleton, Ind. He was Lieut. Col. of 89th Reg. Ind. Vol. Inft. She d. in June, 1909. Ch: I. Eva. II. Jessie. III. Nettie, m. Walter Lewis. IV. Alice. V. Hervy.

 5079. V. Abner, b. 1832.

 5080. VI. Jane, did not m.; d. Oct. 2, 1912.

 5081. VII. Sarah, b. May 11, 1837; m. James Hammond; Ch: I. Cassius. II. Eugenia. III. Elizabeth. IV. Murray.

A–5081. VIII. Maranda, did not m.

 5082. IX. Allen Bond, b. Oct. 6, 1841.

5050. ABNER DOBBINS BOND (Allen-John-John), born in Belmont County, Ohio; died at Cambridge City, Ind., 1863. Married Rebecca Long. Children:

 5083. I. Abner D. Bond, Jr., b. about 1838.

 5084. II. Harry.

 5085. III. Margaret.

 5086. IV. J. Russell Bond, d. at Cambridge City.

5051. REBECCA BOND (Allen-John-John), born ——; married a man named Broomhall. Children:

 5083. I. Elihu Broomhall; m. and had ch: Wilbur, Allen, Joseph, Clinton, Allie. N. f. k.

 5084. II. Allen Broomhall; m. ——; ch: Ella (Titus), Elizabeth, Mary Allen, Anna.

 5085. III. Olinda Broomhall; m. a Mr. Palmer; ch: Josie, Lizzie, Henry and Lewis Palmer.

 5086. IV. Lizzie Broomhall; m. a Mr. Gregg. Their ch: Rodney, Allen, Lewis and Ella Gregg. Ella married a man named Craig.

5055. GEORGE WASHINGTON BARR (Mary (Bond)-John-John), only son of George and Mary (Bond) Barr, was born in Virginia, Feb. 24, 1804, and in 1886 was still living at Woodstock, Shenandoah County, Va. He married in 1829, Mariah Henning, and reared a family of twelve. Four of his sons, I am informed, were soldiers in the southern army during the civil war, viz.: Joseph, Reuben, William, Elijah. Children:

 5087. I. Elizabeth M. Barr, b. March 10, 1830; m. Amos Dillinger.

 5088. II. Richard Pickering Barr, b. Aug. 25, 1831; m. Catherine Sprinkle. Res., Edgar County, Ill. Ch: George, Ida, perhaps others.

5089. III. Sarah Catherine Barr, b. Nov. 20, 1832; m. Daniel Dillinger. Ch: Adam, Robert and others.

5090. IV. John Samuel Barr, b. Sept. 11, 1835; m. Minerva Nott. Res. (1912) Blountsville, Henry Co., Ind. Ch: I. Memphis. II. Franklin. III. Della.

5091. V. William Harrison Barr, b. March 30, 1838; m. Jane Smootz. Ch: William L. and others.

5092. VI. Reuben H. Barr, b. March 30, 1838; m. Nancy Johnson. Res. (1885) New Castle, Ind. Ch: Grace L., Mary F. and Charles Barr.

5093. VII. Hannah Barr, b. Dec. 8, 1840; m. Philip Lentz and had six children: William K., Anna M., Virginia A., Charles Della M. and Hubert Lentz.

5094. VIII. Joseph Marshall Barr, b. Oct. 25, 1842; d. s. p. July 25, 1869.

5095. IX. Elijah Anderson Barr, b. Feb. 4, 1845; m. Sarah Kibler. Children: William H., John A., Mary C., Abbie A., Rebecca F.

5096. X. Benjamin Franklin Barr, b. Aug. 1, 1847; d. April 16, 1880; m. Rebecca Hollar (?). Children: Virginia, Verne, Franklin Mary.

5097. XI. Henry Solon Barr, b. June 23, 1849; m. Mariah Lentz. Children: Ellen, John, Alpha, Minnie M. and others.

5098. XII. Jacob Dillman Barr, b. Feb. 3, 1852; m. Anna Huddle. Children: Charles, Oceola.

5056. ABNER BOND (John-John-John), born Oct. 10, 1801; died Dec. 1, 1884, in Frederick County, Va., two miles north of Winchester; married, 1834: Mary Beale, born April 4, 1801, daughter of William Beale. Children:

5099. I. Rachel Ann, b. Jan. 3, 1835; m. Jacob Madison Harman. N. f. k.

5100. II. John Lupton Bond, b. Jan. 4, 1837.

5101. III. Isaac, b. April 24, 1838; d. March 11, 1845.

5102. IV. William A., b. April 16, 1841; d. Nov. 11, 1843.

5057. HANNAH BOND (John-John-John), born Sept. 20, 1804, in Virginia; died Jan. 20, 1880; married Jan. 12, 1825: Evan George, born Dec. 4, 1794; died Dec. 26, 1863. They first moved to Highland County, O., in 1829, and in 1851 settled in Hamilton County, Ind., near Boxleytown. Their children:

Richard, John P., Margaret, Rachel, Mary, Ellis, Enos

5058. LEAH BOND (John-John-John), born Dec. 4, 1807; married Dec. 24, 1828: John George, son of Richard and Mary. They settled in Hamilton County, Ind., in 1851. Their children:

Sarah L., Isaac C., Abner B., Amy (Baker), David, Lydia, Cyrus, Mary (Kellam), Leah (Bales) and John L. George.

5061. MARGARET BOND (John-John-John), born in Virginia July 27, 1830; moved to Highland County, O., and in 1851 moved to Hamilton County, Ind., north of the town of Westfield. She married George H. Baker. Their children:

I. Amby Baker, m. a Mr. Catterson, of Westfield, Ind.

II. Mary Baker, m. Dr. E. T. Mendenhall, of New Castle, Ind.

5064. EDWARD BOND (Benjamin-Edward-John), married Rachel (?) Woolman. Children:

5120. I. Asher, moved to Iowa.

5121. II. John, dec.

5122. III. Mary.

5123. IV. Rebecca (Marshall).

5124. V. Lizzie. N. f. k.

5068. MOSES BOND (Benjamin-Edward-John), born near Lynchburg, Va., Dec. 7, 1807; died in Grant County, Ind., Aug. 11, 1853; married March 5, 1829: Mary Sears, born Dec. 12, 1809; died Feb. 15, 1900, daughter of John and Penelope Sears. Children:

5125. I. John, b. in Ohio, Feb. 10, 1832; d. 1853.

5126. II. Joseph, b. in Ohio, May 13, 1834.

5127. III. Margaret (Jackson), b. in Indiana, July 26, 1836; d. 1869. N. f. k.

5128. IV. Benjamin, b. Nov. 29, 1838.

5129. V. Elizabeth (Cox), b. Jan. 6, 1841.

5130. VI. Penelope, b. 1843; d. inft.

5131. VII. Amos, b. Oct. 9, 1845; d. at Memphis, Tenn., in army, March 26, 1863.

5132. VIII. Mary (Comer), b. March 10, 1848.

5133. IX. Edward, b. 1851; d. infant, 1853.

5070. SUSANNAH BOND (Benjamin-Edward-John), married Samuel McNairy. Children:

Mary (Doan), Perry, Sarah, Margaret, Elizabeth; the latter married Dillon Cox, of Marion, Ind.

A=5077. CALVIN BOND (John-Allen-John-John), born Dec. 28, 1829; died Jan. 24, 1903, near Cambridge City, Ind.; married first, about 1858: Elizabeth Ball. Children:

    I. Virginia (Baumgardner).

    II. Alice (Silverstone).

He married Oct. 2, 1873: Martha Burkett. Two children by second wife:

    III. (1) Sanford Howard Bond, b. June 8, 1877, in Taylorville, Ill.; m. June 27, 1905, Cora Wissler. Res., 1912, Richmond, Ind. Sanford has three ch.:

      1. Ruth Elizabeth.

      2. Alise Virginia.

      3. Martha Sylvania.

    IV. (2) Lillian Agnes (Berry).

5079. ABNER BOND (John-Allen-John-John), born 1832 in Ohio; moved to Wayne County, Ind.; married Elizabeth Hall; he died 1883. Children:

    I. Elbridge.

    II. Mary.

    III. Nellie.

    IV. Dixon.

    V. Fay.

5082. ALLEN BOND (John-Allen-John-John), born in Wayne County, Ind., Oct. 6, 1841; married Anna E. Moore; he died April 19, 1896; served as sheriff of Wayne County, Ind., several years. Children:

    I. Edna.

    II. Jessie. N. f. k.

5100. JOHN LUPTON BOND (Abner-John-John-John), born Jan. 4, 1837; married Sept. 7, 1873: Ann M. Lupton. Residence, near Winchester, Va. Occupation, farmer and pomologist. Children:

  5134. I. Howell McPherson, b. Aug. 22, 1874.

  5135. II. Walter McClun, b. Dec. 2, 1875.

  5136. III. Allen Beal, b. Oct. 9, 1877.

  5137. IV. Edward Lupton, b. June 16, 1881.

  5138. V. Anna Sidwell, b. Sept. 18, 1882; d. Aug. 27, 1883.

  5139. VI. Mary Emma, b. May 9, 1884; d. Oct. 12, 1884, infant.

  5126. JOSEPH BOND (Moses - Benjamin - Edward - John),

born May 13, 1834, in Ohio; reared and resided in Grant County, Ind. He was a soldier during the civil war. Married Susannah Rich. Children:

    5140.   I.   Asher Bond, of Marion, Ind.

Joseph married second, Anna Wright. Children:

    5141.   II.   Morton.

    5142.   III.   Emma Delight.

    5143.   IV.   May (m. Arthur Baldwin).

    5144.   V.   Lewellen (m. Charles Bisk).

5128. BENJAMIN BOND (Moses-Benjamin-Edward-John), born Oct. 29, 1838, in Grant County, Ind.; died 1901; married August, 1858: Elizabeth Cox. Residence, Marion, Ind. Children:

    5145.   I.   Luther, b. Aug. 13, 1859.

    5146.   II.   Dr. Dillon, b. Oct. 23, 1864; optician. Residence, St. Louis, Mo.

    5147.   III.   Evaline, b. July 22, 1870; d. Sept. 2, 1878.

    5148.   IV.   Laura, b. Oct. 14, 1875; d. Dec. 3, 1903.

5129. ELIZABETH BOND (Moses - Benjamin - Edward-John), born Jan. 6, 1841: married Oliver Cox. Residence, Marion, Ind. Children:

    5149.   I.   William Cox, b. July 15, 1859; m.

    5155.   II.   Arthur Cox, b. Sept. 10, 1861.

    5151.   III.   Laura Cox, b. May 14, 1864; m. Matthew Fenimore.

    5152.   IV.   Mary Cox, b. Nov. 4, 1868.

    5153.   V.   Ella Cox, b. Oct. 22, 1873; m. Chester Ault.

    5154.   VI.   Anna Eliza Cox, b. June 6, 1876.

(The End.)

Joseph, b. 1704; m. Martha Rogers.
Edward Bond, b. 1740 (Son of Joseph); m. Ann Mills.

Benjamin, b. 1765.
m.
Mary Williams.

Edward, Jonathan, Jedediah,
Tabitha, Nathan.

Keziah,
m.
Daniel North.

John, b. 1769.
m.
Mary Huff.

William, Anna, John,
Nathan, Mary, Elizabeth,
Jesse, Joshua, Caleb,
Joseph.

William, b. 1771.
m.
Charlotte Hough.

Anna, Mary, Sarah,
Lydia, Jesse, Charlotte,
William, John, Ira.

Edward, b. 1774.
m.
Anna Huff.

Daniel, Benjamin, Keziah,
Elizabeth, Rachel, Edward,
John, Huldah, Anna,
Elias, Gideon.

Anna Bond, b. 1776.
m.
Abram Bunker.

Keziah, Thomas,
Phoebe, David,
Anna, Daniel.

Jesse, 1779.
m.
Phoebe Commons.

Nathan, Robert, John,
William, Enos, Isom,
Ruth, Hannah, Isaac,
Jesse, Lydia.

Joshua, 1781.
m.
Ruth Coffin.

Anna, Abijah, Deborah,
Phoebe, William, John,
Hepzibah, Elizabeth, Joshua
Daniel, Mary.

Joseph, 1785.
m.
Sarah Mendenhall.

Aaron, Isaac, Achsah,
Dinah, Mahlon, Marian,
Ann, Peter, Susannah,
Esther.

Samuel Bond, 1753–1812 (Son of Joseph and Martha); m. Elizabeth Beales.

Joseph Bond, b. 1704; m. Martha Rogers.

Martha, b. 1775.
m.
Nathan Ballard.

{ Ahira, Sarah, Rhoda,
Samuel, David,
Elizabeth.

Margaret, 1777–1862.
m.
Welcome Garrett.

{ Rachel, Jonathan, Hiram.
Jesse A.

Joseph S., 1779.
m.
Rachel Harrold.

{ Darius, Eunice, John,
Mordecai, Joseph, Amos,
Levi, Elihu, Rachel,
Zimri, Levina.

Thomas, 1781.
m.
Mary Nation.

{ Amer, Betsey, Jesse,
Thomas, Hiram, Pleasant,
Asenath, Phoebe Mary.

Sarah Bond, died, s. p.

Samuel, b. 1786.
m.
Charity Beeson.

{ Amasa, Samuel, Ellis,
Ann, Ruth, Jonathan,
Rhoda, Lydia, Jesse.

Dorcas, b. 1788.
m.
John Baldwin.

{ Joel, Eli, Rhoda,
Ann, Eliza, George.

Rachel, b. 1790.
m.
Thomas Teagle.

{ Ornon, Diadama, Margaret,
Lorenzo, Delila, Orthaniel,
Elmina, Isaac.

Elizabeth, b. 1795.
m.
Isaiah Baldwin.

{ Nathan I., Elizabeth,
Ann, Eunice, Rachel.

Ornon, b. 1798.
m.
Anna Hunt.

{ Riley, Eliza, Asher,
Jane, Nathan, John,
Jesse, Joel, Martha.

Ruth, b. 1802.
M. Joseph Teagle.
M. second: Ezekiel Haisley.

{ Matilda, Elizabeth, Martha,
Allen, Agatha, Eli.
And by second: Mary.

BOND INDEX.

Aaron.....................35, 63
Abel.................50, 102, 179
Abijah......................34, 62
Abner, 59, 125, 232, 233, 235, 236, 238
Abraham..........14, 230, 231, 232
Adam.................51, 105, 232
Ahijah...............80, 157, 218
Albert, 62, 69, 77, 79, 130, 137, 142,
   146, 147, 148, 149, 153, 158,
   162, 167, 199, 204, 207, 209,
   212, 213, 218.
Alfred........53, 95, 101, 105, 110
Alistus...................147, 208
Allen, 13, 127, 156, 173, 230, 232, 234,
   235, 238.
Alonzo.........................94
Alpheus..................80, 156
Alma....................147, 208
Alva....................159, 205
Alvin.........98, 140, 170, 222, 228
Amasa................41, 80, 157
Amer.....................40, 77
Amos, 14, 40, 76, 95, 173, 230, 232, 237
Andrew..................107, 177
Aquilla......................180
Archie.......................143
Ardo.........................210
Arlo.........................199
Arment...................37, 70
Arnold.......................107
Arthur, 61, 93, 124, 130, 140, 142,
   168, 202, 225.
Artemas..............57, 122, 191
Asa.................75, 146, 205
Asbury...................91, 168
Asher...............42, 84, 237, 239
Augustus.....................102
Austin, 109, 122, 123, 140, 152, 191,
   192, 202, 211.
Barclay..........80, 153, 158, 219
Barton...................46, 92
Beal.........................238
Beeson...................46, 93
Benjamin (Mary Walton).....14, 17
Benjamin (Mary Williams).......24
Benjamin (Ellen Goldsmith)......53
Benjamin (Lydia Test).........67
Benjamin (Martha Burt).........71
Benjamin (Rosanna Miller).....230
Benjamin (Elizabeth Cox).......239
Benjamin, 7, 8, 9, 10, 11, 14, 15, 16,
   17, 19, 21, 23, 24, 25, 28, 35,
   37, 43, 44, 45, 47, 53, 54, 62,
   67, 69, 71, 90, 94, 95, 112,
   131, 139, 142, 147, 171, 173,
   200, 207, 230, 231, 233, 237,
   239.

Berry....................88, 166
Bert, or Bertie, 98, 159, 174, 199, 204,
   222, 225.
Boughton.....................140
Bowman.......................114
Brose....................205, 229
Brown........................114
Byron........................210
Caleb.........27, 78, 112, 150, 188
Calvin, 37, 53, 60, 71, 78, 127, 144,
   152, 159, 211, 223, 234, 238.
Carey........................225
Carl.................142, 182, 203
Carlos.......................227
Caswell.................103, 181
Charles, 66, 68, 71, 85, 98, 103, 105,
   108, 111, 112, 126, 130,
   138, 140, 152, 153, 158, 171,
   187, 188, 195, 202, 205, 212,
   218.
Cecil...................193, 209
Chester......................159
Chlorice.....................209
Christian....................181
Christopher.............53, 110
Clair........................156
Clarence....123, 157, 217, 219, 227
Clark, or Clarkson......82, 98, 174
Cleo.........................202
Clement...............127, 195
Clifford.......71, 140, 175, 201, 212
Clifton......................153
Clinton.................83, 161
Clovesta...........84, 162, 163
Coffe........................89
Coin.........................173
Cornelius............79, 153, 180
Curtis.......................136
C. C.........................71
Cyril........................218
Cyrus.........53, 64, 110, 111
Daniel, 28, 35, 51, 53, 54, 68, 94, 105,
   113, 140' 158, 159, 171, 202,
   222.
Darius..............40, 75, 147
David..............54, 61, 130
Dayton.......................79
Dee..........................171
Delbert.............98, 175, 225
Demming.............159, 223
Desford......................156
DeWitt.............83, 153, 161
Dick.........................175
Dickson, or Dixon.........89, 238
Dillon.......................239
Dobbins................232, 235
Domel.................122, 191

Dora.........................170
Drewry........................93
Earl.....101, 157, **177, 178, 179,** 205
Earlington...................149
Earnest, 128, 140, 174, **196,** 197, **201,**
    202.
E. Bert.....................204
Eddie L......................219
Edgar, 142, 147, 149, 152, 177, 178,
    204, 205, 208, 209.
Edmund......................114
Edward (Ann Mills).............11
Edward (Anna Huff)............27
Edward (Nancy Hayworth)......47
Edward (Mary E. Knight)......114
Edward (Mary Fox)............**231**
Edward (Rachel Woolman)......**237**
Edward, 7, 9, 10, 11, **12,** 13, 16, 17,
    20, 23, 25, **27,** 28, 31, 47, 54,
    57, 95, 101, 105, **114, 123,**
    144, 162, 169, **172,** 230, **231,**
    234, **237, 238.**
Edwin...........167, 205, 208, **225**
Elam.......**24,** 79, 80, **154, 156,** 205
Elbert..........**102, 180,** 205, **229**
Elbridge.....................**238**
Eli, 18, **35, 37,** 60, 67, 75, 103, 140,
    146.
Elias..........28, 57, 122, **123,** 191
Elihu................**40, 48, 76,** 98
Elkanah......................89
Elisha........................52
Ellis....**41,** 80, 81, 82, 159, **161, 222**
Ellsworth.....................98
Elmer........................138
Elmore..................159, **221**
Elvin........................220
Elwood....................**69,** 75
Emmet..................168, 171
Enos, 30, 50, **60,** 76, 81, 98, **102,** 159
Erastus...............**54,** 66, 137
Ernest (see Earnest).
Evan.........................149
Everett...........174, 205, 218
Exum...................79, **155**
Ezra....................65, 136
Finley.......................210
Forice........................77
Fountain.....................171
Prancis, 66, 123, 138, 190, **192,** 205,
    227.
Franklin, or Frank, 47, 69, 85, 107, 109,
    139, 140, **142,** 152, **164, 166,**
    178, **200,** 201, 202, **203, 211.**
Fred, or Frederick, 77, 126, 140, 149,
    180, 208, 210, **229.**
Garton.......................167
Garver.......................109
George, **101,** 140, 150, 158, 169, 187,
    202, 225.

Gerald................**133, 177**
Gideon.......................28
Gilbert.....................**174**
Greely......................159
Greenwood..................175
Guy.........................168
Dr. H. A.....................71
Happy......................175
Harlan..................**126, 162**
Harold...........**133, 137,** 180
Harry, 98, 109, 122, 126, **174,** 191,
    195, 206, 212, 235.
Hartman................**153,** 212
Harvey..............159, **221, 227**
Herbert................159, 218
Henry, 47, 52, 59, 64, 67, 79, 102, 103,
    108, 110, 124, 140, 145, 153,
    162, 163, 182, 188, 193, 207.
Herald......................219
Hershal................**143, 211**
Hezekiah................**54, 113**
Hillyard................179, **227**
Hiram, 40, 75, 79, 80, **147, 155,** 180
Horace......................159
Houston....................168
Howard.................140, **238**
Howell.................168, **238**
Howland....................188
Huff........................**105**
Ira, 27, 52, 62, 105, 107, **156, 158,** 218
Irva...................179, **227**
Isaac, 13, 19, 21, 23, 30, 35, 43, **45,**
    46, 52, **61,** 64, 80, 87, **93,**
    94, 107, 156, **157, 166, 171,**
    230, 231, 232, 236.
Isom..........30, 60, 102, **128, 178**
Israel......................231
Jackson...........87, 91, **165, 167**
Jacob.................**54,** 80, **157**
James, 45, 80, 83, 84, 88, 90, 91, 114,
    115, 124, 147, 156, 164, 166,
    167, 168, 179, 193, 203, **207,**
    224, 225, 227.
Jasper......................172
Jedediah.......**25, 47, 95,** 173, **226**
Jefferson............91, **168, 225**
Jehiel................76, **148, 176**
Jehu.........................79
Jeremiah................57, **123**
Jesse (Phoebe Commons)........**29**
Jesse (Rachel Hobson)..........**49**
Jesse (Elizabeth Pitts)..........**82**
Jesse (Emily Randall)..........**84**
Jesse, 15, 17, 26, 27, **29,** 30, 36, 40, **41,**
    42, **49, 52,** 53, 60, **61, 69,** 75,
    78, 82, 84, 85, 107, **109,** 125,
    128, 130, 132, 137, 142, 152,
    155, **211, 215.**
Joel, 21, 23, **42,** 43, **44, 45,** 79, **85, 87,**
    88, **91,** 98, 154, **168, 175.**

John (Sarah Cadwallader)....9, 230
John (Jane Beeson)..........21, 22
John (Mary Huff)...........25, 26
John (Nancy Kennedy and Nancy
    Barnett)...............52
John H. (Emily Hockett)........75
John (Rhoda Stanbro)...........84
John (Marian Brady)...........87
John W. (Margaret Hinds).......93
John (Lucinda Adams)..........98
John (Rachel M. King)........101
John (Lydia Smith)............103
John (Thornzy Cheesman).....124
John J. (Mary Bone)..........132
John W. (Ellen J. Morrow)......141
John (Mary Magee)............142
John S. (Elizabeth Claborne)....145
John R. (America Hudson)......169
John W. (Cora M. Rowe).......171
John A. (Jane Brown)..........175
John S. (Jennie E. Blood)......180
John H. (Rosa Murdock).......182
John (Lula Wood).............182
John M. (Emily Boland).......193
John W. (Isabelle Price)........201
John A. (Fannie A. Wright).....206
John E. (Mary Hollingshead)....208
John M. (Jennie Cheesman)....212
John (Cora E. Fleming).........218
John (Nannie Moore)..........225
John (Margaret Allen)..........230
John (Rachel Lupton)..........233
John (Elizabeth McMillan).....234
John L. (Anna M. Lupton)......238
John, 7, 8, 9, 10, 11, 13, 14, 17, 21, 22,
    25, 26, 27, 28, 30, 35, 36, 40,
    42, 44, 46, 48, 49, 50, 51, 52,
    59, 62, 68, 69, 75, 80, 83, 84,
    87, 88, 91, 93, 94, 98, 101, 102,
    103, 105, 124, 126, 132, 140,
    141, 142, 145, 146, 147, 152,
    158, 163, 166, 167, 169, 170,
    171, 175, 178, 180, 182, 193,
    201, 202, 203, 206, 208, 212,
    218, 224, 230, 231, 232, 233,
    234, 236, 237.
Jonathan, 24, 25, 41, 47, 59, 77, 79,
    124, 232, 234.
Joseph (the immigrant), 7, 9, 10, 12,
    19, 20.
Joseph (Sarah Mendenhall).......35
Joseph S. (Rachel Harrold) 40
Joseph (Abigail Hinds)...........43
Joseph (Naomi Cox)............50
Joseph (Charity Hinds).........89
Joseph H. (Fannie Conley)......166
Joseph, 7, 9, 10, 12, 15, 16, 17, 19, 20,
    21, 23, 27, 31, 35, 40, 43, 44,
    50, 64, 75, 76, 87, 89, 95, 166,
    167, 225, 232, 234, 237, 238.

Joshua, 9, 16, 17, 26, 30, 31, 32, 33,
    34, 35, 50, 75, 102, 132, 148,
    179, 228, 231.
Josiah..................66, 68, 140
Kenneth.......................140
King...........................101
Laban.........................112
Lane..........................105
Larkin..............59, 60, 126, 127
Lawrence......................125
Lee..........94, 108, 125, 158, 171
Leigh.........................101
Leland....................205, 210
Leon..........................205
Leonard...................137, 206
Leonidas.............52, 108, 109
Leroy.......155, 163, 205, 217, 218
Leslie.......140, 150, 201, 208, 210
Lester...................156, 224
Levi, 14, 40, 75, 76, 98, 146, 175, 230,
    231, 232.
Lewis, or Louis, 45, 59, 61, 82, 87, 88,
    91, 94, 111, 125, 130, 140,
    161, 165, 167, 170, 171, 193,
    203, 225.
Lindley......79, 84, 146, 153, 164
Lon..........................146, 205
Lorenzo..................53, 109
Loring...................176, 227
Louis (see Lewis).
Lowell........................180
Lupton...................236, 238
Luther........................239
Luverne.......................202
Lyman.........................199
McClun........................238
McPherson.....................238
Mahlon, 35, 51, 65, 66, 78, 81, 105,
    137, 150, 158, 219.
Marcus........................175
Margaret...................13, 15
Marion...................109, 206
Mark.....................147, 207
Marshall..................88, 167
Martin....87, 94, 95, 166, 170, 173
Marvin........................222
Maxwell.......................217
Melvin........................171
Meritt........................149
Merton........................193
Micajah...........89, 152, 167
Miles.....................158, 220
Milford.......................218
Milton, 36, 59, 68, 79, 80, 84, 114,
    124, 125, 159, 163, 193, 203,
    221.
Monroe...................91, 168
Mordecai...............21, 40, 75
Morick........................156
Morris........................173

Morton...................239
Moses.............110, 234, 237
Murray.....................223
Nathan, 19, 25, 26, 30, 42, 48, 49, 51,
    58, 83, 84, 103, 104, 112,
    146, 163, 188, 205, 208.
Nelson......................147
Newton.....................156
Nolen.......................171
Oliver, 60, 78, 125, 126, 147, 152, 154,
    193, 208, 211, 213, 225.
Omer........................130
O'Neil..................101, 177
Ornon...........21, 42, 85, 164
Orville..................174, 180
Osborn......................122
Oscar, 130, 157, 169, 172, 199, 203,
    220, 228.
Otho........................156
Otis...........136, 150, 158, 210
Owen.....................79, 154
Palin.......................210
Parvin..................147, 209
Paul........................171
Pelatiah................54, 112
Penn.....48, 122, 152, 162, 175, 212
Perry...........46, 66, 88, 93, 137
Peter...........35, 66, 91, 167, 168
Philander...............103, 181
Philip..................52, 108, 147
Pleasant....40, 53, 79, 112, 147, 208
Porter...................159, 223
Prentice................142, 204
Quincy..................52, 108
Ralph......160, 173, 205, 210, 223
Raymond, 140, 165, 173, 190, 201,
    206, 226.
Reuben......75, 112, 145, 205, 231
Riley...................42, 61, 83
Robert, 14, 30, 59, 61, 101, 102, 124,
    130, 153, 154, 158, 177, 178,
    193, 219, 232.
Rodney..................91, 169
Roger.......................209
Roscoe...................69, 203
Ross.............169, 205, 223
Roy............174, 211, 218, 223
Rufus.......................211
Russell............166, 174, 235
Sale........................188
Samson..................54, 112
Samuel (Elizabeth Beals).......20
Samuel (Charity Beeson).......41
Samuel (Mary Harrold).......80
Samuel (Nancy Wilhoite).......88
Samuel, 11, 19, 20, 21, 41, 44, 80, 38, 94,
    109, 114, 158, 167, 170, 190,
    207, 218, 220
Sanford.....................238
Sanders.....................162

Scipio..................113, 190
Scott..................126, 168
S. Edgar....................209
Sedley..................101, 178
Shelby..........46, 87, 89, 166
Shelley.................140, 202
Silas, 18, 35, 52, 68, 79, 81, 107, 108,
    140, 154, 159, 183, 202
Simeon..................166, 167
Simon................53, 89, 111
Simpson.................50, 103
Smith.......................103
Solomon.........36, 57, 69, 122
Stephen, 11, 18, 19, 20, 36, 45, 50, 69,
    75, 91, 101, 169
Sylvanus..............54, 81, 218
Sylvester.........84, 141, 162, 203
Sumner.................112, 187
Susley......................231
Theodore....................175
Thomas (Mary Nation)..........40
Thomas (Ann Hawkins)........79
Thomas L. (Alice Garver)......109
Thomas (Alice Hosier)..........150
Thomas (Nancy Fard)..........155
Thomas (Rachel E. Vancil).....160
Thomas M. (Amanda E. Wilson) 169
Thomas J. (Catherine Black)....211
Thomas, 14, 21, 40, 52, 77, 79, 80, 81,
    91, 94, 109, 150, 152, 153,
    155, 159, 160, 166, 169, 170,
    211, 212, 232.
Thompson............88, 159, 221
Tilden......................94
Titus...................37, 70
Ulysses.................91, 169
Vore........................107
Waldo.......................150
Walter, 108, 112, 126, 130, 137, 140,
    183, 187, 188, 198, 201, 202,
    203, 207.
Ward........................171
Warren......................94
Washington...............46, 91
Watson...................98, 174
Wayne...................205, 229
Wesley..84, 87, 140, 152, 171, 201,
    210.
Wilbur.....177, 190, 195, 203, 208
Willard..................66, 137
William (Charlotte Hough).....27
William (Charity Hinds).......46
William (Elizabeth Wiles).......48
William (Mary Hitchcock).......52
William C. (Hannah Locke).....59
William (Lavina McCoy).......63
William A. (Abigail A. Reeder)...70
William M. (Sarah M. Sullins)....91
William S. (Mary S. Stephens)...94
William P. (Emeline Binford)....97

William (Rebecca Hobson)......102
William (Sarah Ann Giles)......108
William (Josephine Fisher)......108
William H. (Ellen Ebersole).....126
William (Phebe Cadwallader....139
William M. (Caroline Beeson)...148
William (Sarah A. Jessop)......152
William S. (Nancy England)....166
William M. (Leona Scott)......168
William E. (Susie A. Wilcher)...172
William B. (Bertha B. Caswell)..175
William S. (Ada Belle West)....178
William H. (Catherine Shrade)..193
William C. (Mary Elliott)......195
William H. (Lora Snider)......199
William A. (Ollie Smith)........209
William C. (Clara Siler)........210
William P. (Subina Miller)......212
William A. (Estella Irvin)......212
William A. (Cora Thomas)......213
William H. (Carrie King)......228

William, 15, 17, 21, 23, 26, **27**, 29, 30,
   35, 37, 43, 45, 46, **48**, 50, 51,
   52, 53, 57, **59**, 60, 61, **63**, 67,
   68, 69, **70**, 76, 78, 84, 85, 87,
   90, **91**, **94**, 95, **97**, 98, 101,
   102, 103, 107, **108**, 110, 111,
   112, 124, **126**, 127, 132, 139,
   140, 144, 145, 146, **148**, **152**,
   153, 157, 158, 161, 162, **166**,
   167, **168**, 169, **170**, 171, **172**,
   175, **178**, 180, 188, 191, **193**,
   195, 199, 202, **209**, **210**, 211,
   212, 213, 219, **223**, **228**, 234,
   236.
Willis................**69**, **76**, **142**
Wilmer.......................101
Wilson...........80, 146, **205**, **229**
Winfield................**140**, **201**
Wright.........................64
Zimri.................**40**, **76**, 149

INDEX TO OTHER NAMES.

Abbott......................108
Abel.......................177
Abrems.....................142
Adams.................**99**, **190**
Adamson.......**155**, **204**, **213**, **214**
Addington..................148
Adkins (See also Atkins).........37
Albertson...................124
Albright....................147
Alden......................186
Allen, 13, 55, 100, **164**, 176, 230, 234
Alloway.....................35
Alvey......................211
Amburn....................**209**
Amos.......................225
Andrews..............**106**, 117
Applegate...................151
Arnett.....................148
Ashby...................**192**, **193**
Ashe.......................195
Ashton...............113, 191
Atkins......................161
Austin.....................116
Babcock....................136
Bailey..................23, **132**
Bakehorn....................81
Baker......118, **165**, 168, 186, **237**
Baldwin, 12, **41**, 42, **71**, **82**, **83**, 138,
   153, 219, 220, 239.
Bales (See Beals-Beales).
Ball....................161, 238
Ballard...............**39**, **73**, 192
Ballenger...................83
Bamber....................140
Bantham..............138, 134
Bardwell...................228

Barker...................88, 220
Barnard.....................59
Barnes.....................153
Barnett.................53, 155
Barngrass..................228
Barnhart............**134**, **221**, 222
Barr............**201**, **233**, **235**, **236**
Barrett....................183
Bartl......................218
Barton.................221, 230
Bartow....................204
Batten....................199
Baxter....................227
Beals or Beales, 10, 12, 16, 20, 31, 177,
   236.
Beard......................48
Beck................**165**, **203**
Beeson.......12, 21, 22, 41, 148
Bell................126, **194**, 195
Bellangee..................117
Benbow.....................41
Bennett....................65
Benton....................200
Berry..............**163**, **225**, **238**
Bick.......................119
Bicknell...................200
Biddinger..............136, 137
Bimberger..................177
Binford................97, 197
Bisk......................239
Black.....................174
Bland.....................196
Blank.....................170
Blanton...................100
Blood.....................180
Boaz......................220

Bogenrief.................141
Boggs...................213
Bogue...................141
Boland..................193
Bone....................132
Boren...................226
Borton..................160
Boucher.................145
Boughton................140
Bowater.................16
Bowers.............119, 155
Bowman............114, 143
Boyd........124, 125, 129, 187
Boyer...................213
Bradford...........105, 183
Bradway.................234
Branson..............51, 77
Brattain................181
Brice...................203
Brindle.................118
Brinson.................101
Brooks...........86, 87, 229
Broomhall..........232, 235
Brower.............119, 120
Brown, 23, 49, 67, 130, 138, 139, 162,
    175.
Bryant..................20
Bullard.................220
Bumgardner.............238
Bunch...................33
Bunker, 16, 28, 29, 57, 58, 133, 199
Burgett.................104
Burk....................96
Burkett............234, 238
Burnsides...............84
Burrill.................190
Burris..................143
Burt....................71
Busby..............138, 200
Butler......129, 139, 144, 197, 198
Byers...................128
Cadwallader.....9, 105, 139, 230
Cain....................83
Caldwell................141
Callaway................8
Calvert.................130
Cameron.................226
Cammack............144, 196
Campbell...........187, 225
Cannaday............93, 127
Carey..............157, 176
Carlson.................222
Carman..................121
Carr................20, 107
Carrender...............89
Carter..................51
Case....................97
Cassey..................75
Caswell.................175
Catherman...............221

Catterson...............237
Caty....................161
Caulkins................162
Cecil...................208
Chandler................38
Chapin..................117
Chamness................23
Chapman.................211
Charles.................29
Chase...............28, 194
Cheesman...........124, 212
Christie............25, 27
Claborne................145
Clark...................101
Claybaugh...............165
Clayton.................16
Claypool................150
Clevenger..........142, 229
Cliburn.................170
Cloud...................152
Coats..........92, 100, 136
Coffin.........30, 62, 100
Coggeshall......24, 76, 82
Cohorn..................11
Coleman.................28
Coles...................214
Collett.................130
Collins.................70
Comer..........24, 80, 237
Commons.............29, 120
Compton.................176
Cone....................183
Conlee..................114
Conley..................166
Conner..................210
Cook.........68, 78, 154, 215
Cooper..................120
Cope....................179
Cornell.................70
Cowen...................224
Cowgill.................208
Cox, 50, 61, 106, 146, 217, 218, 219,
    237, 239.
Craig...................235
Craford.................23
Craven..................235
Criss...................38
Crosby..................183
Crouch..................186
Crowe...................63
Crull...................118
Crumley.................214
Cummings................154
Daily...................113
Dalton..................195
Darnell.................223
Davis, 15, 22, 50, 74, 81, 83, 87, 99,
    137, 145, 146, 165, 176, 177,
    185, 192, 193, 219.
Dawson..................123

Deck..........................193
Decker........................121
Deering.......................188
Dees..........................204
De Long.......................187
Denio..........................68
Dennis........................188
Denny.....................98, 191
DeVine........................191
Dickason......................203
Dicks......................11, 23
Dillinger................235, 236
Dimmick.......................200
Dinza..........................18
Dixon.........................143
Doan..........103, 104, 210, 237
Dobbins...................27, 232
Downey........................223
Draper........................124
Dresser.......................202
Drew..........................116
Duncan.........................93
Durkee........................206
Eagan.........................227
Eargood........................61
Earl..........153, 154, 185, 213
Early.........................119
Eaton.........................191
Ebersole......................126
Eckberg.......................215
Eckman........................118
Edge...........................16
Edwards..................113, 131
Ehrman........................120
Eigenbrodt....................153
Eikenberry....................199
Eliason.......................195
Elliott...................23, 195
Ellis.....................76, 181
Emery....................189, 216
Emmons........................211
England.......................166
Englert.......................130
Enloe.........................167
Etter....................165, 166
Evans....................110, 199
Fairbank......................174
Fairfield.....................195
Fard..........................155
Farrington....................135
Feagans.......................146
Feasel........................212
Fetta.........................121
Fetters.......................142
Field.........................207
Fisher.......57, 58, 108, 162, 198
Fleming.......................218
Flory.........................223
Foreman........................96
Ford..........................103

Fosdick...................51, 106
Fouts.........................175
Fox......................206, 231
Fraiser.......................212
Frantz........................118
French........................184
Froggatt......................138
Fry.....................152, 209
Fulghum...............66, 72, 73
Fuller..........110, 184, 209
Fulton..................169, 170
Furnace........................73
Gaines........................234
Galley........................201
Garn..........................213
Garner........................174
Garrett, 39, 56, 73, 74, 75, 115, 119,
    121, 122, 156.
Garretson................119, 127
Garringer................214, 215
Garver........................109
Garwood.......................143
Gause..........................70
George...........230, 236, 237
Gerrard.......................201
Gibson.........................74
Giles.........................108
Glascock......................186
Goodwin................115, 201
Goldsmith......................53
Gowan.........................184
Grace.........................160
Grafft........................198
Graham.........................69
Gray................73, 100, 137
Graves........................234
Gregg.........................235
Green...................161, 192
Griffin.......................183
Griffith......................224
Grinnell......................173
Griswold......................109
Gurley...............122, 123, 191
Guy.............................8
Guyer..........................95
Guyton........................194
Hadley..................210, 214
Haisley..............24, 43, 100
Hall...........180, 197, 211, 238
Hammer........................145
Hammond................149, 235
Hanby.........................163
Haner.........................222
Hanley........................197
Hanson............85, 165, 185
Harman........................236
Harris....86, 112, 173, 187, 193, 227
Harrold, 12, 40, 41. 76, 77, 80, 119,
    127, 149.
Harvey........................120

Haskett........................23
Haskins.......................182
Hastings........24, 95, 96, 173, 174
Hawkins....................79, 175
Haworth, or Hayworth..47, 141, 209
Hays..........................167
Hazelhurst....................202
Heagy.........................137
Heald..........................37
Healton....................99, 177
Heath.........................121
Heilman.......................104
Henderson.................162, 224
Henning.......................235
Henry.........................151
Herring.......................145
Hewitt...................128, 129
Hiatt..........20, 64, 65, 100, 128
Hicks.........................234
Higgins.......................223
Hildebrand....................178
Hill............167, 176, 210, 225
Hinds, 44, 45, 46, 87, 89, 92, 93, 169,
    205.
Hinkley.......................191
Hinshaw.......................190
Hippard.......................138
Hitchcock......................52
Hite..........................217
Hobson...........26, 49, 50, 102
Hockett..............51, 75, 148
Hodgen........................146
Hodson.............82, 150, 196
Hoel..........................204
Hoggatt........................12
Hogue.........................186
Holden........................167
Holderman.....................125
Holland.......................234
Holliday..................200, 203
Hollingshead..................208
Hollingsworth.................111
Holloway......................134
Holmes.............46, 92, 210
Honey.........................217
Hood.....................131, 198
Hoover.........................60
Horney.........................70
Horton....................80, 157
Hosier...................131, 150
Hoskins............122, 143, 199
Hoskinson.................180, 228
Hough..............27, 62, 113
Howe.....................198, 216
Howland.......................188
Hudson........................169
Huff......................25, 27
Hull........110, 111, 136, 186, 187
Hunt, 11, 12, 25, 42, 58, 147, 150, 179,
    189.

Hurst.........................194
Hussey.........................53
Hutchins, 26, 49, 57, 99, 102, 114,
    115, 179, 181.
Hutchinson................93, 170
Ingram........................180
Ingmire.......................182
Irvin.........................212
Jackson....23, 112, 173, 181, 227, 237
James....................134, 207
Jay...........36, 67, 153, 203, 212
Jefferis......................223
Jeffries......................125
Jessop, or Jessup, 13, 20, 23, 49, 147,
    149, 152, 207.
Jester........................226
Johnson, 71, 82, 139, 140, 169, 204,
    216, 219, 222, 224, 233, 236.
Johnston......................187
Jones, 20, 24, 64, 66, 67, 107, 117,
    135, 151, 169, 183, 194, 203,
    220, 227.
Jordon........................171
Julian...................125, 150
Kean, or Keene.......114, 115, 119
Keener.........................42
Keever........................189
Kellam........................237
Kelley...................134, 170
Kennard........................35
Kennedy........................53
Kenworthy.............47, 58, 60
Kettlewood....................204
Keys..........27, 49, 100, 101, 206
Kibler........................236
King......8, 62, 101, 125, 126, 228
Kirkhart......................228
Kirkwood......................174
Kist..........................207
Knight.....................12, 114
Knowlton......................154
Kohli.........................217
Kolling.......................195
Koons.........................177
Koontz........................232
Kuhns.........................123
Kinzie........................224
Kyte..........................205
Laflin.........................86
Laid..........................155
Lamb....23, 41, 146, 147, 182, 218
Lancaster.....................158
Larkins.......................168
Lawler...................173, 227
League........................216
LeClair.......................229
Leedy..........................63
Lentz.........................236
Leonard..............130, 131, 195
Lewelling.....................136

Lewis.............127, 183, 235
Lienbarger....................97
Little.................66, 183, 213
Lively........................215
Locke..........................59
Long....................125, 235
Longanecker..................222
Louk.........................194
Lower........................233
Lowry......................47, 96
Lough........................116
Ludlow........................44
Lukens.......................192
Lundy........................176
Lupton..................233, 238
Lyon.........................217
McAfee.......................129
McAvoy.......................211
McCallister..................200
McCown........................90
McCoy......................63, 71
McHenry.................166, 184
McKinney.............46, 73, 92
McLain.......................167
McMeans......................126
McMillan.....................234
McNairy.................234, 237
McNeil.......................195
McPherson.....................13
Macy..............13, 26, 28, 102
Magee........................142
Mahin........................182
Manlove.......................24
Marine.......................161
Markey.......................134
Marshall, 50, 75, 99, 137, 148, 149,
    234, 237.
Martin.......................163
Mason...................106, 107
Maxwell......................156
May..........................180
Means........................229
Mendenhall, 12, 35, 61, 62, 77, 81,
    116, 131, 132, 158, 159, 160,
    161, 220, 237.
Mercer.....................89, 90
Merritt......................216
Mesenhimer.........161, 221, 224
Metzker......................162
Miller......163, 164, 197, 212, 230
Millhollen...................109
Millican.....................177
Millikan.....................194
Milligan.....................196
Mills.........12, 16, 20, 31, 145, 220
Milner..........156, 157, 216, 217
Mitchell......................52
Moad.........................226
Modlin..................131, 132
Molen.................87, 88, 89

Montgomery.....................95
Moore.....8, 160, 196, 199, 225, 238
Morgan..............155, 194, 215
Morris..........107, 142, 185, 211
Morrow.................141, 142
Mort.........................186
Mower........................175
Mullin.............65, 135, 136
Munden.......................132
Murdock......................182
Murphy, 127, 152, 197, 198, 199, 225
Murray..............137, 145, 157
Myers........................203
Myrick.......................201
Nation........................40
Neal.........................205
Newby.....................48, 161
Newman.......................145
Newton.......................166
Nicholson......60, 61, 129, 130, 194
Noel....................190, 191
North.........................16
Norton........................23
Norvell......................178
Nott.........................236
Nugent.......................111
Nunn.........................108
O'Brien...............135, 136
O'Donnell....................145
Odell..................170, 171
O'Hara.......................129
Olds.........................130
O'Neil.......................232
Ortwine......................211
Osborn..............26, 97, 220
Overman......................161
Paddock..................30, 211
Painter......................210
Palin.........78, 150, 151, 152, 209
Palmer..................193, 235
Paradise....................7, 10
Parish..................121, 169
Parker.......................149
Parry........................117
Parshall.....................121
Pascoe.......................189
Patterson.................24, 104
Patty........................173
Paulus.......................194
Payne.........54, 56, 96, 118, 119
Paxson.......................199
Pearch.......................119
Pearson......................179
Peele.........................79
Pegg.........................143
Pennington..............138, 200
Penny........................202
Perdue.......................207
Perry.........................62
Phelps........................97

Pickett..............49, 77, 212
Pierce......................194
Pike........................24
Pitts.....................82, 86
Pool.......................226
Pope........................96
Porter.....................223
Potter.....................207
Powell......................23
Price......................201
Purdy......................174
Putnam.....................192
Quickell...................161
Quigg......................160
Quigley...............108, 191
Raffensbarger..............198
Randall......84, 101, 149, 157, 164
Randolph...................183
Ransdell...................133
Ratcliff...................220
Ratliff....................105
Rawlins....................204
Raymond....................126
Rector.....................105
Reece.......................94
Reed.......................103
Reeder......................70
Regester....................71
Remington..................176
Ressler....................192
Reynolds...........23, 49, 74
Rhynolds...................148
Rich.......................239
Ridgeway....................51
Rigby..................34, 133
Rinard, or Reynard, 110, 115, 116, 184, 185.
Risk........................83
Roberts, 55, 80, 85, 86, 93, 116, 117, 118.
Roberson...................144
Robertson..................215
Robson.....................204
Rogers...........7, 9, 10, 31, 107
Rohrer.....................159
Roller.....................193
Ross...................91, 207
Rowe.......................171
Royalty....................151
Ruble......................114
Ruggles....................143
Runyan.....................197
Rupe........................67
Russell...............188, 189
Rush........................67
Rutty........................8
Sanders....................211
Sanger.......................8
Sarber......................97
Sauer......................221

Schooley....................24
Scott......125, 126, 130, 168, 225
Sears.................175, 237
Sell........................24
Shade......................223
Shaffer................97, 124
Sharp......................119
Shaul.................123, 191
Shaw...........104, 140, 186
Sheard.....................164
Sheets.....................186
Sheidler...................107
Sheldon.....................98
Sheppard..............111, 211
Sherwood...................184
Shirk......................131
Shrade.....................193
Shrock.....................111
Shutes......................73
Siler......................210
Silverstone................238
Simon......................156
Simmons....................116
Simpson....................170
Sizemore...................102
Skinner.....................67
Slusher....................118
Slyter.....................181
Small.................83, 205
Smith, 7, 72, 84, 103, 113, 140, 149, 166, 188, 205, 209, 215, 227, 232.
Snider............86, 127, 199
Spellman...................226
Sprinkle...................235
Spurrier..............137, 169
Stacy......................216
Stafford..............178, 196
Stainbrook.................220
Stake......................224
Stanbro...............84, 122
Stanfield..................190
Stanley......17, 47, 48, 78, 84, 181
Stanton.....................52
Staples....................188
Starbuck....................30
Steenbarger................171
Steinmetz..................144
Stephens.........37, 71, 94, 167
Stevens....................225
Stevenson..................165
Stigleman..................124
Stone......................213
Stout.................179, 227
Strattan...........128, 196, 221
Strawbridge.................36
Stroud.....................130
Stubbs.....................198
Studt................120, 121
Sturdevant.................145

Sullivan...................70
Sullins....................91
Sumner....................39
Sutfin....................186
Sutton....................180
Swallers...................33
Swinney...................168
Tafelmeyer................229
Tanner....................164
Taylor..........70, 114, 208, 225
Teagle................42, 43, 86
Teague....................183
Templeton.................174
Terree....................206
Test......................66, 67
Teter.....................143
Thomas, 20, 91, 130, 185, 186, 209, 213, 216.
Thompson.........204, 213, 229
Thornburg, 11, 59, 95, 142, 172, 206, 208, 229.
Thornton..............158, 218
Throckmorton..............137
Titus......................62
Tomlinson.................210
Towne.....................192
Townsend..................15, 37
Toye......................218
Tracy...........111, 151, 166
Trader....................229
Tribett...................171
Tripp.....................161
Tuttle....................150
Twinkle...................220
Ulrich....................142
Upton.................185, 187
Underwood, 54, 108, 109, 114, 115, 164, 183, 184, 190.
Unthank...................196
Valentine.................149
Van Etten.................208
Vancil....................160
Varney................188, 189
Vaughan...................171
Vetter....................216
Vernon....................191
Vore......36, 37, 52, 69, 70, 71, 72
Wadkins...................212
Wales.....................150
Walker............120, 121, 192
Wall......................190
Walters...........118, 119, 165
Walton, 10, 11, 15, 17, 18, 30, 37, 38, 39.
Ward..................104, 202
Warriner..................191
Wasson.........51, 105, 106, 107

Wathey.....................38
Watlands..................185
Watson....................168
Webber....................222
Weeks.................144, 145
Weightman.................201
Weir......................180
Wells.....................221
Wesler....................120
West.........111, 118, 178, 202
Westerfield................97
Wheeler...................123
Whipple...................117
Whisler...................131
Whitacre........147, 148, 199
White...........73, 189, 201
Whitson..............159, 160
Wickersham..13, 127, 128, 195, 196
Wilcher...................172
Wildman...................234
Wiles......................48
Wiley.....................182
Wilhoite...................88
Wilkerson.................163
Wilkinson.............176, 177
Willitts...............85, 125
Williams, 10, 24, 68, 69, 76, 86, 156, 231.
Wilson, 13, 60, 83, 112, 169, 186, 187
Wiltsie...................200
Wing......................181
Winnie....................150
Winterbotham..............130
Winters...................229
Winslow...............139, 158
Wise..................109, 217
Wisehart..................129
Wiseman....................38
Wissler...................238
Wood..................182, 205
Woodhurst.................107
Woodrow...................183
Woodruff..................194
Woolman...............234, 237
Wray.......................88
Wright, 63, 66, 69, 126, 127, 134, 135, 137, 142, 206, 239.
Wylis.....................168
Wynkoop...............172, 173
Yauky.................175, 197
Yeager....................196
Yockey....................163
Young.................108, 173
Zaph......................204
Zeek.......................68
Zehring...................134

CPSIA information can be obtained
at www.ICGtesting.com
Printed in the USA
BVHW09s0258090718
521072BV00008B/149/P

9 781334 331558